D1210222

MAY 3 0 2007

U.S. DOCUMENTS REPOSITORY

CENTRAL ARKANSAS LIBRARY SYSTEM
LITTLE ROCK PUBLIC LIBRARY
100 ROCK STREET
LITTLE ROCK, ARKANSAS 72201

For sale by the Superintendent of Documents, U.S. Government Printing Office
Internet: bookstore.gpo.gov   Phone: toll free (866) 512-1800;   DC area (202) 512-1800
Fax: (202) 512-2104 Mail: Stop IDCC, Washington, DC 20402-0001

ISBN 0-16-075223-X

DESIGNING THE NATION'S CAPITAL

THE 1901 PLAN FOR WASHINGTON, D.C.

Sue Kohler and Pamela Scott, Editors

U.S. COMMISSION OF FINE ARTS

Washington, D.C.

2006

LITTLE ROCK PUBLIC LIBRARY

U.S. COMMISSION OF FINE ARTS
www.cfa.gov

ISBN: 0-16-075223-X

CONTENTS

PREFACE By Charles H. Atherton vii

FOREWORD By David M. Childs ix

INTRODUCTION By Sue Kohler xi

ACKNOWLEDGMENTS xv

THE SENATE PARK COMMISSION PLAN FOR WASHINGTON, D.C.:
A NEW VISION FOR THE CAPITAL AND THE NATION
By Jon A. Peterson 1

THE AMERICAN INSTITUTE OF ARCHITECTS CONVENTION OF 1900:
ITS INFLUENCE ON THE SENATE PARK COMMISSION PLAN
By Tony P. Wrenn 49

"A CITY DESIGNED AS A WORK OF ART":
THE EMERGENCE OF THE SENATE PARK COMMISSION'S MONUMENTAL CORE
By Pamela Scott 75

BEYOND THE MALL:
THE SENATE PARK COMMISSION'S PLANS FOR WASHINGTON'S PARK SYSTEM
By Timothy Davis 137

PLATES 183

AGRICULTURE, ARCHITECTS, AND THE MALL, 1901-1905:
THE PLAN IS TESTED
By Dana G. Dalrymple 207

THE COMMISSION OF FINE ARTS:
IMPLEMENTING THE SENATE PARK COMMISSION'S VISION
By Sue Kohler 245

"BELOVED ANCIEN": WILLIAM T. PARTRIDGE'S RECOLLECTIONS OF THE
SENATE PARK COMMISSION AND THE SUBSEQUENT MALL DEVELOPMENT
By Kurt G.F. Helfrich 275

APPENDICES 337

PREFACE

By Charles H. Atherton, *FAIA, Secretary (1965-2004)*
Commission of Fine Arts

FROM the inception of the Commission of Fine Arts in 1910 to the present day, there has been a splendid written record of its activities, especially regarding the implementation of the Senate Park (McMillan) Commission's recommendations for the development of Washington. Having itself been an outgrowth of this commission, it was only natural that out of respect for its origin, the major decisions on the realization of the designs for the monumental core were carefully chronicled.

The Commission's Secretary from 1922 to 1954, H.P. Caemmerer, wrote a brief description of each new public building as it was completed, and in 1932 the Commission published his 715-page book, *Washington, the National Capital*, which outlined the history of the development of the capital from L'Enfant's plan to the Federal Triangle project, including public architecture of all kinds, governmental and private, as well as memorials, statues, and parks.

There was, however, nothing written on the architectural history of Washington outside the monumental core. The impetus to do this came as a result of the passage in 1950 of legislation creating the Old Georgetown Historic District, which the Commission was to administer. Authorization was given to do a survey of the area's architecture, but as is often the case, no appropriation was attached. After more than fifteen years of trying to obtain funds, the Commission decided it had to employ a different approach, utilizing volunteers, student interns, and loans of personnel and services from other agencies, in particular the Historic American Buildings Survey. Thus a new publication program was born, first focusing on Historic Georgetown and later, with congressional funding, branching out to include books covering the early development of Washington architecture (1791-1861), the bridges of Washington, and the industrial and mercantile structures of the Georgetown waterfront. These were followed by major works on the architecture of Massachusetts Avenue and Sixteenth Street. There were some sixteen publications in all. And so, when the 100th anniversary of the Senate Park Commission's report occurred in 2002, it seemed appropriate that it be celebrated with a publication of its own. Happily, Congress agreed.

As with any successful program, there is always one person involved who deserves the lion's share of the credit. Sue Kohler joined the Commission's staff in 1974 and was first associated with the Massachusetts Avenue books and the volumes on Sixteenth Street. It should be noted that her work on these publications was in addition to her regular duties which included the recording of the minutes of Commission meetings, a most arduous and demanding task, as well as the writing of the Commission's Brief History series, updated every five years or so. She was a rare find when she joined our small staff, seven persons for most of these years. Her remarkable role in these publications, including this one, represents a unique contribution to the scholarship of the architecture of our national capital.

FOREWORD

By David M. Childs, *FAIA, Chairman (2003–2005)*
Commission of Fine Arts

O VER the past forty years, the Commission of Fine Arts has written and published a series of scholarly volumes on the architecture and history of significant places of interest in Washington, most notably a four-volume set devoted to Massachusetts Avenue and Sixteenth Street. With this current volume, the Commission has chosen to explore its own origins with a look into the events and people leading up to the creation of the Senate Park (McMillan) Commission in 1901 and the resulting plan for the redevelopment of the city.

The publication is especially timely from several perspectives. We are commemorating the recent centennial of the Park Commission Plan as well as bringing to light aspects of and insights into the plan not generally or clearly understood by the public. The plan was and still is a work in progress. Its creation was a lofty endeavor born of the spirit of the times in a political and social climate that seemed to frown on any enterprise that required the spending of public funds or called for a change in the accepted appearance of the Capital. The participants faced formidable obstacles not unlike those that reverberate today whenever a change to the familiar is contemplated.

My colleagues on the Commission and I are pleased to present these essays to the people of Washington and all who find the creation of cities a subject of fascination. No one enjoyed the subject more or contributed more to it than the late J. Carter Brown, our Chairman for over thirty years, and it is to his memory that we dedicate this volume.

INTRODUCTION

By Sue Kohler, *Historian*
Commission of Fine Arts

ANYONE who joins the staff of the Commission of Fine Arts is immediately made aware of the close connection that still exists between the Commission and its predecessor, the Senate Park Commission, popularly known as the McMillan Commission, of 1901. Surrounded by such reminders as the one hundred mounted 33 by 43-inch photographs of European scenes, Frederick Law Olmsted, Jr.'s scrapbook of snapshots taken during the commission's European trip, and the remaining large watercolor renderings used in the 1902 exhibition at the Corcoran Gallery of Art, it is hard not to feel the kinship, and to ponder what was in the minds of these four men as they set out, in the heady atmosphere of the City Beautiful movement, to draft a plan that would make Washington one of the most beautiful capitals in the world.

Fortunately there are letters, primarily in the manuscript collections of the Library of Congress, the Art Institute of Chicago, and the New-York Historical Society, as well as the books on Burnham and McKim by Charles Moore, Senator McMillan's aide who accompanied three of the commission members on their trip to Europe. Reading from these sources makes one realize what a tremendous amount of work was packed into ten months' time—and this included planning and producing the exhibition at the Corcoran in January 1902, a major effort in itself. The six-week European trip, which some referred to as a "junket", was extremely productive; the days at sea with no interruptions, and the first-hand experience of the best Europe had to offer in examples of urban planning and landscaping were invaluable.

It should be understood that the Park Commission's plan did not take shape "out of the blue" in 1901. For the past two decades, in concert with the City Beautiful movement, there had been articles in the press pointing out the capital's shortcomings in regard to public architecture and public spaces, as well as demands for some kind of entity to exercise control over the quality of these civic improvements once funds were appropriated for them. The members of the Park Commission were not unaware of this criticism, and it undoubtedly shaped their thinking. More influential was the series of talks on the subject given at the American Institute of Architects convention of 1900, which took place in Washington, and during which Olmsted himself spoke on landscape, particularly in regard to the Mall.

The plan has been criticized because it seems to ignore the city beyond the monumental core, but this was the case only because of time limitations. As it was, the commission's report devoted 100 pages to the "Outlying Parks and Their Connections" versus 71 pages to the Mall area and the grouping of public buildings in the monumental core. It was, after all, charged with developing a park system for the entire District of Columbia. Especially interesting, in light of the renewed interest today, was the extensive discussion of the Anacostia River, the deplorable condition of the flats, and the advisability of creating a water park to rehabilitate that part of the city. Providing adequate public bathing places and playgrounds for children also occupied the commission members; a reading of the report makes it clear that they were not solely concerned with developing a grand Beaux-Arts plan for the Mall.

After the Corcoran exhibition and the publication of the report, the Park Commission was officially disbanded, but its hardest work actually lay ahead. Almost immediately, and all too frequently, they were called in to advise on the implementation of some aspect of their plan. When specific buildings were proposed and designed for the Mall, the members fought doggedly to assure that the design would be Roman and not contemporary French, and of utmost importance, that the width of the Mall as they had specified it would be maintained, and that the buildings would be placed on the grade established to maintain the correct relationship to the Washington Monument. This continued until the Commission of Fine Arts was finally established in 1910 to take over these duties.

Considering its close association with the complexities of the plan, the Commission of Fine Arts decided to celebrate the Park Commission's 100th anniversary by publishing a series of essays. They have been written by experts in their fields, and we hope they will give the reader a deeper, more three-dimensional—if one can use that word—understanding of what the four members of the commission were planning for the nation's capital. It is fitting that, one hundred years afterward, we look back and see what they accomplished, what they failed to do, and determine what our task is for the next one hundred years.

These are the essays included in this publication:

The Senate Park Commission Plan for Washington: A New Vision for the Capital and Nation, by Jon Peterson, is an overview of the commission and its work, as well as the political setting in which it took place. Dr. Peterson is presently professor of history emeritus at Queens College of the City University of New York. His book, *The Birth of City Planning in the United States, 1840-1917*, was published in 2003 by the Johns Hopkins University Press, and received the Society of Architectural Historians' Spiro Kostoff Award in 2005.

The American Institute of Architects Convention of 1900: Its Influence on the Senate Park Commission Plan, by Tony P. Wrenn, documents the events leading up to the establishment of the Senate Park Commission under the leadership of Senator James McMillan of Michigan. Mr. Wrenn is an honorary member of the AIA and was for many years the archivist of that organization.

"A City Designed as a Work of Art": The Emergence of the Senate Park Commission's Monumental Core, by Pamela Scott, investigates preliminary site and design plans made between the beginning of March and the end of 1901, which have not previously been considered in studies of the Park Commission Plan. Ms. Scott is an independent architectural historian who teaches the history of Washington architecture for Cornell University in Washington, D.C. and has written and lectured extensively on this subject.

Beyond the Mall: The Senate Park Commission's Plans for Washington's Park System, by Timothy Davis, discusses proposals for Washington's parks, a largely untold aspect of the plan. Dr. Davis, a historian with the National Park Service's Park Historic Structures and Cultural Landscapes Division, has a special interest in American landscape history, with an emphasis on parkways and roads, and is a recognized authority in this field.

Agriculture, Architects, and the Mall, 1901-1905: The Plan Is Tested, by Dana Dalrymple, unravels the complicated history of the current Department of Agriculture building on the Mall, a pivotal case in the implementation of the Park Commission Plan. Dr. Dalrymple is a USDA agricultural economist by profession and an architectural historian by avocation; he has been researching the history of the Mall and the Agriculture building for over twenty-five years.

The Commission of Fine Arts: Implementing the Senate Park Commission's Vision, by Sue Kohler, documents the events leading to the establishment by Congress in 1910 of the Commission of Fine Arts, and the Commission's work during its early years to implement the Park Commission Plan. Ms. Kohler, the historian of the Commission of Fine Arts for many years, is the author of *The Commission of Fine Arts: A Brief History*, and the co-author of several other books on Washington architecture.

"Beloved Ancien": William T. Partridge's Recollection of the Senate Park Commission and the Subsequent Mall Development, by Kurt G.F. Helfrich, is an annotation of selected portions of a little-known manuscript by Partridge recalling his work for the Park Commission, and later on as an architectural consultant to the National Capital Park and Planning Commission on the Mall development. Dr. Helfrich is the curator of the architectural drawings collection of the University Art Museum, University of California, Santa Barbara.

ACKNOWLEDGMENTS

My co-editor, Pamela Scott, and I would like to place the name of the late Charles Atherton, secretary of the Commission of Fine Arts from 1965 to 2004, at the beginning of our acknowledgments list. It was Mr. Atherton who suggested that a book would be the most suitable way to commemorate the 100th anniversary of the Senate Park Commission, and he followed its progress until his death in December 2005. His knowledge of the development of Washington was extensive, and he will be sorely missed.

We thank the following individuals and institutions who have been so helpful to us and the other authors of the essays in this book: Jeffrey R. Carson, former assistant secretary of the Commission of Fine Arts and first editor of this book, for his work in getting the project started; my fellow co-workers at the Commission of Fine Arts, for their support; the staff of the Prints and Photographs Division, Manuscript Division, and Geography and Maps Division of the Library of Congress; the staff of the National Archives and Records Administration; the staff of the Washingtoniana Division, Martin Luther King Jr. Memorial Library; the staff of the American Institute of Architects Library and Archives, and the American Architectural Foundation, especially Sherry Birk; Eleanor Gillers and Mary Beth Kavanaugh of the New-York Historical Society; Mary Woolever of the Ryerson and Burnham Archives of the Art Institute of Chicago; T. Michele Clark and Michael Dosch of the Frederick Law Olmsted Historic Site; Gregory C. Schwarz of the Augustus Saint-Gaudens Historic Site; and Arleyn Levee, landscape historian.

Several of the authors have thanked people who have been especially helpful to them at the beginning of the Notes section at the end of their essays.

We would also like to thank picture researcher Peter Penczer, copy editor Gail Spilsbury, and the staff of the Government Printing Office, who worked uncomplainingly with us to give form to this book: Sarah Trucksis, Clint Howard, Patrick Jacobs, and especially designer Amanda Drake.

Generally, I think all of us would like to take this time to express our thanks to John Reps for his pioneering work on the Senate Park Commission, as evidenced in his book, *Monumental Washington*, published in 1967 and still a primary reference for all students of city planning in the nation's capital.

SUE KOHLER

Senator James McMillan of Michigan (1838-1902). Commission of Fine Arts

The Senate Park Commission Plan for Washington, D.C.:
A NEW VISION FOR THE CAPITAL AND THE NATION

By Jon A. Peterson[1]

THE 1901 to 1902 Senate Park Commission plan for Washington, D.C., ranks among the most significant urban plans in American history. Its novel blending and adroit elaboration of city-making ideas then current in the United States made it a benchmark for modern urbanism and triggered a national city-planning movement. The consummate artistry and professionalism of its designers, together with their boldness of vision and willingness to address local needs, established its potential benefit to the national capital. Ultimately, the plan-makers' deep and enduring commitment to implementation, fortified by the tactical shrewdness of their backers—and their plain good luck—in negotiating Washington politics, against a backdrop of mounting public support, brought success: a capital city recast as a symbol of national authority and of the nation's emergence as a world power. All of these considerations, taken together, establish the importance of the Senate Park Commission plan, often called the McMillan Plan after its sponsor, James McMillan of Michigan, chairman of the Senate Committee on the District of Columbia from 1890 until his death in 1902 (frontispiece).[2]

A design of such note might be presumed to reflect a strong, well-established urban planning tradition in the United States. But this was not the case. Since the mid-eighteenth century, most American towns and cities had been laid out on grids by a society more eager to promote land sales than civic order. And big-city growth, once it had begun on a sustained basis from the mid-nineteenth century onward, had occurred in boom-and-bust surges subject to little or no public regulation. Everywhere in the United States, market forces had set the terms of growth, in land subdivision at the city's fringe and in building up the city proper: its stores, shops, offices, factories, and private residences. In transportation, the powerful railroad corporations that had tied the nation's towns and cities into vast networks by the 1880s, and the city transit firms that had laced urban America with trolley lines in the 1890s had dictated the routes and hence the directions of city growth.

During the Gilded Age, large-scale, systematic public planning for existing cities had focused on water supply, sewerage systems, and public parks. Because these services, though urgent, had offered scant opportunity for profit, they usually had been addressed by public authorities as specialized interventions. As to generalized planning for all aspects of the built city, or what is now called comprehensive city planning, it was all but unknown in the United States of 1900.

THE PUZZLE OF WASHINGTON

To all of this, one city stood out as a partial exception. Alone among major urban centers in the United States, Washington rested on a grandly conceived foundation. In 1791 Pierre Charles L'Enfant, in the employ of President George Washington, had conceived the capital as the seat of a "vast empire," designing it as an enormous grid of streets crisscrossed by wide diagonal avenues. The many points of crossing and convergence had, with artful forethought as to placement, yielded over two dozen public squares and spaces and, together with the avenues, had made the city a symbol of nationhood. By 1900 the capital had filled out its frame, but the Victorian city that had emerged differed fundamentally from L'Enfant's and Washington's vision.

When the Mall as the physical and symbolic heart of L'Enfant's plan began to be developed in the 1840s, the neoclassical design principles of harmony and regularity that had guided him had given way to ones predicated on irregularity and intricacy derived from medieval art. L'Enfant had envisioned the Mall as a partially sunken, axial corridor lined by museums and theaters and extending about a mile due west from Capitol Hill. This major axis would have formed the stem of a vast, L-shaped public space, its crossing arm running due south from the President's House. L'Enfant had marked this juncture point with an equestrian statue of George Washington (pl. I). Yet in 1848, Robert Mills's obelisk monument was placed well away from that point, in the middle of the central vista between James Renwick's Smithsonian Institution, begun on the south side of the Mall in 1847, and a canal, which occupied a wide swath along the Mall's north side. Although the Mall still looked like "a marshy and desolate waste," these structures, in concert with the Botanic Garden at the foot of Capitol Hill, would soon define the western "vista" when viewed from the Capitol terrace. Picturesque landscaping for the Mall was considered as early as 1841 and began to be carried out in 1851, to the plans of America's most prominent landscape gardener, Andrew Jackson Downing, filling L'Enfant's corridor with dense tree plantings of many species. The monument itself, built to a height of 170 feet by 1855, remained an unfinished shaft for the next quarter of a century, as if representing the city itself.[3]

Fig. 1 Victorian Washington, ca. 1900. Foreground: The Mall, with its curving paths and random planting of trees, in the vicinity of the Smithsonian Institution building. Middle ground, far left: Center Market, which stood between 7th and 9th streets, facing North B Street (Constitution Avenue). Midddle ground, near right: The B & P Railroad terminal, marked by a Victorian-style tower, now the site of the National Gallery of Art. Commission of Fine Arts

By 1900 the Mall had become a chain of individual public parks, each associated with a different Victorian building, most of them built of red brick. The passenger shed of the Victorian gothic terminal of the Baltimore and Potomac Railroad, built in 1873 to 1878, extended nearly halfway across the Mall at Sixth Street; the canal had been filled during the 1870s.[4] (See Helfrich fig. 3 and Wrenn fig. 6) Beyond the tracks, from Seventh to Twelfth streets, lay the picturesque grounds of the Smithsonian Institution, where a multitude of footpaths meandered through a forest of trees (fig. 1). From Twelfth to Fourteenth streets, the Agriculture Department maintained an open and formal parterre in the center of the Mall, but extensive greenhouses and sheds to the west of its building struck residents and visitors alike as an eyesore. (See Dalrymple fig. 4) Terminating the chain, scattered clumps of trees dotted the meadow around the Washington Monument, completed in 1884.

By 1900, to the west and southwest of the Monument lay "Potomac Park," a 739-acre swath of newly made public ground that, as landfill, covered the old tidal flats of the Potomac River. This project, begun in 1882 by the Army Corps of Engineers, included a long spit of land stretching southeastward along the eastern bank of the Potomac, later named East Potomac Park.[5] What was to be done with this new land and its connections, if any, to the Mall park chain had not been decided (pl. XVI).

Washington itself by 1900 had become a city of considerable stature. From a population of 75,000 in 1860, it had grown to 278,000. Beginning in 1871 the city center and its built-up neighborhoods acquired their first modern infrastructure, including gas and electric lines, water and sewer service, and street paving. These improvements, initiated during the city's brief territorial government (1871–74), had continued under a board of commissioners directly answerable to Congress.

Inevitably, the various House and Senate committees on the District of Columbia that oversaw the city's day-to-day affairs, along with other committees that designated sites for new federal and city buildings or privately sponsored monuments, exerted a fragmented and unpredictable control over Washington's development. For example, beginning in 1892 to 1893, Congress, after years of splitting costs with local taxpayers, suddenly refused to finance the extension of streets and squares into the "county" lands lying between the city's original boundary and the District of Columbia line. Nonetheless, Washington by the 1890s was increasingly perceived as a source of national pride, especially for its government buildings, many of which contained small museums or spaces commemorating American achievements, none more lavishly than the new Library of Congress.

Against this backdrop, the Senate Park Commission plan when displayed at the Corcoran Gallery for nearly six weeks beginning in mid-January 1902, drew rapt attention. On view, first and foremost, was a spectacular design for the city's core, featuring the Mall as a two-and-one-half-mile-long corridor, beginning at the foot of Capitol Hill and extending westward to reach what is now the Lincoln Memorial. Gone was the miscellany of verdant parks and grounds; gone was the railroad station; and gone also were all the brick and brownstone Victorian buildings along the Mall's southern edge, including the Smithsonian Institution. In their place, a unified green space controlled the scene, accented by parterre gardens, water basins, and monuments and flanked by rows of trees in front of new, white, neoclassical buildings—with everything located in concert rather than by happenstance (pl. VIII).[6]

What the Senate Park Commission plan contemplated was a unified ceremonial core, scaled to early twentieth-century urbanism and reflective of a cosmopolitan vision of national culture. Besides the renewed Mall, the core scheme also included formal groups of public buildings around Capitol Square, around Lafayette Square just north of the White House, and between the Mall and Pennsylvania Avenue (an area now known as the Federal Triangle). The newly made Potomac Park contained two monuments, one to terminate the Capitol axis, the other the White House axis. Also integral to the core were a new union railroad station and a memorial bridge across the Potomac River.[7]

A second phase of the plan called for a vast, new park system joining together the outer reaches of the city (pl. IV). From the Mall core, a shore drive ran along the Potomac River leading to a parkway through the valley of Rock Creek that connected to both a multilane boulevard and a beltway across the northern reaches of the city. These roads provided access to several federal sites, including Civil War forts and the grounds of the U.S. Soldiers Home. Further on, additional park and road connections led to the Anacostia River, and to an array of Civil War forts in the southeastern portion of the district, yielding a park chain that encircled most of the city. This phase of the plan also called for the inauguration of a playground system; the transformation of the malarial Anacostia flats into an immense water park; the more "sober treatment" and better regulation of Arlington cemetery; the preservation of the Potomac River palisades and the Chesapeake and Ohio Canal; the establishment of the Great Falls of the Potomac as a national park, of a quay for the Georgetown waterfront, and of a memorial drive to Mount Vernon.[8]

The great puzzle of the Senate Park Commission plan is why a scheme of such remarkable sweep and boldness ever appeared. It followed no European model, despite specific borrowings from European civic and garden design. No American city had ever contemplated anything like it. It was, in fact, *sui generis*: a new and comprehensive vision for the capital and the nation. As such, it reflected an extraordinary convergence of events whose interactions could hardly have been forecast even twelve months earlier. And because it was so idealistically framed and swiftly formulated at a time of fiscal stringency, its prospect for survival and influence was anything but certain. Yet it had appeared in the one city whose planning had always been an American exception.

The story, in outline, unfolded as follows. After several prominent Washingtonians, most of them members of the Board of Trade, had organized a lavish, patriotic celebration to mark the 100th anniversary of the federal government's move to Washington in 1800, their initiative became entangled with city-development issues sparked by a power struggle between Senator McMillan and the entrenched U.S. Army Corps of Engineers. The latter had held executive authority over public buildings and grounds, including the Mall, since 1867. The root question was how to eliminate dangerous railroad grade crossings throughout the city. The controversies that ensued placed the entire urban fabric at issue, most especially the civic core, establishing quite by accident the citywide and multipurpose character of the struggle and hence of the Senate Park Commission plan as its ultimate outcome.

The American Institute of Architects (AIA), well into these controversies, seized hold of the 12 December 1900 centennial event to showcase their profession's most advanced ideas about civic art. Interested in much more than theory, they immediately allied themselves with Senator McMillan and the Board of Trade against the engineers to attain their goals in an unprecedented way: by means of a park system plan for the entire city. Once the Senate Park Commission was named, Chicago architect Daniel H. Burnham played a catalytic role by disregarding McMillan's initial instructions to produce a "preliminary" scheme, pushing instead for an ideal solution. Burnham's leadership, in turn, engendered a deep commitment among all the plan-makers, including McMillan and his political aide, Charles Moore, to the plan itself. Consequently, its creators became its chief advocates in the struggles that followed its release. Finally, the architectural profession through the AIA and a host of civic arts-advocacy groups brought together by the burgeoning City Beautiful Movement established a national constituency for the plan outside of Washington that proved crucial to its survival.

MARKING THE CENTENNIAL

By any telling, the story begins with the effort to celebrate the centennial. The initiators were leaders of the Board of Trade, the most powerful civic promotional body in the capital. After organizing in October 1898, they approached President William McKinley in mid-November, suggesting several ideas: a memorial hall, a majestic bridge across the Potomac River, or some other durable work that would "inspire patriotism and a broader love of country."[9] These conventional, if costly, ideas typified the rituals and piecemeal methods of city-making then commonplace in the United States.

When neither the House nor the Senate authorized a specific project, the Board of Trade called a meeting of local, congressional, and national centennial committees for 21 February 1900. This was to be a glittering occasion, staged as much to honor the state governors who comprised the national committee as to make major decisions. It would culminate in a lavish banquet that would feature the surprise illumination of a huge "American flag of electric lights," emblematic of the unabashed patriotism of the era. Prior to the event, the local sponsors had agreed among themselves to push the Potomac River bridge as their most popular goal. The centennial, they hoped, would climax with the laying of its cornerstone. But to everyone's surprise, the assemblage substituted entirely new objectives.[10]

This turnabout was the work of Senator McMillan, a millionaire and, by reputation, "one of the five senators who 'practically run the United States.' "[11] McMillan was appointed to the Senate

Centennial Committee on 16 February 1900, and five days later became chairman and spokesman of an ad hoc group to evaluate centennial projects. Instead of promoting the bridge, the favorite project of local leaders, McMillan called for the enlargement of the White House, an idea of long standing in Washington, and proposed the building of a three-mile-long Centennial Avenue to begin at the foot of Capitol Hill and to run obliquely through the Mall to the Potomac River (fig. 2). The latter idea, said the next day's *Evening Star*, was "a new scheme, unverified by official surveys, virtually unheralded and unknown."[12]

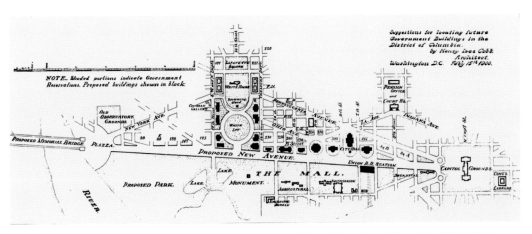

Fig. 2 The avenue plan, called Centennial Avenue by its promoters, designed by architect Henry Ives Cobb, 15 February 1900. *The Inland Architect and News Record*, 35 (Mar. 1900). Photo courtesy The Fine Arts Library, Harvard College Library.

THE AVENUE PLAN AND THE PENNSYLVANIA RAILROAD

McMillan's sponsorship of the avenue plan signaled a critical turning point in the centennial discussions. On the surface, he had raised a genuine, if far-fetched, civic art issue being debated chiefly among Washington architects: whether the original design of the Mall should be reinstated. When McMillan publicly announced the avenue plan, he upheld it as a fulfillment of L'Enfant's dream and as an opportunity to group public buildings, a civic art issue also current among architects.[13] But he was not being candid. The avenue plan had much less to do with L'Enfant and civic art than with two major pieces of railroad legislation that he had recently introduced in the Senate in December to January, 1899 to 1900. Both bills represented complex bargains hammered out during the previous three years with the two railroads that entered the capital, the Baltimore and Potomac (B & P), which was owned by the powerful Pennsylvania Railroad, and the Baltimore and Ohio Railroad (B & O), which operated a terminal at New Jersey Avenue and C Street, NW.[14]

The laws committed the railroads to eliminate grade crossings by removing tracks from the city streets. This hazard, common to most American cities, had killed annually as many as three people and had yielded "a steady stream of serious accidents, one occurring roughly every three weeks."[15] The laws, in turn, authorized each railroad to build new passenger terminals. The old, crowded B & P depot on the Mall would be replaced by an enormous, up-to-date facility in the same location but on a much expanded, fourteen-acre site between Sixth and Seventh streets. The existing tracks across the Mall would be ripped up and rebuilt nearby on a massive, elevated structure to be thrown across the Mall.[16]

Never before had anything so fundamentally destructive to the Mall—or to L'Enfant's vision of it—been contemplated. Yet as sponsor of the legislation, McMillan had wedded himself to the scheme for as long as the Pennsylvania Railroad refused to budge from its coveted position. Viewed in this light, the proposed avenue represented a grand approach street to the new terminal. Its curiously oblique alignment would offer travelers a direct route eastward toward Capitol Hill and westward toward the White House, making the new terminal "so … easy of access as if it were the very pivotal point to all else" in the city.[17] Why McMillan introduced the idea is a significant puzzle. Even the Pennsylvania Railroad opposed it.[18]

LOCAL ORIGINS: THE BATTLE OF PLANS

The Army Corps of Engineers within the War Department became McMillan's first and most determined antagonists. Routinely, Army engineers assigned to duty anywhere in the country reviewed federal public works and reported their findings to the president, who submitted them to Congress. As early as 29 January 1900, the Corps in Washington responded to an official request by McMillan for their technical judgment of his railroad bills.[19] They more than replied: they exploded. Colonel Theodore A. Bingham, the outspoken superintendent of the Office of Buildings and Grounds (since 1867 under the War Department), denounced the proposed terminal as a desecration of the Mall, a travesty of L'Enfant's "noble plan," and an "unpatriotic" rebuke to the memory of George Washington.[20] McMillan's diagonal avenue plan further outraged the engineers.[21] On 5 March 1900, less than two weeks after McMillan unveiled his scheme, Bingham submitted an alternative Mall plan to President McKinley. In it, he banned the proposed terminal to a position south of the Mall, called for a mid-Mall boulevard between Capitol Hill and the Washington Monument, and suggested that any new public buildings be erected along Pennsylvania Avenue.[22]

Meanwhile, the avenue plan had alarmed other Washingtonians, especially businessmen who had long favored upgrading the triangle of land between the Mall and Pennsylvania Avenue. "Given up almost wholly to slumdom," with prostitution along Thirteenth and Fourteenth streets, this area disgraced respectable Washington.[23] By 1900 downtown interests clearly wanted the area upgraded by erecting new government buildings—an incremental slum-removal program.[24] But McMillan's proposed avenue and the building sites he favored along it lay far enough to the south to undercut that hope while stirring fears that Pennsylvania Avenue might become a "back street."[25] Thus, the fate of the Triangle slum and of Pennsylvania Avenue also became entangled in the battle and, ultimately, in the Senate Park Commission plan.

Finally, the avenue plan impinged upon a park system initiated by the Washington Board of Trade in 1899. Following the lead of many American cities in the 1890s, the board had contemplated a great chain of parks and parkways as proof of civic stature. Washington, they claimed, already possessed magnificent resources: the newly made 739-acre Potomac Park; the National Zoological Park in the southern end of Rock Creek valley; the immense Rock Creek Park, just north of the zoo; the parklike grounds of the U.S. Soldiers Home; and various Civil War hilltop fortifications. But except for the zoo, none of these parcels had been developed yet for regular public use, let alone linked by parkways.[26]

Well before McMillan had proposed his avenue plan, the Senate's District of Columbia Committee had aired these ideas and had even readied legislation authorizing a park commission to devise a scheme.[27] But McMillan's proposed avenue raised awkward questions about how such a "grand thoroughfare" could serve public needs and railroad interests simultaneously. Also under scrutiny was the free grant of Mall land to the Pennsylvania Railroad by the proposed grade crossing legislation.[28] These unresolved and conflicting goals resulted in a broad battle over the future development of the nation's capital. Senators, congressmen, army engineers, centennial promoters, downtown businessmen, Civil War veterans, the Washington press, and numerous civic leaders had joined the fray, all disputing basic questions of civic art, park system design, and even slum removal, as if these were interrelated considerations.

THE VICTORIOUS ENGINEERS

To reconcile these divergent viewpoints, McMillan, on 14 May 1900, introduced in the Senate a resolution asking the president to appoint a panel of art professionals. An architect, a landscape architect,

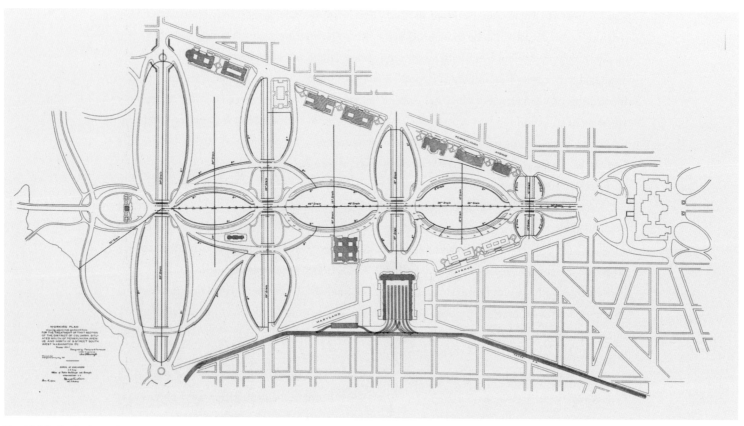

Fig. 3 Mall plan by Samuel Parsons, Jr., 1900. Collection: Pamela Scott

and a sculptor would work with Army engineers to devise a plan for the entire Mall-Triangle area and also to devise a "suitable connection" between Potomac Park and the zoo.[29] The same experts would design the enlargement of the White House. In effect, McMillan sought to reinstate the architects' and artists' traditional right to oversee construction of their own works. The Army engineers had usurped this role in 1867 when Congress had relegated architects to the task of providing only the first drafts of public buildings while asking engineers to both provide technical expertise and wield executive authority over construction, including any design changes they deemed necessary.

In the House version of the bill, the Army engineers, not a panel of art professionals, would carry out the work. On 6 June a House-Senate conference resolved the impasse, with the engineers maintaining the executive role they had played for the past three decades. The chief of engineers then assigned Bingham to the tasks of redesigning the White House—as the president's aide-de-camp, he had worked out of that building since 1897—and of hiring a landscape architect to plan the Mall-Triangle area and the parkway link to the zoo.

In October the *Ladies Home Journal* published Bingham's massive, if truncated, version of Frederick Dale Owen's 1890 plan for White House enlargement.[30] On 5 December the War Department issued a Mall design by Samuel Parsons Jr., the New York landscape architect chosen by Bingham (fig. 3). The Parsons plan, though idiosyncratic, fulfilled one purpose of the engineers by relegating the railroad terminal to the south of the Mall. "A lightning express," Parsons remarked, "is quite incompatible with a green garden and singing birds."[31]

THE ARCHITECTS INTERVENE

The American Institute of Architects assembled in Washington for its annual convention on Centennial Day, 12 December 1900, having rescheduled its meetings to address the issues provoked by the Centennial Avenue scheme. Above all, the AIA wanted Congress to entrust the shaping of the capital core to the nation's premier architects and artists, the same aesthetic elite that had crystallized civic art aspirations in America at the Chicago World's Fair of 1893, or World's Columbian Exposition as it was formally called.

Glenn Brown, the secretary of the AIA who masterminded this strategy, was well prepared professionally and politically.[32] About ten years earlier, while making an exhaustive study of the U.S. Capitol, Brown had recognized L'Enfant's Mall as the true vista to and from the Capitol. As early as 1894 he had launched a personal crusade to arouse his profession to reclaim the Mall in accord with L'Enfant's intentions. Even then, he had opposed the Army Corps of Engineers for the job, reflecting an enmity toward engineers endemic to his profession and notably virulent among AIA members. That body, Brown remarked acidly in 1894, had "never been accused of being artistic."[33] In 1887 Brown had also organized the Washington AIA chapter and in 1895 to 1897, with other chapter members, had established the Public Art League, the first organization to advocate the creation of a national fine arts commission.[34]

As national secretary of the AIA, Brown served an organization already steeped in pressure-group tactics learned from its long struggle to enact and then enforce the Tarsney Act of 1893, a law that stipulated open competitions for federal buildings.[35] Alarmed by the ill-fated Centennial Avenue, he quickly persuaded the AIA to stage its annual meeting as a protest against haphazard city building in the nation's capital.[36] Brown made the "Grouping of Government Buildings, Landscape, and Statuary" the meeting's organizing theme, evoking the growing enthusiasm of his profession for ensembles of buildings utilizing classical architecture with baroque spatial effects, especially when achieved by collaborating architects, sculptors, painters, and fine craftsmen.[37] Many American architects, most especially the AIA elite, had absorbed this Renaissance ideal from studies at the École des Beaux-Arts in Paris.[38] In all, Beaux-Arts classicism in the United States, sometimes called the American Renaissance, conveyed a host of ideas then emergent in national culture: public order, progress; civilization, refined taste; civic pride; and national wealth and power.

From March to November 1900 Brown recruited speakers for the AIA convention and orchestrated their assault, alerting them to Bingham's article in the *Ladies Home Journal* and even cautioning sculptor H. K. Bush-Brown against proposing any commission "dominated in any way by the army engineers."[39] When the architects assembled, they scorned Bingham's White House scheme and on 13 December staged an evening session on the design of the capital city that was reported in local papers.[40] Every AIA speaker sought a formal, monumental, aesthetically unified composition of buildings, statuary, and public grounds, all done in a grand manner and all rendered consistent with the L'Enfant plan as they understood it. "The city of to-day has grown too large to be picturesque," C. Howard Walker proclaimed.[41] No speaker that evening discussed the park system of the city or the suburban districts through which it would reach.[42]

Earlier that day, however, five representatives of the AIA had met with McMillan or his aide Moore, and, almost certainly, someone from the Board of Trade.[43] The Board, long accustomed to working with McMillan, had wanted backing for its park ideas.[44] Not only had the architects denounced Bingham, but they would ignore the Bingham-commissioned Parsons plan for the Mall-Triangle at their public session on the design of the city that evening. McMillan, for his part, still had his eyes riveted on his grade-crossing legislation, especially his bill authorizing the Mall terminal. Even as they met, his opponents in the House of Representatives were preparing to cite engineering criticism and the Parsons plan as justifications for voting down McMillan's legislation.[45] McMillan wanted the architects to sanction his claim that he had the beauty of Washington at heart. The architects, in turn, satisfied the senator's needs in one critical respect: they accepted, as a matter of realism, his terminal in the Mall.[46]

Once allied with McMillan, the AIA had no choice but to embrace park planning. Powerful as McMillan was in Washington affairs, his District of Columbia committee lacked authority over building location, which belonged to the Senate Committee on Public Buildings and Grounds, or over statuary, which lay with a Joint (House-Senate) Committee on the Library.[47] But McMillan did have power over park matters and had already worked with the Board of

Trade to prepare park legislation. Thus the AIA agreed to address this issue, and the Board of Trade, the chief promoter of the park system, agreed to add the subjects of building and bridge placement to its publicly stated goals for the city.[48] Ostensibly, McMillan had fathered a new coalition for the physical improvement of Washington and a strategy for seizing the planning initiative from the engineers.

In fulfillment of this bargain, McMillan introduced Joint Resolution No. 139 in the U.S. Senate. Intended to win the support of both houses of Congress for the planning of Washington, this measure authorized the President of the United States to appoint a commission consisting of two architects and one landscape architect to "consider the subject of the location and grouping of public buildings and monuments … and the development and improvement of the park system" of the district. An appropriation of $10,000 was sought for expenses.[49]

SENATOR McMILLAN FULFILLS THE BARGAIN

Joint Resolution No. 139 would never clear the Senate let alone the House. In the House, Joseph Cannon, the chairman of the House Appropriations Committee, already loomed as a predictable adversary, notorious for his "skinflint" proclivities and distrust of artists.[50] Nonetheless, McMillan found a way to honor his bargain.[51] After 12 February 1901, when his B & P railroad bill was finally enacted, McMillan's trusted aide and confidant, Charles Moore, suggested a new strategy (fig. 4).[52]

Fig. 4 Charles Moore (1855-1942). Commission of Fine Arts

Accordingly, on 8 March during an executive session of the Senate held after the adjournment of Congress, McMillan obtained last minute passage of a resolution authorizing his committee to "report to the Senate plans for the development and improvement of the entire park system of the District of Columbia." Appropriate "experts" might be consulted and expenses defrayed from "the contingent fund of the Senate."[53] These experts, once appointed, would become known as the Senate Park Commission (later, often known as the McMillan Commission). But their authority, it must be emphasized, rested on a far more tenuous base than had been envisioned in Joint Resolution No. 139 back in December. Furthermore, the new measure said nothing whatsoever about public buildings and monuments.

Following through on 19 March, McMillan and Senator Jacob H. Gallinger of New Hampshire, acting as a subcommittee of the Senate Committee on the District of Columbia, held an informal hearing with representatives of the AIA. Their purpose was to discuss, as McMillan put it, the "improvement of the park system" and, "incidentally," the placement of public buildings.[54] Landscape architect Frederick Law Olmsted Jr. also attended, making a detailed record.[55] Everyone present agreed that three experts should be appointed, but no one articulated just what sort of plan they should formulate.

As the hearing proceeded, however, a very definite objective emerged: the commission should devise a "preliminary plan" as distinct from a "matured one."[56] Because the scheme would be tentative, it could then be negotiated through the three Senate and House committees that had jurisdiction over parks, buildings, and statuary—or through a joint committee representing all three bodies.[57] A final, amended plan would be developed later. In light of the tenuous mandate McMillan had won for his commission, this cautious, consensus-building strategy made excellent sense. As Olmsted Jr. noted, McMillan wanted a "comprehensive scheme" but feared that "it might be turned down by the other Committees if it were made too complete and pushed too far."[58]

DANIEL H. BURNHAM: CATALYST

Daniel H. Burnham, the Chicago architect nationally known for having orchestrated the planning and construction of the Chicago World's Fair in 1893, played the catalytic role in redefining this mission. As Moore later recalled, he had proposed Burnham, then age 54, as a member, and McMillan, in turn, had suggested Frederick Law Olmsted Jr., then only 30, recognizing him as the mantle bearer for his eminent father. They then communicated their wishes to the AIA, which nominated them on 19 March 1901.[59] These two men, once enlisted, also took their cues from McMillan and Moore, choosing as the third member, Charles F. McKim, the celebrated New York architect who epitomized the conservative wing of the American Renaissance with its preferences for Roman and Renaissance modes of civic art over more recent and flamboyant French variants. "Only your association with the Washington work," McKim later telegramed Burnham, "made it possible for me to accept." Not until early June did Augustus Saint-Gaudens, the eminent

Fig. 5 Members of the Senate Park Commission

Daniel Hudson Burnham (1844-1912), Chairman
Commission of Fine Arts

Charles Follen McKim (1847-1909)
Photograph by Frances Benjamin Johnston, courtesy
The American Institute of Architects Library and
Archives, Washington, D.C.

Frederick Law Olmsted, Jr. (1870-1957)
U.S. Department of the Interior, National Park Service,
Frederick Law Olmsted National Historic Site

Augustus Saint-Gaudens (1848-1907)
U.S. Department of the Interior, National Park Service,
Saint-Gaudens National Historic Site, Cornish, NH

sculptor, become the fourth commissioner, at the suggestion of McKim.[60] Due to illness, he would play a limited but not insignificant role. All four men were veterans of the Chicago World's Fair; even "young Olmsted" had worked there assisting Burnham (fig. 5).[61]

At the 19 March hearing, McMillan and Gallinger made clear that they wanted a "preliminary plan" so as to avoid heavy expenses. When Burnham and Olmsted had first conferred on 22 March with McMillan, they had quickly estimated $22,600 as their "maximum expense." But McMillan wanted "between $15,000 and $20,000,"[62] and he publicized a still lower sum, reported by the *Washington Post* as "about $10,000."[63] These dollar figures provide benchmarks for gauging how far the commission would soon exceed its instructions.

From the outset, Burnham's powerful personality and expansive outlook dominated, with McMillan treating Burnham as if he were the chairman of the commission, though Burnham would later ask Moore to confirm this unstated fact.[64] Burnham declared that he would serve without compensation. The others followed suit. Burnham wanted every aspect of Washington's urban setting to be considered, just as at the Chicago Fair, when he had overseen everything from sewerage to color effects. In early May, for example, he wrote out eleven pages of topics to explore, including public grounds and buildings, a "general plan of roads" issued by the army engineers in 1898, building-height limits, and even the appearance of private lawns and gardens, public markets, and street vendors.[65] As he had explained to Olmsted in mid-April, on another matter, "My own belief is that instead of arranging for less we should plan for rather more extensive treatment than we are likely to find in any other city."[66]

Action more than words defined Burnham's role. Early on McMillan informed Burnham that the new B & P terminal to be built by the Pennsylvania Railroad must be regarded as "a fixture upon the Mall."[67] But Burnham refused to accept this reality. Since September he had known that Alexander Cassatt, the president of the Pennsylvania Railroad, might employ his firm to design that very structure.[68] To Burnham this spelled opportunity, not conflict of interest. When Burnham reached Washington, 5 April, before seeing anyone and not having spoken to McKim in the interval, he "drove to the location of the Obelisk." And the next day, before making a trolley tour of the city outskirts prearranged by Moore and McMillan, the commission, led by Burnham, "drove to the Obelisk-Capitol axis."[69] Back in Chicago, on 10 April, Burnham wrote Olmsted asking if they were ready to design the Mall's main axis "on a large scale."[70] The second of two of the Commission's earliest sketch plans both dated 27 April, diagramed precisely this area, reasserting L'Enfant's Mall and relegating the railroad station to the south side of the Mall (pl. V).[71]

Fig. 6 Union Station, after erection of the Columbus Monument and the City Post Office (far left), c. 1915. *The Architectural Work of Graham Anderson Probst & White* (London, 1933), vol. 2, pl. 89.

On 20 May Burnham shifted from thought to deed. That day, he arrived at the Philadelphia headquarters of the Pennsylvania Railroad empire, hoping for the assignment to design the terminal.[72] But he did not come as a passive supplicant. He brought rough plans for the alternative site south of the Mall. Afterwards that same day in two excited letters to McKim, whom he addressed as a coconspirator, Burnham reported that Cassatt and his chief engineers had "no idea of the development we had worked out" and had still been thinking of "the old location." "The new idea," he stated with relief and some amazement, "has been received with much more open-mindedness than I had hope of." In fact, the railroad had agreed to halt land purchases "for the old scheme," at least until a more detailed proposal for "the new location" could be presented.[73]

Suddenly, the "fixture upon the Mall" seemed less secure. The railroad certainly had its own reasons and interests and, in fact, had long opposed that particular site.[74] The actual direction of Cassatt's thinking soon became apparent to Burnham. On 8 June he reached Philadelphia, carrying "a hundred or more sketches for the Washington station as part of the new plan," only to discover the following day Cassatt's interest in the new terminal site granted to the Baltimore and Ohio Railroad, just north of the Capitol.[75] As Burnham explained to Cassatt, writing from the commission drafting room in Washington two days later, "The frontage of the B & O plaza toward the Capitol, on which you suggested that a great union depot could be built, is 780 feet; this would be ample for a monumental treatment."[76]

The commission did not know that during their trip to Europe from mid-June to mid-August 1901, McMillan would follow up Burnham's initiative by inviting Cassatt to "Eagle Head," his vacation home at Manchester-by-the Sea on the Massachusetts coast north of Boston. As Moore recalled the story off the record years later, the two men had settled the much-vexed terminal question while playing a game of golf, before Burnham's later, better-known July conference with Cassatt on the same matter in London.[77] Whatever precisely was agreed to, much remained to be done, with key negotiations still to take place between Burnham and Cassatt in late September and between Cassatt and McMillan in early December. "Mr. Burnham has accomplished a great deal in procuring this agreement from Mr. Cassatt," McMillan remarked to Moore after the late September meeting.[78] During the fall of 1901, Burnham and his chief designer Peirce Anderson concentrated on the layout and location of the terminal.

Cassatt's decision to remove the proposed terminal from the Mall, even after obtaining the 12 February legislation guaranteeing the site, stemmed from many factors: McMillan's offer to persuade Congress to meet the increased expenses involved in building a tunnel under the Mall or Capitol grounds; the existence of an alternative site north of the Capitol, made available to the B & O by the newly enacted grade-crossing legislation; and a recent decision by the Pennsylvania to purchase "a controlling interest" in the B & O, which thus gave it access to the alternative site, and Cassatt's own largeness of vision.[79] But without Burnham's initiative in May, boldly suggesting the relocation of the terminal in the first place, neither Cassatt nor McMillan would have altered their course, nor would the Commission have been as zealous in pursuing "the very finest plans their minds could conceive" (fig. 6).[80]

THE COMMISSION AS A FORCE

McMillan and Moore became advisors, facilitators, and ultimately advocates. At McMillan's command a committee room in the Capitol became the commission's headquarters, and Moore commandeered the north-facing Senate Press Gallery as its drafting room manned by James G. Langdon from Olmsted Jr.'s office.[81] When Burnham, McKim, and Olmsted gathered as a team for the first time on 6 April, they traversed Washington in a luxury trolley car obtained by Moore from the president of the street railway system.[82] The following day they visited Secretary of War Elihu Root and other newly appointed members of the Grant Memorial Commission.[83] Congress had authorized $250,000—an immense sum—for a statue or memorial to Ulysses S. Grant as Commanding General of the Union Army, its location yet to be determined.[84] Root then escorted the architects to the White House to be greeted by President McKinley.[85] A reception followed at the home of Senator McMillan.

All this heartened the commission. "The Washington business opens with great promise," McKim reported soon thereafter, noting the probable support of the president, Root, and Treasury secretary Lyman Gage, the latter a personal friend of Burnham. "If half of what is talked of can be carried through, it will make the Capital City one of the most beautiful centers in the world." "I do not think you will hear any more of the proposed alterations of the White House," he added.[86] Burnham returned to Chicago full of enthusiasm. "The Washington work is a stupendous job, full of the deepest interest, and it appeals to me as nothing else ever has. I have the best fellows with me, and we have the sympathy of all officials in Washington."[87]

Burnham, McKim, and Olmsted all focused on the Mall, even as they began to differentiate their roles in shaping the overall plan. Olmsted, who in the 1890s had advised on street extensions and the layout of the National Zoo and St. Elizabeth's Hospital, had already favored the Mall as an open, axial corridor flanked by "masses of foliage and architecture" when he had addressed the 1900 AIA convention.[88] In contrast, neither Burnham nor McKim had had prior Washington commissions. But the thrust of the AIA convention, their shared experience at the Chicago World's Fair, as well as their own architectural and planning principles inevitably drew them to L'Enfant's plan and the antecedents of his ideas.

When the commission gathered for the second time on 19 April, "Senator McMillan himself launched the enterprise by giving a large dinner at which Senators, Cabinet members, and influential citizens" met the designers informally.[89] The three men then took a three-day excursion aboard a U.S. Navy steamer down the Potomac River and up the James River to observe the remnants of southern civic design at Williamsburg and several Virginia plantations and to catch the afterglow of the late eighteenth century in America.[90] The respective roles of Burnham and McKim began to emerge, with Burnham focusing on railroad matters and McKim on the design of the Mall. The architects met again on 14 to 19 May and 10 to 11 June and took a second boat trip to the eastern shore of Maryland on 15 to 16 May to visit the Wye and Whitehall estates.[91] There is no better measure of their growing cohesion and commitment than their personal advances of about $1,000 each to George C. Curtis, the Boston model maker, to get him started on two sizable representations of the capital, one to show existing conditions, the other the proposed changes.[92]

By the first week of June Burnham, McKim, and Olmsted Jr. had conceptualized the Mall as a great corridor extending from Capitol Hill west to the Potomac River—its axis realigned to bisect the Washington Monument—and crossed by a second corridor running due south from the White House (pl. VI).[93] With placement of the Grant and Lincoln memorials under consideration, McKim proposed Saint-Gaudens as a fourth member of the commission.[94] About this time, the commission also resolved the precise width of the Mall's central greensward by requesting "the Supervising Architect of the Treasury to erect some flag poles where we could see them from the steps of the Capitol and from the Washington Monument itself.... We tried 250 feet, and we tried 400 feet, and we tried 300 feet, and the 300-foot space was most plainly the best."[95]

THE EUROPEAN TOUR: PERFECTING THE MALL

When the commission, including Moore, departed for Europe on 13 June 1901 aboard the *Deutschland,* their goal was to refine the Mall's design and to find inspiration for its special features. Abroad, they immersed themselves in the baroque antecedents to their own thinking, mostly from the seventeenth century, with bows to ancient Rome and Haussmann's Paris. The trip had been Burnham's idea, but Olmsted had laid out the itinerary, emphasizing gardens associated with André Le Nôtre.[96] From their landing at Cherbourg, France, 19 June, until their departure from Southampton, England, 26 July, the commission visited Rome, Venice, Vienna, Budapest, Paris and environs, and London and nearby stately homes.[97] Olmsted took photographs, recording in and near Rome the Vatican gardens, Hadrian's Villa and the Villa d'Este at Tivoli, the Villa Albani, the Villa Medici, and the Villa Lante. In Paris and vicinity, they studied the Tuileries gardens, the shores of the Seine, the Luxembourg gardens, Fountainebleau, and Vaux-le-Vicomte. The last, a masterpiece of Le Nôtre, received special attention. These specific places accounted for half of the 396 photographs that survive as a legacy of the trip.[98]

These pictures also reveal a preoccupation with architectonic garden details at every park, estate, and villa the travelers visited: terraces, stair systems, balustrades, statuary placement, garden vistas (fig. 7). Certain aspects of the Washington problem, it is worth noting, did not preoccupy them. At no point did they study railroad stations or their siting, although Burnham did visit the Gare d'Orsay in Paris and made a personal side trip for this purpose to Frankfurt, Germany, at the behest of Cassatt.[99] Nor did they explore the issues that concerned Olmsted, vis-à-vis a city-wide park system for Washington, except to study river quays in Budapest and Paris.[100] The United States, after all, already excelled in "park-making as a national art."[101]

Recollections made years later bear out these observations. Burnham, testifying before Congress in 1904, recalled the commission studying "every notable plantation where trees were used and an open space left between them" and finding at Bushy Park and Hatfield House in England the most satisfying approximations for the Mall's width, 300 feet between the inner rows of trees. They had also examined "every notable avenue in Europe" before settling on four rows of trees for each side of the Mall's central greensward.[102] Similarly, Olmsted recorded in 1935 that he and McKim, en route from Budapest to Paris, had decided how to lay out plantations of elms to frame the Washington Monument terrace.[103] And Moore, whose biographies of Burnham and McKim best record the trip, recollected that at the Villa Borghese, it was agreed that the proposed Memorial Bridge would be a low structure crossing the Potomac from the west end of the Mall on axis with the Robert E. Lee mansion in Arlington Cemetery.[104]

On 18 July 1901, Burnham conferred with Cassatt in London, learning that he was willing to move the train depot off the Mall, provided that the government helped to meet the costs.[105] The commission returned to the United States in high spirits, each member ready to fulfill his part of the undertaking.

EACH MAN TO HIS TASK

When the team disembarked at New York on 1 August Moore, by now a virtual member, immediately wrote McMillan, then at his seaside vacation home, describing the plan and, on 12 August personally briefed him for two hours.[106] "Everything is wonderfully propitious," he also reported to McKim. The Senator was "much pleased." In fact, he was already "working out in his own mind a scheme for the adjustment of the Pennsylvania railroad matter."[107] Before the commission visited McMillan at Eagle Head on 20 August, McKim recruited William T. Partridge as head draftsman.[108] Burnham, for his part, headed back to Chicago to oversee his affairs before returning to Washington on 16 August for a tour of Rock Creek Park.[109] Olmsted returned to Brookline, Massachusetts, checked up on Curtis, who was building the models in an old pool hall in nearby Roxbury, and then made his way to Washington on 11 August to confer with Langdon.[110] Since April Langdon had been assembling baseline maps and data, exploring "every foot of the District on foot or bicycle," and devising plans. And since June, he had been relaying photographs to Curtis for use in building the models.[111]

On 19 August Burnham, McKim, and Olmsted reassembled for the first time since their return from Europe, inspecting Curtis's models in Boston and travelling the next day to Manchester.[112] "On the wide veranda overlooking the sea," they recounted their trip to McMillan, his wife and his daughter, several neighbors, and Senator William B. Allison of Iowa. At dinner, to impress Allison,

McMillan repeatedly hailed Burnham as "General Burnham," Moore recalled years later, because a "man who could persuade President Cassatt to take the Pennsylvania Railroad out of the Mall, deserves to be a general."[113] Moore, in his memoirs, confessed that even he did not learn until long after McMillan's death that the Senator himself had played a significant role.[114]

Late that evening, after the designers had departed, McMillan lavished praise on them to Allison, and McKim, hearing of this from Moore, was delighted "that the heavy weights of the Senate got so fired up." "Things are, indeed, taking a shape which no-one would have dreamed of," McKim confessed. If the commission were "allowed to perfect the scheme" and "present it in the best possible guise," he predicted, it would "arouse the interest of Congress and the public, to a degree which we can not at present realize."[115] McMillan, now wholly committed, advanced $3,000 of his personal funds in mid-September to support the cash-needy Curtis; ultimately he would loan over $12,000 to insure that the models were completed.[116]

Olmsted and Langdon faced the challenge of framing a system of parks and parkways for the entire Washington area. A host of issues confronted them, including boundary realignments for Rock Creek Park, the treatment of the Georgetown waterfront, and the sanitary reclamation of the Anacostia wetlands. The most controversial was the treatment of the lower Rock Creek valley between Georgetown and Washington. The Board of Trade had been promoting an open valley park to replace the refuse-choked banks of Rock Creek as it ran about a mile through a shabby, low-income, industrial area, mostly populated by African Americans. The Army Corps of Engineers had urged filling the entire valley and running its stream through a buried sewer, a proposal favored by land developers who saw the valley as an eyesore, a health menace, and a dangerous haven for drifters and blacks.[117]

As Olmsted and Langdon developed the park system for the outer areas, they drew heavily on their firm's long experience with such design, especially in park-rich Boston. Between 1855 and 1881, Back Bay had been filled in, ending noisome conditions quite similar to Washington's Anacostia flats.[118] And by 1898, Boston had begun the nation's first playground system, utilizing school-based sites, an idea Olmsted would apply to Washington.[119] Finally, the State of Massachusetts, since 1893, had undertaken a vast metropolitan system of reservations for Boston, the first of its kind in the nation, emphasizing scenic and shoreline preservation and bathing beaches, all of which Olmsted Jr. ultimately adapted to Washington.[120]

On 3 December 1901 McMillan and Cassatt agreed to place the B & P railroad station on the north side of Massachusetts Avenue, a block east of North Capitol Street and facing the Capitol.[121] Although Burnham lavished attention on the station and its forecourt plaza, this complex would not be featured in the many drawings made that fall to illustrate the plan, probably because it was a private commission beyond the Senate Park Commission's mandate. But to Burnham, the "Grand Court" to be built in front of the depot as a "vestibule" to the city was "as important as the work around the Monument in the Mall" and just as "essential to the broad scheme of improvement."[122] Burnham also initiated a very significant component of the plan quite late in the process. On 27 November he suggested grouping legislative buildings around Capitol Square and executive buildings around Lafayette Square north of the White House.[123] In addition, McKim sent Burnham a telegram on 29 November which suggests that the Chicago firm contributed to the design of the proposed Memorial Bridge.[124]

Burnham also labored over the text of the Senate Park Commission's report, even hiring a Chicago writer, but Moore eventually took charge, pleasing McKim but deeply distressing Burnham who wanted a more popular style.[125] "I do not see how any of the matter that has been prepared can go into the report without being entirely rewritten," Moore confided to McKim in mid-December. "The tone of much that I have is that of flippant criticism." If published, it would "rob the Commission of the result of their very arduous and intelligent labors."[126] Olmsted matched Moore's clear, simple, and direct prose and the two produced the final draft, Olmsted writing the longer section relating to "park matters" with Moore presenting the rationale for reforming Washington's monumental core.[127] (see Appendices for Burnham's version)

Well before the report appeared, in June 1902, Moore had established himself as the public voice of the Senate Park Commission, publishing "The Improvement of Washington City" in the February and March 1902 issues of the *Century Magazine*, the plan's first public description.[128]

CHARLES F. McKIM: IMAGE MAKER AND DISPLAY ARTIST

As the planning unfolded, McKim steadily emerged as a key figure. From August onward, he took charge of the visual representation of the redesign of central Washington. The images soon created under his direction would win widespread support for the plan and powerfully influence the City Beautiful Movement just then emerging in the United States. Another turning point occurred in August, on the 26th, when McKim conferred with Root about the Grant Memorial, standing in for Burnham, who could not be present. Seeking support for placing the Grant Memorial at the Potomac end of the Mall, McKim discovered the depth of Root's backing and the lucidity of his advice.[129] A meeting between the representatives of the two commissions that might have been adversarial resulted in a long-term liaison.

Fig. 7 A selection of photographs taken by Frederick Law Olmsted, Jr. during the Senate Park Commission's trip to Europe in 1901. Collection: Commission of Fine Arts

Paris: the Louvre and the Pont Royal

Paris: the octagonal basin in the Tuileries. One suspects that architectural details, such as this one of the pool coping, were taken by Olmsted at the request of architect Charles McKim.

Vaux-le-Vicomte, the gardens. The man on the steps is Charles McKim. (Moore, *Burnham*, I, facing pg. 156)

Rome: Villa Albani

Bagnaia: Villa Lante

Tivoli: Villa d'Este

Vienna: Donau Kanal; work on quay and subway

Vienna: Restaurant in the Prater gardens. Perhaps McKim was again posing for Olmsted's camera.

Root, a man of brilliant legal talent and cosmopolitan sensibilities, made clear to McKim that he understood the multiple issues facing the Senate Park Commission, including conflicts with Army engineers.[130] Root personally accepted placement of the Grant Memorial (previously located near the White House) at the Potomac end of the Mall. In turn, he urged the Park Commission to address the Triangle slum for the sake of local business interests who wanted to see the area upgraded and to safeguard the historic stature of Pennsylvania Avenue. McKim listened. And the plan ultimately reflected Root's advice, specifying municipal structures for this locale. Root also forcefully suggested a major publicity campaign, with a simultaneous news release about the plan in key urban centers across the nation, even naming specific cities and newspapermen.[131] And something like it was soon attempted.

That fall McKim lavished attention on the Mall's details, especially the Washington Monument gardens, which one acquaintance lampooned as the "holy of holies."[132] About 13 October, the portion of the Curtis model devoted to the new Mall arrived from Boston and was installed on the sixth floor of McKim's offices.[133] Eventually, seventeen men, in addition to McKim and his chief draftsman Partridge, labored on the model and drawings, developing a notable esprit de corps.[134] "The firm complained that they never saw McKim unless they went upstairs," Partridge recalled.[135]

In late November McKim relocated the Grant Memorial from the Potomac end of the Mall to the foot of Capitol Hill, probably at the suggestion of Augustus Saint-Gaudens. Although a sculptor had yet to be chosen, McKim imagined this new setting, which he called "Union Square," as Washington's analogue to Place de la Concorde in Paris (pl. X).[136] This decision, endorsed by Root but not yet by the Grant Memorial Commission, led to the shifting of the Lincoln Memorial from the south end of the White House axis (now, the Jefferson memorial site) to the Potomac site, all because Grenville Dodge, chairman of the Grant Memorial Commission, had stubbornly opposed McKim's insistence that a triumphal arch be used to honor Grant at this latter site, instead of a sculptural group as mandated by Congress and favored by Dodge.[137]

That the Lincoln Memorial was decided so late underscores a fundamental aspect of the story that is easily overlooked: that the Senate Park commissioners proceeded as artists, giving precedence to design over symbolic content. From the outset, they had chosen to reinstate the original Mall from the Capitol to the Monument and to make its axis their organizing principle. By June they had elaborated a general framework, projecting the original Mall westward to the Potomac, identifying the accent points along its course, and reestablishing the White House cross axis as a central focus. By the time the team returned from Europe, if not before, McKim had settled on the principle that the Capitol axis must be terminated by a unique architectural feature. In contrast to the "arch" of the Capitol dome and the "pier" or vertical line of the Monument, the western end should be closed by a flat-topped structure, or "lintel," after the Arc de Triomphe in Paris or the Brandenburg Gate in Berlin.[138] That the architects wanted at first to honor Grant, not Lincoln, on the Potomac site startles the modern reader. In 1901, however, the placement of the Grant Memorial was a more urgent question.

As these decisions unfolded, McKim also became preoccupied with the upcoming exhibit of the models, drawings, and photographs. By late August he began urging "the right kind of drawings and enough of them"—watercolor renderings—to supplement the Curtis models.[139] McMillan, asked to countenance yet another expense, replied, says Moore, "Go ahead. If the Government will not pay for it, I will."[140] Moore arranged a dinner party on 22 October for the architects to meet the trustees of the Corcoran Gallery of Art and discuss a major exhibit.[141] Eventually a dozen illustrators and architectural renderers, including Henry Bacon and Jules Guerin, produced bird's-eye perspectives and ground-level views from multiple vantage points.[142] Olmsted compiled photographs for the exhibit as well as drawings that compared parks in six major American and European cities.[143]

On 15 January 1902 the Corcoran exhibit opened, with the still unfinished Curtis models in the "Hemicycle" room so that visitors might walk beside them or look down on them from a raised platform.[144] On the walls and in adjoining galleries 179 illustrations offered a compelling pictorial tour of what Washington might become, supplemented by photographs of the European settings that had inspired the commission.[145] For the heart of the city, the plan proposed a vast new ceremonial core, arranged as a kite-shaped expanse bounded by the Capitol and its building group to the east, the Lincoln memorial to the west, the White House and the executive buildings clustered about Lafayette Square to the north, and a complex of recreational buildings to the south. Immediately west of the Washington Monument where the two great axes of the plan crossed lay McKim's elaborate sunken garden.[146] Ironically, the proposed Union Station, the key to the entire scheme, had only a shadowy presence in three overview illustrations (pls. VII, VIII, XIII).[147] For the periphery, Olmsted provided a state-of-the art park system, including a Potomac parkway link from the Mall. Less prescriptive than McKim's monumental core, it suggested broad treatments more than detailed and completed designs.

Nothing like this exhibit had ever before been mounted in the United States: a spectacular display of a new vision for an already built city, specifying the future direction its development should take on a comprehensive basis. With the whole of Washington as its object, it captured the entire trajectory of the Senate Park Commission since March 1901: what its final report would describe as "the treatment of the city as a work of civic art."[148] Visitors could attend the exhibit free of charge on Tuesdays, Thursdays, Saturdays, and Sundays or pay a twenty-five cent fee all other days.[149]

THE POLITICS OF THE PLAN

By framing an ideal scheme, the Senate Park Commission had embraced one horn of a then insolvable political dilemma. If it had followed its original instructions to produce a "preliminary plan," subject to negotiation with other Senate committees, the result, at best, would have been a politically brokered, lackluster outcome. Almost certainly, the railroad would have remained in the Mall. But opting for a perfected plan had entailed great risks, financially and politically. By mid-December 1901 the commission had already "entirely used up the contingent fund of the Senate."[150] And by September 1902, when all its expenses had been accounted for, the price of its idealism had become apparent. The Curtis models alone, originally estimated at $13,000, had cost nearly $24,500. McKim had spent over $17,000, mostly for draftsmen and illustrators; Olmsted, about $4,300 on expenses and assistants; and Burnham, $1,550. Altogether, an undertaking originally estimated by McMillan publicly at $10,000 and privately at $15,000 to 20,000, had consumed almost $55,500.[151]

These excesses made the commission an easy political target, giving rise to myths of its wanton, almost dissolute ways. Repeated and embellished from year to year, they would find expression in 1904 in the *Chicago Chronicle*. Senator McMillan, so the story ran, had believed the cost would not exceed $5,000. But the commission had "immediately entered upon a career of extravagant expenditure that has few parallels," hiring a huge staff that occupied "nearly an entire floor of the new Willard Hotel, the most expensive in Washington," and then sailing "for Europe with a large and expensive retinue." McMillan, though a man of "sincerity and patriotism," had become "a victim of bad faith." Significantly, one fact in the tale was correct, or nearly so: that "Burnham, McKim, and Olmstead [sic] contracted obligations aggregating $60,000."[152] This reality kept the myths alive.

The only escape, politically, was to avoid head-on debate over the plan as a whole. Although the commission had assuaged local advocates of a memorial bridge, of Triangle slum redevelopment, and of Civil War fort sites, it also had made enemies, beginning with Colonel Bingham and the Army Corps of Engineers and now, potentially, those who spoke for institutions already present on the Mall, especially the Botanic Garden and the Department of Agriculture. Furthermore, any adversary could count on support from the plan's most powerful opponent, Joseph G. Cannon, of Illinois, a Congressman since 1873, the chairman of the House Appropriations Committee, a leader of Old Guard Republicans, and, beginning in 1903, Speaker of the House.[153]

In December 1901, well before this line-up of forces had become fully visible, Glenn Brown, working with Robert S. Peabody, president of the AIA, began to advocate a permanent art commission to enforce the plan, enlisting McKim and activating the Public Art League (PAL).

With the Senate Park Commission about to complete its work, Brown feared that Congress might assign its implementation to "the Commissioner of Public Buildings, an army engineer, or may place it under … the Chief Engineer of the Army."[154] Significantly, the first full-dress discussion of this proposal took place in New York, then the center of public art advocacy in the United States. On 16 December, at the office of architect George B. Post, McKim, together with Richard Watson Gilder, editor of *Century Magazine*, and Saint-Gaudens—both of them PAL officers—and Frederick Crowninshield, president of the Fine Arts Federation of New York, decided to defer to the judgment of Senator McMillan, as conveyed by Moore in a letter sent to McKim for use at the meeting.[155]

Although McMillan nine months earlier had foreseen the need for a permanent commission, the politics of the plan now looked very different.[156] Noting the poor shape of District finances and "a disposition in some quarters … to criticize the cost of your present plans," Moore, speaking for McMillan, thought it "unwise to give jealous and disgruntled people an opportunity at this time to say that the architects propose to run the country and shut out all others." McMillan was dealing with "500 individuals from all parts of the country" with diverse opinions. "The only thing to do is to overcome them in an easy fashion that will leave no bad blood…."[157] In short, the backers of the plan should offer no easy targets, especially measures that might jeopardize the entire effort. When Peabody revisited the issue in mid-March 1902, Moore again delivered McMillan's verdict through McKim. "Any movement at this time to secure a permanent Commission will be bad policy…. The present situation can not be improved, and may be seriously impaired by the proposed legislation."[158]

Only a gradualist approach offered an escape from the dilemma, keeping the plan alive by advancing it piecemeal. For McMillan, this meant pushing his Union Station bill, which he regarded "as the foundation of all the work."[159] Once that was settled, then he would consider a permanent commission, he told Moore in April.[160] Because the railroad in the Mall had long been recognized as a mistake, the Senator got his bill through the Senate by 15 May 1902, shortly before Congress adjourned.[161]

Then, unexpectedly, Senator McMillan died, 10 August, while at his vacation home in Massachusetts. Suddenly, the political mainspring of the plan was gone. In shock and grief, Olmsted wrote to Moore from Paris, where he had been studying European zoos. "I fell at once to wondering, fearfully, how seriously his irreplaceable loss would set back the movement upon which we have all come to set our hearts," he confessed.[162] McKim and Burnham, with Moore, joined the McMillan family in Detroit. Moore, his patron now dead and his career disrupted, would return to Washington, at the family's request, to settle the Senator's affairs and to shepherd the Union Station bill through

Congress, almost as a memorial.[163] On 4 December the House District Committee approved the bill; on 28 February 1903, Congress enacted it.[164] By 16 March Moore had left the capital for new employment in the far northern reaches of Michigan, at Sault Sainte Marie.[165] With his departure, the plan stood exposed to its enemies as never before. New political tactics would be needed if anything more than a new railroad station was to be its outcome.

THE CITY BEAUTIFUL AND THE SENATE PARK COMMISSION PLAN

To its good fortune, the Senate Park Commission plan coincided with the emergence of the City Beautiful Movement in the United States, quickly becoming one of its icons. Absent this development, the new vision of the Mall set forth in 1902 might never have been carried out. As a cause, the City Beautiful championed town and city beauty, drawing its support from the same native-born, business and professional groups that had been energizing municipal reform in efforts in the Northeast, Midwest, South, and West Coast since the mid-1890s. What had begun with local calls for efficient and honest governance in opposition to ward bosses and venal business interests, had blossomed by 1900 into a multifaceted campaign to address the city itself as the critical arena of national life. To many reformers, the forces then wrenching the nation and its cities—immigration, industrialization, ever-larger transit and railroad empires, big business mergers, and transformative technologies, such as electricity—necessitated the fashioning of a new civic order, to be achieved through a revitalized sense of citizenship or what many called a new civic consciousness. The City Beautiful, as one expression of this ethos, became something of a crusade as the twentieth century opened.[166]

As a movement, the City Beautiful wove together many threads of American aesthetic culture. The oldest of these, "village improvement," dated back to the mid-nineteenth century ideas of Andrew Jackson Downing about the upgrading of often bleak country towns and villages. By 1900, as "civic improvement," it had spread across the nation. Its activists, often women, demanded clean streets, tidy waterfronts, garbage incineration, municipal flower beds, public libraries, street trees, indeed almost anything that would make an ordinary place more visibly appealing.[167] A second thread involved "outdoor art," namely the naturalistic values that had been pushed forward by the movement for scenic urban parks, beginning with Central Park in New York before the Civil War and, after the war, exemplified by the city park system idea in Buffalo and Chicago by the late 1860s, in Boston and Minneapolis by the 1880s, and in Kansas City and Louisville by the 1890s, and culminating with the vast metropolitan system of Boston begun in the 1890s.[168]

Fig . 8 Court of Honor, Chicago Fair of 1893. Commission of Fine Arts

A more recent and more cosmopolitan thread, then called municipal art, had emerged among the New York artists and architects who had helped design and execute the Chicago World's Fair. The Chicago spectacle, they hoped, just might persuade city officials to make greater use of murals, statuary, artistic street fixtures, and other embellishments in public places. More profoundly, they sought to turn the post–Civil War pursuit of art and culture, which had long been the preserve of the rich and wealthy, toward the adornment of the public realm. From their vantage, the Chicago World's Fair had represented a breakthrough for public art, with its great Court-of-Honor basin, framed by white, classic buildings and adorned throughout with lavish outdoor sculptural and mural displays (fig. 8).[169] After the fair, a devastating economic depression had thwarted the impulse to translate this model into the fabric of real cities until the return of prosperity, about 1897.

As the new century dawned, the City Beautiful, just then coalescing as a national movement, favored piecemeal undertakings, not citywide planning. For example, the National League of Improvement Associations, founded in October 1900 in Springfield, Ohio, promoted virtually any action that would physically upgrade a town or small city. A year later, it renamed itself the American League for Civic Improvement, reflecting the new civic reform ethos. Yet another body, the American Park and Outdoor Art Association, begun in 1897, voiced the landscape-art tradition.[170] It groped at first for ways to uphold its values. One became the promotion of children's gardens; another was opposition to outdoor advertising. Meanwhile, municipal art societies in Cincinnati, Chicago, and Baltimore—all following New York's lead and emboldened by the new prosperity—together with various art and architectural organizations, envisioned bigger and ever more daring projects: a lakefront park in Chicago, a radial boulevard in Philadelphia, a public building group in Cleveland.

That all these efforts comprised a national movement first became apparent in the writings of Charles Mulford Robinson, a Rochester, New York newspaperman and magazine columnist. In 1901 he published *The Improvement of Towns and Cities,* soon dubbed "the bible of the believers in the city beautiful."[171] In it, he brought all threads of beautification effort together. Issued by a skeptical publisher who forced Robinson to bear the cost, it sold immediately and well, going through eleven reprints by 1916.[172] In fact, the diverse organizations which Robinson upheld as parts of a common cause were just then exploding in number, rising from about 300 "improvement" groups in 1901, to over 700 by 1902, to 1,740 in 1904, and reaching 2,426 in 1905. In these same years, the popular Chautauqua movement added its support as did great numbers of women's clubs, whose 300,000 members were organized through the General Federation of Women's Clubs.[173] Robinson had written his book as a manual for all these groups. Its success elevated him to the top ranks of the national organizations then promoting civic beautification.

Precisely as this "great civic awakening," as its advocates called it, gathered momentum, the Senate Park Commission displayed its spectacular plan for the national capital at the Corcoran Gallery in Washington, knowing that its fate hinged directly on its public reception.[174] On 15 January, with the finest photographs, the most artful renderings, the best possible display of the three-dimensional Curtis models, and maximum press coverage—locally and nationally—all arranged, President Roosevelt and his party and, soon thereafter, key members of Congress and the commissioners of the District of Columbia toured the displays. Knowingly or not, they commenced a publicity blitz intended to place the future of Washington squarely on the nation's public agenda.[175]

Although the Senate Park Commission had risked everything on a perfected scheme and Senator McMillan had been won over to this course, neither he nor his experts could have known that their idealism almost perfectly suited the mood underlying the City Beautiful. Fortunately for the plan, it cleared its first hurdle. The president, his cabinet, the congressmen, and the District commissioners liked what they saw.[176] Then in February, March, and April and with reduced frequency for the rest of the year, the national magazine press lavished attention on the scheme. Key journals of polite opinion and genteel culture—*Harper's Weekly*, *Outlook*, and *Century Magazine*, all of them esteemed by the nation's reform-minded groups—paid immediate heed.[177] Others, less prestigious and more specialized also offered major coverage, virtually guaranteeing the attention of the college-educated middle class throughout the nation.[178] Without exception, all of these accounts highlighted the spectacular aspects, especially the new Mall with its promised grandeur and patriotic appeal.

Meanwhile, the architectural profession, proud of its role in generating the plan, inundated its members with reports. Every one of its major publications and nearly every minor one provided detailed, authoritative coverage, sufficient to prime the rank and file for proselytizing interested laymen.[179] In addition, a lantern-slide lecture circulated, reaching about twenty cities by year's end. Daniel Burnham, Charles Moore, Frederick Law Olmsted, as well as William Partridge and Glenn Brown, all spoke to select groups in different cities.[180] As one Boston architect remarked of the plans after the first year of publicity, "almost everybody who reads only as he runs knows something about them."[181]

Many writers and editors instantly grasped the national significance of the Senate Park Commission plan. "We have the same opportunities here," said the *Inland Architect* of Chicago, upholding Washington "as an example for municipal improvement."[182] "What a tantalizing prospect this must be for an artistically sensitive New Yorker!" enthused the *New York Times*, urging that a "board of experts" be appointed to study "the general treatment of New York."[183] "The good work planned for the capital city," said the editors of *Century Magazine*, prophetically, "will give impetus to the advancing tide of civic improvement now passing over the United States." "The more these plans and pictures are studied," they added, "the more thorough, the more significant, the nobler, do they seem."[184]

Big-city art organizations swung into action, nowhere more swiftly than in New York where much of the actual preparatory work for the Senate Park Commission plan had taken place, especially for the design of the Mall.[185] Thus, only a few weeks into the publicity blitz, the Fine Arts Federation, speaking for the city's—and the nation's—artistic establishment, petitioned reform Mayor Seth Low, requesting that the Municipal Art Commission determine "the advisability of employing a commission of distinguished experts, as was done recently by Congress for the city of Washington."[186] Soon, the Municipal Art Society endorsed the effort, set up its own City Plan committee, and took charge of the campaign.[187] Efforts were even made to enlist McKim as the planner, to no avail.[188]

Other art centers began to stir. In Cincinnati, the Municipal Art Society arranged for a lecture on the Washington plan.[189] Similarly, the Boston Society of Architects discussed comprehensive planning for their city. "Somebody that knows has got to show the way to the City Beautiful," the principal speaker asserted. "The architects are of the cognoscenti; if they can not, no one can."[190] And in Chicago, the Municipal Art League by early 1903 foresaw "the necessity of the appointment of a similar commission … to offer a comprehensive plan for developing the natural advantages of Chicago."[191]

Charles Mulford Robinson, the master scrivener of the City Beautiful, caught the shift perfectly. In 1902 he was drafting his second major work, *Modern Civic Art or the City Made Beautiful*, to be issued in 1903. Recognizing the limitations of piecemeal action, he now recast his approach, concluding that "in an effort for civic improvement…the first step is to secure a comprehensive plan" and pointing to Washington. "Unless there be a well thought out, artistically conceived, general plan to work on," he emphasized, "our civic art will go astray, with lack of completeness or continuity."[192]

This embrace of the larger planning idea embedded in the Senate Park Commission plan soon yielded results. The prosperity and optimism of the nation at the opening of the new century and the proliferation of ambitious public works proposals and projects in many cities, together with the pursuit of beauty as a public value, had created a receptive climate for big ideas. By 1904 to 1905 New York, San Francisco, and Detroit were seeking expert advice on physical development. By 1909 over thirty-five cities in the United States had obtained comprehensive plans, some quite bold and elaborate such as Daniel H. Burnham's Plan of Chicago, issued in 1909, and others more modest, such as the many schemes devised by Charles Mulford Robinson. All of these reports, including those of such landscape architects as John Nolen and Frederick Law Olmsted, characteristically had one trait in common: they adhered to the Senate Park Commission plan idea of combining both suggestions for public building groups, usually in the form of civic centers, with proposals for parks and park systems. In bigger cities, a union railroad station often figured in the scheme.[193] A national pattern had been set.

The many organizations and enthusiasts who embraced city planning as the best vehicle for fulfilling the goals of the City Beautiful also became a resource for defending the Senate Park Commission plan itself, especially during the critical battle fought in early 1904 over the placement of the Department of Agriculture's proposed new building in the Mall, a struggle detailed elsewhere in this volume. Had this structure been built as originally intended, the commission's vision of the Mall and ultimately its overall plan would have suffered irreparable defeat. Worth noting here is the fact that in late February and early March 1904, even as Olmsted despaired that "the matter has been settled against us," he and others summoned every scrap of support from around the country. Glenn Brown, as AIA secretary, prepared and sent out thousands of circulars alerting AIA chapters and art organizations.[194] Olmsted himself enlisted Charles Eliot, president of Harvard, to write to Joseph Cannon.[195] He also worked with Boston-area architects to contact Senator Henry Cabot Lodge and wrote to his House representative, Samuel Powers, who defended the architects and the plan in a House speech in early March.[196] In addition, Olmsted fed information to the *Boston Herald* and *Boston Transcript*, to Senator Francis G. Newlands, and to Charles Mulford Robinson, who had caught wind of what was afoot.[197]

The defenders at first did not know their own strength, having never fought such a national battle before. Moore, by then based in Detroit and eager to reenter the fray, had by 7 March enlisted William McMillan, the deceased Senator's brother, to appeal to all Michigan congressmen in behalf of the plan. "I believe that the plans have got enough popular support by this time to bring about the right result if we can only bring the sentiment to bear," he told McKim.[198] The American Park and Outdoor Art Association, though crippled by an office fire in Rochester at this time, became a resource, thanks to Robinson, its secretary, and to Warren Manning, a Boston-area landscape architect with strong ties to Olmsted.[199]

Had there been no prior publicity blitz for the plan in 1902 and no City Beautiful Movement already alert to its significance, these appeals for support might have been far less successful. But on short notice, a lot could be done. For example, in Philadelphia, Charles Mulford Robinson, on 18 March, alerted Andrew Crawford Wright, an ardent civic reformer and experienced park promoter, who in turn summoned twenty representatives of local art and architectural groups. Meeting at the office of AIA architect Edgar Seeler, architect Frank Miles Day explained the situation and, together, they all agreed to contact local congressmen as well as place articles in the press.[200] The effect of such efforts is suggested by the experience of Massachusetts Congressman Powers who later told Olmsted that his speech defending the plan had brought forth "more letters and inquiries and seemed, to his surprise, to rouse a more widespread interest in the country than any speech he had ever made."[201]

In essence, the Senate Park Commission plan through the City Beautiful Movement was reflected back upon itself, helping to authenticate the case being made for its survival in Washington. Through such processes, the Senate Park Commission plan became more than a paper scheme: it became a new vision deeply expressive of what was possible for the capital and the nation.

The Lincoln Memorial and the Reflecting Pool soon after their completion and before the construction of Memorial Bridge. Commission of Fine Arts

NOTES

[1] Portions of this essay are based on Jon A. Peterson, "The Hidden Origins of the McMillan Plan for Washington, D.C., 1900–1902," in *Historical Perspectives on Urban Design: Washington, D.C., 1890–1910*, ed. Antoinette J. Lee, (Washington, D.C.: George Washington University Center for Washington Area Studies, Occasional Paper No. 1, 1983) and Jon A. Peterson, "The Nation's First Comprehensive City Plan: A Political Analysis of the McMillan Plan for Washington, D.C., 1900–1902," *Journal of the American Planning Association* 51 (spring, 1985), 134–50; and Jon A. Peterson, *The Birth of City Planning in the United States, 1840–1917* (Baltimore: Johns Hopkins University Press, 2003).

For their assistance with this essay, I should like to thank Pamela Scott, Fred Bauman of the Manuscript Division, Library of Congress, and Charles Atherton and Sue Kohler of the Commission of Fine Arts.

[2] Charles Moore, McMillan's political aide, was a participant as well as recorder and archivist of the plan. See especially Charles Moore, *Daniel H. Burnham: Architect, Planner of Cities*, 2 vols. (Boston: Houghton Mifflin Co., 1921); and idem, *The Life and Times of Charles Follen McKim* (Boston: Houghton Mifflin Co., 1929). Architect Glenn Brown was another key participant; see Glenn Brown, *Memories, 1860–1930: A Winning Crusade to Revive George Washington's Vision of a Capital City* (Washington, D.C.: W. F. Roberts, 1931). Important secondary works include Thomas S. Hines, *Burnham of Chicago: Architect and Planner* (New York: Oxford University Press, 1974); Howard Gillette Jr., *Between Justice and Beauty: Race, Planning, and the Failure of Urban Policy in Washington, D.C.* (Baltimore: Johns Hopkins University Press, 1995); Alan Lessoff, *The Nation and Its City: Politics, "Corruption," and Progress in Washington, D.C., 1862–1902* (Baltimore: Johns Hopkins University Press, 1994); Richard Longstreth, ed., *The Mall in Washington, 1791–1991* (Washington, D.C.: National Gallery of Art, 1991, 2002); and John W. Reps, *Monumental Washington: The Planning and Development of the Capital Center* (Princeton: Princeton University Press, 1967).

[3] For the Mall as a "waste" ca. 1852, see Anne C. Lynch, "A Sketch of Washington City," *Harper's Monthly Magazine* 31 (December 1852): 3. For the new taste for the picturesque, see Therese O'Malley, "'A Public Museum of Trees': Mid-Nineteenth Century Plans for the Mall," in *Mall in Washington*, Longstreth, ed., 61–76. For a history of the Mall, emphasizing its buildings and monuments, see Pamela Scott, "The Mall (ML)," in Pamela Scott and Antoinette J. Lee, *Buildings of the District of Columbia* (New York: Oxford University, 1993), 62–90.

[4] Dian Olson Belanger, "The Railroad in the Park: Washington's Baltimore & Potomac Railroad Station, 1872–1907," *Washington History* 2 (spring 1990): 5–15.

[5] Charles Moore, "Park Improvement Paper No. 6, Notes on the Parks and their Connections," in *Park Improvement Papers: A Series of Twenty Papers Relating to the Improvement of the Park System of the District of Columbia*, ed. Charles Moore (Washington, D.C.: Washington: Government Printing Office, 1903), 83–84. Government Printing Office hereafter abbreviated GPO.

[6] Senate Park Committee on the District of Columbia, *The Improvement of the Park System of the District of Columbia*, 57 Cong., 1st Sess., 1902, S. Rept. 166 (Washington, D.C.: GPO, 1902), 35–36, hereafter cited as *Senate Park Commission Report*.

[7] Ibid., 37–71.

[8] Ibid., 58–59, 73–122. Also proposed: a complex of hilltop, fort-site, and valley parks west of Rock Creek Park, a fort-park chain through the northern reaches of the city, new parks for northeast Washington, and development of East Potomac Park as a national arboretum. The park system proposals are discussed in detail by Timothy Davis elsewhere in this volume.

[9] William V. Cox, comp., *Celebration of the One Hundredth Anniversary of the Establishment of the Seat of Government in the District of Columbia* (Washington, D.C.: GPO, 1901), 21.

[10] "Scene of Splendor," *Evening Star*, 22 February 1901, 1. "Memorial Bridge, Too," *Washington Post*, 22 February 1900, 10. *Evening Star* and *Washington Post* hereafter cited as *Star* and *Post*, respectively.

[11] News clipping "Senator McMillan," enclosed with 7 August 1902 material, Box 1, Charles Moore Papers, Library of Congress, Manuscript Division, hereafter cited as Moore Papers, LC. See also David J. Rothman, *Politics and Power: The United States Senate, 1869–1901* (Cambridge: Harvard University Press, 1966), 45–50.

[12] "December Selected," *Star*, 21 February 1900; "Centennial Avenue," *Star*, 22 February 1900, 4. For Henry Ives Cobb's identity as designer of Centennial Avenue, see F. W. Fitzpatrick, "Beautifying the Nation's Capital," *Inland Architect and Building News* 35 (March 1900): 13–14; and F. W. Fitzpatrick, "Centennial of the Nation's Capital," *The Cosmopolitan* 30 (December 1900): 112. At this time Cobb was under official censure of the AIA for violating professional ethics during a design competition for the Pennsylvania statehouse.

[13] For McMillan's rationale, see "Boulevard to Bridge," *Post*, 26 February 1900, 3.

[14] The grade crossing bill (S.1929) for the B & P Railroad was introduced to the Senate 20 December 1899. "Bill and Joint Resolutions," *Senate Journal*, 56th

Cong., 1st Sess. (Washington, D.C.: GPO, 1900), 57. A comparable bill (S.2329) for the B & O Railroad reached the Senate District Committee, 11 January 1901. Ibid., 75.

[15] Accident data, courtesy of William Wright, historian of Union Station, Ph.D. diss. draft, University of North Carolina, chap. 1. See also Constance McLaughlin Green, *Washington: Capital City, 1879–1950* (Princeton: Princeton University Press, 1963), 2:53.

[16] For details about the B & P bill (S.1929), see *Grade Crossings of the Baltimore and Potomac Railroad Company in the District of Columbia*, 56th Cong., 1st Sess., S. Rept. 928, 3–32 (hereafter cited as *Grade Crossings of the B & P*). For Senatorial debate of both bills, see "Baltimore and Potomac Railroad" and "Baltimore and Ohio Railroad," *Cong. Record*, 56th Cong., 1st Sess., vol. 32 (Washington, D.C.: GPO, 1900), 6088–95.

[17] Fitzpatrick, "Beautifying," 14.

[18] On 28 February Alexander Cassatt telegramed Senator McMillan, opposing the avenue plan as jeopardizing the lot-space available for a Mall terminal. See Gillette Jr., *Between Justice and Beauty*, 92–93; and telegram from A. J. Cassatt to Gen. William J. Sewell, 28 February 1900, National Archives and Records Administration (NARA)., Record Group (RG) 46, 56A-F-7. The avenue plan may reflect McMillan's infighting with Col. Theodore Bingham, *infra* and n. 21.

[19] "Report of the War Department on the Bill (S.1929) to Provide for Eliminating Certain Road Crossings on the Baltimore and Potomac Railroad," in *Grade Crossings of the B & P*, 18–21.

[20] *Grade Crossings of the B & P*, 20–21. Lansing H. Beach, Engineer-Commissioner of the District of Columbia, fully supported the bill. "Report of the Commissioners of the District of Columbia" in *Grade Crossings of the B & P*, 9–17.

[21] Because the avenue plan did not reflect the Pennsylvania Railroad interests (see n. 18), McMillan may have introduced it on 21 February, together with the White House proposal, in retaliation against Bingham. No direct evidence for this explanation exists, however.

[22] "Plan for Boulevard," *Post*, 6 March 1900, 2; "Plans for Avenue," *Post*, 29 April 1900, 20.

[23] Moore, "Notes on the Parks," 94; Fitzpatrick, "Beautifying the Nation's Capital," 11. For the sobriquet "Murder Bay" often applied to this area, see William M. Maury, *Alexander "Boss" Shepherd and the Board of Public Works*, GW Washington Studies, No. 3 (Washington, D.C.: George Washington University, 1975), 31; and Lessoff, *The Nation and Its City*, 22, 90, 252.

[24] For the slum-removal role of the then new post office, see Moore, "Notes on the Parks," 94. For views of major businessmen, see remarks of C. C. Glover quoted in "Plan for Boulevard," 2. The *Star* favored the triangle as a site for new public buildings: "Centennial Avenue Scheme Again,"

26 May 1900, 6.

[25] "Why Two National Avenues," *Star*, 23 February 1900, 4.

[26] W[illiam]. V. Cox, "Park Improvement Paper No. 1. Action of the Wahsington Board of Trade in Relation to the Park System of the District of Columbia," in *Park Improvement Papers*, ed. Moore, 5–21. Also: Moore, "Notes on the Parks," 79–97.

[27] Cox, "Action of the Washington Board of Trade," 10.

[28] "Report of the Committee on Railroads," Washington Board of Trade, *Annual Report* (1901) (Washington, D.C.: Washington Printing Co., 1902), 102–3. For the Board of Trade's involvement with park promotion and beautification, see Jessica I. Elfenbein, *Civics, Commerce, and Community: The History of the Greater Washington Board of Trade, 1889–1989*, Center for Washington Area Studies of the George Washington University (Dubuque, Iowa: Kendall/Hunt Publishing Co., 1989), 13–15. Lessoff, *The Nation and Its City*, 197.

[29] Reps, *Monumental Washington*, 74.

[30] The original plan was done in cooperation with first lady, Caroline Harrison. Bingham wanted elaborate circular office and public reception wings to be attached to the east and west sides of the White House as first steps in a truly massive complex.

[31] "Plans for Treatment of that Portion of the District of Columbia South of Pennsylvania Avenue and North of B Street, SW., and for a Connection between Potomac and Zoological Parks," 56th Cong., 2d Sess., 1900, H. Doc. 135, 8, reprinted in *Celebration*, comp. Cox, 324–28.

[32] Reps, *Monumental Washington*, 82–83. For detailed analysis of Brown and the AIA, see Tony Wrenn's essay elsewhere in this volume. See also William Bushong, Judith Helm Robinson, and Julie Mueller, *A Centennial History of the Washington Chapter, The American Institute of Architects, 1887–1897* (Washington, D.C.: Washington Architectural Foundation Press, 1987), 1–19; also valuable: William Brian Bushong, "Glenn Brown, the American Institute of Architects, and the Development of the Civic Core of Washington, D.C." (Ph.D. diss., George Washington University, 1988).

[33] Glenn Brown, "The Selection of Sites for Federal Buildings," *Architectural Review* 3 (1894): 27–29, quote, 29.

[34] For Brown's career and Washington work, see Bushong, "Glenn Brown," and Bushong, et al. *A Centennial History*.

[35] Hines, *Burnham of Chicago*, 126–33.

[36] Bushong, et al., *A Centennial History*, 24–25.

[37] American Institute of Architects (AIA), *Proceedings* (1900): 92.

[38] Oliver Larkin, *Art and Life in America* (New York: Holt, Rinehart and Winston, 1960), 293–300. See especially Richard Guy Wilson, "The Great Civilization," in *The American Renaissance, 1876–1917*, (New York: Brooklyn Museum, 1979), 11–25, 28, 45.

[39] Glenn Brown to H. K. Bush-Brown, 9 and 18 October 1900, in Brown, Outgoing Correspondence, Archives of the American Institute of Architects, secretary office files, Outgoing Letter Books, Washington, hereafter cited as Brown, Outgoing Correspondence.

[40] George B. Post lambasted Bingham as making the White House into "a banquet for the Philistines," in "A Residence for the President," *Post,* 15 December 1900, 6. St. Louis architect William S. Eames worried that "the entire machinery of the army lobby" was seeking the White House job. "Capital's Chief Need," *Post,* 14 December 1900, 2, 9.

[41] C. Howard Walker, "The Grouping of Public Buildings in a Great City," in *Papers Relating to the Improvement of the City of Washington,* comp. Glenn Brown, 56th Cong., 2d Sess., 1901, S. Doc. 94 (Washington, D.C.: GPO, 1901), 36.

[42] This analysis of the evening session viewpoint is based strictly on the papers given on that occasion, not those of Cass Gilbert, Paul J. Pelz, and George O. Totten, which were published later with the evening-session papers. Landscape architect, Frederick Law Olmsted Jr., who spoke that evening, scorned the then existing Mall with its "wiggling road and confused informal planting," favoring its treatment as a broad corridor of turf as suggested by the Tapis Vert at Versailles, to be flanked in Washington by "masses of foliage and architecture and shaded drives." Olmsted Jr., who became a member of the Senate Park (McMillan) Commission, later strongly influenced its thinking on this crucial feature. Only Paul J. Pelz, a local architect, wanted to preserve the Mall as series of picturesque gardens. Ibid., 3, 30. For a list of those who actually spoke, see AIA, *Proceedings* (1900): 92.

[43] For the 13 December meeting, see AIA, *Proceedings* (1900): 47–48, 113. The presence of the Board of Trade is inferred from the fact that it voted the very next day to adopt the policies set 13 December. See Cox, "Action of the Board of Trade," 17. For the Board's resolution, see Washington Board of Trade, Proceedings (unpublished), 14 December 1900, in Archives of the Greater Washington Board of Trade, Gellman Library, Special Collections, George Washington University. For additional confirmation, see Elfenbein, *Civics, Commerce, and Community,* 15. Elfenbein notes that the Board later took much of the credit for creation of the Senate Park Commission. For direct reference to the understanding reached between McMillan, the AIA, and the Board of Trade, see "Commission to Consider Certain Improvements in the District of Columbia," 18 January 1901, Calendar No. 1897, 56th Cong., 2d Sess., 1901, S. Rept. 1919, 2.

[44] For analysis of the "alliance between politics and business" in promoting public utilities, parks, and suburban improvements, which centered on McMillan and the Board of Trade beginning in the 1890s, including their shared "skepticism" toward the Army Corps, see Lessoff, *The Nation and Its City,* 151–52, 162, 197–98.

[45] "Grade Bills in Committee," *Post,* 12 December 1900, 4; "To Save the Mall," *Star,* 15 December 1900. See also W. S. Cowherd, T. W. Sims, "Views of the Minority," 15 December 1900, in *Grade Crossings of the Baltimore and Potomac Railroad Company,* 56th Cong., 2d Sess., 1900, H. Rept. 2026, Pt. 2.

[46] See Mall plan drawings, accompanying *Papers Relating to the Improvement of Washington,* comp. Brown. The design by Edgar V. Seeler, reproduced by Reps, *Monumental Washington,* 88, is especially revealing of Brown's acceptance of the Mall site of the proposed terminal because Brown personally escorted Seeler over the Mall grounds before Seeler prepared his paper. See Seeler to Brown, 30 October and 21 November 1900, in Brown, Incoming Correspondence. Frederick Law Olmsted Jr., when addressing the AIA convention, 13 December, also approached the railroad terminal as a fait accompli, in "Landscape in Connection with Public Buildings in Washington, *Papers Relating to the Improvement of Washington,* comp. Brown, 31.

[47] "Improvement Paper No. 5. Informal Hearing before the Subcommittee on the Committee on the District of Columbia, United States Senate," in *Park Improvement Papers,* ed. Moore, 68.

[48] Cox, "Action of the Washington Board of Trade," 17.

[49] Brown, comp., *Papers Relating to the Improvement of Washington,* 9; "A Commission for the Artistic Development of Washington," *American Architect and Building News* 71 (9 February 1901): 47–48 (hereafter abbreviated *AABN*).

[50] Lessoff, *The Nation and Its City,* 183, 260.

[51] Between 17 December 1900 and mid-January 1901, at least two other commissions were proposed in the Senate and the House to address roughly the same tasks. "To Beautify the District," *Star,* 17 December 1900; "Control by Permits," *Post,* 16 January 1901, 12; "District in Congress," *Star,* 15 January 1901, 4. By early February, three additional bills had emerged, each designating sites for new buildings. Brown, Outgoing Correspondence, February to March 1901.

[52] The grade crossing bill for the B & O was also enacted 12 April 1900. For dates of both bills, see *Catalogue of the United States Public Documents* (Washington, D.C.: GPO, 1901). Charles Moore toward the end of his life took

credit for suggesting this resolution and, after McMillan agreed, writing it. See Charles Moore, "Memoirs of Charles Moore" (typescript), 75, Box 21, Moore Papers, LC. For Moore's special relationship to McMillan, see Alan Lessoff, "Washington Insider: the Early Career of Charles Moore," *Washington History* 6 (fall/winter 1994–95): 64–80. Essentially, the two men worked as a team, with McMillan the final arbiter for any proposed action.

[53] *Senate Park Commission Report*, 7; American Institute of Architects, "The Commission on Parks and the Future Grouping of Government Buildings in Washington," *Quarterly Bulletin* 2 (April 1901): 6, 8; and Moore, *Burnham*, 1:137.

[54] "Informal Hearing," 67, 70.

[55] Frederick Law Olmsted Jr., "Washington Park System, 19th March, 1901." Box 134, FF: "Capitol Grounds," Olmsted Associates Papers, Library of Congress, Manuscript Division, hereafter cited as Olmsted Papers, LC.

[56] Although McMillan made clear that any work done must be "preliminary," Olmsted Jr. crystallized the "preliminary plan" approach, upholding Charles Eliot's 1893 plan for the Boston metropolitan park system as a model "general scheme" versus a detailed one. See "Informal Hearing," 71, 75–76, 78.

[57] "A Great Park System," *Post*, 23 March 1901, 12.

[58] Olmsted Jr., "Washington Park System, 19th March."

[59] That the AIA understood McMillan's wishes is implied, not stated, by Moore, *Burnham*, 1:137–38.

[60] All four had had roles at the fair. Even Olmsted Jr., age 30 when appointed to the commission as a stand-in for his father, had worked with Burnham at the fair in 1891 and later recalled it as a high point of his professional career. See "Insertion A" in "Biographical Notes FLO, Jr.," Box 176, Olmsted Papers, LC. For the addition of Saint-Gaudens, see Moore, *Burnham*, 1:147–48 and Moore, *McKim*, 185–86.

[61] Daniel H. Burnham to Charles F. McKim, 15 April 1901. McKim, Mead & White Papers, New-York Historical Society, hereafter cited as MM&W Papers, NYHS.

[62] Olmsted Jr., "Washington Park System, March 22, 1901." Box 134; FF; "Capitol Grounds," Olmsted Papers, LC.

[63] "A Great Park System," *Post*, 23 March 1901, 12. The $10,000 sum echoed Joint Resolution No. 139 and the June 6, 1900 House-Senate conference resolution of the Mall-Triangle impasse.

[64] Moore recorded that he offered Burnham the chairmanship when they met the evening of 21 March, but Cynthia Field, on the basis of Burnham's later correspondence, establishes that this matter remained unsettled in Burnham's mind. See Cynthia R. Field, "The City Planning of Daniel H. Burnham" (Ph.D. diss., Columbia University, 1974), 138. For McMillan's treatment of Burnham as de facto chairman, see Olmsted Jr., "Washington Park System, March 22."

[65] Burnham to McKim, 8 May 1901, MM&W Papers, NYHS.

[66] Burnham to Frederick Law Olmsted Jr., 15 April 1901, MM&W Papers, NYHS. Burnham was contrasting his views to those of architect C. Howard Walker.

[67] Brown, *Memories*, 79.

[68] Daniel H. Burnham to Frederick Law Olmsted Jr., 27 May 1901, refers to an agreement with Cassatt made eight months ago. Letterbook VIII, Daniel H. Burnham Papers, Ryerson & Burnham Library, Chicago Art Institute, hereafter cited as Burnham Papers, Art Institute.

[69] Burnham diary for 5 April, quoted by Moore, *Burnham*, 1:142. Burnham's entry for the fifth as recorded by Moore includes events of the sixth.

[70] Burnham to Olmsted Jr., 10 April 1901. Burnham Papers, Art Institute.

[71] Burnham placed the station at the juncture of Virginia and Maryland avenues between Sixth and Seventh streets, SW.

[72] Burnham diary for 20 May, quoted by Moore, *Burnham*, 1:147.

[73] Two letters, Burnham to McKim, 20 May 1901, record the talks (sent from Washington and from the Pennsylvania Limited en route). MM&W Papers, NYHS.

[74] The newfound flexibility of the Pennsylvania Railroad did not reflect direct interest in the station site proposed by Burnham. For over a year, Theodore Bingham and other enemies of the grade-crossing bill had urged this site, to no avail. William Wright notes the long-standing opposition of the Pennsylvania to the southern site, at the juncture of Maryland and Virginia avenues, as too far from the downtown and also quotes Pennsylvania Railroad Vice-President Samuel Rea, as recalling in 1908 that "our possession and use of the Mall for railroad purposes was very insecure" and that Cassatt feared "that in the course of time they would be forced off the Mall, and there would then be no suitable place for the location of their station." William M. Wright, "Who's Driving? The Origins of Union Station," unpublished paper, Society of Architectural Historians Convention, 1998; and dissertation draft. This evidence does not alter the judgment offered here about Burnham's role. Wright establishes that the railroad had its own concerns and fears. But no evidence supports the view that the railroad initiated its own retreat from the Mall. Wright is now completing his history of the station as a doctoral dissertation at the University of North Carolina.

[75] Moore, *Burnham*, n. 1, 148–49.

[76] Daniel H. Burnham to Alexander Cassatt, 11 June 1901, James McMillan Papers, Detroit Public Library, hereafter cited as McMillan Papers, DPL.

[77] William T. Partridge, "McMillan Commission: Personal Recollections," 3, 15, in NARA, RG 328, hereafter cited as Partridge Papers, NARA. For a discussion

of Partridge and his work, and for excerpts from his "Recollections," see Kurt Helfrich's essay elsewhere in this volume. For Burnham's mid-July conference with Cassatt in London, see Hines, *Burnham of Chicago,* 149; and Moore, *McKim,* 191–92, 198.

[78] James McMillan to Charles Moore, 30 September 1901, Box 1, Moore Papers, LC.

[79] James McMillan, *Union Railroad Station at Washington, D.C.,* 3 April 1902, U.S. Congress, Senate, Committee on the District of Columbia, 57th Cong., 1st Sess., 1902, S. Rept. 982, reprinted in U.S. Congress, House, Committee on District of Columbia, 57th Cong., 2d Sess., 1902, H. Rept. 2788, 11.

[80] Moore, *McKim,* 188.

[81] For drafting room arrangements, see Olmsted Jr., "Washington Park System, March 22," and Moore to Frederick Law Olmsted Jr., 27 March and 1 April 1901. McMillan Papers, DPL.

[82] "District Park System," *Star,* 6 April 1901, 1; Moore, "Memoirs," 79.

[83] Burnham diary entry in Moore, *Burnham,* 1:143.

[84] Dennis Robert Montagna, "Henry Merwin Shrady's Ulysses S. Grant Memorial in Washington, D.C.: A Study in Iconography, Content and Patronage" (Ph.D. diss., University of Delaware, 1987), 1, 4–5, 60–61, 70.

[85] Charles F. McKim to Wendell P. Garrison, 10 April 1901, Charles F. McKim Correspondence, New York Public Library, Manuscript Division. Also quoted by Moore, *McKim,* 185.

[86] Ibid.

[87] Burnham to Albert R. Wells, 10 April 1891, Burnham Papers, Art Institute.

[88] For Olmsted Jr.'s 1890 work in Washington, see "Statement of F. L. Olmsted Jr.," *The Mall Parkway Hearing before the Committee on the District of Columbia* (Washington, D.C.: GPO, 1904), 30; and Frederick Law Olmsted Jr., "Government Hospital for the Insane," typescript, 26 December 1900, Olmsted Papers, LC; Lessoff, *The Nation and Its City,* 246–47. Olmsted Jr., in 1895 to 1896, provided street extension plans for the District. See payment voucher of 25 January 1897, in Olmsted Papers, LC. For his convention views, see Frederick Law Olmsted Jr., "Landscape in Connection with Public Buildings in Washington," *Papers Relating to the Improvement of Washington,* comp., Brown, 30.

[89] Moore, "Memoirs," 81. For Burnham's diary record and identity of some guests, see Moore, *Burnham,* 1:144.

[90] Moore details the trip in *Burnham,* 1:144–46. Moore records that W. E. Curtis, a Chicago newsman and close friend of Burnham, accompanied the party.

[91] Before going abroad, the commission met four times for at least thirteen days together: 6 to 7, 19 to 22 April; 14 to 19 May; and 10 to 11 June. Burnham worked

in Washington until afternoon 19 May; the presence of Olmsted and McKim on the eighteenth and nineteenth is unclear. Burnham diary, Moore, *Burnham,* 1:146. For the Maryland trip, chiefly 15 May, see ibid.

[92] Burnham and Olmsted Jr. agreed to this first; McKim followed suit. Burnham and McKim each provided $1,000, Olmsted Jr., $950. See Olmsted Jr. to James G. Langdon, 6 June 1901; and Olmsted Jr. to Moore, 27 August 1901. Box 3, Moore Papers, LC.

[93] McKim, Mead & White, Plan for the Mall dated 3 June 1901, MM&W Papers, NYHS.

[94] For Saint-Gaudens early interactions with the Commission, see Moore, *Burnham,* 1:147–48.

[95] Testimony of Daniel H. Burnham, *Mall Parkway Hearing,* 14–15. James G. Langdon to Charles McKim, 29 May 1901, reported discussing "the flag business with Mr. Moore" and the decision "to have these [flags] put up one or two days before you arrive." See MM&W Papers, NYHS. This means that either McKim studied them alone during a quick visit to the capital, 4 June, or, more likely, that the commission did so during its June 10 to 11 gathering. Burnham's diary records that the commission plus Moore and Secretary Gage ascended the Washington Monument, 10 June. See Moore, *Burnham,* 1:149. No evidence exists that flag-pole experiment occurred after going abroad.

[96] For McKim's role, see Charles F. McKim to Moore, 16 April 1901 and 10 May 1901, Box 2, Moore Papers, LC. For Olmsted Jr.'s role, see Moore, *McKim,* 187.

[97] For accounts of the trip, see Cynthia F. Field, "The McMillan Commission's Trip to Europe," in *Historical Perspectives on Urban Design,* ed. Lee, 19–24; Moore, *Burnham,* 1:149–57; Moore, *McKim,* 187–99. Of value if used with care, William A. Bogan, "The McMillan Plan for Washington, D.C.: European Influences in the Origins and Development," unpublished manuscript, ca. 1974 Commission of Fine Arts, Washington, D.C.

[98] Frederick Law Olmsted Jr., "European Photographs Taken during the Study for the Washington Park System in 1901," manuscript, Commission of Fine Arts, Washington, D.C.

[99] See Burnham diary record and Moore's notes, in *Burnham,* 1:153–54; and Moore, *McKim,* 196.

[100] For lists of recorded itinerary sites, see Bogan, "The McMillan Plan," Appendix A.

[101] Mary Caroline Robbins, "Park-Making as a National Art," *Atlantic Monthly* 79 (July 1897): 86–98.

[102] Burnham, *Mall Parkway Hearing,* 14–15.

[103] Frederick Law Olmsted [Jr.], "Note on Githens' Caricature Coat of Arms for the So-Called 'Senate Park Commission of 1901,'" November 1935, attached to "Personal Recollections," McMillan Commission, 1901–1928" 18, Partridge Papers, NARA. (see pl. XX)

[104] Moore, *McKim,* 193.

[105] Moore, *Burnham*, 1:154; Moore, *McKim*, 198.

[106] McMillan to Moore, 7 August 1901, Box 1, Moore papers, LC.

[107] Charles Moore to McKim, 12 August 1901, MM&W Papers, NYHS.

[108] James Knox Taylor to McKim, 6 August 1901. MM&W Papers, NYHS; McKim to Daniel H. Burnham, 10 August 1901; and to Moore, 14 August 1901, Box 2, Moore Papers, LC. McKim states in the last letter that he leased "St. Gauden's old studio, at 107 East 27th Street, size 14 x 26," apparently for work on the Curtis model. The model did not reach New York for two months. There is no evidence that this space was ever used.

[109] Burnham diary in Moore, *Burnham*, 1:156–57.

[110] Olmsted Jr. inspected the Curtis model the evening of 2 August, sending a lengthy report to McKim the following day. Olmsted Jr. to McKim, 3 August 1901, Box 2, Moore Papers, LC. For the pool hall, see Moore, "Memoirs," 82. For departure date, see Olmsted Jr. to Moore, 10 August 1901, Moore Papers, LC.

[111] Olmsted Jr to Moore, 13 April 1901, hand-delivered by Langdon as he took up his post; Olmsted Jr. to Langdon, 30 April 1901, listing needed information; and six letters Olmsted Brothers to Langdon, 27 June to 8 July 1901, revealing initial difficulties in supplying photographs to Curtis, Box 2, Moore Papers, LC. For quote, see Acting Director, Department of Interior, to Col. C. O. Sherrill, 14 April 1925, Olmsted Papers, LC.

[112] Burnham diary for 19 and 20 August, in Moore, *Burnham*, 1:158.

[113] Ibid.

[114] Moore states that he learned of this "by chance from McMillan's grandson." "Memoirs," 102. He told the same story to William T. Partridge. See "Personal Recollections," 15, Partridge Papers, NARA.

[115] McKim to Moore, 26 August 1901, Box 2, Moore Papers, LC.

[116] McMillan to Hon. Charles G. Bennett, Secretary of the Senate, 12 September 1901, Box 1, Moore Papers, LC; "Memorandum of amounts paid to George Carroll Curtis for personal services in connection with models," accompanying letter from Olmsted Jr. to Moore, 14 May 1902, Box 2, Moore Papers, LC. This memorandum credits Charles Moore with paying $12,354.78 to George C. Curtis. Since Moore always handled McMillan's personal disbursements, this is a reliable measure of McMillan's loans in support of the commission effort.

[117] For Rock Creek issue, see Frederick Law Olmsted Jr., "Washington: Report of Interview on Rock Creek Parkway with Capt. [Lansing] Beech, Engineer Commission," 25 September 1901," typescript, Box 134, Olmsted Papers, LC. For a detailed analysis of this issue, see Timothy Davis, "Rock Creek and the Potomac Parkway, Washington, D.C.: The Evolution of a Contested Urban Landscape," *Studies in the History of Gardens & Design Landscapes* 19 (Summer 1999): 145–58.

[118] For remarks on this parallel, see Olmsted Jr. to Hon. Sydney E. Mudd, House of Representatives, 19 June 1902, 3, Moore Papers, LC. For the filling of Back Bay, see Nancy S. Seasholes, "Gaining Ground: Boston's Topographical Development in Maps," in Alex Krieger and David Cobb, with Amy Turner, *Mapping Boston* (Cambridge: Massachusetts Institute of Technology Press, 1999), 124–28.

[119] Lawrence W. Kennedy, *Planning a City upon a Hill: Boston since 1630* (Amherst: University of Massachusetts Press, 1992), 104; Cynthia Zaitzevsky, *Frederick Law Olmsted and the Boston Park System* (Cambridge: Belknap Press of Harvard University Press, 1882), 105–7.

[120] Norman T. Newton, *Design on the Land: The Development of Landscape Architecture* (Cambridge: Belknap Press of Harvard University Press, 1971), 326–32.

[121] Moore, *Burnham*, 1:160–61, 163–64.

[122] Burnham to Moore, 13 December 1901, in Moore, *Burnham*, 1:164.

[123] J. G. Langdon to McKim, 29 November 1901, relaying Burnham's request of 27 November to McKim; and to Burnham, 29 November 1901, McMillan Papers, DPL.

[124] "Hearty concurrence in Bridge scheme received this morning. Will complete immediately." Telegram, McKim to Burnham, 29 November 1901, McKim Papers, NYHS.

[125] For analysis of Burnham's disagreements over writing style with Moore and McKim, see Hines, *Burnham of Chicago*, 150–51. Burnham's disappointment lingered, affecting his views of the battle over the Department of Agriculture building in 1904. See John Charles Olmsted to Frederick Law Olmsted Jr., 5 March 1904, Job No. 2825-5, Olmsted Papers, LC.

[126] Charles Moore to Charles F. McKim, 19 December 1901, McMillan Papers, DPL.

[127] For Olmsted Jr.'s role, see Frederick Law Olmsted Jr. to Burnham, Sept. 3, 1901, McMillan Papers, DPL. See also Moore, *Burnham*, 1:166. McKim also contributed draft material on the Mall, and Langdon helped Olmsted Jr. write his portion.

[128] Charles Moore, "The Improvement of Washington City, pt. 1," *Century Magazine*, 58 (February 1902): 621–28, and pt. 2, 58 (March 1902): 747–57.

[129] McKim to Burnham, 28 August 1901, Box 2, Moore Papers, LC. Charles F. McKim to Elihu Root, 24 August 1901, Elihu Root Papers, Library of Congress.

[130] Ibid.; John Braeman, "Root, Elihu," in John A. Garratty and Marck C. Carnes, eds., *American National Biography* (New York: Oxford University Press, 1999), 16:838–40.

[131] For McKim's talks with Root, McKim to Burnham, 28 August 1901, and attachments headed "Grant Memorial," "Additional Property," and "Public Support."

[132] William Hudson Harper to McKim, 11 December 1901, MM&W papers, NYHS. Harper's tone probably reflects his banishment as Burnham's hired writer of the commission report.

[133] This middle section of the model measured 3 x 17 feet. See Olmsted Jr. to McKim, 3 August 1901, Box 2, Moore Papers, LC. The model was railway-expressed back to Boston in twelve cases, 31 December 1901. See telegram, McKim to Moore, 31 December 1901, Box 2, Moore Papers, LC. The same procedure probably had been used for sending the model to New York in October. McKim to Moore, 11 October 1901, Box 2, Moore Papers, LC.

[134] Senate Park Commission Report, 123; and Moore, Burnham, 1:165.

[135] "Second Installment from William Partridge, Received March 8, 1918," 3 in the Papers of William T. Partridge, Avery Library, Columbia University.

[136] McKim to Moore, 21 November 1901, Box 2, Moore Papers, LC. For detailed discussion and Root's support, see Montagna, "Shrady's Ulysses S. Grant Memorial," 76–79.

[137] Montagna, "Shrady's Ulysses G. Grant Memorial," 76. Also, see Montagna for detailed discussion of interactions between the two commissions over the Grant site location and subsequent battles, from April 1901 to 1908, 60–110.

[138] "William T. Partridge's Personal Recollections," 43, Partridge Papers, NARA.

[139] At this point, McKim anticipated thirty to fifty "illustrations, large and small" and already had two men at work on them. McKim to Moore, 26 August 1901, Box 2, Moore Papers, LC. Written the morning of his trip to see Root in Washington.

[140] McMillan quoted by Moore, from memory, Moore, Burnham, 1:165. Moore provides a variation of this same quote and story in his "Memoirs," 103.

[141] Burnham diary for 21 to 22 October and Moore's note, in Burnham, 1:162.

[142] Moore formally thanked twelve contributing artists in Senate Park Commission Report, 123: Otto H. Bacher, Henry Bacon, Robert Blum, Curtis, F. L. V. Hoppin, Sears Gallagher, Percival Gallagher, Charles Graham, Jules Guerin, Henry McCarter, Rodeman, and A. R. Ross. First names, if available, supplied from Moore, Burnham, 1:165; and McKim, 200–201. Curtis is almost certainly George Curtis, the model builder. The list omits artist Carleton T. Chapman. Ibid.

[143] Key letters attesting to Olmsted Jr.'s role include Olmsted Jr. to Langdon, 27 November 1901; and McKim to Moore, 10 December 1901, Box 2, Moore Papers, LC.

[144] Worries about whether the Curtis models would be finished for the exhibit became intense by 23 December. McKim to Moore, 23 December 1901. Curtis wanted an extension to 1 February. George Carroll Curtis to McKim, 26 December 1901. The McKim portion of the model was returned from New York to Roxbury on 31 December. Telegram, McKim to Moore, 31 December 1901. By 2 January McKim was desperate and demanded "the model, finished or unfinished, in time for the exhibition on the 15th." McKim to Moore, 2 January 1902, Box 2, Moore Papers, LC. Curtis arrived in Washington "with his models," 11 January 1902. See Charles Moore Diary, University of Michigan Library.

[145] "List of Drawings, Designs, and Models Illustrating the Report of the Commission on the Improvement of the Park System of the District of Columbia," in Senate Park Commission Report, 147–54.

[146] The Senate Park Commission Report, issued in June, summarized these features.

[147] Illustrations 19 to 29, as listed in the Senate Park Commission Report, Appendix F, 148.

[148] Ibid., 12.

[149] "The New Washington," Post, 15 January 1902. A twenty-five-cent admission, inflation adjusted for historical cost-of-living increases, would have been about $5.00 in 2001.

[150] Moore to McKim, 12 December 1901, McMillan Papers, DPL.

[151] The following totals were disbursed from the contingent fund: to Daniel H. Burnham, $1556; to Frederick Law Olmsted Jr., $1698; to James G. Langdon (head draftsman for Olmsted Jr.), $1,971; to R. A. Outhet (draftsman for Olmsted Jr.), $600; to Charles F. McKim (who in turn paid draftsmen and illustrators), $17,066; to Charles Moore, who personally handled McMillan's advances, $6,099; to George C. Curtis (who paid his assistants), $24,482; to Jules Guerin (artist-illustrator), $425; to H. A. Zeck (photographer), $444; to L. C. Handy (photographer), $356; to Senator Gallinger, $83; for hotel expenses, $456; to the Architectural Press, $243. Because none of the entries is specifically identified as a commission expense, my overall cost-estimate may understate the total. See U.S. Senate, Contingent Expenses, 1897–1901 [ledger], Vol. C-41, RG 46, NARA. The $55,500 expended in 1901, adjusted for cost-of-living increases, would have been 1.1 to 1.2 million in 2001.

[152] Newspaper clipping, from the Detroit Journal, 20 May 1904, quoting the Chicago Chronicle, Olmsted Associates Papers, LC. For identity of the clipping, see Olmsted Jr. to Moore, 25 May 1904, Box 7, Moore Papers, LC.

[153] For Cannon's opposition in the wake of the January exhibit, see editorial, "To Beautify Washington," New York Times, 3 April 1902.

[154] Glenn Brown to McKim, 4, 11, 12 (quoted), and 13 December 1901. See also McKim to Brown, 7 December

1901, MM&W Papers, NYHS.

[155] McKim to Moore, 18 December 1901, Box 2, Moore Papers, LC.

[156] For McMillan's views, 19 March 1901, see "Informal Hearing," 78.

[157] Moore to McKim, 16 December 1901, McMillan Papers, DPL.

[158] Moore to McKim, 25 March 1902, MM&W Papers, NYHS.

[159] Charles Moore to Charles F. McKim, 12 March 1902, Charles F. McKim Papers, Library of Congress, Manuscript Division, hereafter cited as McKim Papers, LC.

[160] Moore to McKim, 14 April 1902, McKim Papers, LC.

[161] "Union Station Bill passed Senate today 45 to 24." See telegram, Charles Moore to Charles F. McKim, 15 May 1902. MM&W Papers, NYHS.

[162] Olmsted Jr. to Moore, 28 August 1902; McKim to Moore, 5 December 1902, Boxes 7 and 2, Moore Papers, LC.

[163] Moore, "Memoirs," 111–12.

[164] Moore to Mrs. James McMillan, 4 December 1902, Box 3, Moore Papers, LC. "An Act To provide for a union railroad station," in *Acts of Congress of 1901 and 1903 Providing for Elimination of Grade-Crossings of Railroads in the District of Columbia, and Authorizing Construction of Union Station and Terminals* (Washington, D.C.: Judd & Detweiler, 1905), 34.

[165] Moore to Oscar F. Billingsley, 25 February 1903, Box 3, Moore Papers, LC. Moore, "Memoirs," 132–33.

[166] For the origins of the City Beautiful Movement, see Jon A. Peterson, "The City Beautiful Movement: Forgotten Origins and Lost Meanings," *Journal of Urban History* 2 (November 1976): 415–34; and William H. Wilson, *The City Beautiful Movement* (Baltimore: Johns Hopkins University Press, 1989). See also Peterson, *The Birth of City Planning*, 98-127.

[167] Peterson, "City Beautiful Movement" and *The Birth of City Planning, 108-115*; Wilson, *City Beautiful Movement*, 35–52.

[168] For histories of park systems, see David Schuyler, *The New Urban Landscape: The Redefinition of City Form in Nineteenth-Century America* (Baltimore: Johns Hopkins University Press, 1986), 126–46; and Newton, *Design on the Land*, 290–336. For outdoor art, see Peterson. *The Birth of City Planning, 115-118*

[169] Peterson, "City Beautiful Movement" and *The Birth of City Planning, 102-108"*

[170] For the naturalistic tradition of landscape design, especially as applied to cities, see Schuyler, *The New Urban Landscape*; and Newton, *Design on the Land*, 267–336.

[171] Marion Louise McCall, "What Organization Has Done for St. Louis," in *Nation-Wide Civic Betterment: A Report of the Third Annual Convention of the American League for Civic Improvement* (Chicago, n.p., 1903), 50.

[172] Charles Mulford Robinson, *The Improvement of Towns and Cities or the Practical Basis of Civic Aesthetics* (New York: G. P. Putnam's Sons, 1901); "American Society of Landscape Architects, Minute on the Life and Services of Charles Mulford Robinson, Associate Member," *Landscape Architecture* 9 (1919): 180–89.

[173] D. J. Thomas, "Report of Corresponding Secretary," in American League for Civic Improvement, *Proceedings of the Annual Convention of the American League for Civic Improvement* (Springfield, Ohio: The Home Florist, October 1901): 59; Clinton Rogers Woodruff, "Awakening America," American Park and Outdoor Art Association, *Proceedings, Part I* (1903): 75; "Civic Improvement, The American Civic Association in Convention," *Park and Cemetery and Landscape Gardening*, 15 (October 1905): 372; and Mary I. Wood, *The History of the General Federation of Women's Clubs, for the First Twenty-two Years of Its Organization* (New York: History Department, General Federation of Women's Clubs, 1912), 166, 170.

[174] Sylvester Baxter, "Great Civic Awakening," *Century Magazine* 64 (June 1902): 255; J. Horace McFarland, "The Great Civic Awakening," *Outlook* 73 (18 April 1903): 917.

[175] Reps, *Monumental Washington*, 105–8; Moore, *Burnham*, 1:167–68.

[176] Hines, *Burnham of Chicago*, 154–55.

[177] The Beautifying of Washington," *Harper's Weekly* 66 (1 February 1902): 146; Elbert F. Baldwin, "Washington Fifty Years Hence," *Outlook* 70 (5 April 1902): 817–29; Charles Moore, "The Improvement of Washington City," *Century Magazine* 43 (February 1902): 621–28 and (March 1902): 747–57.

[178] "The Fair White City: The Beautifying of the Nation's Capital," *Current Literature* 32 (March 1902): 276–77; John Brent, "Washington, The Capital City," *Munsey's Magazine* 27 (May 1902): 228–29; Frederick Law Olmsted, Jr., "Beautifying a City," *Independent* 54 (2 August 1902): 1870–77; Charles Moore, "Washington as a Work of Art," *Municipal Journal and Engineer* 13 (July 1902): 1–5; "The Improvement of the City of Washington," *Popular Science Monthly* 63 (June 1903): 149–58; and "The Improvement of Washington," *Scientific American* 86 (15 February 1902): 108–9. See also Montgomery Schuyler, "The Nation's New Capital," *New York Times Magazine* 19 January 1902, 4–5. For a digest of early responses, see "The Park Commission and the Improvement of the City of Washington," The American Institute of Architects, *Quarterly Bulletin* 3 (April 1902): 5–16.

[179] "Washington: The Development and Improvement of the Park System," Parts 1 and 2, *AABN* 75 (1 February 1902): 35–36 and (8 March 1902): 75–77; Charles Moore, "The Improvement of Washington,"

AABN 78 (27 December 1902): 101–2; "Beautifying the Nation's Capital," *Inland Architect and News Record* 39 (February 1902): 2–3; Montgomery Schuyler, "Proposed Sites for Future Buildings," *Architectural Record* 12 (May 1902): 1–26; Charles Moore, "Improvement of Washington City," *Architectural Record* 12 (September 1902): 456–58; Editorial, *Architectural Review* 9 (February 1902): 69 and (June 1902): 116.

[180] "The Thirty-sixth Annual Convention of the American Institute of Architects," Part 1, *AABN* 78 (20 December 1902): 92. For Brown's lecture in New York to the National Arts Club, see "To Beautify Washington," *New York Times*, 13 February 1902, 2.

[181] H. A. Caparn, "The Development of Washington," *AABN* 79 (3 January 1903): 4.

[182] Editorial, "Washington: An Example for Municipal Improvement," *Inland Architect and Building News*, 34 (February 1902): 1.

[183] Editorial, "The Art of City Making," *New York Times*, 19 January 1902, 8.

[184] "Civic Improvement a Phase of Patriotism," *Century Magazine* 58 (March 1902): 793.

[185] For the drafting in New York of the Mall portion of the plan, see William T. Partridge, "McMillan Commission, Personal Recollections," Partridge Papers, NARA.

[186] For the Fine Arts Federation resolution, see "To Beautify the City," *New York Times*, 1 February 1902, 2. See also editorial, *AABN* 75 (Feb. 15, 1902): 49. See also Gregory F. Gilmartin, *Shaping the City: New York and the Municipal Art Society* (New York: Clarkson Potter, Publishers, 1995), 84–85.

[187] At this point, the Municipal Art Society was publicly focused on specific, practical embellishments, but it quickly lent support. See "Embellishing the City," *New York Times*, 30 January 1902, 8; "To Embellish the City," *New York Times*, 1 February 1902, 8; Harvey A. Kantor, "The City Beautiful in New York," *New-York Historical Society Quarterly* 57 (April 1973): 154; and "New York Municipal Art Society," *Municipal Journal and Engineer* 14 (March 1903): 97–99.

[188] McKim to Moore, 8 January 1903, Box 2, Moore Papers, LC. Significantly, McKim stressed to Mayor Seth Low the importance of independent action and of making "the work comprehensive" by including all the boroughs as well as real estate and transportation interests, revealing the far-reaching lessons he drew from his Senate Park Commission experience.

[189] The Municipal Art Society of Cincinnati, *Annual Report* (28 April 1902).

[190] Walter H. Kilham, "Boston's New Opportunities," *AABN* 79 (17 January 1903): 22.

[191] Municipal Art League of Chicago, *Yearbook* (1901–1904): 16.

[192] Charles Mulford Robinson, *Modern Civic Art or, the City Made Beautiful* (New York: G. P. Putnam's Sons, 1903), 32.

[193] Peterson, *The Birth of City Planning*, 151-223. See also Mel Scott, *American City Planning since 1890* (Berkeley: University of California Press, 1969), 47–82.

[194] Bushong, "Glenn Brown," 149–50.

[195] Charles Eliot to Olmsted Jr., 15 February 1904, Olmsted Papers, LC.

[196] J. R. Coolidge Jr. to Olmsted Jr., 25 February 1904; Olmsted Jr. to Samuel Powers, 16 February 1904; and Olmsted Jr. to Glenn Brown, 17 March 1904, Olmsted Papers, LC.

[197] Charles Mulford Robinson to Frederick Law Olmsted Jr., 25 February 1904; Olmsted Jr. to Robinson, 1 March 1904; Olmsted Jr. to Francis Newlands, 3 March 1904. Olmsted Papers, LC. A 14 March 1904 article in the *Boston Herald*, "Building Plan for Washington" utilizes the same language Olmsted Jr. used in his 1 March letter to Robinson. The support of the *Boston Transcript* is noted by Moore in a letter to McKim, 7 March 1904, MM&W Papers, NYHS.

[198] Ibid. In this letter, Moore also stated "I am going to have some Skull and Bones men make an appeal to Secretary Taft."

[199] Olmsted Jr. to Daniel H. Burnham, 8 March 1904; to Francis Newlands, 8 March 1904; and Charles Mulford Robinson to Olmsted Jr., 9 March 1904, Olmsted Papers, LC.

[200] Robinson to Olmsted Jr., 10 March 1904. See also Robinson to Olmsted Jr., 18 and 21 March 1904, for other efforts by Robinson, including writing to the president and to congressmen and his work with Clinton Rogers Woodruff, president of the American Park and Outdoor Art Association, Olmsted Papers, LC.

[201] Olmsted Jr. to Charles Moore, 28 November 1904, Olmsted Papers, LC.

The Mall, ca. 1937. Commission of Fine Arts

Glenn Brown, architect and secretary of the American Institute of Architects, photographed in his office in the Octagon, Washington, D.C., ca. 1900, by Frances Benjamin Johnston. Library of Congress, Prints and Photographs Division.

The American Institute of Architects Convention of 1900:
ITS INFLUENCE ON THE SENATE PARK COMMISSION PLAN

By Tony P. Wrenn

 ARLIER studies have discussed the American Institute of Architects' (AIA) convention in 1900 as a seminal event leading to the 1901 Senate Park Commission plan for Washington, D.C., yet none has closely studied the events and architects of the period who used the convention to lay the groundwork for the modernization of the capital city.[1] At the same time, these individuals actively organized local and national arts-related professional groups to exert pressure on Congress and the president to establish a federal arts bureau to oversee Washington's continuing development. What becomes clear as one studies the era, is that the research accomplished in the 1890s gave the Senate Park Commission, once it was formed, the data it needed to base its plan on Pierre Charles L'Enfant's 1791 plan for Washington. The ideas and concepts discussed at the 1900 AIA convention provided the basic outline and goals for the Senate Park Commission plan, and the art and architecture organizations already mobilized provided the plan, when completed, with a national support base. It is equally clear that the members of the 1901 commission came to their work with full knowledge of this existing base, for all had been involved in building it, and could therefore, in a relatively short time, produce a plan which would not just shape the next century of Washington architecture but have enormous influence on the City Beautiful Movement worldwide.

The federal government was then (and has continuously been) the greatest source of funding for the design and construction of new buildings and for the maintenance of existing structures built for public, government, or military uses. Federal buildings had, since 1853, been designed and constructed by government architects in the Office of the Supervising Architect in the Treasury Department.[2] In the 1870s the AIA first sought a federal bureau or commission to secure designs from private architects, especially those who belonged to the AIA, an effort it intensified in the 1890s.[3] The role that the AIA later played in promoting the Senate Park Commission's 1901 plan for Washington was an extension of that policy of promoting the best design for America's public buildings.

GLENN BROWN AS COORDINATOR OF THE AIA'S INVOLVEMENT WITH THE SENATE PARK COMMISSION PLAN

Perhaps the most important factor influencing the AIA in the 1890s was the friendship forged among a group of men of divergent occupations but similar interests in the arts. At the center of this group was Washington architect Glenn Brown (1854–1932), who as a public historian, and after 1898 secretary of the AIA, supervised its local and national program (frontispiece).[4] Earlier in the decade Brown had studied L'Enfant's plan for Washington and led a crusade to revitalize the city's central core based on that plan.[5] He was especially suited for this leadership, for, as the son of a prominent Alexandria, Virginia, physician, and the grandson of a United States senator, he had been raised in a privileged world. He studied at Washington and Lee University (1871–73), where his classmates included George E. Chamberlain, who was elected to the U.S. Senate from Oregon in 1908, and James L. Slayden, who served in the House as a representative from Texas beginning in 1897. Both were important Capitol Hill contacts and supporters of Brown. Author and ambassador Thomas Nelson Page, who served as president of the Washington Fine Arts Society and as an officer of the Committee of One Hundred for the District of Columbia, two powerful local lobbying groups, was another Washington and Lee classmate of Brown's.[6] Page lent his Washington residence, designed by the New York firm McKim Mead & White, for meetings and for entertaining visitors important to the campaign to revitalize the L'Enfant plan. At the Massachusetts Institute of Technology (MIT), where Brown studied after he left Washington and Lee, William Robert Ware, the father of American architectural education, became Brown's mentor and friend. Ware later sponsored Brown for membership in the AIA, and Fellow of the American Institute of Architects (FAIA), the institute's highest membership category. One of Brown's MIT classmates was Francis Bacon, brother of Henry Bacon, the architect of the Lincoln Memorial, one crucial element of the Senate Park Commission's 1901 Mall design.[7]

When Brown established his practice in Washington in 1880, he readily found clients, the majority of whom were in Washington's Elite List. He designed a number of buildings at the National Zoo and naturalistic bridges for Rock Creek Park during the next two decades (fig. 1). He was a finalist in several important competitions, his works were widely illustrated in the architectural press, and his reputation as an architect and designer was secure before he turned to administrative work related to public architecture and planning.[8] In 1887, Brown had been a founding member of the Washington chapter of the AIA. It would become one of the leading AIA chapters, important not just in defining the role of the professional architect, but also in organizing national support for AIA causes, including, ultimately, the Senate Park Commission plan for Washington.

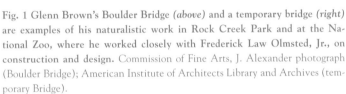

Fig. 1 Glenn Brown's Boulder Bridge *(above)* and a temporary bridge *(right)* are examples of his naturalistic work in Rock Creek Park and at the National Zoo, where he worked closely with Frederick Law Olmsted, Jr., on construction and design. Commission of Fine Arts, J. Alexander photograph (Boulder Bridge); American Institute of Architects Library and Archives (temporary Bridge).

One of Brown's most important contributions to Washington's architecture was his study of the U.S. Capitol. This project developed as a result of his interest in the Octagon, a distinguished early-nineteenth-century house completed in 1801 to the designs of William Thornton, whom Brown would establish as the Capitol's first architect.[9] The Capitol had additional significance for Brown. His great grandfather, Peter Lenox, had been the Capitol's superintendent of construction between 1817 and 1829, and his grandfather, Bedford Brown, had served there as a senator from North Carolina from 1829 to 1840. Portions of Brown's history of the Capitol, serialized in the *American Architect and Building News* in 1896 and 1897, caught the attention of Senator James McMillan of Michigan, chairman of the Senate Committee on the District of Columbia, and McMillan's aide, Charles Moore. They suggested that Brown's essays be published as a Senate document, and the first volume of his *History of the United States Capitol* was issued in 1900, with the second volume appearing in 1903.[10] The work established Brown as one of the most prominent historians of public architecture in America (fig. 2).

At the Cosmos Club, a private organization of Washington's intellectual elite, Brown often talked about L'Enfant and the growing movement to revitalize Washington's original plan. Architect Cass Gilbert later wrote "that it was Charles Moore and Glenn Brown, who, talking to a group of architects one evening at the Cosmos Club, urged that the architects should throw their fullest efforts in favor of the return to the L'Enfant plan, and by their earnest persistence prevailed upon those present to interest themselves in the subject."[11] Ultimately Brown's ability to manage the movement to resurrect key elements of L'Enfant's plan depended as much on his social and professional contacts as on his organizational ability. It was fortunate for the cause that Brown spoke as a successful and knowledgeable architect and historian.

Fig. 2 One of William Thornton's 1793 drawings for the U.S. Capitol. Brown, whose research reestablished Thornton as the original architect of the Capitol, became, with his 1900 and 1903 volumes, *History of the United States Capitol,* one of the nation's preeminent public historians. Prints and Drawings Collection, the Octagon Museum, the American Architectural Foundation.

THE DECADE OF THE 1890s

In his 1894 article "The Selection of Sites for Federal Buildings," published in *Architectural Review,* Brown lauded L'Enfant's placement of the Capitol and White House. "It is difficult to realize the pleasure produced by the sight of the [Capitol] building as seen from the hills of the District, Maryland, and Virginia. The Dome is constantly peeping out through the trees down the valleys in the most unexpected places as one drives or wanders through the country…."[12] Brown argued for restoration of the Mall, noting that it was feasible, but that "the probability of such wise action without a competent Bureau of Fine Arts is infinitesimal." In his autobiography, *Memories,*

Fig. 3 Although no photograph of the Senate Park Commission members together is known to exist, this 1892 view of architects and officials of the World's Columbian Exposition shows Daniel H. Burnham, far left; Charles F. McKim, third from right; and Augustus Saint Gaudens, sixth from right (with top hat). The fourth member, Frederick Law Olmsted, Jr., was an undergraduate student at Harvard at the time. George Browne Post, president of the AIA in 1896-97 and an important figure in the planning of the 1900 AIA Annual Meeting, is second from the left. *Chicago Tribune*, 26 January 1930. Photograph courtesy the American Institute of Architects Library and Archives.

published in 1931, Brown recalled that the 1893 World's Columbian Exposition held in Chicago provided inspiration for what might happen in Washington. "A plan…if carried out under the direction of artists, equal to the corps employed at the World's Columbian Exposition, would give the country a parked avenue in Washington unequaled by anything in the world,—a triumph of the arts" (fig. 3). Brown had visited the Chicago exposition as architect Daniel Burnham's guest and the two men worked closely together when Burnham was president of the AIA in 1894 to 1895.[13]

In 1895 the Washington Chapter of the AIA and the Cosmos Club organized the Public Art League, a national body with a national membership, to lobby for the fine arts. Richard Watson Gilder, editor of *Century Magazine*, was elected president, architect Charles Follen McKim,

Fig. 4 This ca.1872 photograph of the Octagon, designed by William Thornton and completed in 1801, is the oldest known photograph of the house. The Octagon became the headquarters of the AIA in 1898 and is still owned by the architects. American Institute of Architects Library and Archives.

first vice-president, and sculptor Augustus Saint-Gaudens, second vice-president. Landscape architect Frederick Law Olmsted Jr. and Daniel Burnham were among the directors, and Brown was corresponding secretary. He later wrote: "We found appeals to Congress by our small local body accomplished nothing. The way to the legislator's brain was through marked interest from their home voters."[14] The organization's main goal was to establish a national fine arts commission composed of the country's leading artists. In a related move, Brown and the Washington chapter of AIA argued that the headquarters of the AIA, a national organization, should be moved from New York to Washington.[15] This was accomplished in 1898, when the Octagon House was rented, and as of January 1899 became AIA national headquaters The building was purchased in 1902 and is still owned by the AIA (fig. 4).[16]

Brown was elected secretary of the AIA at its 32d convention held in Washington 1–3 November 1898. The convention proceedings for that year noted that "promptly at 2 o'clock the members, with their wives and lady friends, went in a body to the White House and were received in the East Room, each member being introduced by the Secretary of the Institute to President McKinley by whom they were cordially greeted." From the White House they went to the Treasury Department to meet Secretary of the Treasury Lyman Gage and visit the Office of Supervising Architect. A reception at the Octagon followed where they viewed an exhibition of architectural drawings and inspected the house, then being prepared to serve as AIA headquarters. A special feature of the exhibition was "many of the original drawings of the Capitol, which had been found, after diligent research by Mr. Glenn Brown."[17]

In accordance with newly adopted organizational policies, Brown's position as the AIA's secretary, beginning in 1898, combined most of the duties of the modern Chief Executive Officer, Chief Operating Officer, and Chief Financial Officer. At the same time, a term limit of two years was set for AIA presidents, effectively reducing their power.[18] During Brown's tenure as secretary (1898–1913), nine AIA annual conventions were held in Washington. Brown was able to offer visiting dignitaries and distinguished architects special privileges, including guided tours of the White House "through the basement, then through the principal floor…ending up by taking them out on the south portico and calling their attention to the beauty of the grounds and to the charming view of the Potomac."[19]

It proved most useful in the decade after 1898 to have the AIA, the Washington chapter of the AIA, and the Washington Architectural Club under one roof in the Octagon. These three would soon be joined there in the decade after 1898 by the Archaeological Society of America, the American Academy in Rome, the American Federation of Arts, the National Society of Fine Arts, and The Washington Society of Fine Arts. This last organization had been founded by members of the Washington chapter of the AIA, and its 1914 yearbook noted that the group had "lent its aid in developing Washington into the most beautiful city in America, if not the world, strongly advocating the adoption of the Park Commission Plan."[20] Though other organizations were involved, these constituted the core that orchestrated a national advocacy by artists and architects for revitalization of the L'Enfant plan for Washington.

Adjacent to the Octagon was the Lemon Building where, in the decade following the presentation of the Senate Park Commission plan in 1902, the Rock Creek Parkway Commission, the Lincoln Memorial Commission, and the Fine Arts Commission established their headquarters. The War Department's Office of Public Buildings and Grounds, which had legal authority over development in Washington and daily faced pressing pragmatic problems, also had offices in the Lemon Building. The White House was two blocks away; the Office of Supervising Architect in the Treasury Department three blocks away; and the Cosmos Club, four blocks away. It is unlikely that any other area in the nation possessed such a concentrated collection of professional, political, and social organizations. It is certain that this concentration made coordination easier, and response time quicker, both important in the crusade over Washington's future.

As the 1890s ended, Brown met with McKim at the Century Club in New York to talk about Washington's future. Brown later recalled that McKim "lauded the beauties of the L'Enfant plan… and urged the feasibility of returning to it in the future development of the city…. McKim forcibly expressed his regret that this great plan should be destroyed by indifference and want of knowledge. Then we discussed the great need of a commission to study and plan a scheme for the future growth of the National Capital. I left him determined to make a demonstration that would arouse the attention of thoughtful people to the crime our nation was committing."[21]

At its first meeting in the Octagon on 5 January 1899, just five days after the AIA had moved its headquarters there from New York, the AIA board of directors authorized publication of a quarterly magazine, *The American Institute of Architects Quarterly Bulletin*, which Brown would edit.[22] From the magazine's first issue in April 1900 until its last in 1913, the status of Washington's development was a frequent subject. The magazine was initially sent to all members of the AIA and to forty-three foreign societies, forty American societies and institutions, and fifty-nine periodicals in the field. Both its circulation base and influence expanded over the next 13 years.

PLANNING THE AIA CONVENTION OF 1900

The year 1900 was an important one in Washington, for it marked the centennial of the federal government's move from Philadelphia to its permanent seat in the District of Columbia. Numerous plans were being formulated to celebrate, not just with parades, but with commemorative building. Suggestions included a Centennial Avenue which would run from the Capitol diagonally across the Mall to the Potomac River, where it would cross the river on a memorial bridge. Enlarging the White House was a second important proposal. Both projects would become major points of discussion at the AIA's annual convention in 1900, to be held in Washington. One convention session was earmarked for discussion of federal buildings and their grouping. In March Brown wrote architects Thomas Hastings and Cass Gilbert, asking them to present papers. Frederick Law Olmsted Jr. was evidently asked at the same time. Henry Van Brunt, architect and president of the AIA in 1899, was asked to participate, but he was in Europe and would not return in time. On 18 May sculptor John Quincy Adams Ward declined Brown's invitation to present a paper while "thanking you for the opportunity."[23] From the beginning, Brown's intent was to have architects, landscape architects, and sculptors participate, each approaching the subject of "grouping buildings" from the point of view of his respective profession.

Even as convention sessions were being planned, drawings that could be exhibited during the convention were sought. These included the University of California competition sponsored by Phoebe A. Hearst.[24] The firm Boring & Tilton supplied drawings of their work at Ellis Island; George Browne Post loaned drawings of the proposed Justice Department building in Washington; and Hornblower & Marshall drawings of the Baltimore Custom House. These were exhibited at the Octagon, and at the Cosmos Club while the AIA convention was in session.[25]

McKim's firm was asked on 22 June to participate. "Be kind enough to let me know if you or Mr. Mead or Mr. White will not prepare such a paper," Brown wrote. Brown noted that the convention would be in early December in Washington and that "Mr. F. L. Olmsted, Jr., has agreed to give a paper on the Landscape feature of the project." McKim held his reply until 31 July, when he responded that he would be sailing for Europe the next day, and could neither participate nor attend the convention. "I wish that it were in my power to contribute to the occasion," he wrote. A May letter to architect Howard Walker asking him to be a presenter finally reached him in Italy and he replied on 12 June accepting.[26] Walker noted that he had already visited Amsterdam, Munich, London, Rome, Venice, Budapest, Milan, and many smaller cities, and would be going to Paris, Dresden, and Berlin "with a view to studying municipal improvements." Brown, requesting a paper from architect Edgar V. Seeler, wrote: "It is intended by these papers to call the attention of Congress forcibly to the need of some harmonious scheme to be followed in the future development of Washington. We propose to have the reading and discussion open to the public and invite all Congressmen and officials to attend." Brown continued: "I will be pleased to furnish data about the original scheme of the city and buildings, as well as get you maps or other information you may desire."[27]

During July 1900 Brown continued to contact possible participants. He asked Daniel Burnham, William A. Boring, Cass Gilbert, and Thomas R. Kimball, noting that "we propose to make a prominent feature of papers on the grouping of Federal Buildings in Washington City."[28] Gilbert did participate and Boring and Kimball attended the convention. Burnham, however, was too busy to attend. The sculptor H. K. Bush-Brown agreed, when Brown asked him, to prepare a paper.[29] When the program was set, Brown organized the papers in a session entitled "On the General Subject of the Grouping of Government Buildings, Landscape, and Statuary in the City of Washington," to proceed from general to specific topics. Walker delivered a paper on the topic of "Grouping of Buildings in a Great City" and Seeler one on "Monumental Grouping of Buildings in Washington." Olmsted spoke on "Landscape in Washington" and Bush-Brown on "Sculpture in Washington." Walker and Seeler were both MIT graduates and practicing architects as well as teachers of architecture. All four speakers had traveled abroad, were well known in their professions, and well known public speakers.

Also in July 1900 Brown sent speakers background information. He noted in a letter to Olmsted that he was sending:

> ...a copy of the Report of the Committee on the Centennial of the Establishment of the Seat of Government in Washington, D.C., with early map of the City, copy of the Report on the Designs for a Memorial Bridge across the Potomac River at Washington, D.C., a blue print map of the portion of Washington showing the present location of government buildings, and a map of the city of Washington at the present time...I call to

your attention the article by Mr. F. W. Fitzpatrick on beautifying the Nation's Capital, in the March No of Inland Architect. The same periodical also contains the diagram of the proposed new Avenue, by Mr. Henry Ives Cobb. I have just written an article on this same subject, which is to appear in the August Number of the Architectural Review.[30]

In September Brown and the Committee on Arrangements "determined to fix the 12th, 13th, 14th, and 15th of December as the days of the convention." The 12th was the day on which the Centennial would be celebrated. Brown wrote that including the 12th in the convention calendar would "give an opportunity to all architects who wish to see the different sights connected with the Centennial" and "follow it up by the Convention the next three days."[31]

On 22 September Brown wrote Bush-Brown alerting him to Brown's "Suggestions for the Grouping of Buildings, Monuments, and Statuary, with Landscape in Washington," appearing in the *Architectural Review*. Brown noted that it was "written…as a preliminary to our convention work, thinking it might serve to call attention to the subject." He wrote again, after queries from Bush-Brown, that "we wish to call the attention of Congress to the fact that a grouping or massing of landscape, sculpture and buildings would be a great addition to the Capital City; also that a Commission should be appointed composed of architects, landscape architects, and sculptors to consider the subject, before any one of the schemes at present under consideration should be adopted."[32]

Brown suggested emphasizing the importance of establishing an art commission to oversee development within the city and he stressed the importance of "not having it [the commission] dominated in any way by the Army engineers." Bush-Brown rewrote his speech in accordance with Brown's suggestions, but he still wanted to confer with Walker, who would not return from Europe until November, in case Walker might desire changes also. He agreed with Brown that the "several papers should compliment each other." They exchanged papers and Seeler modified his after reading Walker's.[33]

All participants were invited to Washington to tour the area under discussion; Brown wanted no surprises and no deviations. He wanted each speaker to have extensive background material that included knowledge of the views of the other presenters and also familiarity with the locations in question. These areas included the White House and Ellipse, Capitol Hill, the Mall to the Potomac River, and areas abutting the south and north sides of the Mall. On 21 November Seeler sent Brown a copy of his speech noting that in preparing it, "the tour over the ground under your guidance a couple of weeks ago was of the greatest assistance to me."[34] Olmsted would already have been familiar with the area, and the others either toured it earlier or did so before the convention. In October, Brown had called the attention of his speakers to an article in the November *Ladies Home*

Journal by Col. Theodore Bingham relating his plans for the enlargement of the White House. The article included a drawing that showed massive, multistory wings that clashed with the style of the original White House, and also dwarfed it.[35] Gilbert responded almost immediately, noting that the convention "would seem to me a very proper occasion…to take the matter up officially and see what action could be taken to preserve this fine old public monument." Boring replied humorously that he would "purchase now the first number of this valuable periodical that I have ever invested in, and hope to be much edified by Colonel Bingham's Architecture." Olmsted, too, sought out the magazine.[36] This solidified a second motive of the 1900 convention, to wrest control of the White House from Bingham and the Army engineers and foil the proposed enlargement.

Bingham was preparing a model of his proposed addition to the White House and was asked to lend it to the AIA for exhibition during the convention. He replied that he could not "assist your committee with designs for the White House and treatment of the Mall" because the drawings would not have been officially published by then. He did, however, thank Brown for the invitation to attend the session, which he noted he would "be glad to accept, if possible." When pressed to lend the model, Bingham responded "in order to make clear the position of this Office in the matter, your attention is respectfully called to the fact that the work being done in this Office in regard to an extension to the Executive Mansion is entirely official in its character, and is, therefore not subject to general inspection by law and regulations until it has been officially made public."[37] Bingham's model was actually exhibited, but at the White House (12 December 1900), where he explained it to the guests assembled for the centennial celebration.

Discussions on illustrating the AIA session were extensive, with Brown offering to produce lantern slides, either from materials provided by the speakers or from other sources. In August and early September 1900, Brown and Joseph C. Hornblower of the AIA's Washington chapter traveled to Europe to attend the Paris Exposition. "I procured a large collection of photographs," Brown wrote, "covering sculpture, landscape and buildings and their combinations which, in form of lantern slides, we could use in our crusade."[38] These photographs were reproduced as lantern slides and many of them were used in lectures at the 1900 convention. They also appeared in the published papers of the convention and in the 1902 Senate Park Commission report. These and other lantern slides from the Senate Park Commission's report were, between 1902 and 1913, frequently used in prepackaged slide lectures distributed across the nation in support of the commission plan for the Mall.

The dean of Washington architecture, Hornblower, would chair the 13 December session on grouping Washington's public buildings and introduce the individual speakers. A former student of Jean-Louis Pascal in Paris, Hornblower had served as president of the AIA's Washington chapter in 1897 and was on the faculty of the School of Architecture at Columbian University [now George Washington University] since 1897. He and his partner, James Rush Marshall, had won the Baltimore Custom House competition in 1900 and, in 1904, they were commissioned to design the Smithsonian's National Museum (Natural History Museum), one of the first two buildings on the Mall to respond to the parameters established by the Senate Park Commission's report.[39] Three other architects were asked to prepare responses to the principal papers: Cass Gilbert of New York, (initially asked to be a speaker), Paul J. Pelz, and George Oakley Totten Jr., the last two both prominent Washington architects. When Pelz replied affirmatively, he noted that he had "as a member of the Board of Trade given this subject [grouping buildings in Washington] some study...and [had] produced a suggestive plan to that effect which met the unanimous approval of the Com. on Publ. Bldgs. of the Board of Trade."[40] The discussants were well known to the national AIA audience, and all had designed major government buildings. Gilbert's New York Custom House was already considered a modern masterpiece. Totten had been the chief designer in the Office of the Supervising Architect of the Treasury, designing the Philadelphia Mint and several post offices, before opening a Washington office in 1898. Five years earlier he had won the McKim Traveling Scholarship and attended the École des Beaux-Arts in Paris. He also served as president of the Washington Architectural Club from 1897 to 1898. Pelz, in partnership with John L. Smithmeyer, had designed the Library of Congress (1871–97), which brought Beaux-Arts design to Washington and was much in the public eye in 1900.[41]

Everything was ready for the beginning of a battle with Colonel Bingham and the Army engineers, with the first skirmish set for the White House celebration on 12 December. Brown had been invited by President and Mrs. William McKinley to "an informal luncheon following the exercises at the Executive Mansion."[42] It is probable that at least the AIA convention speakers and AIA officers were also invited to the luncheon, for George Browne Post telegraphed Brown, "I accept luncheon invitation with pleasure."[43]

THE 1900 ANNUAL MEETING AND IMMEDIATE AFTERMATH

Celebration of the 100th anniversary of the establishment of the seat of government in the District of Columbia took place officially on 12 December 1900. President McKinley met the state governors and other guests in the White House's Blue Room, where they were presented by Colonel Bingham in his official capacity as the president's aide. All were ultimately seated in the East Room where, "on a raised decorated platform in the center was a plaster model of the Executive Mansion

Fig. 5 Army Corps of Engineers Colonel Theodore Bingham, superintendent of public buildings and grounds, was in charge of White House care and championed his own design, unveiled in 1900, for the restoration and enlargement of the house. The AIA used the design to wrest control from the Corps while engaging architects, artists, and sculptors in Washington design. Library of Congress, Manuscript Division.

with the proposed additions." (fig. 5) Bingham, the engineer officer in charge of Public Buildings and Grounds, delivered an address on the history of the Executive Mansion during the nineteenth century. He spoke principally on the proposed enlargement of the Executive Mansion, which, he noted, he had begun to study in 1897. He lauded his plan for retaining the original building, asserting his extensions would accentuate the character of Hoban's original design by being architecturally harmonious with it. The rationale for the extensions was to relieve the pressure of use on the building for the next quarter century. He closed his address by stating "We have endeavored to imbue ourselves with a part, at least of the spirit of the first architect of this house and have worked for the entire country; and if these results please you, its representatives, that is our sufficient reward."[44]

The next day, 13 December, at the opening session of the AIA convention, AIA president Robert Peabody stated that "if the White House in which we all take such pleasure and pride, needs to be increased in size, we want…[the work] carried out by the best artistic skill that the country can produce and by nothing less efficient." On the following day the convention adopted a resolution on the White House aimed at preventing its disfigurement "by allowing its proposed enlargement to be carried out by parties unfamiliar with architectural design." The convention voted overwhelmingly for the resolution.[45] Two days earlier the Fine Arts Union of Washington, another AIA ally, had protested against Bingham's design to the House and Senate committees on Public Buildings and Grounds. The group wrote that "[the Union] wishes to call your attention to the enclosed protest and recommendations from various Art societies in reference to additions to the Executive Mansion and request your earnest consideration of the same."[46] Brown, through the Public Art League, had collected protests from forty art associations around the country, from local AIA chapters, and from individual architects. These, too, were presented to the congressional committees.[47]

Brown also took advantage of the national press's presence in Washington because of the centennial celebrations and distributed information packets about the nationwide protests to the reporters.[48] Also on 14 December the Washington Board of Trade resolved to support a commission to study the future development of the capital city.[49] Philadelphia's T-Square Club, an architectural society and AIA supporter, followed on the 20th with a resolution demanding that any White House changes take place only after a professional commission had been appointed and had agreed to the change.[50] Brown later wrote that "the people were interested in keeping intact their historic Presidential home and responded to the appeal for its preservation. McKinley listened to the public demand and ordered the model removed from the East Room. It was stored in the cellar of the Corcoran Gallery and neither [Bingham's] scheme nor model was heard of again."[51] Because Brown was the recognized scholar on the Capitol and White House his criticism was taken seriously.

While confronting the White House issue, the AIA simultaneously considered the future development of Washington, when on Thursday evening 13 December the convention opened the floor to discussion of grouping government buildings on the Mall. In his opening remarks Hornblower gave a short history of planning in Washington, noting that L'Enfant's plan was not derivative but original. He suggested that the plans which would be proposed at the convention for the Mall might have credit, but he suggested that all should be questioned until a "more comprehensive study has been made of the whole matter of arrangement of parks and disposition of buildings." He suggested public buildings for the triangle between Constitution and Pennsylvania avenues, and a building for the Supreme Court. "The plan of the city as originally projected has been sufficient for the requirements of [its] first century. Now, at the end of the first…it is proper to consider fully and studiously the requirements of the second."[52]

Olmsted discussed existing landscape features of the area, especially the Mall: "The solution of the general problem involved in the revision of the Mall demands months of careful study and consideration by able and appreciative men, while the suggestions given here are the crude produce of a few days' thought. But one thing is clear: The fundamental importance of living up to the greatness of the original plan."[53]

Architect Howard Walker illustrated his presentation with slides from European cities, most of them the capitals of their countries. "It is apparent," he asserted, "that the most attractive cities are those where some broad comprehensive plan of treatment has been conceived and adhered to, and when if poor surroundings or inferior architecture forced itself into prominence, its effect was minimized either by planting out with trees or by interrupting continuous vistas by a monument or building." He recommended extending the White House and Capitol vistas beyond the Washington Monument to the Potomac River.[54]

Edgar Seeler began his presentation with a history of Washington's founding, ending with: "This, then, is a site selected after much thought and conscientious deliberation by Washington, a plan developed under his guidance by the foremost engineer of the time; the whole endorsed by Jefferson and Madison and the territorial commissioners. A plan which, in its essential scheme, the intervening years have stamped with their approval. And yet a plan which was practically forgotten after the Capitol and White House were located until within a few years.... We architects are just beginning to see that there is a mission for our organization." Seeler suggested the following criteria for a new plan: strict height limitations along Pennsylvania Avenue; retaining only the Smithsonian Institution and Washington Monument among the Mall's structures; the construction of a memorial bridge on a direct axis from the Capitol through the Washington Monument; removal of the railroad station from the Mall; purchasing the triangle between Sixth and Fifteenth streets and Pennsylvania Avenue and North B Street (now Constitution Avenue) for federal construction; placement of buildings on the outer limits of the Mall; and the formation of a Commission of Fine Arts. "The American Institute of Architects should pledge itself to the formation of a commission, powerful, authoritative, and beyond question in its judgments, in whose hands the artistic development of the city of Washington shall be placed, and whose decisions shall be without recourse." In discussing the proposed memorial bridge on the Capitol–Washington Monument axis, he suggested that "at the transition from boulevard to bridge should be a vigorous architectural accent—a memorial or monumental group."[55]

Sculptor H. K. Bush-Brown, reminded the convention in his speech "Sculpture in Washington," that monuments were erected to "keep alive in the mind of the community the ideals that have moved the souls of men in the past. Commendable as are the monuments in Washington, do we find that any plan of selecting subjects or grouping them has been adopted? No, quite the contrary...[but] art made Athens and Rome and Florence and Venice, each in turn, the center of the world.... We have in Washington one of the finest city plans in the world...." Bush-Brown also suggested formation of a fine arts commission, noting that "to judge of military tactics and national policies requires years of training and experience. Is it too much to assume that art is worthy of the same consideration?"[56]

After the AIA meeting Olmsted wrote Brown that "as to forwarding the movement for doing the right thing at Washington, I doubt if such meetings have any very considerable weight except as they may set a few people to work to personally talk to the right people in just the right way." He warned that Bingham would be a problem and that Secretary of Agriculture James Wilson was "distinctly hostile."[57] The AIA convention directed Peabody to appoint a special committee of seven members to consider the formation of an art commission "to advise regarding the improvement of the National Capital." William A. Boring of New York was appointed as chairman of the first of these committees, with its members including G. F. Shepley from Boston, Frank Miles Day from Philadelphia, W. S. Eames from St. Louis, Edward Green from Buffalo, Joseph C. Hornblower from Washington, and George Browne Post from New York its members. Eames was appointed to chair a second committee, with Post and R. W. Gibson of New York as members asked to communicate to Congress the AIA resolutions regarding the White House.[58]

These AIA committees met with Senator McMillan's aide Charles Moore almost immediately, and on 19 December, just six days after the papers had been read to the convention, McMillan introduced a congressional resolution to print the AIA papers as a Senate document. Printed as a government document the AIA papers and their viewpoint would become available to architects nationwide and abroad.[59] The publication would be sent to AIA members, forty American societies and institutions, forty-three foreign societies, and to fifty-nine periodicals on architecture and the allied arts. Equally important, the collected papers would be accessible to politicians at all levels. Moore, in his introduction to the convention papers, noted that "The Report of the Centennial Celebration, now in press, will show the ideas of the laity; this publication contains the tentative plans of the experts," leaving no doubt where his and Senator McMillan's sympathies lay.[60]

Brown's article from the *Architectural Review* of August 1900, although not read at the convention, was also included. This piece discussed a number of building topics: the proposed Centennial Avenue; future development in the triangles of land between Pennsylvania and Maryland avenues and the Mall; a memorial at the foot of the Capitol; another memorial on the banks of the Potomac on axis with the Capitol and the Washington Monument; a memorial bridge; and parkland in the area between the Washington Monument and the Tidal Basin. Rock Creek Park and the National Zoo (with four illustrations of Brown's own work) were suggested as parkland to be permanently preserved. Brown also mentioned railroads and the need to remove the existing station to the Mall's south side, with its entrances below street level and confined to Sixth and Seventh streets. To oversee all this, he wrote, "it appears to me that a carefully selected commission of architects, sculptors and landscape architects should be given charge of the subject."[61]

The collected convention presentations by Gilbert, Totten, and Pelz on grouping buildings were labeled "discussion following the papers read before the Institute," although they had not actually been read. Gilbert had proposed building a new residence for the president on Meridian Hill, eighteen blocks north of the White House, allowing the older building to be used exclusively for offices.[62] Totten, in presenting his plan, acknowledged his indebtedness "to the inspiring writings of Mr. Glenn Brown. It is to Mr. Brown, I believe, more than to any other one person we are indebted for the revival of Major L'Enfant's beautiful scheme."[63] In the collected papers Pelz reported that a campaign to purchase all the property between Pennsylvania Avenue and the Mall had been suggested by the Washington Board of Trade in 1899, and had found support in the local press. He suggested a Treasury Annex along Fifteenth Street, NW, and at Center Market between Seventh and Ninth streets, today's National Archives, Pelz envisioned "a most central site between the Capitol and all the departments [suitable for] a hall of records." (figs. 6-11) [64]

On 17 December 1900 Boring, Peabody, and Brown met with Moore and the Senate Committee on the District of Columbia. Together they agreed on what would become Senate Resolution 139, authorizing the president to "appoint a commission, to consist of two architects and one landscape architect eminent in their profession, who shall consider the subject of the location and grouping of public buildings and monuments to be erected in the District of Columbia and the development and improvement of the entire park system of said District, and shall report to Congress thereon."[65] Boring recommended Peabody, Burnham, McKim, Post, and Olmsted as "suitable men to serve on such a commission."[66] Resolution 139 was introduced into the Senate that same day. It included an appended statement prepared by Brown stating: "Now is the time, on the hundredth anniversary of the foundation of the Capitol [sic] to consider the propriety of another plan on which future buildings shall be erected, by which parks shall be laid out so as to enhance the effect and beauty of the buildings, and by which groupings of monuments may add to the effectiveness of the whole." Almost immediately Boring's committee sent a letter to members and chapters suggesting that all possible pressure be brought to bear on the Congress to insure passage of the resolution.[67] Moore later recalled the subsequent events:

> The resolution having been adopted, a Subcommittee consisting of Senators McMillan, Gallinger and Martin was named; and on March 19 this Subcommittee met Mr. Robert S. Peabody and the legislative committee of that body [the AIA]. After a discussion of the problem Mr. Boring, for the Institute Committee, recommended that Mr. Daniel H. Burnham, of Chicago and Mr. Frederick Law Olmsted, Jr., of Brookline, Massachusetts be requested to prepare the contemplated plan, and that they have the power to select a third member to act with them. These recommendations having been adopted by the Subcommittee, Mr. Charles F. McKim, of New York City, was requested and consented to serve as the third member.[68]

Internationally known sculptor Augustus Saint-Gaudens, a friend of Brown's and a wintertime resident of Washington, was added to the commission by McKim and Burnham.[69]

During the lengthy discussion at the 19 March 1901 hearing, McMillan noted that the "architects...are as much interested in the park system as they are in the public buildings."[70] They wished the Senate Park Commission members to benefit from the professional opinions expressed by the authors of the talks and papers prepared for the AIA's convention in 1900. In his obituary in 1932 of Brown, Moore wrote that the Senate Park Commission's "textbook was Glenn Brown's History of the United States Capitol and the presentations he made of the fundamental and vital value of the L'Enfant Plan were instrumental in leading members of the Senate Commission to base their report and their plans on the plan L'Enfant had designed and George Washington had approved, and which was already the underlying plan of the capital."[71]

In discussing efforts to insure the adoption of the Senate Park Commission plan, the AIA magazine asked in an editorial of 1913: "Why should individuals band themselves together into societies? Is personal benefit the object?" The editorial went on to answer: "The basis of such association should be public service, not individual gain, otherwise it were much better not to organize."[72] The last decade of the nineteenth and first decade of the twentieth centuries certainly provide one of this country's best examples of continued public service by artists and architects. It has never since been equaled.

Fig. 6 Trains crossing the Mall were a visual and actual impediment to the vista between the Capitol and the Washington Monument that L'Enfant had intended. The AIA campaigned for the clearing of stations and tracks from the Mall, work accomplished in accordance with the Park Commission's 1901 plan. The architects also proposed more careful siting of buildings, pointing out the effect of the Library of Congress dome on this view of the Capitol from the Mall at 6th Street. *Papers Relating to the Improvement of the City of Washington*, Senate Document No. 94, 56th Congress, 2nd Session, 1901, fig. 25.

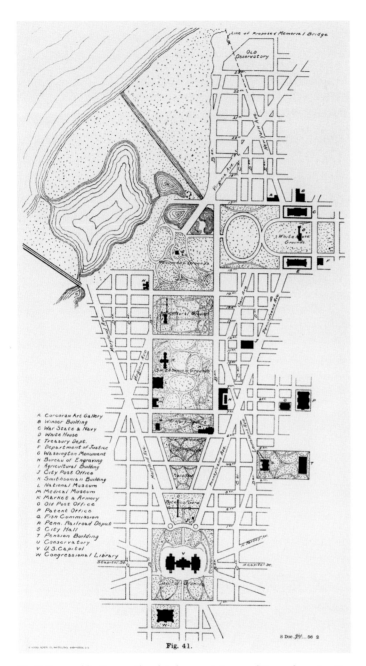

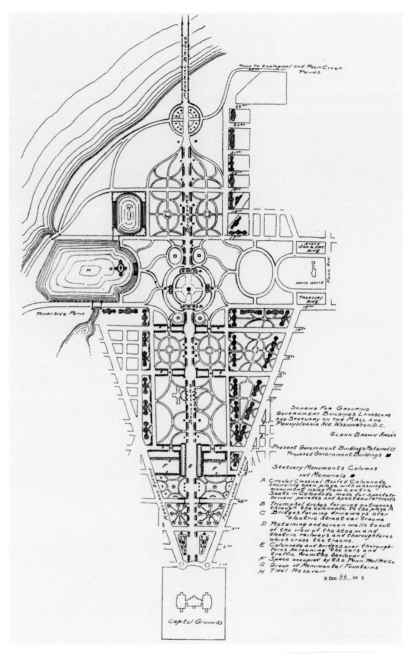

Fig. 7 Prepared by Brown, the plat shows existing conditions of construction on and around the Mall. This was used by all speakers at the 1900 AIA meeting as a starting point for their discussion. *Papers Relating to the Improvement of the City of Washington*, Senate Document 94, 56th Congress, 2nd Session, 1901, fig. 41.

Fig. 8 Brown's suggested plan for development of the Mall with government buildings constructed along both sides and an extension from the Washington Monument to a memorial bridge across the Potomac. The plan was prepared for the August 1895 *Architectural Record* and later included in the Senate document which printed the papers of the 1900 AIA Annual Meeting. *Papers Relating to the Improvement of the City of Washington*, Senate Document No. 94, 56th Congress, 2nd Session, 1901, fig. 42.

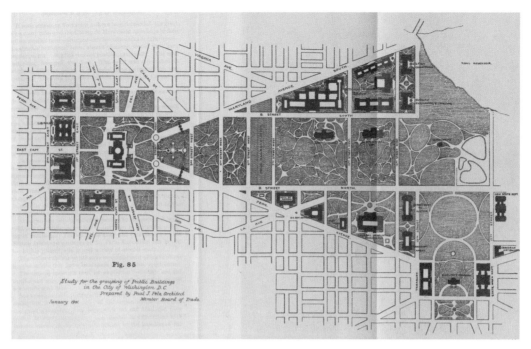

Fig. 9 Paul Pelz's study for the grouping of government buildings on the Mall was prepared for the 1900 AIA Annual Meeting and refined for use in the 1901 Senate printing of the annual meeting papers. *Papers Relating to the Improvement of the City of Washington*, Senate Document No. 94, 56th Congress, 2nd Session, 1901, fig. 85.

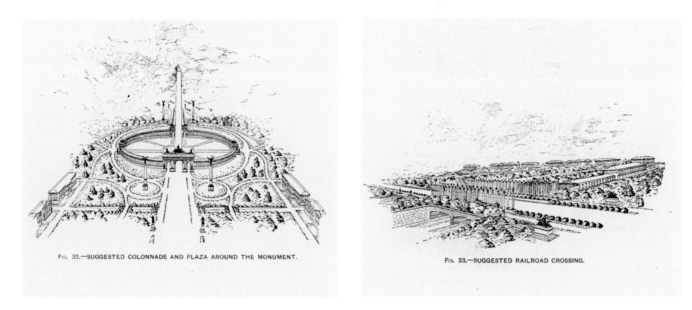

Fig. 10 Brown's drawing for a proposed colonnade and plaza around the Washington Monument and for depressed rail crossing of the Mall indicate the manner in which landscape, sculpture, and public parks were basic to AIA suggestions for reaffirming L'Enfant's plan. These and other plans and proposals provided grounding and ideas for the Senate Park Commission's subsequent plan. *Papers Relating to the Improvement of the City of Washington*, Senate Document No. 94, 56th Congress, 2nd Session, 1901, fig. 12.

Fig. 11 In the late 19th century the Potomac and its marshes lapped at the base of the Washington Monument. In 1900 the architects suggested extending the Mall from the Monument to the Potomac, work which became a part of the Senate Park Commission's 1901 plan. Dredging and fill of wetlands shown here provided the land where the Park Commission's Reflecting Pool and Lincoln Memorial would later be located. Photograph taken in 1885, soon after the Washington Monument was completed. Commission of Fine Arts.

NOTES

I should like to thank James F. Olmsted, Sue Kohler, and Pamela Scott for their assistance, material, and leads as this essay was being written.

[1] John W. Reps, *Monumental Washington: The Planning and Development of the Capital Center* (Princeton: Princeton University Press, 1967); Jon A Peterson, "The Hidden Origins of the McMillan Plan for Washington, D.C., 1900–1902," in *Historical Perspectives on Urban Design: Washington, D.C.*, ed. Antoinette J. Lee, Conference Proceedings, 7 October 1983, Center for Washington Area Studies, Occasional Paper No. l; Sue A. Kohler, *The Commission of Fine Arts, A Brief History, 1910–1995* (Washington, D.C.: Government Printing Office, 1996; Sue A. Kohler, "Artists and Architects in Government Planning: The Beginnings of the Commission of Fine Arts," a paper read at the National Collection of Fine Arts (today's Smithsonian American Art Museum) symposium, *Art in Washington: Some Artists, Patrons, and Institutions in the Nineteenth and Early Twentieth Centuries*, 15 May 1980. Kohler, as the title of her paper suggests, has looked more closely at the involvement of artists and architects locally and nationally in the Senate Park Commission and Commission of Fine Arts movements than have other authors.

[2] Antoinette J. Lee, *Architects to the Nation—The Rise and Decline of the Supervising Architect's Office* (New York: Oxford University Press, 2000), 163–88.

[3] American Institute of Architects Archives 801/1.2B, "Bureau of Architecture, 1875–76." This Record Group also contains files on President Theodore Roosevelt's later creation, by executive order, of a "Council of Fine Arts/ Bureau of Architecture, 1908–09."

[4] Glenn Brown, *Memories, 1860–1930: A Winning Crusade to Revive George Washington's Vision of a Capital City* (Washington, D.C.: W. F. Roberts, 1931). This is a basic source on Brown's efforts and those of the AIA to reestablish the L'Enfant plan for Washington; William Brian Bushong, "Glenn Brown, The American Institute of Architects, and the Development of the Civic Core of Washington, D.C.," (Ph.D. diss., George Washington University, 1988). This is the best biography of Glenn Brown and the most complete study of the involvement of the American Institute of Architects 1890–1913 in the evolution and carrying out of the Senate Park Commission plan for Washington.

[5] William Brian Bushong, Judith Helm Robinson, Julie Mueller, *A Centennial History of the Washington Chapter of The American Institute of Architects, 1887–1987* (Wash-

ington, D.C.: Architectural Foundation Press, 1987). This study of a major Washington, D.C., organization, of which Glenn Brown was a founder and important member, contains important data on the work of Brown and the chapter in focusing national attention on the L'Enfant and Senate Park Commission plans. It also offers good, short biographies of most of the Washington architects mentioned in this paper.

[6] Bushong, "Glenn Brown," 8–15; Brown, *Memories*, 87–88 (Chamberlain); 91–95 (Slayden); 497–99 (Page).

[7] Ibid., 18–22; 23.

[8] Bushong, "Glenn Brown," 8–39, for a survey of Brown's training and practice; 295–301 for a list of his projects.

[9] Glenn Brown, "The Tayloe Mansion, The Octagon House, Washington, D.C.," *American Architect and Building News* 23 (7 January 1888): 6–7. Glenn Brown, "Dr. William Thornton, Architect," *Architectural Record* 6 (July 1896): 52–70.

[10] Glenn Brown, *The History of the United States Capitol*, 2 vols. (Washington, D.C.: Government Printing Office, 1900–1903).

[11] Cass Gilbert, foreword to Glenn Brown, "Roosevelt and the Fine Arts," *American Architect*, 116 no. 2294 (10 December 1919): 709–10; Brown's article appears in two parts: "Roosevelt and the Fine Arts, Part 1," in ibid., 711–19, and "Roosevelt and the Fine Arts, Part 2," in ibid., 116 no. 2295 (17 December 1919), 739–52. Brown, *Memories*, 138–77.

[12] Glenn Brown, "The Selection of Sites for Federal Buildings," *American Architect* 3 no. 4 (August 1894): 27–29. The first sentence of this article became the first sentence of Brown's *The History of the United States Capitol*, and its title provided the theme for the American Institute of Architects Convention of 1900.

[13] Brown, *Memories*, 345.

[14] Ibid., 357–63.

[15] AIA Archives 509/2, "American Institute of Architects Board of Directors, Minutes," 16 January 1896; AIA Archives 505, "American Institute of Architects Proceedings, 30th Convention, Nashville, Tennessee, 20–22 October 1896."

[16] AIA Archives 505, "American Institute of Architects Proceedings, 31st Convention, Detroit, Michigan, 29–30 September, 1 October 1897."

[17] AIA Archives 505, "American Institute of Architects Proceedings, 32d Convention, Washington, D.C., 1–3 November 1898."

[18] AIA Archives 501, "American Institute of Architects, Constitution and By-Laws," 1898.

[19] Brown, *Memories*, 104–5.

[20] The Historical Society of Washington, D.C., Archives, "The Washington Society of Fine Arts Yearbook, 1914."

[21] Brown, *Memories*, 265–66.

[22] AIA Archives 505, "American Institute of Architects Proceedings, 33d Convention, Pittsburgh, Pennsylvania, 13–16 November 1899," 18.

[23] AIA Archives 801/1/17/1900H, Thomas Hastings to Glenn Brown, 26 March 1900; 801/1/17/1900G, Cass Gilbert to Brown, 31 March 1900; 801/1/17/1900N–O, Frederick Law Olmsted Jr. to Brown, 2 April 1900; 801/1/17/1900N–O, Olmsted to Brown, 1 May 1900; 801/1/17/1900U–Z, Henry Van Brunt to Brown, 13 April 1900; 801/1/18/1900U-Z, John Quincy Adams Ward to Brown, 18 May 1900.

[24] AIA Archives 801/1/18/1900T, Paul B. Tuzo to Brown, 18 May 1900, 16 June 1900, and 21 June 1900. AIA Archives 801/1/18/1900P, Brown to Robert Peabody, 18 June 1900, and return to Brown marked approved.

[25] AIA Archives 801/1/1/6/1A/91, Brown to Boring & Tilton, 22 June 1900; 80l/1/1/6/1A/163, 14 July 1900; 801/1/1/6/1A/417, 8 December 1900. Correspondence with George Browne Post, Hornblower & Marshall, and others asked to supply drawings is similar and can be found in this letterbook.

[26] AIA Archives 801/1/1/6/1A/65, Brown to Charles F. McKim, 22 June 1900; 801/1/17/1900/L–M, McKim to Brown, 31 July 1900; 801/1/18/1900U–Z, Howard Walker to Brown, 12 June 1900.

[27] AIA Archives 801/1.1/6/1A/84, Brown to Edgar V. Seeler, 16 June 1900; 801/1/18/1900S, Seeler to Brown, 9 July 1900.

[28] AIA Archives 801/1.1/6/1A/130, Brown to Daniel Burnham, 6 July 1900. In the same letterbook records identical letters to Thomas Kimball on 128, to Gilbert on 129, and to Boring on 131.

[29] AIA Archives 801/1/17/1900B, Burnham to Brown, 4 December 1900; 801/1/17/1900B, H.K. Bush-Brown to Brown, 14 July 1900.

[30] AIA Archives 801/1.1/6/1A/152, Brown to Olmsted, 12 July 1900.

[31] AIA Archives 801/1.1/6/1A/295–98, Brown to R. S. Peabody, 15 September 1900.

[32] AIA Archives 801/1.1/6/1A/324, Brown to Bush-Brown, 22 September 1900; 801/1.1/6/1A/373, Brown to Bush-Brown, 11 September 1900.

[33] AIA Archives 801/1.1/6/1A/389, Brown to Bush-Brown 18 October 1900; 801/1/17/1900B, Bush-Brown to Brown, 27 October 1900; 801/1/18/1900S, Seeler to Brown, 1 December 1900.

[34] AIA Archives 801/1/18/1900S, Seeler to Brown, 21 November 1900.

[35] AIA Archives 801/1/18/1900S, Brown to Seeler, 29 October 1900. Other speakers were also notified, as were Cass Gilbert, E. B. Green and Wm. A. Boring.

[36] AIA Archives 801/1/17/1900G, Gilbert to Brown, 31 October 1900; 801/1/17/1900B, Boring to Brown, 31 October 1900; 801/1/17/1900N–O, Olmsted to Brown 8 November 1900.

[37] AIA Archives 801/1/17/1900B, Col. Theodore Bingham to Brown, 13 November 1900; 801/1/17/1900B, Bingham to Brown 15 November 1900.

[38] Brown, *Memories*, 260.

[39] Bushong, *Centennial History*, 132.

[40] AIA Archives 801/1/18/1900P, Paul Pelz to Brown, 4 December 1900.

[41] Bushong, *Centennial History*, 168.

[42] AIA Archives, Glenn Brown Papers 804/5/5A. The invitation and other materials concerning Brown's relations with presidents William McKinley, Theodore Roosevelt, and William Howard Taft are in this collection in 804/5/4, 804/5/5A, 804/5/5B, and 804/5/5C.

[43] AIA Archives 801/1/18/1900P, Post to Brown, 11 December 1900. This clearly refers to the White House luncheon since Post noted, "I arrive in Washington tonight. Must return to New York tomorrow night."

[44] William V. Cox, comp., *1899–1900 Celebration of the One Hundredth Anniversary of the Establishment of the Seat of Government in the District of Columbia*, (Washington, D.C.: Government Printing Office, 1901), 59, 60–64.

[45] AIA Archives 509, "American Institute of Architects Proceedings, 34th Convention, Washington, D.C., 12–15 December 1900," 3, 112.

[46] National Archives and Record Administration (NARA) HR 56A–H23.1, "Letter with enclosed protests," Theodore F. Laist, Secretary of the Fine Arts Union of Washington, D.C., 11 December 1900. The President of the Union is listed on its letterhead as Glenn Brown, the organization address given as The Octagon.

[47] Brown, *Memories*, 109.

[48] Ibid. , 106.

[49] Washington Board of Trade Records, "Minutes," 14 December 1900, George Washington University, Gelman Library, Special Collections Division.

[50] NARA HR 56A–H23.1, "Resolution," T-Square Club of Philadelphia, 20 December 1900.

[51] Brown, *Memories*, 109.

[52] Glenn Brown, comp., *Papers Relating to the Improvement of the City of Washington*, (Washington, D.C.: Government Printing Office, 1901) 13–21.

[53] Brown, *Papers*, 33; for Olmsted's entire speech see 22–34.

[54] Ibid., 44; for Walker's entire speech see 35–47.

[55] Ibid., 49; for Seeler's entire speech see 48–58.

[56] Brown, *Memories*, 77; for Bush-Brown's entire speech see 70–77.

[57] AIA Archives 801/1/10/1901N–O, Olmsted to Brown, 13 December 1900.

[58] AIA Archives 505, "American Institute of Architects Proceedings, 34th Convention, Washington, D.C., 12–15 December 1900," 120.

[59] *The American Institute of Architects Quarterly Bulletin* 1 no. 4 (January 1901): 162.

[60] Brown, Papers, 7.

[61] Ibid., 62. For Brown's entire paper, reprinted from the August 1900 *Architectural Review*, see 59–69.

[62] Brown, Papers, Gilbert's plan appears between 80–81.

[63] Ibid., 86.

[64] Ibid., 87–91.

[65] Ibid., 9.

[66] AIA Archives 509, "American Institute of Architects Board of Directors, Minutes," 7 January 1901.

[67] AIA Archives 801/1/2B/2.1, papers concerning Resolution 139.

[68] Brown, *Papers*, 10.

[69] "Informal Hearing Before the Subcommittee of the Committee on the District of Columbia, United States Senate, Park Improvement Paper No. 5," in *Park Improvement Papers: A Series of Twenty Papers Relating to the Improvement of the Park System of the District of Columbia*, ed. Charles Moore (Washington, D.C.: Government Printing Office, 1903).

[70] *Park Improvement Papers*, ed. Charles Moore, 5, 69.

[71] Charles Moore, "Glenn Brown," *Journal of the Royal Institute of British Architects* 15 (October 1932): 39.

[72] Unsigned editorial, *Journal of the American Institute of Architects* 1 no. 2 (1913): 59.

The long walk at Windsor

The *tapis vert* at Versailles

In his paper read at the 1900 convention of the American Institute of Architects entitled "Landscape in Connection with Public Buildings in Washington", Frederick Law Olmsted, Jr. commented on "the importance of treating the Mall in such a way as to relate strongly and visibly to the Capitol." He showed two examples that merited further study: the long walk at Windsor Castle, "with its expanse of open turf instead of pavement", and the *tapis vert* at Versailles. During their European tour, the Senate Park Commission visited both places, drawing from aspects of each as they planned the final design for the Mall. *Papers Relating to the Improvement of the City of Washington*, Senate Document No. 94, 56th Congress, 2nd Session, 1901, figs. 15, 16.

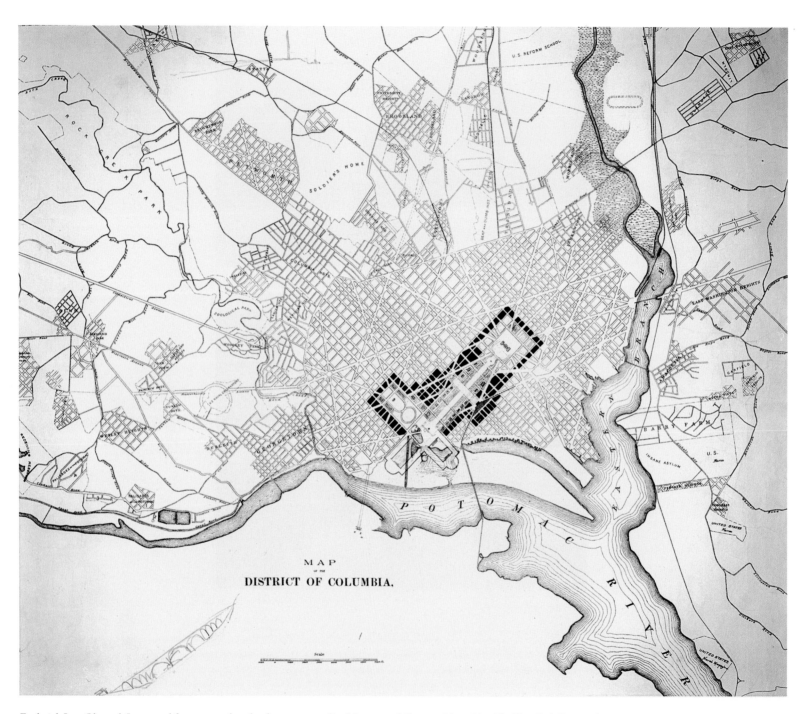

MAP

OF THE

DISTRICT OF COLUMBIA.

Scale

Frederick Law Olmsted, Jr., second figure-ground study of area surrounding Monumental Core, ca. May 1901. The New-York Historical Society, McKim, Mead & White Collection, Neg. #75564.

"A City Designed as a Work of Art":
THE EMERGENCE OF THE SENATE PARK COMMISSION'S MONUMENTAL CORE

By Pamela Scott

O N 6 January 1902, nine days before the Senate Park Commission exhibit opened at the Corcoran Gallery of Art, Glenn Brown and Charles Moore spoke at a meeting of the Columbia Historical Society. Their goal was to prepare Washington's historically minded community to accept imminent changes planned for the city. In his illustrated lecture, "The Making of a Plan for Washington City," Brown drew on his professional education as an architect and his avocation as a local historian to recount Peter Charles L'Enfant's sources for his plan of Washington. He enumerated the maps of the eleven European cities Thomas Jefferson sent L'Enfant on 10 April 1791, but singled out Paris and London as the "capital cities of the two most powerful countries of the world in L'Enfant's time." Paris was L'Enfant's native city and Sir Christopher Wren's 1666 plan for rebuilding London exhibited key elements of L'Enfant's Washington: long, broad boulevards and public squares or circles from which streets radiated.[1]

After Brown set the historic stage, Moore, Michigan Senator James McMillan's secretary, gave a lecture describing the Senate Park Commission's proposed improvements to all parts of the outlying areas of the District of Columbia. Moore, defender and apologist of Congress's administration of Washington's municipal affairs, toured his audience around the city's outskirts, interweaving recent public services (sewers, water supply, purchase of park lands) with the proposed parkways, driveways, parks, and land reclamation projects. Throughout his lecture Moore emphasized Congress's preservation of the area's natural beauty for future generations. He concluded by emphasizing the honesty, efficiency, and non-partisan "enlightened spirit" with which Congress dealt with District of Columbia affairs.[2]

Brown wanted L'Enfant's Paris and nearby royal gardens to be major influences on the original design for Washington because the Paris, Versailles, and Vaux-le-Vicomte of 1901 were major influences on the Senate Park Commission's "revival" of L'Enfant's plan to be made public in just a few days. He wanted Wren's London and near-by country estates to be prototypes because he wanted English (and hence Anglo-American) traditions to have also been part of the city's original design process. Moore wanted to reassure his local audience that city residents were to benefit materially from the Senate Park Commission's plan, their substitute "city council" in the form of the House and Senate Committees on the District of Columbia, responding to their needs and wishes. Moore, writing nearly three decades after the event, likened Paris—"a city designed as a work of art"—to the Senate Park Commission's vision for the Mall.[3]

Brown and Moore were an accomplished public relations team who had been at the epicenter of Washington's modernization for the past several years. As its secretary, Brown had galvanized the American Institute of Architects to take an active role in Washington's future development, beginning with its 1900 annual meeting. Moore, trained as a journalist, had come to Washington from Detroit in 1889 with the newly-elected McMillan and worked closely with him on improving fundamental city services after the senator was appointed to the Committee on the District of Columbia in 1891. Brown's and Moore's joint goal on 6 January 1902 was to convince Washingtonians that the Senate Park Commission's plan was the perfect solution to the capital's future growth because it revived the city's original design and conserved large parts of the surrounding countryside where subdivisions were rapidly being laid out on former farmland or country estates. Their strategy was imbedded in the history of Washington's founding and the acknowledged beauty of the federal city's original design.

L'Enfant's plan (pl. I) was well-known locally in the 1890s because it had been periodically discussed in Washington newspapers and even national journals. In 1887 Army engineer Colonel John Wilson, head of the Office of Public Buildings and Grounds which had legal possession of L'Enfant's fading manuscript, persuaded the Coast and Geodetic Survey to make a facsimile. This effort led to extensive research about the plan's origins, much of which was duly noted in the *Evening Star*. The *American Architect and Building News* considered Washington reporter Frank Sewell's articles on Washington's public buildings (which mentioned L'Enfant's plan) important enough to reprint in its 13 February and 7 May 1892 issues. At a time when both the city and federal governments were discussing new buildings to serve a variety of functions—a municipal building, a public library, a judiciary building (that included rooms for the Supreme Court), a government printing office, an auditor's office, a geological survey, and even a national university—Sewall was urging that they be grouped coherently on the south side of Pennsylvania Avenue between the White House and Capitol. In 1900, North Dakota Senator Henry Clay Hansborough, a member of the Committee on the District of Columbia, praised the idea of placing public buildings south of Pennsylvania Avenue, especially if they were surrounded by parks and brought the Mall up to the avenue. Moreover, "almost a unanimity of opinion prevails in the House for putting public buildings hereafter south of Pennsylvania Avenue." [4]

As part of his study of the U.S. Capitol during the early 1890s, Brown had carefully examined the characteristics of L'Enfant's plan, considering himself to be both its champion and resurrector. The opening chapter in the first volume of his *History of the United States Capitol* (1900) is a slightly shortened version of his "The Selection and Sites for Federal Buildings," published in the *Architectural Review* in 1894. Brown's thoughtful look at L'Enfant's plan and the many reports and correspondence relating to it led to him to conclude that the "the more the scheme laid out by Washington and L'Enfant is studied, the more forcibly it strikes one as the best." In both 1894 and 1900, Brown likened the Mall to the Champs Élysées, his only discussion of L'Enfant's sources prior to his championing of the Senate Park Commission plan before the Columbia Historical Society in January 1902. As early as 1894, Brown criticized the random placement of federal buildings in Washington during the nineteenth century, claiming they depended "on cost, influence, whim, or the advice of men in no way prepared to advise." L'Enfant's 1791 plan offered a model to counteract the continuing fragmentation that characterized post-Civil War placement of Washington's public buildings.[5]

On 13 December 1900 Frederick Law Olmsted, Jr., who was to be the landscape architect on the Senate Park Commission, concluded his paper delivered at the AIA meeting, "Landscape in Connection with Public Buildings in Washington," with the point of view that was to become a fundamental tenet of the commission and its adherents:

> Here is a plan not hastily sketched, nor by a man of narrow view and little foresight. It is a plan with the authority of a century behind it, to which we can all demand undeviating adherence in the future; a plan prepared by the hand of L'Enfant, but under the constant, direct, personal guidance of one whose technical knowledge of surveying placed the problem completely within his grasp, and who brought to its solution the same clear insight, deep wisdom, and forethought that gave pre-eminence in the broader fields of war and statesmanship to the name of George Washington.[6]

During the next few years, Washington as L'Enfant's active design partner grew from a conviction to a propaganda tool, a patriotic shield to fend off potential critics of the Senate Park Commission's radical redesign of Washington's Victorian monumental core. Thomas Jefferson's role in the federal city's design, (arguably more important than Washington's from an examination of extensive surviving documentation) was rarely mentioned although his role in the city's founding was acknowledged. The Federalist Washington was the political ancestor of early nineteenth-century Republicans then in power; the Democratic-Republican Jefferson's role was undoubtedly invoked to garner support among contemporary Democrats in addition to maintaining some historical credibility.

With the collaboration and advice of the Senate Park Commission, Moore wrote a two-part article for the February and March 1902 issues of *Century Magazine* entitled "The Improvement of Washington City" to coincide with publication of the commission's report entitled "The Improvement of the Park System of the District of Columbia." Moore began with the history of the founding of the federal city:

> Arriving in Georgetown in the March of 1791, L'Enfant was soon joined by Washington, and the two tramped over hills and through forests to discover the most advantageous sites for the Congress house and the President's palace. These two points having been located, L'Enfant began his congenial task of laying out a city, reporting by mail twice a week to Thomas Jefferson, then Secretary of State.

Moore concluded his overview by noting that "Washington and Jefferson not only adopted L'Enfant's plan, but so long as they were in power they protected it from perversions. . . and by the time these two worthies had passed from the scene the main features of the original scheme were fixed beyond possibility of loss, although not beyond neglect and temporary perversion." Yet when Moore spoke before Washington's historians in January 1902 he was unwilling to deviate from the evidence of government records. "Two plans were submitted by the young architect and rejected. The third was accepted, and although the original development and general scheme belong alone to L'Enfant, both Washington and Jefferson made known their views on the subject." [7]

Moore's articles and lectures delivered by Brown, Moore, and members of the commission were very effective, calculatingly so. On 28 August 1901, New Yorker Charles F. McKim reported to Chicagoan Daniel H. Burnham (the two architect members of the Senate Park Commission) the outcome of a meeting with Secretary of War Elihu Root:

> He suggested the propriety of an introductory chapter in the report, which should deal with the conditions as we found them, with the history of the inception of the plan and the laying out of the City of Washington, as proof that the scheme proposed by the Commission was in consequence of what had been already done, and a natural development of his (Washington's) aims and views. Mr. Root said he felt that if the Commission could prove their case in this regard, that it would go far towards winning it; that, in this way public acceptance would be assured, and opposition removed. He further suggested that the editors of selected newspapers…, should be interviewed, and furnished with copies of the report, before its publication, … These numerous editorials, appearing on the same date, in various parts of the country, would be far-reaching in their result—the smaller journals, in remoter communities, being guided by them. . . . Members of Congress would be largely

influenced by the editorials of the leading papers, and the approval of their constituents, in country districts, thus made easier, would prepare them to espouse a project, and vote for the very appropriations which they might, on account of the opposition of their constituents, otherwise oppose.[8]

Section four in the 13-page introduction to the commission's report presented the city's original design history in terms of what Burnham, Olmsted, and McKim wanted it to be in order to coincide with the major elements of their own plan:

When the city of Washington was planned under the direct and minute supervision of Washington and Jefferson, the relations that should subsist between the Capitol and the President's House were closely studied. Indeed the whole city was planned with a view to the reciprocal relations that should exist among public buildings. Vistas and axes; sites for monuments and museums; parks and pleasure gardens; fountains and canals; in a word, all that goes to make a city a magnificent and consistent work of art were regarded as essentials in the plans made by L'Enfant under the direction of the first President and his Secretary of State.[9]

McKim, very much an architect who championed the role of architects, may not have believed as fervently as the other commission members in Washington's prominent role in the actual design of the city. On 6 April 1901 Root had introduced the commission to President William McKinley, who "received us cordially and spoke, without hesitation, in favor of preserving the works of Washington's time," McKim wrote a few days later. "I trust you are not out of sympathy with your friends who are struggling in the cause of Peter Charles L'Enfant," he appended in a postscript to a letter sent to President Theodore Roosevelt on 20 March 1904.[10]

Burnham, however, was a true believer. After Roosevelt became embroiled in the debate about locating the Department of Agriculture Building, Burnham wrote Secretary of Treasury Leslie M. Shaw on 24 March 1903 that:

General Washington himself dictated the plan of the Mall in all its essential features.

1st. A grand avenue in the center of the Mall.

2nd. A line of white palaces, one on each side of the Avenue, extending along its entire length.

This arrangement cannot be surpassed and after advising with everyone whose judgment we found of value we incorporated Washington's arrangment into our plan, or rather, we considered his plan best and adopted it.[11]

On 9 August 1903 Burnham wrote Secretary of Agriculture James Wilson: "I have the honor to send you a copy of the general plan, made by the Senate Commission, on which I have marked the true axis referred to. This plan carries out General Washington's, which is L'Enfant's." Burnham continued to gather evidence to support his thesis. "By-the-by! I was told in Pennsylvania a few months ago," he wrote Olmsted the following November, "that there is a small town in the vicinity of Connellsville, which was laid out by General Washington when he was a young man, and that it has the same system of radiating streets as the City of Washington. This, if true, will prove that the plan of the Capital of the country is Washington's own and not Major L'Enfant's. I am going to investigate it more carefully." In testimony before Congress on 12 March 1904, Burnham declared: "We examined the documents, among others the well-known L'Enfant plan, which was prepared under the direction of and in participation with General Washington. Washington himself selected this location and then employed L'Enfant to carry out his ideas."[12]

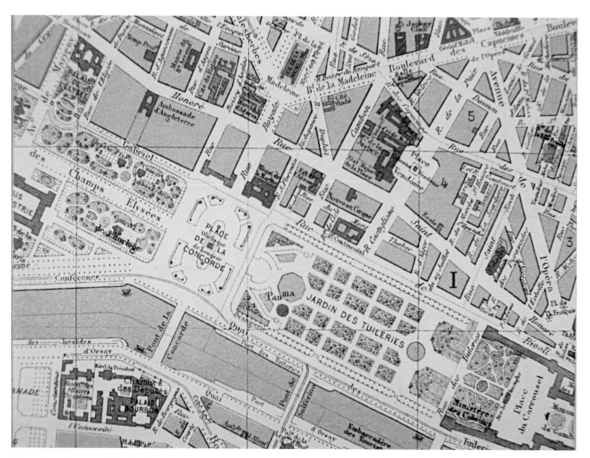

Fig. 1 Ange-Jacques Gabriel. Place Louis XV, 1783; renamed Place de la Concorde, 1793. Library of Congress, Geography and Map Division.

How did the commissioners' understanding of L'Enfant's plan, and the political era that produced it, influence their own designs for Washington's monumental core during 1901? When he spoke before the Columbia Historical Society in January 1902, Brown knew L'Enfant's Paris was not the same city Burnham, Olmsted, and McKim had visited with Moore during the summer of 1901.[13] Brown's lecture, therefore, abounds in contradictory statements as he tries to resolve the conundrum of L'Enfant's multiple sources of inspiration. Paris's "numerous small squares and the parked way of the Champs Élysées may have suggested and probably did suggest the many small parks as well as the treatment of the Mall, which he adopted in his plan" (fig. 1). Brown's brief account of Versailles focused on the landscape setting André Le Nôtre created for it from 1661-1668:

> In this garden we have a highly developed plan showing points of interest and beauty from which radiate avenues and walks. We can not question but that L'Enfant was familiar with this piece of landscape architecture, and it, together with the suggestion of Wren, we may reasonably assume, induced L'Enfant to try the same idea in the building of a city, instead of a garden, with radiating avenues; and also influenced him in the principal and most imposing feature of the Mall.

Yet, a few sentences earlier: "The Mall, as the grand garden approach to the Capitol, would naturally have suggested itself from a study of the Champs Élysées and of the more beautiful garden approach to Versailles."[14]

To appeal to those who opposed Beaux-Arts classicism and favored "American" sources for civic design, Brown emphasized that the *"most unique and distinctive feature of Washington, its numerous focal points of interest and beauty from which radiate the principal streets and avenues was not suggested by any city of Europe."* He sought and found two American antecedents—Annapolis and Williamsburg—that he stated "influenced [George Washington] in approving and modifying the scheme submitted by L'Enfant." Annapolis's "two focal points from which several streets radiate," Brown believed, had been taken from Wren's plan of London, and Williamsburg "had a mall, a dignified tract of green around which imposing buildings were grouped and toward which the principal streets converged." L'Enfant himself had almost surely been to Annapolis because it was a major Chesapeake Bay port near Washington. It is unknown if he ever saw Williamsburg; he was a prisoner of war on Haddrel's Island, South Carolina, when the French troops engaged in the battle of Yorktown, Virginia, in 1781. In April 1902, Buffalo architect George Cary chastised those who were "narrow-minded enough to criticize the [plan] and to say that it is Frenchy….should remember that in beautifying the city of Washington along the lines adopted by the special park commission, that body is simply carrying out the plans of Maj. L'Enfant."[15]

A month after the Senate Park Commission was formally created on 19 March 1901, and while they were in the midst of preparations for a summer trip to Europe, Chicago reporter William E. Curtis arranged for them to visit Chesapeake Bay towns and plantations. From 20-24 April, Burnham, Olmsted, McKim, Moore, and Curtis, accompanied by several government officials and prominent businessmen, visited seven Virginia sites. "Williamsburg had its lesson," Burnham wrote his wife on 24 April," for here in outline is the plan of the Mall in Washington with the Capitol at one end of the broad parkway; the College of William and Mary at the other end of the main axis, and the Governor's Palace at the head of the cross-axis, a location similar to that of the White House." Three weeks later the same party spent a day visiting Annapolis and two Maryland plantations. The immediate political purpose of these two trips was to reinforce the link between George Washington, Anglo-American planning traditions, L'Enfant's plan, and the Senate Park Commission's initiatives as well as to forestall criticism of a European bias in their thinking.[16]

The relative contributions of the European and American journeys made by the Senate Park Commission vary greatly: some specific experiences that impressed them all were recorded in correspondence and drawings, others can be inferred, and yet others were so synthesized into their general design tenets as to be totally absorbed. The following detailed examination of visual and textual documents produced during, or relating to, the ten months when the Senate Park Commission was actively designing, seeks to clarify these varied contributions.

Congressional committee report #1919, "Commission to Consider Certain Improvements in the District of Columbia," dated 18 January 1901, was the first formal step towards establishing the Senate Park Commission. It summarized Congress's accomplishments during the 1890s (which coincided with most of McMillan's tenure on the District committee), claiming they "provided the means for the artistic development of the District of Columbia in a manner befitting the capital city of the nation." From the purchase of Rock Creek Park (1890) to the adoption of a permanent system of highways for the entire District of Columbia (1898), these projects "betoken[ed] the desire and intention of Congress to carry out the original idea of making Washington a beautiful capital city."[17]

The purpose of the Senate's proposed commission was to "get up a comprehensive scheme 'a plan to work to,'" according to Olmsted's notes of the 19 March 1901 Senate subcommittee hearing attended by himself, Burnham, and an AIA committee. Olmsted noted that "Mr. McMillan made a brief, clear statement from which it appeared that the subject which most interested him was parks although placing of public buildings was part of the project." Olmsted (and other attendees) recognized that the chief difficulty was that the "diverse authorities over different parks and over public buildings, grounds and statuary" was not just confined to the jurisdictions of different executive departments, but extended to congressional committees as well. To get a consensus of what constituted an "artistic" plan for Washington's future development, a matter of taste and therefore peculiarly personal and strongly felt, would be very difficult. "The sub-committee [consisting of McMillan and New Hampshire Senator Joseph Gallinger]," Olmsted concluded, "does not know just what it wants to do nor how to do it."[18]

Olmsted succinctly expressed his point of view about the outcome of the 19 March hearing:

Any such committee or commission or board of experts should proceed first to an investigation leading to a preliminary report, with plans not very definite in character—necessarily not very definite in character, but embodying the results of a few months of investigation of the subject—and from those plans, after a conference with your committee and with other committees that are concerned with the whole problem, a basis might be laid for the detailed plans that would be necessary for the carrying out of any scheme.[19]

Burnham and Olmsted met with McMillan and Moore on 22 March and "agreed that report and plans must be as general in terms as possible so as not to tie things up too tight and so as not to offer many points for attack, but I thought that in dealing with Mall and public buildings we should be forced to be somewhat specific. Mr. B. did not see why we should." By 27 March when McKim had accepted Burnham's invitation to be the Park Commission's third member, Olmsted was already at work asking Moore two days earlier to obtain a set of ordinance survey maps of London and its suburbs "with the parks and other public spaces outlined and so marked as to indicate the authority in control of each." Olmsted had access in Boston to a map of the Paris parks.[20]

On 29 March Burnham wrote Olmsted that the first business of the commission's initial meeting scheduled to begin on 6 April would be to "organize" and "to comprehend the work, its scope and limitations." He stressed that the three members must "fix the rules governing our official actions" and that not even a draftsman should be hired until they had decided on the division of responsibilities. Although many contributions of individual members can be identified, much of their work was a team effort. Burnham wrote a second note to Olmsted the same day: "I am trying to arrange for a run across the water this summer. Will you go and will you be able to leave by the middle or end of June? I am writing to Mr. McKim by this post, asking the same questions. We can decide when we meet." Thus, almost immediately after the establishment of the commission, Burnham thought in terms of European inspiration.[21]

The commissioners met for three days beginning on 6 April when they visited Arlington National Cemetery and the following day spent the "morning on the Potomac," lunched at the Library of Congress, and in the afternoon and the following day advised the Grant Memorial Commission.

In 1904, in testimony before Congress on the work of the Senate Park Commission, Burnham recalled its initial "optical survey." "We encircled the city on the hills, spending a great deal of time, keeping our minds open as far as possible, without going to the documents or attempting to examine what had already been done. In this way we expected to become familiar without prejudice from anything that had already been done with the situation." McKim, immediately after his return to New York, wrote: "If half of what is talked of can be carried through it will make the Capital City one of the most beautiful centers in the world. The work of education still requires many years, but the essential thing…is to bring about a general plan." On 10 April Olmsted hired James G. Langdon, a landscape architect in his office, as the commission's first draftsman and three days later dispatched him to Washington. Langdon's drawings produced during the next two months are the best record of what the Senate Park Commission accomplished during its initial meetings.[22]

Langdon's first map for the use of the commission members was of the entire District of Columbia, compiled from ones obtained from the Corps of Engineers, Coast and Geodetic Survey, and District Commissioners (pl. III). This lithograph showed graphically the results of all current legislation concerning the city, with color coding indicating the extent and jurisdiction of all large plots of land in public and quasi-public hands. The War Department controlled the Mall and East and West Potomac Parks and all the public reservations—the squares, circles, and parklets—within L'Enfant's original city boundaries. It was also responsible for the Soldiers Home, Washington Barracks (formerly the Arsenal), Reservoir, and Arlington National Cemetery. The District Commissioners, the Interior Department, the Navy Department, the Smithsonian Institution, Gallaudet College and others controlled scattered tracts throughout the city. Langdon overlaid on this map the 1898 version of the "permanent system of highways," developed over the previous decade to extend L'Enfant's grid streets, diagonal avenues, and public circles into all areas between Florida Avenue (Boundary Avenue before 1890) and the District of Columbia-Maryland line. The third important documentation that Langdon included on his map were the streets and city squares that Congress had determined during the 1890s might be used for railroads. Public schools were indicated by circles because recreational facilities for schools were one of the many local issues the Senate Park Commission was to address. The boundaries and street patterns of Washington's 101 subdivisions that had been laid out during the previous half century were also indicated on Langdon's map.

Thus, the Senate Park Commission designers had in one place valuable information about what public lands were available for outlying parks (and which federal agency was responsible for them) and where future circles, squares, and avenues would be. Moreover, they knew where Burnham's recently commissioned Baltimore & Potomac (hereafter B&P) Railroad station could legally be located. Langdon identified the possible railroad corridors along existing tracks in the city's southwest, southeast, and northeast quadrants and the entire width of the Mall between 6th and 7th streets. A railroad bridge parallel to Long Bridge carried existing tracks across the Potomac River that originated southeast of the city (crossing the Anacostia River at M Street SE) and ran along Virginia Avenue SE and Virginia Avenue SW until they made a 130 degree turn at the intersection of Maryland Avenue SW, a block south of the Mall. Tracts of land comprising several city squares were proposed at three points along this route for railroad expansion: at the landfall of Long Bridge at 14th Street SW; south of the intersection of Maryland and Virginia avenues between 6th and 10th streets SW (the Senate Park Commission initially located the B&P station partially within these boundaries); and between Virginia Avenue, South Capitol, M, and 2nd streets SE.

The land for possible railroad expansion in the relatively undeveloped northeast sector was concentrated along the corridor of tracks that served the Baltimore & Ohio (hereafter B&O) station at New Jersey Avenue and C Street NW and its freight depot in Eckington, a northeast subdivision just beyond Florida Avenue. A wide swath from North Capitol to 2nd Street NE gradually narrowed above Massachusetts Avenue diminishing to just a corridor above R Street. In June and July 1901, B&P railroad president Alexander Cassatt (who had just acquired control of the B&O railroad) chose to place his new Union Station within this precinct. Legally he could have built a new station on the Mall; the Park Commission wanted the station south of the Mall but was delighted that Cassatt found it advantageous to locate it on Massachusetts Avenue NE. For a brief time in October 1902, when Congress could not agree on a site, Cassett was willing to have the station south of the Mall: "he says he wants this thing settled now without any further delay," Burnham reported to Curtis.[23]

Several preparatory drawings for the Senate Park Commission plan have survived among McKim's papers in the New-York Historical Society. On 10 April 1901 Burnham wrote Olmsted suggesting that they "begin to lay out the work between the capital Obelisk and the dome of the Capitol on a large scale," that is, that they make drawings of a large size. Among McKim's papers are two Mall plans dated 27 April 1901 which he acknowledged receiving (along with photographs of the Mall) from Langdon on 2 May. The base plan isolated the Capitol grounds and the two blocks directly east of it; the Mall and the pertinent areas north and south of it roughly between Pennsylvania and Maryland avenues; the White House complex including greater Lafayette Park; and, several blocks between the White Lot (now called the Ellipse) and the Potomac River. In these areas, streets and buildings were shown in detail but East and West Potomac Parks, the Tidal Basin, and Hain's Point were shown in outline only, probably because the commission was not yet ready to concentrate on these areas.[24]

On the first 27 April plan (fig. 2) Langdon inserted the elevations of the Mall along nine north-south lines and at several other points including within the Mall-Pennsylvania Avenue triangle (later called the Mall Triangle by the Park Commission), east of the Capitol, and at the foots of 17th through 23rd streets, NW. The disparity in height between the north and south sides of the Mall was considerable, the south side varying from 22.8 feet at 7th and B streets, SW, to 37.3 feet at 14th and B streets, SW, while the corresponding intersections on the Mall's north side ranged from about 6.5 to 7 feet above sea level. The elevation along the Mall's center line gradually rose from about 20 feet at 7th Street to 24.5 feet at 14th Street; the Washington Monument sat exactly 40 feet above sea level on the summit of a conical mound, its grounds to the west falling rapidly to 8.5 feet.

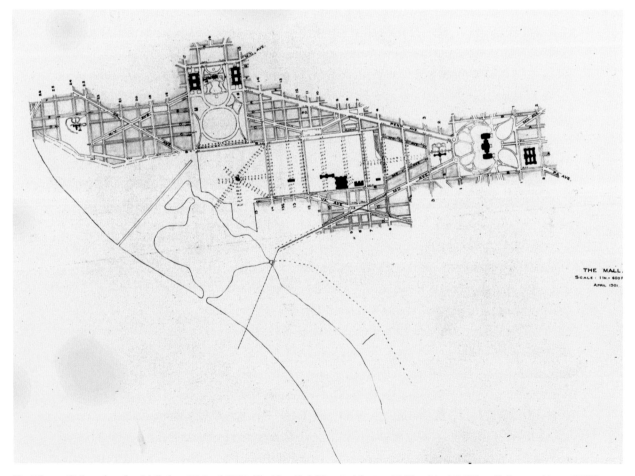

Fig. 2 James G. Langdon, first Mall plan, 27 April 1901. The New-York Historical Society, McKim, Mead & White Collection, Neg. # 75565.

On April 30, apparently in response to receiving his copy of this 27 April 1901 plan, Olmsted wrote Glenn Brown asking him to send Langdon a Coast and Geodetic Survey facsimile of a map that dated from about 1798 and showed buildings only on the Mall's south side. Writing to Langdon on 4 May about this map, Olmsted noted that it was "not the L'Enfant Plan of 1791 and is one which Mr. Brown had not discovered in his researches," but was one Olmsted had lent Brown. Soon after 16 May Olmsted investigated this map further and concluded that the "differences may be the fancies of the engraver," but the episode shows how carefully the team investigated L'Enfant's (and his contemporaries') intentions as they conceptualized the new plan. With the exception of the B&P station built at 6th Street, NW, in 1872, all of the Mall's nineteenth-century buildings were scattered irregularly along the high ridge on its south side. The earth works necessary to level the Mall would be a considerable undertaking, an issue that the Senate Park Commission seems to have addressed immediately.[25]

Langdon's second Mall plan (pl. V) dated 27 April 1901 depicts the effects of reinstituting L'Enfant's Mall and accommodating some proposed new buildings. The Park Commission maintained the existing cross streets but divided the Mall into seven east-west zones, the outer one colored green but presumably planned for buildings in landscaped settings. This building zone fronted walkways backed by a grove of five rows of trees planted in a formal quincunx pattern in a 225-foot-wide swath. These three zones framed an open, central space 350 feet in width colored yellow rather than green to indicate that a boulevard or carriageway was initially considered rather than a greensward or parkway. (In 1900, both Colonel Theodore Bingham of the Corps of Engineers and Olmsted had suggested running a broad carriageway down the Mall's center.) A major purpose of Langdon's drawing was to determine the effect on existing buildings and adjoining private property if the Mall were to be realigned on the Washington Monument with each of its sides equidistant from a central axis. It demonstrated that the government would have to purchase all the squares facing B Street South between 6th and 15th streets, if both sides of the realigned Mall were to be equal in width.[26]

Langdon's second 27 April plan also showed a proposed major cross axis, a graveled boulevard, between 7th and 9th streets in the same location where L'Enfant had proposed breaking up the Mall's great length by placing a water element on its north side. This blueline also placed Burnham's new B&P railroad station south of the intersection of Maryland and Virginia avenues, SW, a logical early decision because the tracks already were laid through the intersection and it could be legally located on part of it. Another result of the Senate Park Commission's April meeting recorded on the 27 April blueline was the proposal to incorporate the land within the wide triangle facing the Mall formed by Virginia and Maryland avenues (about half the Mall's length) to function as a plaza vestibule for the station. Three new buildings for the Department of Agriculture were penciled in on the Mall's north side between 12th and 14th streets, NW; the 2 March 1901 congressional appropriation stipulated that they be "erected on the grounds of the Department of Agriculture" which spanned the Mall's width between these two blocks. Dark pencil hatching of several blocks north and south of the Mall and east of the Capitol may mean that these areas were already being considered for an expanded public precinct.

McKim wrote Moore on 10 May noting that Langdon's "plans…have been most useful" and that when the commissioners next met they would be "in a better position to discuss [the treatment of the Mall more] intelligently than was the case on our last visit." Their next meeting began on 15 May with their second Chesapeake Bay trip to Maryland sites followed by four days of intense work on the Mall's redesign. The results of that charrette are recorded on a plan dated 3 June 1901 but seem to have been preceded by a set of unsigned and undated figure-ground (high contrast black areas placed on a light background) studies of Washington's monumental core made on small printed maps of the District of Columbia. These two altered maps were probably made by Olmsted in response to Langdon's 27 April Mall plans that recorded the commission's "what if's". When the tin case of plans that Olmsted planned to take to Europe did not arrive in time, he sent for several printed maps of Washington, apparently his favored method of quickly recording his thoughts vis-à-vis actual conditions. Moreover, Olmsted used the same graphic figure-ground convention for the plans of parks in urban settings that his firm contributed to in the Senate Park Commission's report published in January, 1902. Olmsted may have brought the two surviving figure-ground studies to the commission's May meeting; they are preserved among McKim's papers.

The first of Olmsted's figure-ground drawings (fig. 3) has inked in black the Mall and President's grounds, in grey the larger public reservations, in red the smaller ones, and outlined in green Rock Creek Park, the Soldier's Home, the Reform School and other outlying government properties that encompassed large land areas. This study graphically illustrated the concentrated mass, but irregular configuration, of Washington's L-shaped monumental core in 1901. The spatial homogeneity of the Mall's east end had first been compromised in 1808 when the canal was cut across it at 4 ½ Street and again when the Botanic Garden was laid out at the foot of Capitol Hill in 1823, three years after Congress granted the site. The canal was slowly filled in during the 1870s and in 1872 the B&P railroad tracks were laid along Sixth Street. The east end of the Mall was further interrupted when Missouri and Maine avenues were inserted parallel to Pennsylvania and Maryland avenues for the two blocks between 4th and 6th streets.

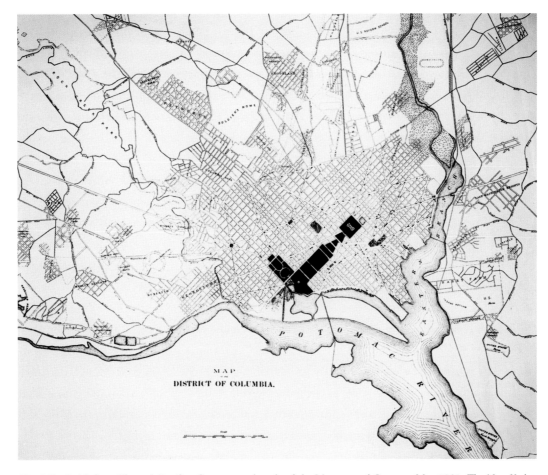

Fig. 3 Frederick Law Olmsted, Jr., first figure-ground study of the Monumental Core, ca. May 1901. The New-York Historical Society, McKim, Mead & White Collection, Neg. # 75563

The black inked areas on Olmsted's second undated figure-ground study (frontispiece) outlined not just the accepted monumental core but expanded its boundaries to include the squares framing the Capitol grounds; the triangle between the Mall and Pennsylvania Avenue; the entire X-shaped crossing of Virginia and Maryland avenues south of the Mall; the residential blocks facing the east and west sides of Lafayette Square; and, several privately held blocks on both sides of the Mall's east end where it joined the Capitol grounds. If the blacked-out blocks do indeed represent proposed expropriation of private land for public use (as they seem to), the Senate Park Commission considered early on nearly doubling the monumental core not counting East and West Potomac Parks created when the Potomac River was dredged during the 1880s.

On 15 April Burnham wrote Olmsted: "my own belief is that instead of arranging for less, we should plan for rather more extensive treatment than we are likely to find in any other way. Washington is likely to grow very rapidly from this time on, and be the home of all the wealthy people of the United States."[27] At the 19 March 1901 Senate subcommittee hearing, New York architect George B. Post, who had just secured the commission to design the new Department of Justice building (which was to contain the Supreme Court) on Lafayette Square spoke about the rapidly increasing number of proposed government buildings:

> [I]t seems to me that the buildings for the departments that have direct and daily and hourly business with each other and with the President must be concentrated around the White House, and the buildings where the offices and functions are necessarily connected with the general legislative branch of the Government must be concentrated more or less about, or be in direct connection with, Capitol Hill.[28]

In the final report, the Park Commission decided to place the Supreme Court on square 728 on the corner of First and East Capitol streets, NE which had been suggested by Senate bill 697 in 1889.[29]

Other prescient aspects of Olmsted's second figure-ground drawing include realigning the Mall to place the Washington Monument in its visual center but retaining it within its original boundaries formed by B streets North and South. Thus the south building zone became increasingly narrower and the north one increasingly wider as one moved west from the Capitol, a factor in locating large buildings such as the Agriculture Department which was considered for both sides of the Mall. The Mall's central and cross vistas were still colored tan or yellow to indicate graveled boulevards. Buildings located in park-like settings were shown lining the Mall's edges and were separated from the central vista by groves of trees. The location of the B&P railroad station south of the Mall at the convergence of Virginia and Maryland avenues remained as shown on the 27 April plan. The major change on Olmsted's second figure-ground drawing was the introduction of important water features south and west of the Washington Monument. Two proposed large rectangular pools terminating in semicircular ends were each one-third the length of the public grounds on its respective eastern or northern sides of the Washington Monument. They would have replaced the Fisheries Commission's spawning ponds located between the White Lot and the Washington Monument as well as the irregularly shaped Tidal Basin, designed by Army engineers to flush out the Washington Channel, its inlet on the Potomac River and its outlet at the head of the new channel.

The Senate Park Commission's productive May meeting is recorded in the third preliminary drawing dated 3 June 1901 (pl. VI). Having earlier focused on the Mall, they turned their attention to central Washington's greater landscape, not only the new parkland resulting from the Potomac's dredging during the 1880s, but to a vast kite-shaped polygon encompassing triangles of land south of Pennsylvania and New York avenues, NW, and north of Maryland Avenue, SW. Thus, within two months of their formation, the Senate Park Commission had conceptualized the visionary extent of their project and all of its salient features. In 1929, Moore noted in his *Washington Past and Present* that "by June a tentative plan had been sketched. As a magnet placed under a sheet of paper covered with a mass of unrelated iron filings brings the particles into symmetry and beauty, so under these organizing minds in close consultation the disordered elements in the District of Columbia fell into their proper relations one with another."[30]

Because the final report discussed each section within this kite as a "division," it is convenient to trace the plan's evolution from June 1901 through January 1902 section by section. Treatment of the Capitol and White House divisions, each framed by appropriate legislative and executive department buildings, was not settled until very late in the commissioners' design process. Therefore, base brownline drawings used beginning in June include only the Capitol and White House grounds and not the squares that surround them. The Park Commission's report divided the east-west Capitol axis into three divisions, the "Mall," "Monument Section," and "Lincoln Division" crossed on the north-south axis by the "White House Division," "Monument Section," and "Washington Common." The Mall Triangle was the only one of the four triangles that abutted this central Latin cross to be dedicated to buildings, the other areas being laid out as parks.[31]

THE WHITE HOUSE

Post's March 1901 suggestion to group future executive buildings near the White House responded to Supervising Architect James Knox Taylor's January 1900 scheme to locate them on the residential blocks that flanked Lafayette Square. In 1901, the future of James Hoban's President's House, whether it would remain as the President's home, official residence, and office, or be enlarged, or become solely the President's office, had been debated for the previous decade. Large public events and general public access to the White House had subjected the building's structure to strains that were not foreseen when it was erected in the 1790s. In 1902, McKim's firm was hired to restore the White House (its interiors dating from several Victorian redecorations) to its original appearance and to design a temporary office building on its west side. On Monday, 27 January 1902 Burnham met with Roosevelt about the new executive offices and Moore recorded in his diary that "he [Burnham or Roosevelt, it is not clear who] favored [the] site of St. Johns Church and John Hay's house," thus conforming to the commission's just completed plan. By 14 April Burnham was advocating locating the "permanent quarters for the President" in the center of Lafayette Park. The second edition of the Senate Park Commission plan did place a building in the square's center.[32]

The legislative and executive groups were not added to the Senate Park Commission's drawings until mid-December 1901. In the interim, the commissioners considered many alternate solutions. On 30 July 1901 soon after returning from Europe, Burnham suggested "that we place the President's House on the site of the old (Naval) Observatory" on a high bluff overlooking the Potomac River between 23rd and 25th streets, NW. After a day at Oxford, Burnham recorded in his diary that the travelers "reached hotel at 11:30 and talked an hour or more about the President's House and grounds;" erecting a new building at 23rd Street was still under consideration at the end of October when Olmsted noted that if it were to happen, the Heurich brewery would have to be removed. This is the third instance where the commission took advantage of elevated positions within the city to create terraced overlooks, apparently an effect that deeply impressed them all during their European trip. The Washington Monument terrace was their most developed and imposing design, but in December 1901, the commission began planning more prominent terraces for the Capitol's west front to extend those erected in the 1880s, designed by Frederick Law Olmsted, Sr., adding a lower terrace enclosing a pool connected to Olmsted's terrace by a second pool (fig. 4).[33]

Fig. 4 Proposed treatment of basin, terraces, and Capitol approaches. *Senate Park Commission Report*, No. 39.

MALL TRIANGLE

In the late nineteenth century the area between the Mall and Pennsylvania Avenue was partly industrial, partly commercial, and partly working-class residential. Its character was a serious impediment to both the development of the Mall as a gracious public space and Pennsylvania Avenue as a world-class boulevard. "A well-known architect of the city," possibly Paul Pelz (architect of the Library of Congress), noted in the 17 April 1886 *Washington Evening Star* that Pennsylvania "avenue should be made a grand driveway, and the government ought to buy the squares at the south of the avenue, and bring the reservation, or park, up to the south side. Then that would allow plenty of space for the public buildings, which will be erected, and, at the same time, beautify one of the grandest driveways in the world."[34]

The sad state of America's main street—and its possible greatness—was Frank Sewell's recurrent theme in 1892 *Evening Star* articles. "Undoubtedly Pennsylvania Avenue, of which the American loves to boast, is, as a roadway, one of the finest in the world, while, as the great central promenade and public thoroughfare of a capital city, it is probably, in its architectural display, the meanest and most insignificant." Sewell advocated the "proper utilization of the avenue for the government and district buildings under a consistent and imposing architectural plan." He noted further that "it is probably not far from the truth to say that had the War, State and Navy, the Interior, the Pension office and Post office and Treasury been built with a single front, instead of in quadrangles, and located on the south side of the avenue, they would have formed a continuous line of palaces extending from the White House to the Capitol." If a national art commission were formed to regulate a coherent and unified design for buildings recently proposed by federal agencies or private groups, Sewell contended, "we might look hopefully forward to seeing not many years hence the avenue graced on either side with beautiful colonnades and arcades lining the front of our new District buildings—public library, museums, auditor's offices, Indian Department, geological survey and musical and art conservatories, and possibly the government's own national university."[35]

An undated article from the *New York Evening Post*, filed with papers dating from March 1901, noted:

> The Press has had occasion heretofore to comment favorably on the project for the purchase by the Government of all the remaining private property lying between Pennsylvania and Maryland avenues, from the Capitol to the White House, and the transformation of this entire tract into a magnificent national park, in which should be located the departmental buildings. This project is now presented for consideration in the form of a joint resolution of the House and Senate, authorizing the President to appoint a commission, consisting "of

two architects and one landscape architect eminent in their professions," and appropriating $10,000 for the use of this commission in the task of devising plans for the improvement of the park system of the District of Columbia.[36]

Thus the Park Commission did not originate the idea of developing the Mall-Pennsylvania Avenue triangle as a campus of public buildings, but it did determine where each individual building should be located within the triangle and their spatial and formal interrelationships. On 21 December 1901 when they were putting the finishing touches on the drawings, McKim wrote that an unspecified building facing Pennsylvania Avenue "adjoining the proposed Armory, was not made parallel to Pennsylvania Avenue, because it faces a Public Square. But for the invasion of the Square, it would have been made parallel with Pennsylvania Avenue. The site of the proposed new Municipal Building is a similar one. There is no doubt that the architecture of the South side of Pennsylvania Avenue should, as far as practicable, be made parallel with the Avenue."[37]

By the spring of 1904, in preparation for legislative action to acquire the land in the Mall triangle, Nevada Senator Francis Newlands (one of the Park Commission's staunchest supporters), proposed changes. "His idea," Washington architect J.R. Marshall reported to McKim, "is to obliterate all minor streets in it, and keep only the necessary thoroughfares. He proposes, for instance, to reserve the section north of the New Museum [Hornblower and Marshall's design] from B street to Pennsylvania Avenue for the growth of the Museum." Newlands advocated similar room for expansion of the Agriculture Department (should it be located on the Mall's north side) and other changes to the Senate Park Commission's plan, including "moving back the building line on the south side of [Pennsylvania] Avenue and planting trees, and making a bridle path under them."[38]

McKim was particularly cognizant that the proposed new buildings in the triangle and on the Mall must have the same kind of definition on the model of the Senate Park Commission's plan as was shown on its drawings prepared for exhibition in order to be convincing. On 15 January 1902 this model went on display at the Corcoran Gallery in an unfinished state; McKim wrote Moore that day:

> Especially the public buildings (for which designs were many weeks ago placed in [model maker George Curtis's] hands) need the detail and color which are required to make them count measurably in finish and effect with the Capitol, Treasury, White House & other existing buildings carefully modelled by him. At present they look like huge unbaked blocks—wholly out of scale & character with their environment. Unless these bldgs are immediately finished Congress will form at the start an erroneous & adverse opinion, which once established will be impossible to overcome.[39]

THE MALL

Once the commission had organized the Mall's length into nine east-west zones (two walkways framing the central space were added to the former seven zones) and determined its axial orientation, the basic issues they addressed were the width of each zone, the relationship of the buildings in the outer zone to their sites, the length of each segment as defined by cross streets, the Mall's grade, and its special features. The 1792 engraved plans of Washington described the Mall's center open space as being 400 feet wide out of a total width of 1,600 feet, with 1,000 feet between façade lines. In March 1904, when building lines for the Department of Agriculture and the National Museum were being debated in the Mall Parkway hearings, Olmsted recalled the problems the commission faced in determining the widths of the Mall's various zones:

> The Commission in its effort to bring the original plan to a more definite and detailed project spent more time and attention on this question of interpreting the meaning of "an avenue 400 feet wide," and of determining the best width for the several parts of the Mall than upon any other item of the whole problem. The plan finally recommended is indicated diagrammatically on the enclosed cross section [not identified]. The central space between the trees was established at 300 feet, which the Commission unanimously regarded as the least which would carry out in a dignified way the original conception. This central open space it was proposed to flank by four rows of trees on either side, the rows being 59 feet apart. The distance of "400 feet" includes the central greensward and the two rows of trees immediately flanking it. On so great a length as the Mall a vista flanked by only two rows of trees on either side would be meagrely furnished, and the Commission felt that the additional rows of trees on either side would be quite essential. Outside of these four rows of trees, after allowing ten feet for a margin of planting space, it was proposed to space the road for access to the buildings and the sidewalk adjacent to this road, and in order to give the buildings a setting commensurate with their monumental character and the scale of the whole project, and in order to provide for adequate porticos, steps and other means of approach, a considerable distance is requisite between this sidewalk and the main walls of the buildings. The Commission therefore recommend a space of 145 between the trunks of the outermost row of trees and the buildings, leaving a total distance between building lines of 890 feet.[40]

Burnham testified during the Mall Parkway Hearing that having designed the central parkway, its width became the burning question:

> What width should a parkway be which was a mile and a half long in the midst of one the great capitals of the world? We made a very thorough examination of every notable plantation where trees were used and an open space left between them, and we found that the nearest approach to the one in the Mall in its dimensions was Bushy Park, near London, and the parkway in front of the residence of the Marquis of Salisbury.[41]

In his 1929 biography of McKim, Moore related that "McKim determined that the width of the grass carpet between the trees at Hatfield House should serve for the space at the Mall. The grouping of four trees on the Mall was suggested by the six rows on either side of a central grass plot at Bushy Park." The experience of visiting English parks in July 1901, may well have confirmed visually the monumental spatial effects created by long plantations of trees, but the commissioners had depended on their visits to American colonial sites, maps of European parks, and their careful study of L'Enfant's plan to determine this aspect of the Mall's character before they embarked for Europe. In his 1904 congressional testimony, Burnham related the Senate Park Commission's experiment of erecting flag poles on the Mall 250 feet, 300 feet, and 400 feet from its center line to determine proportionally the best width; in late May Langdon and Moore worked through the Supervising Architect's office to arrange this demonstration to coincide with the commissioners' next meeting in mid-June. Two dated preliminary plans made by the Senate Park Commission in late April and early June help clarify the sequence of influences.[42]

Langdon's second 27 April 1901 drawing, made subsequent to the Senate Park Commission's first formal meeting, showed the Mall's central space lined with five rows of trees with an inscription in the margin indicating that the groves were 225 feet wide, the rows 45 feet apart (see pl. V). The Senate Park Commission's report noted that plantations of rows of elms were common in many European gardens, "in those towns, North and South, which were laid out during the colonial era," and even the Mall in Central Park.[43] Burnham's 1904 congressional testimony gives both valuable insights about the Park Commission's aesthetic intentions and clarifies the historical record:

> Having determined that a 300-foot opening is necessary between the greatest monument in the world and one of the greatest domes in the world, the discussion went to the supporting of it by trees on each side. There again we examined every notable avenue in Europe. We found that not less than four trees constituted an avenue; three trees produce a bad effect, because no space is left in the center and it becomes lopsided—people walk either on one side or the other—whereas with four trees there is a valley under the trees, with a great

promenade on either side. Then the distance apart for planting elms was considered, and many hundreds of elm trees were measured in order that we might not make a mistake in the distance which the trees should be placed apart, lengthwise or crosswise, and this result represents our conclusion after a careful study. The effect of four trees is rich. There are some notable avenues in England which have six, and even more, and there is a certain richness and beauty that convinced us of the propriety of recommending not less than four trees on either side of the central parkway vista.[44]

The Senate Park Commission's preliminary plan dated 3 June (drawn on the same base map as their 27 April design) had wider plantations of trees than the 27 April design, but the number of rows and their planting widths were not specified. Narrow promenades, however, ran down the centers of these groves as described by Burnham in 1904. Although Burnham's 1904 testimony subtly suggests that this lesson was learned while the designers were in Europe, the decision about the general width of the Mall's zones was made before the event. Certainly avenues of trees are fundamental to European landscape architecture and were the source of the commission's thinking, but the trip to Europe only verified this aspect of their design, apparently determined during their second meeting in mid-May 1901. The issue was so important that it was an ongoing discussion; McKim noted at the Mall Parkway Hearing that the distance between building facades on L'Enfant's Mall had been 1,000 feet:

> We need width more than length. In the language of Lord Elverson—I am quoting Mr. Root—'rather,' he said, in the Canadian controversy, 'rather would I lie down on the floor of this court and die first.' That was not in passion, but in conviction. We have studied this enterprise very carefully, and have give our time and thought to it, and we are firmly of the opinion that a greater rather than a less width is absolutely essential, and that not by a single inch should it be narrowed.[45]

Moore later quoted Burnham speaking on 6 June: "I have talked the matter over with Senator McMillan. The four of us are going to Europe in June to see and to discuss *together* parks in their relations to public buildings—that is our problem in Washington and we must have weeks when we are thinking of nothing else." Plans of square, rectangular, and quadrangular buildings sketched in the outer zones on the 3 June plan nearly filled each block. Footprints of buildings on plans among McKim's papers made after the European trip—unfortunately too light to reproduce—modified the size, shape, and number of the Mall's projected buildings. Their number gradually increased as they were reconfigured in response to projections about the country's growth and the government's future space needs. These numbers took into account the future executive buildings planned to encircle Lafayette Square, legislative ones framing the Capitol Grounds, and a miscellany of buildings projected for the Mall Triangle. Although the sum total of the Senate Park Commission plan was visionary, each of its parts responded to specific mandates rooted in actual needs.[46]

On 23 August 1901 McKim sent Supervising Architect of the Treasury James Knox Taylor, the government's advisor on the Department of Agriculture building, specific widths of streets, curbs, sidewalks, and setbacks:

> The space to the South of the Northerly line of the proposed building, at the centre, is, approximately, 230 feet to the curb. Deducting say 15 feet, for sidewalk on S[outh]. B. Street, would leave (approx.) 215 feet, ample space for the building, and approaches for the B. Street side. As the future buildings of the government, to be placed upon the Mall, will, however, vary from each other, in purpose as well as dimensions, we have thought it wise to confine ourselves to determining the building line on the Mall side only. In the case of the Agriculture Building, we would suggest that 20 to 25 feet, between the lot line and the building, be set aside for approaches on the South.[47]

Olmsted probably solved the problem of realigning the Mall without having the building zones become progressively narrower or wider. He off-set B Street South in the 500 block where it converged with Maryland Avenue and B Street North at 7th Street on the edge of the market-station cross axis, effectively masking the shift from the Mall's east and west ends (see pl. V). On both the 3 June and 30 August drawings the building zone blocks are the same width their entire lengths; the disparity between their respective widths would hardly be noticeable because they were separated by the two groves of trees and the central space, a total of 890 feet. By 3 June the central boulevard had been changed to a parkway flanked by graveled avenues; the 30 August drawing (fig. 5) is not color coded but we know that the central lawn treatment was retained in the final design. In his biography of McKim, Moore suggested that the greensward was a result of the European trip: "Windsor Great Park, with its central driveway, emphasized Olmsted's objection to running a road through the center of the Mall," but the decision had been recorded on a drawing dated two weeks before they embarked.[48]

In proposing its visionary plan, the Senate Park Commission supposed that the historical jurisdictions over the Mall's reservations would to be negated by some future law. In 1901 the Smithsonian Grounds ran from 7th to 12th streets and the Department of Agriculture had jurisdiction between 12th and 14th streets with the 1400 block considered part of the Washington Monument grounds. By 3 June the commission had regularized the Mall's blocks in relation to the city's cross streets, with three blocks east of the market-station cross axis and three blocks west of it. The

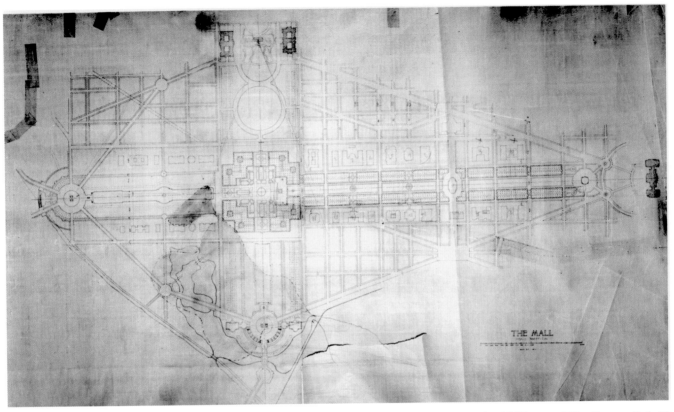

Fig 5. Charles Follen McKim and Frederick Law Olmsted, Jr., design for Mall, Washington Monument Grounds, Tidal Basin, and West Potomac Park, 30 August 1901. The New-York Historical Society, McKim, Mead & White Collection, Neg. # 75562

two easternmost blocks were to be the same length, while the one between 6th and 7th streets was slightly shorter; the circular pool at the head of the mall was surrounded by a circular plaza, the whole enclosed by trees.

West of the market-station cross axis, the Park Commission initially created two long blocks of equal length followed by a short one by running streets across the Mall at 9th, 11th, 14th and 15th streets. By 30 August, however, the designers had divided the two long blocks by inserting three circular elements, possibly fountains or possibly sculpture, in the center of the parkway and amidst the trees. The plan of the Mall included in the Senate Park Commission report (pl. VII) published in the spring of 1902, divides the area west of the cross axis as in late August. The accent elements within the tree line have been deleted but those on the Mall's center line were retained. Both cross streets or vistas between buildings caused breaks in the groves of trees; Park Commission members repeatedly invoked L'Enfant's plan as their source for complementary vistas between buildings. In the end the Park Commission determined that "museums and other buildings containing collections in which the public generally is interested" should be located on the Mall's north side, while those on the south should be dedicated to "buildings in which the scientific and technical work of the Government is done."[49]

The question of how to orient the new Mall buildings in relation to the existing streets was posed by Washington architects Hornblower and Marshall in April and May 1904. Initially the commission suggested that buildings be erected out of square so that their north and south facades would be parallel to either B Street North or South as well as to the Mall's adjusted axis. Hornblower and Marshall argued that the square figure 8 configuration of their National Museum—519 feet long and 375 feet deep—could not be skewed so the decision was made to conform to the Mall's axis and place the museum at an angle within its square.[50]

Regularizing the Mall's grades was one of the commission's earliest concerns but the first textual evidence of the "continuous platform," or terrace, along the Mall's north side is in a letter Olmsted sent McKim on 31 October 1902. Olmsted suggested that a terrace along B Street North, beginning at 6th Street gradually rise to 34 feet in height at 14th Street (and possibly higher in the next block) to form a platform into which the new buildings would be set "forming an extension of the basements of the buildings." Hornblower and Marshall set the basement of the National Museum in a partially sunken well on the Mall side but fully exposed it on the street side to accommodate the *circa* 17-foot height difference (fig. 6). In early February 1905, civil engineer Bernard R. Green, employed by the Corps of Engineers to oversee construction of the museum, noted that "where the present *cross* slope is greatest it is only about 25' in the whole width. Even between the 890 ft. lines, that much cross slope would seem hardly to be noticeable on the ground and amongst the trees." McKim's telegraphed reply was to ask Green to raise the museum's first floor from 24 feet to 25 feet above the street, this small change in McKim's judgment "would essentially appreciate value of base line Capitol to monument." Green worked with Hornblower & Marshall to raise the museum an additional three feet, partly to get a better north entrance, better drainage, better light, and "to get a greater height of cornice and sky line," which satisfied McKim. McKim had been instrumental in persuading the Agriculture Department to lower its grade "so that the whole composition may have reference to the dome and the needle," making both buildings properly subordinate to the Mall's two defining elements. The base line of the Capitol's west façade at 90 feet was McKim's major reference point in determining the Mall's grading.[51]

Fig. 6 John J. Earley. **Plaster model of Hornblower & Marshall's National Museum Design, Mall (left) and B Street (right) facades.** Library of Congress, Prints and Photographs Division.

Olmsted does not mention in his October 1902 letter to McKim how the terrace was to be contained where it abutted North B Street. During the Mall Parkway hearings in 1904 Burnham was questioned about this issue. He calculated that 160,000 cubic yards of fill would be necessary "to build up to the grading line," adding $48,000 to the cost of reclaiming the Mall. "I will add to that a wall, which would perhaps be $30,000." A retaining wall along the Mall's north edge would not require placing the streets crossing the Mall in a viaduct, in Burnham's opinion. Rather, "streets would cross the Mall by a depressed grade, which would be a thing of great beauty, as everyone sees who rides along the Capitol grounds where such a grade exists. You look down, the hill falling away from you. It is a thing of great beauty, and so it would be with the streets coming from the Mall." Frederick Law Olmsted, Sr., had designed these carriageways in the Capitol grounds during the 1880s.[52]

Olmsted's and McKim's manipulation of the Mall's landscape achieved simultaneous pragmatic and aesthetic goals. Olmsted's 29 October 1902 drawing (fig. 7) acknowledged that razing the Smithsonian and other Victorian buildings on the Mall's south side was not likely in the near future. Groves of trees between 9th and 12th streets are shown abutting the Smithsonian Institution, planted on a terrace three feet higher than the Mall's center line (a graduated terrace now makes the transition). Moreover, the green walls created by these groves would effectively mask the building's then-despised architecture. Although it was not the subject of correspondence (which focused on the cross Mall grades), McKim planned forced perspectives for the Mall (and later for West Potomac Park.) The

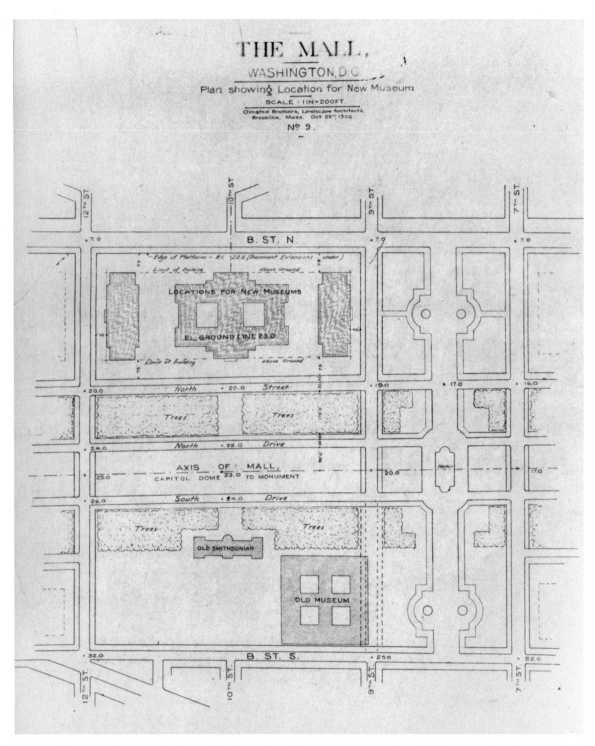

Fig. 7 Olmsted Brothers. Mall plan showing location of Hornblower & Marshall's National Museum, 1902. The New-York Historical Society, McKim, Mead & White Collection, Neg. #75566

Mall's actual length of nearly a mile and a half would be visually lessened by creating an extended bowl, the Capitol grounds terracing down from its 90 foot elevation and the Mall gradually rising to the Washington Monument's 40 foot elevation. Both would appear closer than they actually were to visitors within the central greensward, the "tunnel" of trees giving them even greater prominence.

About 18 November 1901 McKim sent Moore a pencil sketch plan (fig. 8) of the terrace with alternate designs of how to extend the Mall's plane up to the monument's base. He was considering whether to break the Mall's rows of elms at 15th Street or to tunnel the street under the Mall rather than interrupt the grand approach to the Washington Monument. The commission's final report recorded McKim's decision: "The bordering columns of elms march to the Monument grounds, climb the slope, and spreading themselves left and right on extended terraces, form a great body of green strengthening the broad platform from which the obelisk rises in majestic serenity" (p. 47). In 1899, classical scholar

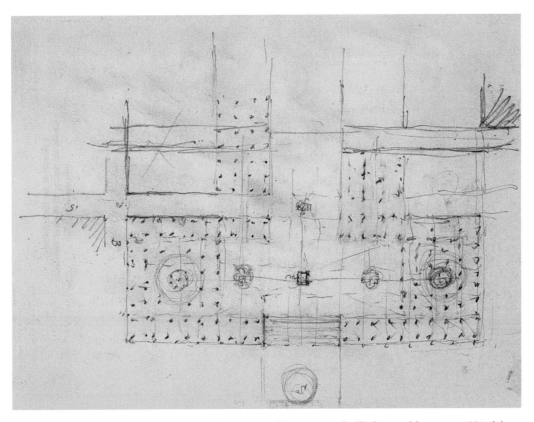

Fig. 8 Charles Follen McKim, sketch of proposed treatment of the terrace at the Washington Monument, 1901. Library of Congress, Manuscript Division, Charles Moore Papers

William H. Goodyear remarked that McKim, Mead & White were the first modern architects to use "the Greek horizontal curves on an extended scale" in their work at Columbia University. McKim applied the same principle to the Mall and West Potomac Park to create these forced perspectives.[53]

MALL CROSS AXIS

By 3 June 1901 the Senate Park Commission had developed the market-station axis into a major Mall element specifically to heighten the experience of those arriving at or leaving from the B&P station. Its center contained five pieces of sculpture out of eleven works planned for the Mall at this time. Two days earlier, McKim wrote Burnham about the value of adding sculptor Augustus Saint-Gaudens to the design team, citing the contributions he had already made:

> His visits to the office and keen interest in the Washington work have been invaluable; and this lead[s] me, knowing well your sentiments towards him, to make the proposition that we join him with us in the work of the Commission, in order that he may assist us, not only for the value of his counsel in many directions, but because the question of 'sites,' demanded in our report, is one which offers as much to sculpture as to architecture, and should be determined by the highest authority in the land. …[his] addition would materially strengthen, and add weight, in the final judgment of Congress, as well as that of the public, to the forthcoming report of the Commission. Saint-Gaudens has already so deeply manifested his interest in the outcome of this enterprise.[54]

Saint-Gaudens was added to the Senate Park Commission, but because of illness he did not join the other members on their European trip when they made substantial changes in the location and nature of the plan's sculpture. In mid-November, McKim reiterated Saint-Gaudens role: "upon his judgment will largely depend the selection of sites, for such monuments as the Lincoln, Grant, Garfield, McKinley, Sherman, Sheridan and McClellan, and the solution of other problems not less essential to the work of the Commission." By 30 August, the sculpture garden initially planned for the Mall cross-axis had been replaced by groves of trees. The designers initially envisaged hansoms entering or leaving the station's forecourt on 7th or 9th streets, a grand vehicular entrance into the city. Visitors would have passed by the monumental sculpture garden in the Mall's center with fleeting glimpses of the Washington Monument and Capitol in the distance. When the railroad station was no longer part of the Mall's equation, the sculpture garden lost its function as a place to be experienced from a moving vehicle and was replaced by parterres to be enjoyed by pedestrians. The

Fig. 9 Daniel Burnham, proposed new Union Station. *Senate Park Commission Report,* ff. p. 28.

commissioners then suggested that a new District government building replace the Center Market at the north end of this intermediary cross axis and the new National Museum occupy its south end; both buildings would be visited by large numbers of pedestrians.[55]

After Union Station was officially relocated to Massachusetts Avenue north of the Capitol at a meeting between McMillan, Cassatt, and Burnham on 3 December 1901, Burnham continued to conceive of the station as a vital element in the commission's plan. He wrote McKim ten days later:

The Government is to fill and finish the Grand Court in front of the depot. Of course, this will cost some money, but it is for the adornment of the city, to produce a vestibule in keeping with the Capitol, and is as important as the work around the Monument in the Mall.

The railways can get along without this Grand Court, but we cannot. It is essential to the broad scheme of improvements, and is for the dignity and beauty of the city, and should be provided for in the railroad bill, so that work on it can proceed early this year.[56]

Burnham's sketch of the Union Station design (fig. 9) published in the Park Commission's report was for the site of the B&O station on New Jersey Avenue, NW, adjacent to the Capitol grounds which he preferred to Massachusetts Avenue NE. He wrote Olmsted: "You probably will change your mind about the beauty of the location when certain considerations are placed before you which McKim and I considered last Sunday....I have a scheme for making a deep fore-court of the terrace wall between the court and the Capitol grounds, which will subordinate the depot and give it its proper artistic relation to the Capitol." Burnham planned a sunken court with two sets of staircases flanking a monumental fountain leading to a terrace at the station's entrance level, one of several echoes of Vaux-le-Vicomte in the commission's work. Once the Massachusetts Avenue NE site was chosen, Burnham designed a semicircular plaza with "three fountains whose locations at the three focal points would place a glistening dome of water in the vista of all the principal streets approaching the plaza, constituting an effect of exceeding beauty." In 1907, Burnham suggested that a monument to Christopher Columbus be erected in the plaza and he later collaborated with Lorado Taft in the design of the *Columbus Fountain*, erected in 1912.[57]

Fig. 10 Arch of Constantine, Rome. The Commission of Fine Arts

In 1903 and 1904 Olmsted critiqued Burnham's site plans for Union Station, suggesting proper angles of streets radiating from this plaza in order to get the best vistas. At the time the Park Commission's report was published, Burnham had conceived of the station's facade based on the Arch of Constantine (fig. 10) as "equally as dignified as that of the public buildings themselves." He felt strongly that although it was located just outside the boundaries of the new plan, "this station is intended to be monumental in every respect and to be in keeping with the dignity of the chief city of America and with its present and future beauty." Only the station's outline plan and that of a large semicircular plaza appeared on the main Senate Park Commission plan (see pl. VII), probably because Burnham's firm had not completed its design in time to be included.[58]

WASHINGTON MONUMENT GARDENS

During its May 1901 meeting the Senate Park Commission determined that the best solution to the Washington Monument's placement 371.6 feet east of the White House axis was to create a positive feature from a negative circumstance. Their 3 June preliminary design replaced the utilitarian Fish Commission's hatcheries north of the monument and greenhouses to its south with a vast public garden comparable in size to the White Lot south of the White House (see pl. VI). Spanning the Mall and the White Lot widths, this square was subdivided into fourteen square units to create a Greek cross at the center of the great Latin cross that regulated the monumental core's overall design. The corner squares were colored deep green on the 3 June plan indicating that they were to be planted with groves of trees. Eight wide boulevards traversing the Monument Gardens connected the Mall's carriageways with those in West Potomac Park and those in the White Lot with drives in the new park south of the monument. After McKim showed Saint-Gaudens this design, the sculptor wrote Burnham that he "thought it so splendid and was so impressed that I want at once to tell you how it struck me. Great Caesar's chariot ought to go through and if my shoulder would be any good at the wheel let me know and I'll push till I'm blind." Until their European trip, the commissioners conceived of the Mall as the center of a vast nexus of carriageways from which one enjoyed the city and explored the surrounding countryside. In 1904 it was estimated that the Park Commission plan gave Washington 8,000 acres of parkland connected by 65 miles of carriage or parkways.[59]

The crossing of the central axes was a series of three concentric squares, possibly a stepped pyramid formed by extending westward and geometrizing and leveling the roughly conical mound on which the Washington Monument stood. A monumental piece of sculpture stood in the center of the inner square, its plaza approached by diagonal pathways leading through the turfed middle square. Four additional sculptural works were located at the corners of the forested outer squares. For the Monument Gardens, McKim applied the same design principles used by his firm for the plan of Low Library and its plaza (1892-1898) at Columbia University. The three-dimensional richness of this campus setting, achieved through terracing and diagonal circulation, resulted in Columbia's premier gathering place and provided multiple connections to adjacent buildings. At Monument Gardens, McKim also introduced the third dimension of graduated height to change the simple geometric forms into a powerful planning device. André Le Nôtre's parterres flanking the central vista at Versailles, each laid out as a Greek cross within a square traversed by diagonals, provided the basic geometry for the plans of both Low Library and Monument Gardens. But the idea of overlooks was McKim's valuable design contribution, in the case of Washington, the monument's already elevated position suggesting such a treatment.[60]

After the Mall's character changed during the European trip from a vast system of lengthy carriage drives to a series of specific park experiences, the Monument Gardens was transformed into a pedestrian enclave laid out on a plane "as extensive as the piazza in front of St. Peter's in Rome." Its geometries laid down on the 30 August drawing had become more complex, two superimposed Greek crosses, each subdivided by pools, parterres, groves of trees, or sites for sculpture. The inner Greek cross was framed by four W-shaped corners densely planted with trees, each containing two circular open spaces for small monuments, their zigzag shapes leaving the four corners as open lawns, a figure-ground reversal from the 3 June design. All four of these W-shaped groves of elm trees were planted on 40-foot high terraces, their inner walls framing an elaborate sunken garden.[61]

On 30 August 1901 Burnham wrote McKim a long critique of four alternate schemes for Monument Gardens McKim had sent him:

> We have been happy with the drawings of the Mall. The interest in this work does not slacken. General schemes B. C. and D. seem, on a hasty inspection, to be inferior to A., because in each of them the Grand Court is walled in, and, therefore, scheme A. appeals to us as more open.
>
> Should you wall in the court at the three hundred foot spaces north and south of it, you would, when approaching it from the White House or the Lincoln Monument [then located at the southern termination of the White House axis], be obliged to climb up and then down to get into it. Would not this disconnect the Grand Court from the compositions north and south of it, and thus destroy the smooth flow of things?

This disconnection would conceal the court from those approaching from the north and south, and especially conceal the fountain and the people about it from the White House itself.

Do you not think that ease of access from the north and south is important; and do you not think that sight of the gay movement of people around the fountain and on the Grand Stairway, should be preserved, as one of the fine elements to be seen from a distance? Then, also, do you not think that we should see through the court from the White House to the Lincoln Monument, or vice versa, thus enriching this vista, and adding the mystery of the larger distance, and of the elements of the design that could thus be taken in?[62]

McKim anticipated Burnham's advice as scheme "A" was recorded on the drawing dated 30 August 1901.

The function of the terraces in the Monument Gardens was the emphasis in the *Senate Park Commission Report*, which considered that the "groves on the terraces become places of rest, from which one gets wide views of the busy city." Paths within the elm groves led to squares containing fountains to the west and classical temples to the east of the obelisk. The report's photograph 175 (fig. 11), a panorama of Rome from the terrace of the Villa Medici, illustrated the "public value of hilltops wisely treated": the dome of St. Peter's in the center is seen framed by trees clipped to enhance the view. The experience of this and other urban terraces during their European trip were particularly noted by the Senate Park Commission because the White House, Capitol, Washington Monument, and buildings on the Mall's south side were already located on elevated grounds. McKim's goal was to take greater advantage of Washington's vast natural panorama and picturesque setting by either creating or reinforcing a series of overlooks from the Capitol to the Potomac River.[63]

The Senate Park Commission also planned vistas towards the city, described by Burnham in his draft of the final report:

Fig. 11 Panorama of Rome from the Villa Medici. *Senate Park Commission Report*, No. 175 .

[T]he high slopes on which [Arlington] house stands should be treated with terraces by which the visitor would ascend easy grades from the Virginia end of [Memorial] bridge to his destination at Arlington. In this way that great reservation would be brought into close relationship with the Potomac Park, so as to be but an extension of it. Moreover, the terraces are not only capable of a treatment intrinsically beautiful, but they will afford the most beautiful view imaginable of Washington and the Potomac. In this way a harmonious, thoughtful, systematic and continuous treatment can be given to a vast area.[64]

McKim suggested that Moore revise the text of his comparison of Washington with European capitals for his *Century Magazine* articles to emphasize its topographical advantages and delete references to all "Royal country seats." He said, "When one recalls the setting of many foreign Capitals and their flat topography, one realizes that with so superb a beginning, and with the majestic Monument in a vista closed by the Potomac and the Virginia Hills, the possibilities for beautiful treatment of Washington are unequalled." He went on to caution about using too many superlatives. "I suggest, as more conservative and in line with the excellent tone and restraint of your article, that the preeminence of the Capital, above other cities in the world, as the *most beautiful*, be avoided, and that the sentence be made to read so that the Capital should stand as *one* of the most beautiful cities of the world? If this could be made true would it not be fine enough?"[65]

"The Washington Monument Division" in the 1902 report includes eleven drawings and a photograph of the model showing views to, from, and within the monument gardens (pl. IX). The designers acknowledged that "no portion of the task set before the Commission has required more study and extended consideration than has the solution of the problem of devising an appropriate setting for the Monument." Further, they believed that their design was the "best adapted to enhance the value of the Monument itself." When Olmsted reported on the history, design, and status of the Senate Park Commission's plan to the AIA convention on 11 December 1902 he explained the intended effect of the sunken court. "The actual intersection of the axes cannot be marked by any object which could be brought into comparison with the supreme shaft of the Monument, so it is proposed to mark it by a void—a great circular water basin set in a sunken garden, flanked and enclosed by terraces. At the head of the great bank of steps, 300 feet in width, which rise on the east from this garden like a great plinth would stand the Monument, related in position to the crossing of the axes like the altar at the crossing of a church." Burnham's critique of McKim's design of the Washington Monument Gardens reinforced these sacred associations. "The Court is a shrine, to which one should climb, *constantly* going up....Are not these open spaces that enclose the Grand Court the Court's real vestibule; and is not the Court itself the real inner vestibule to the stairway that leads up to the monument itself, which is the principle of the whole composition." Saint-Gaudens apparently suggested that Robert Mills's original intention of using the shaft's base for inscriptions be revived by "becoming a monumental 'affiche,' and that the Farewell Address, for example, should be incised upon the shaft."[66]

McKim turned to Vaux-le-Vicomte's terrace wall articulated by fountains (pl. XII) set in niches as the model for Monument Gardens east side (fig. 12). On its center axis at the top of a hill overlooking the French formal garden stood a statue of Hercules, from the 1780s suggested as an appropriate symbol for America, a suggestion first made in France. Washington was seen as the American Hercules whose great strength defeated monsters and tyrants that menaced the state. Although the only textual reference to Vaux-le-Vicomte in the Senate Park Commission report was that its "cascades, canals, and fountains us[e] one-twelfth of the daily water-supply of the District of Columbia," many photographs of its water features were taken by Olmsted during the commission's visit. Moore's biography of McKim, however, emphasized Vaux's iconography and its impact on the visitors, albeit nearly three decades later:

> From the terraces to the far horizon stretched the *tapis-vert*, crossed by a basin presided over by the carved image of Father Nile, and terminated by the golden figure of Hercules silhouetted against the sky....A wicker cart...carried them along the broad driveways, and they pictured what the Washington Mall would be when L'Enfant's design had been restored and American taste had worked its adornment.[67]

Although Moore may have telescoped travel reminiscences and remembered conversations, there were three visual references to Vaux's fountain wall in the final plan, at both ends of the West Potomac Park canal and in the forecourt of Union Station.

Moore's diary entry for 15 January 1902, the day when the exhibit of models and drawings opened, was unusually lengthy: "Went to Corcoran Gallery with Senator McM and Gallinger to meet President. When he saw me he came through the knot of people and thrust out his hand in the old way. He fell foul of the small model of Monument, saying it looked like fussy work. I expostulated but he insisted until Mr. McMillan took him to see the pictures of the Monument. Then he frankly acknowledged his error and took back all he said." Moore felt that artistry reached its highest point in McKim's Monument Gardens design.[68]

Fig. 12 View of Monument Garden, looking towards the White House, rendering by O.H. Bacher. *Senate Park Commission Report*, No. 48

WEST POTOMAC PARK

After the Senate Park Commission expanded the Mall to form a great kite during their May 1901, meeting, vehicular drives throughout the expanded area were fundamental to their thinking. Five miles of carriageways had wound through A.J. Downing's picturesque Mall and the literature concerning Washington's post-Civil War society frequently cited both horseback and carriage rides in and around Washington as major forms of recreation. Although selecting sites for future public buildings was part of the Senate Park Commission's mandate, the development of a comprehensive park system was McMillan's major goal and the commission's primary charge. When the commissioners changed the east Mall's central axis from a boulevard into a turfed parkway in May-June 1901, they concurrently developed West Potomac Park as a series of parallel boulevards. These connected to drives around the kite's perimeter, roads flanking the east Mall's greensward, and the central boulevard west of the monument, in total at least tripling central Washington's carriage and pathways, most adjacent to or through newly proposed parklands.[69]

The 3 June 1901 drawing (see pl. VI) shows building zones on the edges of West Potomac Park facing these wide boulevards, while parterres and pools flanked the central vista. While in Europe the commissioners decided on a long, wide canal framed by walkways and double rows of trees for the center of West Potomac Park. Irregular in shape—its eastern and western ends were widened slightly—the canal's great length was broken on the 19th Street axis by a circular pool. By 30 August the boulevards were narrower because they no longer passed through the redesigned Monument Gardens to connect to the Mall's drives (see fig. 6). Also by 30 August the western edge of the memorial circle had developed into a wide plaza with two roadways leading from it, one to a Potomac River bridge and the second leading to Rock Creek. Between these roadways directly behind the monument a stair, or watergate, descended into the Potomac River. By January 1902, West Potomac Park's building zones had disappeared and all internal references to Washington's street pattern eliminated and replaced by a vast parkland criss-crossed by multiple carriageways. The canal was widened slightly, its form changed to a Latin cross. In this final design, the canal's east end was terminated by an apsidal ended cross canal separated from the main canal by a narrow plaza, the germ of the future Rainbow Pool.

Many of the illustrations in the *Senate Park Commission Report* show variations in details for many sections of their plan. These drawings were done throughout the fall of 1901 while major and minor elements of the design were still in flux. Moreover, there are many indications that the commission's overall design philosophy was to establish basic principles and a broad framework, not dictate individual elements. Commonalities among the commission's design sources reinforce a recurring theme throughout the previous century: America was the inheritor of varied European cultural traditions imported with its pan-European population. The caption of photograph 100 (fig. 13) in the 1902 report reads: "Basin and Great Canal, Fontainebleau, Suggestive of the Treatment of the Canals West of the Monument," yet the text notes that these canals were "similar in character and general treatment to the canals at Versailles and Fontainebleau, in France, and at Hampton Court, in England."[70]

Fig. 13 Basin and Great Canal, Fontainebleau. *Senate Park Commission Report,* No. 100

In mid February 1901, Congress had appropriated an unprecedented $250,000 to erect a Grant Memorial in Washington, specifying that it be sculptural in nature. At the initial meeting of the Grant Memorial Commission on 6 March a site south of the State War & Navy Building was selected but twelve days later Secretary of War Root suggested that the north side of the White Lot was a better location; both sites were included in the 10 April circular soliciting designs. On 7 June Root convinced the Grant Memorial Commission to delay deciding on a site until all designs had been received, not due until 1 April 1902. Root had just asked the Senate Park Commission to serve as official advisors to the Grant Memorial Commission and he wished to leave its members some latitude concerning important monument sites.[71]

In May-June 1901, the commissioners decided to terminate the Mall's west axis with a vast triumphal arch on a scale comparable to Paris's Arc de Triomphe (almost 50 meters high and 45 meters wide) (fig. 14). On 7 June McKim invited Saint-Gaudens to attend the commission meeting

Fig. 14 Arc de Triomphe, Paris. Commission of Fine Arts

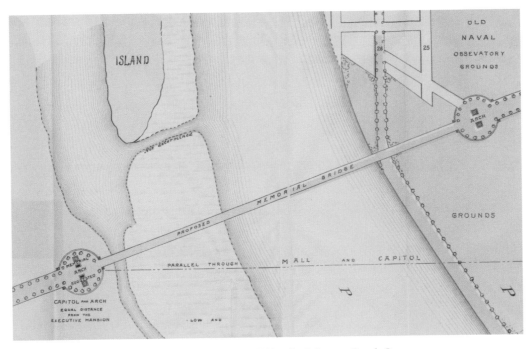

Fig. 15 Colonel Bingham's March 1900 Plan for the Mall (detail). Collection: Pamela Scott

on the 11th, "as the skeleton of the general scheme for the Mall will be discussed, and if possible accepted as the basis for future development. It is of the utmost importance the question of the establishment of permanent sites for the Lincoln and Grant especially should be reached at this meeting, and to do this effectively your presence and authority are most needful." For its siting, McKim looked back to 1894 when his firm in partnership with Olmsted, Sr.'s, redesigned Brooklyn's Grand Army Plaza at the entrance to Prospect Park to reinforce the meaning of John H. Duncan's Soldiers' and Sailors' Memorial Arch as a "national Valhalla for the Civil War." Duncan's arch, based on Rome's Arch of Titus, was located at one end of its plaza's elongated oval to collect and disperse traffic from twelve boulevards. Nine roadways converged on the arch McKim planned for West Potomac Park; it sat in the center of a double circle, a national Civil War memorial he surely intended would vie with Duncan's acknowledged masterpiece.[72]

The Park Commission did not originate the idea of a triumphal arch as part of Washington's monumental core. In 1890, Franklin Webster Smith had proposed a replica of the Brandenburg Gate for a "Lincoln Gate" to be erected on Pennsylvania Avenue at 4 ½ Street NW, and in 1900 he published a design for a bridge with triumphal arches derived from Rome's Arch of Constantine facing extensive plazas at both its landfalls. Commissioner of Public Buildings and Grounds Colonel Bingham's March 1900 plan for the Mall's development included two triumphal arches as entrances to Memorial Bridge. His memorial arch on the Virginia shore was located on the east-west axis of the Capitol (fig. 15). More significantly, Edward Pearce Casey won the 1900 competition for Memorial Bridge to span the Potomac River between the foot of 23rd Street, NW and Arlington Cemetery. The centerpieces of Casey's design were two Roman triumphal arches that masked the working of its central draw. Three months after McKinley's death in 1901 an association was formed to erect a memorial arch to him in Washington.[73]

In his draft of the *Senate Park Commission Report*, Burnham wrote about the symbolic relationship between the Mall's major axis and its connection to Arlington Memorial Cemetery via Memorial Bridge:

> In honor of the great General [Grant] who led the armies of the Union to victory that meant the preservation of the Republic, and in memory of the brave soldiers who fought under him, what more appropriate site than one which holds vital relations on the one hand with the commander of the Revolutionary armies, and on the other hand with the last resting place of so many thousands of the brave men who gave their lives in battle for their country.
>
> …Moreover the sentiment in favor of a memorial bridge to connect the Potomac Park with Arlington is so strong that the project must soon be carried out. The memorial bridge plans sent to Congress, with the approval of the War Department, call for a more elaborate and costly structure than will be necessary or advisable in case a Grant Memorial arch is located as suggested.[74]

Burnham's admiration for Grant was shared by the majority of Americans who considered him the country's greatest nineteenth-century figure. Moreover, Burnham would have linked Grant to Washington because they were the only two American generals to have commanded all the Armies and both were elected President subsequent to their military victories. In 1895, a decade after his death and five years after Grant's Tomb was erected in New York's Riverside Park, the Society of the Army of the Tennessee, Grant's old command, began lobbying Congress for a national monument to Grant. Locating the Grant Memorial was one of the Park Commission's major charges in spite of its stipulated location south of the White House in the 1901 competition guidelines.[75]

In late August 1901, Burnham and McKim brought Root up to date concerning their progress in the Mall's design during their trip to Europe, of great concern to him because the War Department's Corps of Engineers would have to implement the commission's decisions. The architects hoped to convince Root to accept the arch, shown on an even larger scale on the 30 August drawing than on the 3 June one. "We entertain the hope that you will feel as we do regarding the site which was selected for the Grant Monument," Burnham wrote Root on 22 August. "Mr. McKim will explain to you that the site is one of the five great points of the design....We place the Grant Memorial Arch in the center of this concourse, from which point the Memorial Bridge should lead over the river to Arlington, where are the dead of Grant's old army, and the country in which he won those victories which made his name most famous." Root was the first executive officer to be shown the drawings, Senators McMillan and Allison being the only legislators to have seen them.[76]

Memorializing Grant at the west end of the Mall began with the suggestion in May 1886 that a "Grant Memorial Bridge" be erected "over the river which separates the National Capital from Virginia, the great battlefield of the war which he brought to a successful conclusion." The anonymous author "H" of this scheme envisaged the bridge as "a superb arch (or succession of arches) bridging the chasm—no longer bloody, thank God—between the North and the South." A week later Ohio Senator John Sherman introduced a resolution that directed the Secretary of War to report on building such a Potomac River bridge. The following year, Captain T.W. Symons of the Corps of Engineers and the architects John Smithmeyer and Paul Pelz presented to Congress their design for the Grant Memorial Bridge. Their design was based on London Bridge with two high double towers supporting a bascule, or moveable, draw. The high towers—"granite, quarry-faced and rugged, intended to express the character of Gen. Grant"—excited a lot of favorable comment and were revived several times during the next decade with both Union and Confederate veterans, the Grand Army of the Republic, and most Congressmen supporting the concept.[77]

Fig. 16 George Keller, proposed design for Memorial Bridge, 1900; perspective view from Washington side of the bridge. Library of Congress, General Collections

Although a bridge connecting Washington to Arlington Memorial Cemetery (a popular tourist destination) and Fort Myer was a business and military necessity, its final approval by Congress was repeatedly blocked, apparently because its major feature was a memorial to Grant. To break the impasse the National Memorial Bridge Association was formed early in 1899 and a competition organized by the Secretary of War limited to four invited New York engineers was held. In the draft letter sent to the competitors, "a memorial to General Grant" was replaced with "a Memorial to American patriotism," probably at Root's suggestion. The winning design by engineer William H. Burr and architect Edward P. Casey was based on the 1887 bascule model, but its classicizing towers "crowned by bronze statues of Victory" and bronze "statues of men of renown" punctuated its stone balustrade.[78]

In March 1901 Massachusetts Senator George F. Hoar prevented the bridge's passage because he "did not want the design for the structure to be limited to the plan which has been approved by the Secretary of War." The previous November an alternate, post-competition Memorial Bridge design proposed by Hartford architect George Keller went on display at the Hall of the Ancients in Washington. Keller argued that the high bascule draw was neither necessary nor desirable; his single-span Roman triumphal arch standing in the center of a circular esplanade functioned as the Washington approach to the bridge while a "column memorial of consolidation of the Union" marked the Virginia approach (fig. 16). In December 1900 Keller's design was published in the *American Architect and Building News* and he gave an illustrated lecture at the AIA's critical annual meeting in Washington which focused on the city's future development. In late December 1900 and early January 1901 two members of Congress from Connecticut introduced into the House and Senate resolutions to appoint a memorial bridge commission. When the Park Commission began its work, Keller's Memorial Bridge approached by a triumphal arch was the favored design. Immediately after McKinley's assassination in September 1901 either Memorial Bridge or a McKinley Memorial Arch associated with it changed the focus of the site's meaning from one commemorating the preservation of the Union to one dedicated to McKinley's progress in reconciling the North with the South.[79]

Burnham and McKim were apparently unaware of how politically inflammatory a huge Grant Memorial Arch—an architectural type that historically recorded the conquest of enemies—had become when they proposed it less than three weeks before McKinley's assassination. McKinley had included sectional reconciliation as a policy in his inaugural address and had subsequently been criticized by some Northern newspapers for his overtures to southern political and business interests. On 28 August, McKim reported to Burnham on his positive meeting with Root the evening before in Washington. Root, he said, supported an arch to commemorate Grant on the Potomac site but had explained to McKim that "it was best not to disturb the present arrangement," the Grant Memorial's competition for a sculptural work being so far advanced. McKim went on to quote Root concerning General Grenville Dodge's chairmanship of the Grant Memorial Commission. "It seemed wisest not to press [Root] on this point, after his expressions of unwillingness, as he said 'to over-ride a man so near the end of his career, whose public service entitled him to such consideration.'" Root's decision meant *de facto* that the Grant Memorial could not be at the west end of the Mall's axis because the Potomac site required a large architectural structure.[80]

Root probably did not act alone when he adroitly avoided antagonizing the South—especially Southern congressmen—by refusing to nullify the War Department's competition for the Grant Memorial. John Hay, Lincoln's secretary during the Civil War and Secretary of State from 1898 until his death in 1905, consulted with Root and McKim about Lincoln's appropriate recognition in the Park Commission plan. When this initial conversation occurred can only be surmised by the nature of a key quotation attributed to Hay and the timing of the substitution of the Lincoln Memorial peristyle for the Grant Memorial arch in West Potomac Park. In 1912, while Burnham served as its chairman, the annual report of the Commission of Fine Arts quoted Hay concerning the Lincoln Memorial's location:

> As I understand it, the place of honor is on the main axis of the plan. Lincoln of all Americans next to Washington deserves this place of honor. He was of the immortals. You must not approach too close to the immortals. His monument should stand alone, remote from the common habitations of man, apart from the business and turmoil of the city; isolated, distinguished, and serene. Of all the sites, this one, near the Potomac, is most suited to the purpose. [81]

The first sentence in the attributed Hay quote suggests that he has just learned of the plan's schematic outline, information Burnham first gave Root in a 22 August letter. Five days later McKim traveled to Washington and met Root at his home during the evening when they discussed the Grant Memorial competition and other matters relating to the plan's acceptance by Congress and the public. Hay may have been present that evening and influenced McKim to think of Lincoln's life and achievements as more significant than those of Grant. The Lincoln Memorial design published in the Park Commission's report verifies that McKim approached its design as a unique architectural expression to represent "the one man in our history as a nation who is worthy to be named with George Washington." It is certain that Hay hosted a meeting at the State Department on 22 March 1902 to discuss pending legislation about a Lincoln Memorial; the attendees included

Senator McMillan, Root, McKim, and Saint-Gaudens. It "was agreed that the site for the memorial should be that fixed in the plans of the park commission, namely, on the north bank of the Potomac, near the old Observatory. Messrs. St. Gaudens and McKim were charged to prepare rough outlines of the proposed structure as a basis for the ascertainment of the amount of the appropriations which Congress will be requested to make." In preparation for his biography of McKim, Charles Moore in 1927 tried unsuccessfully to locate McKim's 1902 Lincoln Memorial design. Had McKim not died in 1909 he probably would have been the architect of the Lincoln Memorial. In 1911 Glenn Brown illustrated a lecture with "a picture of the proposed Lincoln memorial, as suggested by Charles Follen McKim, just prior to the architect's death. [Brown] favored the McKim plans."

Fig. 17 Henry M. Shrady and Edward P. Casey, revised design for the Grant Memorial, 1907. Commission of Fine Arts

After a lengthy political process deciding its site, Henry Bacon was chosen to design the Lincoln Memorial in 1912 because, Moore reported in his 1929 biography of McKim, "Mr. Burnham regarded him as the man who worked most in the McKim spirit." [82]

Moore, who became chairman of the Commission of Fine Arts in 1915, repeated Hay's quote in his 1921 biography of Burnham, noting that shortly before his death in 1909, McKim recalled his conversation with Hay for architect Cass Gilbert. Gilbert wrote it down and gave it to Richard Watson Gilder, poet and editor of the *Century Magazine*, whose admiration for Lincoln was expressed in his sonnet "On the Life-Mask of Abraham Lincoln," published in the November 1886 issue of the *Century*. In the final three pages of their ten-volume *Abraham Lincoln, A History* (1890), Hay and John G. Nicolay summarized Lincoln's achievements and fame as an expression of "the marvelous symmetry and balance of his intellect and character," a character that was "among the precious heirlooms of the Republic." Their concluding sentence expressed the hope that Lincoln's "name and his renown may be forever a bond of union to the country which he loved with an affection so impartial, and served, in life and in death, with such entire devotion." Roosevelt certainly would have supported Hay's point of view about the character of the Lincoln Memorial although he did not read Nicolay's and Hay's *History* until the summer of 1902. He wrote Hay at that time: "[Lincoln] and Washington stand alone not only in our history, but in the history of mankind during the period covered by their respective lives."[83]

In late November 1901, McKim moved the Grant Memorial to the east end of the Mall, hoping still to influence the Grant Memorial's aesthetic and symbolic character when he created Union Square to be the setting for three equestrian statues of Generals Grant, Sheridan, and Sherman. McKim changed his original sedate circular pool into what he conceived as Washington's version of Paris's Place de la Concorde, an open nexus of many cross roads (see fig. 1). Saint-Gaudens was able to influence the Grant Memorial's aesthetic character when in the spring of 1902 he urged other jury members to choose Shrady and Casey's composition of a huge equestrian statue of Grant flanked by monumental groups representing the artillery and the cavalry, which had been led by Sheridan and Sherman (fig. 17). In 1907 McKim recommended stairs on both sides of Casey's pedestal, a change the younger architect resisted but finally agreed would make the Grant Memorial as accessible from the Capitol grounds as from the Mall.[84]

The Park Commission probably moved the Lincoln Memorial to the Mall's west end in the early winter of 1901. Possibly McKim rejected the Roman arch prototype for the Lincoln Memorial after meeting with Root and Hay because the form was already becoming a common American Beaux Arts memorial type; these Republican statesmen apparently convinced him that he needed to invent

Fig. 18 Brandenburg Gate, Berlin, 1903. Library of Congress, Prints and Photographs Division

Fig. 19 "The Brandenburg Gate as a Lincoln Gate before the Capitol." Franklin Webster Smith, *Designs, Plans and Suggestions for the Aggrandizement of Washington*, 1900, p. 22.

a new memorial typology to commemorate Lincoln's unique character just as Robert Mills had created a new typology for the Washington Monument. The final report described McKim's second Lincoln Memorial project hastily designed that winter:

"Crowning the *rond point*, as the Arc de Triomphe crowns the Place de l'Etoile at Paris, should stand a memorial erected to the memory of that one man in our history as a nation who is worthy to be named with George Washington—Abraham Lincoln.

Whatever may be the exact form selected for the memorial to Lincoln, in type it should possess the quality of universality, and also it should have a character essentially distinct from that of any monument now existing in the District or hereafter to be erected. The type which the Commission has in mind is a great portico of Doric columns rising from an unbroken stylobate."[85]

The temple-shaped "portico," 250 feet by 220 feet, was to stand on a terrace 40 feet tall (level with the Washington Monument), its columns rising yet another 40 feet (pl. XI). Topped by a quadriga, its form was now more reminiscent of Berlin's Brandenburg Gate (1789-1793) (fig. 18), rectangular in outline, its post-and-beam structure derived from Greek rather than the Roman tradition of arches from which Paris's Arc de Triomphe had descended. McKim may have consulted more immediate and local sources: Franklin Webster Smith's 1890 proposed "Lincoln Gate" (fig. 19) or even L'Enfant's 1791 open peristylar monument shown adjacent to the canal on South Capitol Street (see pl. II). Stairs on the west side of McKim's Lincoln Memorial led to the Potomac River watergate while those on the east descended to a terrace overlooking the canal, a standing figure of Lincoln facing the Washington Monument. Saint-Gaudens may have suggested this conjunction of architecture and sculpture but McKim would have known it; at Chicago's 1893 World's Columbian Exposition Saint-Gaudens "said the east end of the composition should be bound together architecturally…. He suggested a statue backed by thirteen columns, typifying the thirteen original states." In his Lincoln Memorial composition McKim again referred to the statue of Hercules and terrace at Vaux le Vicomte. On the east side of Monument Gardens, he equated the military hero Washington with Hercules; at the west end of the Mall he equated the statesman Lincoln with the ancient hero whose defeat of tyrants and monsters was for the civic good. [86]

The landscaping of the triangle between Memorial Bridge, the Rock Creek Park drive, and the Lincoln Memorial's circle also evolved between 30 August 1901 and January 1902. On 27 August George Vanderbilt had invited the commissioners to visit his estate, Biltmore, near Ashville, North Carolina. Olmsted, whose firm began designing Biltmore's vast landscaped park in 1890, thought the trip would be valuable because the climate, soil conditions, and flora of the two places were similar and the trip also offered the chance to study the "possibilities and limitations in certain directions of park work….The work there is for the greater part entirely informal but the approach to the house and its immediate setting is a formal design of some size which would be not without suggestiveness." Burnham met Olmsted at Biltmore on 22 September but McKim was unable to join them.[87]

Fig. 20 View of the Monument and Terraces from the White House, rendered by Jules Guerin. *Senate Park Commission Report*, No. 40

Solutions to the collision of wild and tamed nature at Biltmore might have been applied to the juncture of Rock Creek Parkway and West Potomac Park; between 30 August and 15 January the commission replaced the graveled or paved plaza on the outer ring of the Potomac site's circle with grass to create a more natural transition between the two parks. Langdon (who undoubtedly knew Biltmore's landscape well from his work in the Olmsted office) contributed this soft transition to the Senate Park Commission's design. On 14 December Olmsted wrote Langdon, "I have received your letter of the 11th instant, enclosing sketch of entrance from the Mall to Potomac Park. I think your suggestion a good one and I will forward it to Mr. McKim." McKim replied directly to Langdon on the 18th that he "heartily" agreed to his proposed entrance to Potomac Park. Burnham himself designed the final details of Memorial Bridge's landfall and its Roman character. In great haste, McKim telegraphed him on 25 November: "Large Bird's-eye drawing, Arlington to Capitol, completed, except Memorial Bridge (pl. VIII). Please send immediately rough sketch of Lincoln abutment and several arches as guide." Four days later McKim had Burnham's drawing in hand: "Hearty concurrence in Bridge scheme received this morning. Will incorporate immediately."[88]

THE WASHINGTON COMMON

The Senate Park Commission had not yet determined the building type for the circular plaza at the southern end of the White House axis at the Tidal Basin when the 3 June 1901 drawing was made. The commissioners apparently decided, at least tentatively, at their 11 June meeting to place the Grant Memorial at the west end of the Capitol axis and the Lincoln Memorial in the Tidal Basin plaza. On 22 August Burnham wrote Root outlining the plan's "five great points," the Capitol, Washington Monument, White House, Grant Memorial, "and, we hope, the Lincoln Memorial." McKim's letter to Root two days later is also indefinite, but suggests that the memorial planned for the Tidal Basin was dedicated to Lincoln. ("The sites proposed, for the Monuments to LINCOLN and GRANT, are second only in importance to that of WASHINGTON.") Burnham noted in his draft of the report that the site "may well be reserved for the memorial that surely will be built to Lincoln." [89] (see Appendices)

The 30 August drawing shows a relatively small triumphal arch in the Tidal Basin circle confirmed by a drawing of a single-span arch included in the 1902 report (fig. 20) although it no longer reflected the Park Commission's final designs. Burnham, in an undated note among his papers quoted President McKinley whom the commission members had met in April 1901: "McKinley said, speaking of the

Fig. 21 Arch of Titus, Rome. Commission of Fine Arts

Vista from the White House 'the failure of the engineers to place the monument on the axis may not be without compensation.' He meant that the South View from the White House was too grand to be in[terrupted] by even the Monument." Thus, the smaller scale of the Lincoln Memorial arch was in deference to the view from the White House but also because the slain President was initially perceived, at least by Burnham, to be of lesser relative historical importance than Grant.[90]

Because triumphal arches historically commemorated either great military heroes or civic leaders, the commissioners considered it appropriate to honor both Lincoln and Grant with the architectural type prominent in ancient Rome, made grandiose in Paris, and built in America in increasing numbers after the Civil War. Seemingly, they considered Paris's Arc de Triomphe as the fitting model for the Grant Memorial because it had been erected to commemorate Napoleon's great armies. Rome's Arch of Titus, 81 A.D., (fig. 21) was probably the model for the Lincoln Memorial arch as it had been for Duncan's Soldiers' and Sailors' Memorial Arch (1889-1901) in New York (which included an equestrian statue of Lincoln). Like Lincoln, Titus had suppressed a rebellion. This specific iconography that linked the Civil War's military and civic achievements to European historical events and leaders gave way in the final design to architectural models associated with Washington's founding history.

On the 30 August 1901 drawing, the Lincoln Memorial arch at the Tidal Basin was flanked by two buildings with rotundas facing south, their plans copies of the 1803 outline of William Thornton's Capitol later illustrated in the Park Commission's report. On 14 September McKinley died from an assassin's bullet and Theodore Roosevelt became President. The much expanded enclave of buildings proposed for the Tidal Basin, hastily designed in December after the Lincoln Memorial was moved to the Potomac River site, may reflect the influence of Roosevelt's intense interest in George Washington's presidency as well as his own robust, athletic lifestyle. These buildings in the "Washington Common," as the Tidal Basin group was called in the final report, continued to refer to the city's early federal buildings, almost to the point of caricature.[91] (see Davis, fig. 5)

The Roman Pantheon, which inspired the central memorial building, was dedicated to the "Framers of the Constitution," the same model Jefferson had suggested for the Capitol, the impetus for William Thornton's 1793 winning design. The undigested final design for the buildings in the Washington Common was reflected in the terse commentary in the 1902 report. "Whether this memorial shall take the form of a Pantheon, in which shall be grouped the statues of the illustrious men of the nation, or whether the memory of some individual shall be honored by a monument of the first rank may be left to the future; at least the site will be ready." More than two decades later, Olmsted acknowledged that "this portion of the plan of 1901 was less carefully studied than any other major part of the 'Mall area'" and that "almost at the last moment [the commissioners] agreed on the tentative plan for the southern area."[92]

Six identical buildings flanking the Framers Memorial, based on James Hoban's design for the White House, were hastily inserted during the Park Commission's final weeks. Their placement in relation to the pantheon, moreover, recalled L'Enfant's executive department buildings that framed his presidential palace (see pl. II). These White House clones were surely place-holders, buildings of a scale, form, and historical lineage that McKim found appropriate for the site but that McKinley would have found so large as to spoil the view from the White House. McKim evidently trusted Roosevelt would understand the visual necessity for monumental scale to match the rest of the plan. For both Potomac River memorials—the Grant Arch and subsequently the Lincoln Memorial—McKim envisaged rectilinear buildings that would complete a geometric progression from dome to obelisk to rectangle from east to west. With the introduction of the Framers Memorial in the early winter of 1901 he reversed the progression for the north-south axis: the obelisk stood between the rectangle of the White House and the domical Framers Memorial.

The architectural character of the six White House clones was belied by their anticipated functions; the 1902 report called for expanded recreational uses throughout the Washington Common, proposing a stadium, ball fields, tennis courts, a gymnasium, expanded bathing beaches, and a bath house. In August 1901 local citizens' groups were again lobbying for more public parks including bathing houses and beaches. In at least one of his many lectures promoting the plan soon after it was made public, Moore noted that on 24 March 1902, 12,000 people had visited the Zoo. "More parks must be prepared, and on the shores of the Potomac, south of the Washington Monument, is an ideal place for a park of great proportions. There is room for ball grounds and tennis courts. Then the location along the river is ideal for a great swimming pool, such as Boston has." The ascension to the Presidency by the outdoorsman Roosevelt in September 1901 undoubtedly spurred the Park Commissioners to propose a variety of athletic uses for the Tidal Basin area.[93]

UNION SQUARE

On 21 November 1901, McKim wrote Moore about his epiphany concerning the east end of the Mall, noting that Saint-Gaudens "strongly urges it" and that McKim will seek Burnham's "criticism and approval":

> As a site for the Grant Memorial, likely to be approved by both the Commission and the Grant Committee, it would seem that, thus far despite our many deliberations on

the subject, we had overlooked the spot, which seems to have been waiting for us all the time. Does it not exist in the great Square, at the foot of Capitol Hill, heading the Mall—Washington's Place de la Concorde, to which all avenues and streets converge? Within this area of 1,000 by 400 feet, there is a glorious space for three horsemen abreast, three separate memorials, yet three forming a single composition, in which the central figure, standing upon a raised platform, say 100 feet square, surrounded by a balustrade enriched with sculpture, and approached by steps on four sides, at a cost easily covered by $250,000 would represent Grant. Indeed, some such Memorial would be needed, to give this site its proper monumental character, while yet preserving intact the vistas to Capitol and Monument. It would seem as though no more appropriate sentinel could be found to defend the Capitol and the head of the Avenue, than three great equestrian figures, with their accessories standing for Grant, Sherman, and Sheridan.[94]

"Brilliantly illuminated, embellished with fountains, and commanded by terraces, [Union Square] would compare favorably, in both extent and treatment, with the Place de la Concorde in Paris," summed up the Grant Memorial's site in the Senate Park Commission Report (see pl. X). Moreover, Union Square revived the commission's May-June idea of a Mall cross axis by moving its sculpture, fountains, and parterres bounded by carriageways to the head of the Mall. Equestrian figures of the three Union Army generals were spread across the Mall's central parkway, the focus of a formal landscape that provided an "organic connection between the Capitol and the Mall." Probably designed by McKim, whose knowledge of Paris was matched by his appreciation of the lessons taught by its urbanism, Union Square's genesis in the Place de la Concorde transcended its function as the convergence of several routes. McKim named the new Grant Memorial site "Union Square;" eight statues erected in the 1750s in the Place de la Concorde represented in Paris the unity (and contributions) of France's major provinces. Grant, Sheridan, and Sherman were the three Union Army generals whose Civil War victories preserved the union of American states.[95]

Moore later suggested that the Grant Memorial's figures served as directional markers in the Mall's greater framework:

The first and most important consideration is the height of the long pedestal to the monument. Obviously this height should not be so great as to obstruct the vision from any point in the square. An instructive illustration of the principles which should govern the treatment of this square is to be found in the Place de la Concorde in Paris. There the obelisk occupies a position corresponding to the location of the Grant Statue; and the two fountains may be taken as corresponding to the two subordinate groups in the Shrady [the sculptor of the Grant Memorial] design. There is no point in the entire square at which the vision is arrested by an object within the square itself. The Obelisk [in the Place de la Concorde] itself acts as the sight on a gun-barrel, focusing the attention on the great arch [the Arc de Triomphe] at the end of the vista.[96]

ENDGAME

What did "reviving" L'Enfant's plan actually mean to the Park Commission? Aesthetically and politically it meant the triumph of Beaux-Arts classicism over Victorian historicism brought by nineteenth-century émigré populations to America. L'Enfant and the Park Commissioners shared aesthetic principles rooted in European classicism. In 1904 Burnham argued the aesthetic grounds for replacing the Victorian Mall:

> In regard to the Secretary's feeling that the treatment of the Mall should be natural instead of formal, that is a question of taste; it is a question for educated men to settle for the country; it is a question for this committee. It is a question for the committee to settle whether they would have the most beautiful thing that man can conceive or whether the park shall remain in its natural state. We do not feel that it can with propriety be left in its natural state. We do not think that in the midst of a great city, which has formality all about it, that informality should become the rule. We think with the Capitol at one end and the Monument at the other, which are the most formal things in the world, the treatment between these structures should be equally formal.[97]

In August 1905, Burnham, Olmsted, and McKim all objected to Hornblower & Marshall's "French-exposition entrance" for the National Museum, an homage to Charles-Louis Girault's Petit Palais erected in Paris in 1900. Burnham passionately argued the commission's position again in 1905:

> The Senate Commission declared that all of the architecture of the Mall should be similar in style and treatment and that it should harmonize with the architecture of the Capitol. I still very strongly think so.
>
> Every part of the Mall should be considered a part of the whole design and it is not permissible to introduce a style foreign to the dominating one.[98]

The Mall's six Victorian buildings were unacceptable to the Park Commission because they were not fitting complements to L'Enfant's plan. Five were based on Medieval architectural traditions, were built of brick and terra cotta, and varied in their size and interrelations; three had been designed by the German-trained architect Adolf Cluss. The Park Commission plan signaled the end of the era that had fostered the ad hoc placement and strong individualism of the Victorian Mall and the beginning of centralized planning. An overt attack on the culture that had produced the Mall's Victorian architecture was unacceptable; restoring the Mall as President Washington had intended it to be was laudable.

By early June 1901 (and possibly earlier) the Park Commission began devising an appropriate overarching theme for the monumental core that united the country's two great defining events, the Revolution and the Civil War. The three key buildings associated with the country's founding—the Capitol, White House, and Washington Monument—were untouchable. The Park Commission strengthened and extended the existing axes with new structures commemorative of saving the Union west and south of the Washington Monument. Immediately the commissioners conceived the Capitol axis as the warrior-President line but half-heartedly developed the White House axis as the statesman-President line. Influenced by the political reality of sectional reconciliation and a mature recognition of the relative historical importance of Lincoln over Grant, McKim created Union Square for the Grant Memorial at the Mall's east end and moved the Lincoln Memorial to the Mall's west end. The Park Commission simply ran out of time before it could mature its designs for the Washington Common. In their final design the commissioners merged these two lines into one powerful, seemingly inevitable statement about national union rooted in the Constitution with Lincoln and Grant as its joint defenders.

The Senate Park Commission plan presented to the public on 15 January 1902 was the fruition of ideas and projects that had been suggested or partially implemented during the previous two decades. Mutual respect among the commissioners was based in part on their shared conviction that great cities are works of art and that urban beauty is rationally conceived and a positive force in human life. All the pieces of the puzzle were on the table; the Park Commission arranged them to have an appropriate political armature in an aesthetically appropriate composition guided by a visionary ideal of urban grandeur that still answered foreseeable functional needs. In the pithy extract from his paper "On the Commercial Value of Beauty," printed by the Senate Committee on the District of Columbia in January 1902, Burnham offered Pericles in ancient Athens and Louis Napoleon in modern Paris as exemplars for American officials to study and emulate. Although all four of the commission members contributed to the logic, clarity, and beauty of their plan's monumental core, McKim's critical eyes and mind dominated the final design. Moore, knowledgeable about the commissioners' ideas and influences from the beginning, opined that "Burnham's affection for McKim was evident, as was also his respect for the carefully reasoned opinions that came from McKim's reflective mind. Soon I was to find that while Burnham sat at the head of the table, it was McKim who arranged the feast." [99]

NOTES

[1] Glenn Brown, "The Making of a Plan for Washington City," *Records of the Columbia Historical Society* 6 (1903), 1-10. Hereafter, Brown, "Plan for Washington". "Building the Capital," *Washington Post* 7 January 1902. I wish to thank Sue Kohler who alerted me about the Senate Park Commission's preliminary plans and has advised me on several aspects of this paper. John Reps shared his transcriptions of Charles Moore's diary, Tony Wrenn shared his documents on the AIA's involvement with the Senate Park Commission, John Fondersmith gave me a copy of the *Senate Park Commission Report*, and Kirsten Schaffer kindly transcribed some Burnham letters for me; thank you all.

[2] Charles Moore, "The Making of a Plan for the City of Washington," *Records of the Columbia Historical Society* 6 (1903), 11-23. Republished in *Century Magazine* 58 (Mar. 1902), 747-757.

[3] Charles Moore, *The Life and Times of Charles Follen McKim* (Boston: Houghton Mifflin Company, 1929), 198; hereafter Moore, *McKim*.

[4] *Washington Evening Star*, 10 December 1887, and 5 September 1888. *American Architect and Building News* 35 (13 February 1892), 107-8 and 36 (7 May 1892), 87. *Washington Post*, 7 February 1900.

[5] Glenn Brown, *History of the United States Capitol* (GPO, Washington, D.C., 1900); "The Selection and Sites for Federal Buildings," *Architectural Review* VIII:4 (1894), 89-94.

[6] Frederick Law Olmsted, Jr., "Landscape in Connection with Public Buildings in Washington," in Charles Moore, ed., *Papers Relating to the Improvement of the City of Washington* (GPO: Washington, D.C., 1901), 34.

[7] Charles Moore, "The Improvement of Washington City," *Century Magazine* 63 (Feb. 1902), 628; "Building the Capital," *Washington Post*, 7 January 1902.

[8] Charles Follen McKim to Daniel H. Burnham, 28 August 1901, Charles Moore Papers, Library of Congress Manuscript Division; hereafter Moore Papers, LC

[9] Charles Moore, ed. *The Improvement of the Park System of the District of Columbia*, 57th Cong. 1st Sess, (1902) Sen. Rpt. No. 166, 12. Hereafter *Senate Park Commission Report*.

[10] McKim to Wendell P. Garrison, 10 April 1901, Moore Papers, LC; McKim to Theodore Roosevelt, 20 March 1904, Charles Follen McKim Papers, Library of Congress, Manuscript Division; hereafter McKim Papers, LC.

[11] Daniel H. Burnham to Leslie M. Shaw, 24 July 1903, Olmsted Associates Papers, Library of Congress, Manuscript Division; hereafter Olmsted Papers, LC.

[12] Burnham to James Wilson, 9 August 1903, Olmsted Papers, LC; Burnham to Olmsted, 12 November 1904, Olmsted Papers, LC; *The Mall Parkway Hearing Before the Committee on the District of Columbia* (Washington, D.C.: Government Printing Office, 1904) 13-4; hereafter *Mall Parkway Hearing*.

[13] Ironically, from the 1850s to the 1870s Baron Haussmann had transformed central Paris so that it more resembled L'Enfant's Washington than it did the Paris of 1784 when L'Enfant last saw it.

[14] Brown, "Plan for Washington", 7.

[15] *Ibid*, 6-8. "A Matter of Patriotism," *Washington Post*, 27 April 1902.

[16] Daniel Burnham to Margaret Burnham, 24 April 1901, Daniel H. Burnham Collection, Ryerson & Burnham Archives, Art Institute of Chicago; hereafter Burnham Collection, AIC.

[17] James McMillan, "Commission to Consider Certain Improvements in the District of Columbia," 56th Cong., 2d Sess. (1901) Sen. Rpt. 1919, Calendar No. 1897, 1-2.

[18] Olmsted, 19 March 1901, meeting notes, Olmsted Papers, LC.

[19] Senate Committee on the District of Columbia, *Park Improvement Papers, No. 5*, "Informal Hearing Before the Subcommittee of the Committee on the District of Columbia, United States Senate," April 1, 1901, (GPO: Washington, D.C., 1901), 76.

[20] Olmsted, "Washington Park System," meeting notes, 22 March 1901. Olmsted Papers, L.C.

[21] Burnham to Olmsted, 29 March 1901. Burnham Collection, AIC.

[22] *Mall Parkway Hearing*, 13. McKim to Prescott Butler, 10 April 1901 in Moore, *McKim*,185. Burnham to Olmsted, 12 April 1901, Burnham Collection, AIC.

[23] Burnham to William E. Curtis, 17 October 1902, Burnham Collection, AIC.

[24] The McKim, Mead & White Papers in the New-York Historical Society has many more unsigned drawings for the Senate Park Commission plan than discussed here. Burnham to Olmsted, 10 April 1901, Burnham Collection, AIC. McKim to James G. Langdon, 2 May 1901, Moore Papers, L.C.

[25] Olmsted to Burnham, 30 April 1901, Moore Papers, L.C.; Olmsted to Langdon, 4 May 1901, Moore Papers, L.C; Olmsted to Glenn Brown, 16 May 1901, AIA Archives, 801/1/20/1901 N-O. Olmsted's autograph postscript added to typed letter dated 16 May 1901.

[26] B Street South is today Independence Avenue; B Street North is Constitution Avenue.

[27] Burnham to Olmsted, 15 April 1901. Quoted in Cynthia R. Field, "The City Planning of Daniel Hudson Burnham," Ph.D. diss., Columbia University, 1974, 217.

[28] *Park Improvement Hearing*, 74.

[29] S. 697, 51st Cong. (1889).

[30] Charles Moore, *Washington Past and Present* (New York: The Century Co.. 1929), 262.

[31] *Senate Park Commission Report*, 35-54.

[32] *Washington Post*, 14 January 1900; Charles Moore Diary, 27 January 1902, University of Michigan Library; Burnham to Moore, 14 April 1902, Moore Papers, LC.

[33] Olmsted to Langdon, 29 October 1901, Moore Papers, LC.

[34] *Washington Evening Star*, 17 April 1886.

[35] *Washington Evening Star*, 13 February 1892.

[36] *New York Evening Post*, undated clipping; National Archives and Records Administration, R.G. 46, Records of the U.S. Senate, Committee on the District of Columbia, 56A-F7; hereafter NARA.

[37] The long Armory was to be located on 15th Street overlooking the White Lot where the Commerce Department was built. In a talk that Moore gave before the Brookland Citizens Association in May 1902, he suggested that the District Building should be "placed on the site of the market house, and not on the one selected, that of the old power house." Newspaper clipping inserted in Charles Moore's diary for 7 May 1902, University of Michigan Library. The District Building was built on the site of the old power house which had burned in 1897. "New Armory Project," *Washington Post*, 8 December 1901.

[38] James Rush Marshall to McKim, 31 March 1904, McKim, Mead & White Papers, New-York Historical Society; hereafter MM&W Papers, NYHS.

[39] McKim to Moore, 15 January 1902, Moore Papers, LC.

[40] Olmsted to Charles Mulford Robinson, 1 March 1904, Olmsted Papers, LC.

[41] *Mall Parkway Hearing*,14.

[42] Moore, *McKim*, 199; *Mall Parkway Hearing*,14-15.

[43] *Park Commission Report*, 99.

[44] *Mall Parkway Hearing*,15.

[45] *Ibid.*,31.

[46] Charles Moore, *Daniel H. Burnham, Architect, Planner of Cities* (Boston: Houghton-Mifflin Company, 1921), I:142: hereafter Moore, *Burnham*.

[47] McKim to James Knox Taylor, 23 August 1901. McKim Papers, LC.

[48] Moore, *McKim*,199.

[49] Montgomery Schuyler, "The Nation's New Capital," *New York Times*, 19 January 1902.

[50] Hornblower & Marshall to McKim, 30 April 1904, MM&W Papers, NYHS; Olmsted to Hornblower & Marshall, 5 May 1904, Olmsted Papers, LC; Hornblower & Marshall to Olmsted, 9 May 1904, Olmsted Papers, LC.

[51] Olmsted to McKim, 31 October 1902, Olmsted Papers, LC; Bernard R. Green to McKim, 5 February 1905 and McKim to Green, 15 and 16 February 1901; McKim to George H. Harries, 3 April 1905, MM&W Papers, NYHS.

[52] *Mall Parkway Hearing*,16.

[53] In 1929, Moore quoted an unnamed source that suggests this effect, a quote that varies slightly from the text of the Senate Park Commission report. "Feeling strongly the lack of adequate support given to the towering obelisk perched on a formless mound, the commission so planned that the four rows of elms marching through the Mall should 'climb the slope, and spreading themselves to right and left on extended terraces, form a great body of green strengthening the broad platform on which the Monument should rest and from which this obelisk, like its historic prototypes, shall rise from a plane.'" Moore, *Washington Past and Present*, 266-7. This quote may have been taken from McKim's original (now lost) description before it was edited for the Park Commission report. William H. Goodyear, "Horizontal Curves in Columbia University," *Architectural Record* 9 (July-Sept. 1899): pp. 82-93.

[54] McKim to Burnham, 1 June 1901, Moore, *McKim*, 185-6.

[55] McKim to Rev. E. Winchester Donald, 12 November 1901, McKim Papers, LC; "The Commission's Report," *Washington Post*, 16 January 1902.

[56] Burnham to McKim, 13 December 1901, cited in Moore, *Burnham*, I:163-64.

[57] Burnham to Olmsted, 10 October 1901, Burnham Collection, AIC; Jay J. Morrow to Burnham, 3 June 1907, Olmsted Papers, LC; Burnham to Col. John Biddle, 8 January 1906, Burnham Collection, AIC.

[58] Olmsted to Burnham, 5 November 1903 and 15 March 1904, Olmsted Papers, LC; *Senate Park Commission Report*, 30-1.

[59] McKim to Langdon, 21 December 1901, Moore Papers, LC. The squares on the north side of the monument section were elongated into short rectangles because the Mall's shifted central axis created a wider outer zone on the north side. Augustus Saint-Gaudens to Burnham, 29 May 1901, reproduced in Moore, *Burnham*, 146; "Parks in Washington," *Washington Post*, 22 July 1904.

[60] Mari Nakahara and Katsuhiro Kobayashi, "Analyses on Geometrical Composition of McKim, Mead & Whites's Architectural Works," *Memoirs of Faculty of Engineering, Tokyo Metropolitan University*, No. 45 (1995), 199-209.

[61] Moore, *Burnham*, I:170.

[62] Burnham to McKim, 30 August 1901, Burnham Collection, AIC, quoted in William A. Bogan, "The McMillan Plan for Washington, D.C.: European Influences

in the Origins and Development," undated research paper (ca. 1974) in the files of the Commission of Fine Arts. Bogan discovered the preliminary drawings in the McKim, Mead & White Papers, New York Historical Society, that form the basis of many arguments presented in this paper.

[63] *Senate Park Commission Report*, 47.

[64] Daniel H. Burnham, first draft, "Improvement of the Park System of the District of Columbia", Burnham Collection, AIC; hereafter Burnham draft. See Appendices.

[65] McKim to Moore, 18 November 1901, Moore Papers, LC

[66] *Ibid.*, 48; *Proceedings of the Thirty-Sixth Annual Convention of the American Institute of Architects* (1903), 58; *Senate Park Commission Report*, 27; Burnham to McKim, 30 August 1901, Burnham Collection, AIC, quoted in Bogan, *McMillan Plan*, 21; Schuyler, "Nation's New Capital," *New York Times*, 29 January 1902.

[67] Moore, *McKim,*197.

[68] Charles Moore Diary, 15 January 1902, University of Michigan Library.

[69] "Equestrian Path in the City," *Washington Post*, 4 January 1900.

[70] *Senate Park Commission Report*, 51.

[71] Dennis R. Montagna, "Henry Merwin Shrady's Ulysses S. Grant Memorial in Washington, D.C.: A Study in Iconography, Content and Patronage," Ph.D. diss. University of Delaware, 1987, 60-79. Root to McKim, 1 April 1902, NARA, RG 42, Records of the Grant Memorial Commission.

[72] McKim to Saint-Gaudens, 7 June 1901, quoted in Moore, *McKim,*186. About 5 June 1901, Burnham sent Olmsted a telegram suggesting that Saint-Gaudens join them at their meeting because "we are going to need him much." Burnham letter books, Burnham Collection, AIC.; Richard Guy Wilson, *McKim, Mead & White, Architects* (New York: Rizzoli, 1983),151.

[73] Burnham draft, Burnham Collection, AIC; See Appendices. Donald Beekman Myer, *Bridges and the City of Washington* (Washington: Commission of Fine Arts, 1974): 21. All of Bingham's 1900 plans for the Mall's future development are among the Senate Park Commission project files in the McKim, Mead & White Papers, New-York Historical Society. They are part of the *Report of the Chief of Engineers, U.S. Army, Public Buildings and Grounds*, 57th Cong., 1st sess., H. Exdoc. 1 (30 June 1901). "Legislation for Arch," *Washington Post*, 19 December 1901.

[74] Burnham draft, Burnham Collection, AIC; See Appendices

[75] Kathryn Fanning, "American Temples: Presidential Memorials of the American Renaissance," Ph.D. diss., University of Virginia, 1996, 53-62.

[76] Burnham to Root, 22 August 1901 and McKim to Root, 24 August 1901, Elihu Root Papers, Library of Congress, Manuscript Division; hereafter Root Papers, LC.

[77] *Washington Post*, 16 May 1886 (first quote); 13 & 19 February 1887; 18 October 1889; 13 July 1892; 13 December 1894; and 12 February 1896 (second quote). Joanna S. Zangrando, "Monumental Bridge Design in Washington, D.C., as a Reflection of American Culture, 1886 to 1932," Ph. D. diss., George Washington University, 1974, 20; hereafter Zangrando, "Monumental Bridge".

[78] *Washington Post*, 2 & 23 February, 4 March and 5 July, 1899; 11 April 1900. Zangrando, "Monumental Bridge,"124.

[79] *Washington Post*, 2 March 1901 (first quote), 18 November & 17 December 1900 (second quote), 24, 25 & 29 September and 10 October 1901; Zangrando, "Monumental Bridge," 268-70; George Keller, *The Proposed Memorial Bridge across the Potomac River at Washington, D.C., Designed by George Keller, Architect*, privately printed, 1900.

[80] Lewis L. Gould, *The Presidency of William McKinley* (Lawrence, Kansas: Regents Press of Kansas, 1980) 29,153-7; McKim to Burnham, 28 August 1901, Moore Papers, LC. On 6 April 1901, the members of both the Grant Memorial and Senate Park Commissions "visited the White Lot and adjacent points available for a site for the statue [to Ulysses S. Grant]. Upon reassembling, considerable discussion was had as to the advisability of erecting a statue on any of these sites. Various other points in the city were mentioned and discussed. No decision was made." *Minutes of the Grant Memorial Commission*, 8 April 1901, NARA, RG. 42, entry 344.

[81] *Annual Report of the Commission of Fine Arts* (Washington: GPO, 1912), 20. Moore, *Burnham*, II:133-4.

[82] "Site for the Grant [sic] Memorial," *Washington Post*, 23 March 1902; Zangrando, *Monumental Bridge*, 508; *Senate Park Commission Report*, 52; "Urge a City Beautiful," *Washington Post*, 30 March 1911; Moore, *McKim*, 61.

[83] John G. Nicholay and John Hay, *Abraham Lincoln, A History* (New York: The Century Company, 1917) X: 355-6; Theodore Roosevelt to John Hay, 22 July 1902, Library of Congress, Manuscript Division, John Hay Papers. See also Albert Bushnell Hart and Herbert Ronald Ferleger, eds. *Theodore Roosevelt Cyclopedia* (New York: Theodore Roosevelt Monument Association, 1941), 217, 313-3, 556, 637-9.

[84] McKim to Root, 11 January 1907, Col. Charles S. Bromwell to McKim, 8 March 1907, McKim to Casey, 11 March 1907, and McKim minority report to Grant Memorial Commission, 1 April 1907, Root Papers, LC.

[85] *Senate Park Commission Report*, 51-52.

[86] Quoted in Moore, *Burnham*, I:36. Christopher

Alexander Thomas, "The Lincoln Memorial and Its Architect, Henry Bacon (1866-1924)," Ph.D. diss., Yale University, 1990, 358. Thomas was the first scholar to connect McKim's Lincoln Memorial design with Saint-Gaudens's suggestion.

[87] Olmsted to Moore, 27 August 1901, Moore Papers, L.C.; Burnham to Olmsted, 9 September 1901, Burnham Collection, AIC.

[88] Olmsted to Langdon, 14 December 1901; Moore Papers, LC; McKim to Langdon, 18 December 1901, Moore Papers, LC; McKim to Burnham, 25 and 29 November 1901, MM&W Papers, NYHS.

[89] Burnham to Root, 22 August 1901, and McKim to Root, 24 August 1901, Root Papers, LC; Burnham draft, Burnham Collection, AIC, 16.

[90] Daniel Burnham, undated autograph note. Burnham Collection, AIC, Box 57, folder 25. William Seale, "Theodore Roosevelt's White House," *White House History* 11 (Summer 2002): 29-37; Tony P. Wrenn, "The 'Eye of Guardianship': President Theodore Roosevelt and the American Institute of Architects," *White House History* 11 (Summer 2002): 50-61.

[91] Burnham's printed diagram of the Mall, dated December 1901, did not include a plan of the pantheon. Olmsted Papers, L.C.

[92] *Senate Park Commission Report*, 50. McKim was probably the designer of this complex; his 1892-94 design for New York University's Bronx campus had a similar arrangement with a central rotunda on a terraced overlook flanked by rectangular Colonial Revival buildings. Leland M. Roth, *McKim, Mead & White Architects* (New York: Harper & Row, 1983),187; Sue A. Kohler, *The Commission of Fine Arts. A Brief History, 1910-1995* (Washington: Commission of Fine Arts, 1995), 69.

[93] "Plea for Dark Spots," *Washington Post*, 22 August 1901. "More Playgrounds Needed," *Washington Post*, 25 March 1902.

[94] McKim to Moore, 21 November 1901, Moore Papers, LC.

[95] *Senate Park Commission Report*, 41-2.

[96] Undated draft fragment in Moore's hand among the MM&W Papers, NYHS.

[97] *Mall Parkway Hearing*, 17.

[98] Burnham to Green, 10 August 1905, Olmsted Papers, LC.

[99] "Memoir of Charles Moore," Moore Papers, LC., typescript, 80.

Map showing the existing District of Columbia park system and the additions proposed by the Senate Park Commission. From D.H. Burnham and E. H Bennett, *Plan of Chicago*, Chicago, 1909 (For color version, see pl. IV)

Beyond the Mall:

THE SENATE PARK COMMISSION'S PLANS FOR WASHINGTON'S PARK SYSTEM

By Timothy Davis

 HE Senate Park Commission's proposals for the development of the nation's capital had an enormous impact on the evolution of twentieth-century Washington and significantly influenced city planning efforts throughout the United States. The history of the commission and its plan has generated considerable interest among scholars, planners, architects, and others concerned with the development of the national capital and the evolution of urban form in America. Most of this attention has focused narrowly on the revitalization of Washington's monumental core, however, leaving an important aspect of the Senate Park Commission's story largely untold. The Mall and its architectural accouterments generate study after study, but the commission's equally ambitious proposal for a system of parks, parkways, and playgrounds stretching throughout the metropolitan region has been relegated to obscurity as little more than an historical footnote (frontispiece).[1] This omission is both surprising and unfortunate. Equating the Senate Park Commission plan with its proposals for the monumental core and then presenting this abbreviated construct as a microcosm of City Beautiful-era civic improvement has led to serious misunderstandings, both of the plan itself and of the history of American city planning in general. Not only did the commission devote the greater part of its report to the articulation of a wide-ranging and diversified park system, but these proposals profoundly affected the development of twentieth-century Washington and continue to play a prominent role in shaping the city's image for residents and visitors alike.[2] A more inclusive reading of the commission's report reveals that the park system schemes were at least as significant as the more celebrated Mall proposals and suggests that these humble recreational spaces – and not the grandiose but idiosyncratic monumental core – are what link the Senate Park Commission most firmly to the mainstream of American planning history.

This essay has three goals. By retrieving the park system proposals from obscurity and describing them in the detail usually reserved for the monumental core it seeks to provide additional insights into the Senate Park Commission's plan that more accurately reflect the magnitude of its aspirations and the virtuosity of its execution. By tracing the origins of the park components in various local and national precedents it will underscore the plan's close relationship to contemporary planning efforts, demonstrating that it was not as radically innovative as subsequent commentators have claimed. The concluding section addresses the underlying factors that caused the Mall saga to overshadow the equally compelling park system story and dominate later analyses of the Senate Park Commission and its place in the history of American city planning. Reviewing the commission's efforts from this perspective will restore the park dimensions of the plan to their rightful prominence, while shedding light on the ways in which various intellectual, political, professional, and personal influences have colored interpretations of the Senate Park Commission's goals and achievements in the century since that august body presented its vision for the development of Washington as "a visible expression of the power and taste of the people of the United States."[3]

The commission was composed of Daniel Burnham, Charles McKim, Augustus Saint-Gaudens, and Frederick Law Olmsted, Jr., nationally recognized experts in the fields of architecture, sculpture, and landscape design. The commissioners prefaced their study with two general observations. The first was that the development of a suitable plan for the nation's capital was a "stupendous" undertaking that would take generations to realize and require constant vigilance to perfect and maintain. Second, the commission observed that its mission could be divided into two distinct but related tasks: the restoration of Pierre L'Enfant's vision for the monumental core and the development of a comprehensive park system for the broader metropolitan region. The commission itself acknowledged that L'Enfant's original plan made no provisions for such an expansive park system but insisted that the park proposals were essential because they answered "the need, not recognized a hundred years ago, for large parks to preserve artificially in our cities passages of rural or sylvan scenery and for spaces adapted to various forms of recreation."[4]

By the end of the nineteenth century, virtually every American city with cosmopolitan aspirations was intent on developing a broad-based park system comprised of urban parks and suburban reservations linked together by formal boulevards and informal parkways. Progressive cities such as Chicago and Boston were beginning to provide playgrounds and neighborhood recreation centers as well. These park systems answered a variety of practical, social, and symbolic needs and expressed the hopes and fears of a nation grappling with dramatic social changes.[5] Despite the purported allure of Jeffersonian agrarianism, the nation's cities were growing at a phenomenal rate. Since many Americans remained ambivalent about densely packed European-style urbanism, parks offered attractive means of ameliorating the oppressiveness of large-scale urban development. By affording urban residents opportunities to enjoy the physical and psychological benefits of nature close at hand, park systems extended the promise of a new form of metropolitan landscape that combined the best attributes of city and country. Park development produced more demonstrable public health benefits, as well, transforming noxious dumping grounds, disease-producing swamps, and polluted streams into wholesome recreational landscapes. Additionally— and this was a point that carried significant weight with elected officials and influential civic boosters— parks paid. Park promoters emphasized that park development converted underutilized "wastelands" into public amenities that enhanced surrounding real estate values, increased tax revenues, and elevated a city's prestige as a place of residence, commerce, tourism, and investment. An attractive and wide-ranging park system was seen as a mark of civic attainment that attested to a city's progress from frontier outpost or crass commercial center to mature metropolis. By the time the Senate Park Commission began its deliberations, the mania for park development had reached the point where professional designers were traveling around the country devising park systems for towns of all shapes and sizes while popular periodicals like *Atlantic Monthly* published effusive articles declaring park-making to be "A National Art."[6] If Boston, New York, Chicago and even more modest cities such as Minneapolis, Buffalo, and Kansas City could garner widespread acclaim for the beauty and vitality afforded by their parks and parkways, it was roundly agreed, the nation's capital surely deserved a park system that would answer the recreational demands of its citizens while serving as a shining example of American achievement in landscape design and civic improvement.[7]

Washington was not devoid of parks, by any means (fig. 1). L'Enfant included provisions for both formal and informal park development in his celebrated plan of 1791, distributing green spaces throughout the original city with an ingenious arrangement of boulevards, squares, circles, and triangles. The great American landscape designers Andrew Jackson Downing and Frederick Law Olmsted, Sr. lent their talents to the embellishment of the monumental core, devising romantic treatments for the Mall and Capitol grounds, respectively. The U.S. Army Corps of Engineers had been expanding and improving Washington's parklands since 1867. Among the engineers' most significant accomplishments was the transformation of the Potomac shoreline from a foul-smelling morass of swamps and mud flats into an impressive expanse of well-drained parklands, a process that resulted in the creation of West and East Potomac Parks, which easily doubled the area of centrally located land devoted to park purposes while eliminating a serious public health nuisance. Much of this newly created land lay undeveloped when the Senate Park Commission undertook its assignment and its imminent improvement was much anticipated. The other major building block of the contemplated park system was Rock Creek Park, a 1,600 acre expanse of woodland scenery in northwest Washington, set aside by Congress in 1890 to provide Washington with the grand

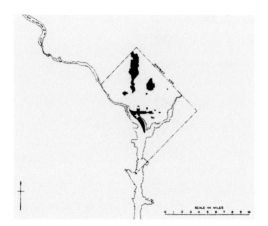 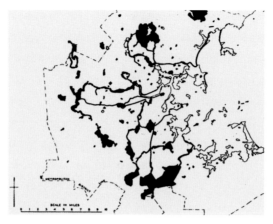 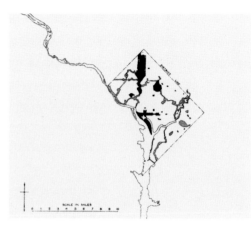

Fig. 1 Diagram of Washington park system, 1901. *Senate Park Commission Report*, Appendix F

Fig. 2 Diagram of Boston park system, 1901. *Senate Park Commission Report*, Appendix F

Fig. 3 Diagram of proposed Washington park system, 1901. *Senate Park Commission Report*, Appendix F

suburban pleasuring ground that had come to be considered an essential component of any well-developed metropolitan landscape.[8]

Late-nineteenth-century Washingtonians also enjoyed the benefits of a number of smaller parks and park-like areas maintained by various government agencies, private organizations, and generous individuals. The romantic cemetery movement had left its mark on the city in the form of Georgetown's picturesque Oak Hill Cemetery and the slightly more removed Rock Creek Cemetery, both of which lured visitors with their scenic beauty and manicured paths. The Soldiers Home, a 500-acre tract located in northwest Washington, also served as a de facto public park, its smooth drives and attractive gardens maintained by the retired veterans in residence. The Smithsonian's Zoological Park, located just south of Rock Creek Park, was one of Washington's most exquisitely configured picturesque landscapes, though, like Rock Creek Park, it was scarcely a decade old. Another relatively recent development was the free public bathing beach on the newly created Tidal Basin, which, though crudely equipped and poorly maintained, received heavy use from local residents desperate for relief from the summer heat.[9] Added to these organized parks and preserves was a diverse array of private and public lands that were used informally by excursionists in search of outdoor amusements. These included the valley of Rock Creek below the Zoo, a mixture of undisturbed forest and heavily polluted industrial zones and dumping grounds; the banks of the Potomac, especially in the area north of the city leading towards Great Falls; the falls themselves, long considered among the most impressive natural spectacles on the Eastern seaboard; Arlington Cemetery, which attracted visitors not just for its memorial associations but because the landscaped grounds afforded cooling shade and outstanding views of the nation's capital; and the string of old Civil War forts that surrounded the city, which combined romantic historical associations with pleasing prospects of Washington and its environs. Several old estates and private gardens also served as places of popular resort and were admirably suited for incorporation in a more formally protected and comprehensively developed park system.

While Washington possessed an assortment of individual parks and park-like areas, there was widespread agreement that the nation's capital lacked any semblance of a coordinated park system, or, for that matter, even the most basic provisions for getting from one park to another without encountering the dangers and disruptions of disorderly urban streets. These shortcomings were underscored in a series of diagrams the commission included in its report, which compared Washington's modest collection of isolated parks with the wide-ranging and well-coordinated park systems to be found in Boston (fig. 2), New York, Paris, and London.[10] A number of proposals were already afoot to remedy this situation, both by developing new parks in key areas and by constructing parkways and boulevards to link major parks and attractions. The U.S. Army Corps of Engineers and local citizens' groups had come up with various schemes — some of them quite detailed and sophisticated — for a wide array of projects ranging from the draining and improvement of the Anacostia marshes to the reclamation of lower Rock Creek Valley, the construction of a grand boulevard between Washington and Mount Vernon, the creation of a circular carriage drive linking the city's abandoned Civil War defenses, and the provision of parks and neighborhood playgrounds in the rapidly growing subdivisions that lay beyond the boundaries of L'Enfant's original plan.[11]

The challenge facing the Senate Park Commission was to survey Washington's potential park resources, scrutinize these pre-existing plans, and then employ its wide-ranging expertise in civic improvement to produce a unified and comprehensive park system that would consider both the practical needs of city residents and the additional demands afforded by Washington's unique role as the nation's capitol. The ultimate goal, the commission maintained, was to create "a modern park system" that would complement the neoclassical grandeur of the monumental core so that the two elements of the plan would together form "one great composition designed to comprehend the entire District of Columbia."[12] (fig. 3)

While all the commissioners participated in this effort, Frederick Law Olmsted, Jr. served as the primary author for the parts of the report that dealt primarily with park-related concerns. As the son of the country's most famous landscape architect, Olmsted was steeped in the tradition of American park planning. He had worked with his father on the landscape design for the Chicago World's Fair and gone on to serve as a consultant to park departments throughout the country. His close association with the Boston park system was considered particularly valuable, since the city's collection of parks, playgrounds, and parkways was widely hailed as the nation's finest. Olmsted delegated one of his firm's senior designers, James Langdon, to serve as onsite coordinator for the project. Langdon's experience with the Olmsted office dated back to Frederick Law Olmsted, Sr.'s work on Boston's renowned park system, where he was responsible for transforming the visionary landscape architect's visionary schemes into detailed plans. Langdon played a vital, if undersung, role in developing the Senate Park Commission's plan for Washington. When Olmsted was not personally in Washington, he stayed in close contact with Langdon, constantly requesting additional information and sending maps, drawings, and photographs down from Boston to aid in the plan's development.[13] Commission secretary Charles Moore also compiled a collection of existing and proposed plans, which Olmsted and his colleagues evaluated and appropriated where they saw fit. The Washington Board of Trade and the Army Corps of Engineers provided studies and proposals for the commission's benefit, as did the American Institute of Architects and a variety of local citizens' associations and prominent individuals.[14]

The Senate Park Commission's plan was not a combination of abstract schemes and pre-existing proposals, however. While none of the members actually lived in Washington, the commission made a concerted effort to explore the city and its environs, gaining an intimate familiarity with its topography, natural history, and social geography. This strong preparation and first-hand knowledge of local conditions enabled the commission to produce a plan that embodied the best principles of contemporary American park development. Following in the footsteps of such noted nineteenth-century park system planners as Frederick Law Olmsted, Sr. and Horace W. S. Cleveland, they called for a unified and comprehensive array of attractive landscapes and recreational amenities spreading throughout the city in a manner that reflected the diverse recreational needs and geographic features of the metropolitan region. What is particularly striking about the broader park plan, especially in light of the common criticism that City Beautiful-era planners tended to impose rigidly formal neoclassical compositions with little concern for local conditions, was the meticulous attention the commission paid to fitting its plan to the particularities of the site, displaying remarkable sensitivity to the natural attributes and recreational requirements of the Washington region.

One of the commission's most basic—and largely overlooked—conclusions was that environmental considerations, most notably Washington's oppressive summer heat, should play a dominant role in shaping the nature and distribution of parks and related features. Since Congress was in session well into the hottest portion of the summer and most of the city's residents had no means to escape to cooler climes at all, the commission declared that the "first and greatest step in the matter

Fig. 4 Basin of Latona, Versailles. *Senate Park Commission Report*, No. 177

of beautifying the District of Columbia" was to ameliorate the mental and physical strain engendered by Washington's notoriously unpleasant combination of heat and humidity. Outlying parks and parkways would contribute to this goal by offering shady groves and breezy hilltops, but much could be done to improve the quality of life in the central city. The commission called for a significant increase in the quality and quantity of fountains in the urban core, observing that Rome and other great cities had long recognized the value of such water features in mitigating the debilitating influence of harsh summer climates. Tying these concerns to the parallel mission of restoring L'Enfant's lost intentions, the commission pointed out that a similar appreciation for practical and aesthetic value of water features had informed the original plan for Washington, which included a diverse array of canals, fountains, pools, and water terraces. The commission illustrated this section of its report with over a dozen photographs of pools, fountains, and other water features in Rome, Versailles, Vaux-le-Vicomte and other notable settings (fig. 4 and pl. XII). Later interpreters of the *Senate Park Commission Report*

Fig. 5 View of the Washington Common and Public Playgrounds, showing proposed memorial buildings, baths, theater, gymnasium, and athletic buildings. *Senate Park Commission Report*, No. 54

tend to skip over these images, or focus on the broader settings as precedents for baroque grandeur envisioned for the Mall, but their frequency and prominent placement reveal the high priority the commission placed on this aspect of its plan. By casting these water features as environmental improvements and public health amenities rather than as gratuitous neoclassical allusions, the commission underscored both its under-appreciated environmental awareness and its commitment to improving the urban landscape through practical as well as aesthetic measures. Another aspect of these illustrations that has been habitually overlooked is that they are the most heavily populated images in the entire volume. In sharp contrast to the monumental emptiness of the monumental core renderings, they depict lively public places being enjoyed by a multitude of citizens.[15]

The commission's plans for transforming the Tidal Basin and its environs into a grand recreational center similarly reflected the desire to cater to the practical needs of local residents, even in the city's central symbolic spaces. Tentatively titled "The Washington Common" this area was intended to accommodate a wide variety of recreational practices (fig. 5). A "great stadium" designed in the reigning neoclassical idiom would provide an impressive venue for athletic events, patriotic celebrations, and fireworks displays. There would be ball fields, tennis courts, an open-air gymnasium, playgrounds for children, and spacious and well-equipped facilities for boating, wading, swimming, and skating.

Given Washington's insalubrious climate, these bathing facilities were described as "secondary in importance" only to the previously mentioned fountains. A detailed appendix addressed the ways in which other cities had provided public bathing facilities, paying particular attention to the Boston Metropolitan Park Commission's widely praised efforts at Revere Beach (fig. 6). The provision of public bathing opportunities was heralded as particularly desirable in the nation's capital, where few attractive natural opportunities existed due to the sluggishness of the local streams and the generally disagreeable character of the largely industrialized Potomac and Anacostia waterfronts. For better or worse, this ambitious recreational development was never constructed. The massive assemblage of buildings and ball fields, no matter how artistically arranged (the report's tentative scheme called for a massive neoclassical composition reminiscent of the Chicago World's Fair's Court of Honor), was incompatible with the increasingly ascendent vision of the monumental core as a symbolic space. Utilitarian structures catering to local recreational concerns had little or no place in the new order, either literally or figuratively. Modest bathing facilities remained at the Tidal Basin for a number of years, but the stadium, gymnasiums, tennis courts and other athletic facilities were relegated to less sacrosanct precincts. A flotilla of plastic paddle-boats and a series of informal softball fields provide a faint echo of this ambitiously conceived recreational amenity.[16]

Fig. 6 Revere Beach Public Bath House, near Boston. *Senate Park Commission Report*. No. 188

The commission was much more successful with its proposals for outlying parks and parkways. These schemes represented the heart, or perhaps more appropriately, the arms and legs, of the Senate Park Commission's plan, without which it would never have been able to pass legislative muster or fulfill its creators' ambitions as the *sine qua non* of American achievement in city planning and civic art. The commission acknowledged that the proposed park system might seem excessive given Washington's relatively small permanent population, but insisted that the city's status as the national capital merited a world-class park system that could be considered the pride of the nation as a whole. While many of Washington's outlying areas remained relatively untouched, the commission warned that the city's rapid growth threatened to defile these lands with unsightly development. "Whatever of natural beauty is to be preserved and whatever park spaces are still to be acquired must be provided for during the next few years," the commission's report admonished, "or it will be forever too late."[17]

The commission began its discussion of the broader park proposals with a number of general observations about Washington's geography. The District of Columbia was comprised of three basic sections, each of which afforded distinctive opportunities for park development. The northwest section, from Rock Creek to the Potomac, was characterized by abrupt hills and narrow valleys, the former providing impressive prospects and the latter offering intimate views of picturesque scenery. The center portion, from the highlands east of Rock Creek to the Anacostia River, could be further divided into a relatively flat inner section, where L'Enfant had located the original city, and an outer section, which, though somewhat hilly, was not as dramatically differentiated as the region west of Rock Creek. The third district, east of the Anacostia, consisted of a series of long, relatively flat ridges affording views of Washington and the surrounding area. The stream valleys that defined these basic regions of-

Fig. 7 **Typical treatment of Potomac Quay.** *Senate Park Commission Report*, No. 10

Fig. 8 Quays and Corso, Budapest. *Senate Park Commission Report*, No. 192

fered considerable potential for park and parkway development, but both were seriously degraded from decades of abuse and needed major aesthetic and environmental rehabilitation. The Potomac shoreline also posed considerable challenges. Though it clearly possessed tremendous potential as a scenic and recreational resource, most of the waterfront outside the newly created Potomac Parks was in private hands and subject to a variety of industrial and commercial indignities. Following this broad summary of the district's reigning characteristics, the commission focused on each section in turn, describing existing features in considerable detail and then outlining proposed treatments designed to maximize each area's scenic and recreational potential.[18]

The commission determined that the Potomac waterfront between West Potomac Park and Georgetown was in such compromised condition that there was no realistic prospect of transforming it into the sort of naturalistic landscape favored by contemporary park designers. The most reasonable approach for this area would be to accept its industrial status and devise a dignified means of securing passage from West Potomac Park to the mouth of Rock Creek. A broad granite quay would define and stabilize the shoreline while bringing order to the existing chaos of wharves and warehouses (fig. 7). Commercial and industrial enterprises could use the quay for their shipping operations while park patrons passed overhead on an elevated promenade wide enough to accommodate carriages and pedestrians in the shade of dignified rows of trees. Making virtue out of necessity, the commission maintained that waterfront shipping activity would "add to the interest of the parkway" and give it a uniquely European character reminiscent of similarly urbanized waterfronts Paris, Vienna, and Budapest (fig. 8). In typical American fashion, the commission insisted Washington would put its Old World predecessors to shame. If the situation warranted and additional funding became available, the quay and promenade scheme could be extended along the Georgetown waterfront, which was similarly blighted with industrial development.[19]

Fig. 9 Rock Creek, looking north from M Street Bridge. *Senate Park Commission Report*, No. 180

Fig. 10 Rock Creek, looking south from P Street. *Senate Park Commission Report*, No. 190

The valley of Rock Creek posed similar challenges, though it promised a more pleasing resolution from a traditional park development point of view. Early proposals for the creation of Rock Creek Park had envisioned preserving the creek valley from the Maryland border all the way down to Georgetown. By the time the park was created in 1890, however, political and economic concerns limited its southern extent to the boundary of the National Zoo, just north of Connecticut Avenue. Attractively wooded hillsides bordered the creek as far south as P Street, but from that point to the Potomac waterfront, the stream valley served as a combination dumping ground and industrial zone (figs. 9, 10). The Washington Board of Trade and Georgetown Citizens' Association had developed competing proposals to remedy the situation, and the Army Corps of Engineers made a study in 1893, but Rock Creek's fate was still very much up in the air when the Senate Park Commission undertook its investigation.[20]

Characterizing the lower valley as "unsightly to the verge of ugliness" the commission placed high priority on improving its condition. In addition to being an urban eyesore and public health menace, the degraded landscape of Rock Creek was a significant obstacle to the commission's goal of creating a unified park system. Since Rock Creek Valley afforded the best means of linking the two primary units of Washington's park system—Rock Creek Park and the monumental core—the commission insisted that the creation of an attractive parkway along the creek was essential to its broader program of linking the city's parks together in a comprehensive and unified system. The commission prepared a lengthy analysis of the available options, devoting more space in its official report to this topic than to more celebrated subjects such as the Mall, the Washington Monument grounds, or the Lincoln Memorial. Another indication of the importance the commission placed on this project was that the report's first two illustrations highlighted the "disagreeable" conditions that the proposed parkway would supplant with an attractive, sanitary, and economically beneficial civic space. As a vivid demonstration of the practical and aesthetic benefits of comprehensive city planning, no other aspect of the 1901 scheme better exemplified the Senate Park Commission's affinity with the mainstream tradition of American park development and civic improvement.[21]

The commission gave due consideration to both proposals, but its affinities clearly lay with Washington Board of Trade's "Open Valley" scheme (fig. 11). Under this alternative, unwanted industries and undesirable residents would be banished from the lower valley, which would be restored to a semblance of its original condition. This would require significant expenditures for excavation and landscaping, but the commission insisted that the end results would justify the initial costs. Not only would a picturesquely winding streamside parkway accord with contemporary preferences for naturalistic scenery, but the combination of a low-level parkway and judicious plantings would be most effective in screening out the sights and sounds of the surrounding city, so that excursionists could travel from one portion of the park system to the other in soothing sylvan surroundings. Locating the main parkway drive at the bottom of the valley would also minimize interference from cross-town traffic, which could be carried overhead on monumental bridges. The practical and aesthetic appeal of this approach was illustrated with a photograph of Boston's Riverway and the similarities between the two projects were detailed in the accompanying text.[22]

The commission acknowledged that the rival "Closed Valley" treatment might also produce a useful and dignified urban improvement, but raised a number of practical and aesthetic objections to this course of action (fig. 12). There were ample precedents for enclosing urban streams in this manner, and districts like Boston's Back Bay had demonstrated that grand formal boulevards could stimulate the development of handsome residential neighborhoods in areas that had earlier been dismissed as noxious wastelands, but the Senate Park Commission was not convinced that this section of Washington would develop in similar fashion. While the commission's report was conspicuously silent on race matters, the lower portion of Rock Creek valley was surrounded by poverty-stricken neighborhoods inhabited primarily by African-Americans. If this area failed to gentrify and the new parkway was surrounded by tenements and factories, the relatively shallow plantings of a formal boulevard would not provide anywhere near the protection afforded by a low-lying parkway lined by thick woodlands. The commissioners also questioned whether the federal government should be entering the real estate business in competition with private investors—an important

Fig. 11 "Open-valley" Plan for Rock Creek Parkway. *Senate Park Commission Report*, No. 11

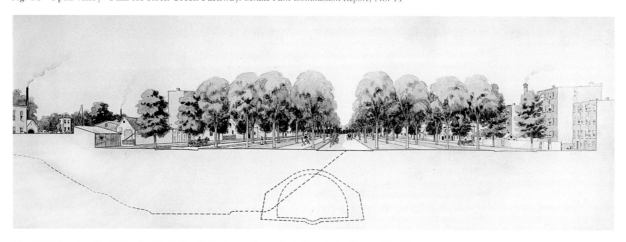

Fig. 12 "Closed-valley" Plan for Rock Creek Parkway. *Senate Park Commission Report*, No. 12

Fig. 13 Typical section of one of the Valley Parkways, such as Piney Branch, Soapstone Creek and Georgetown parkways. *Senate Park Commission Report*, No. 13

consideration given that the implementation of the commission's plan depended on the support of civic boosters and members of Congress, many of whom were heavily involved in local real estate speculation. Another drawback was that a boulevard-style development at street level would provide a less appealing park connection than a low-level parkway, since the inevitable intersections would pose dangers and disruptions for recreational carriage drivers, bicyclists, and pedestrians. After examining the situation in the field and weighing the arguments and financial estimates provided for both alternatives, the Senate Park Commission ruled in favor of the "Open Valley" plan, proclaiming it more desirable "on the grounds of economy, convenience, and beauty."[23]

The commission called for a number of other parkways to link the various elements of the District park system into a unified whole that could be enjoyed without recourse to ordinary city streets. Most of the proposed connections were informal parkways along the lines proposed for Rock Creek, but in situations where the surrounding character was predominantly urban, or where the terrain did not lend itself to naturalistic development, the commission advised that formal boulevards were preferable. In many cases, secondary formal boulevards would flank informally landscaped parkways, serving to delineate the edges and accommodate utilitarian traffic (fig.13). Generally speaking, the commission observed, the narrow stream valleys in the rugged highlands west of Rock Creek were ideally suited to informal parkway development, while the gentler, more developed terrain in the center of the district was more compatible with formal avenues and boulevards.

In the commission's grand plan, a "Georgetown Parkway" would leave Rock Creek Parkway just north of Oak Hill Cemetery and wend its way past the Naval Observatory and Georgetown College to the valley of Foundry Branch, following this stream to its mouth on the Potomac (see pl. IV). Georgetown Parkway would play an important role in the broader park system by connecting proposed parks along the upper Potomac with Rock Creek Park and the central and eastern districts. Along with providing connections between key parks, the Georgetown Parkway would preserve two attractive tracts of undeveloped land: the old estate grounds and adjacent broad ravine leading into Rock Creek Parkway that later became Montrose and Dumbarton Oaks parks, and the wooded valley of Foundry Branch, which was later preserved as part of Glover-Archbold Park. The intervening segments were never realized, though a narrow and abbreviated corridor known as Whitehaven Parkway preserved a rugged ridge and tributary stream valley.[24]

Further north, in the vicinity of Tenleytown, the commission identified the "narrow, well-timbered, and beautiful" valley formed by Soapstone Branch as an ideal location for an informal parkway providing access to Rock Creek Park from Connecticut Avenue. This parkway would also help preserve two small hills just west of Connecticut Avenue that afforded extended views of the

Fig. 14 View from the Terraces, St. Germain, Paris. *Senate Park Commission Report*, No. 72

Fig. 15 Fort Reno, view to the west. *Senate Park Commission Report*, opposite page 92

central city and the Washington Monument. At Yuma Street the parkway crested a distinct ridge, taking advantage of this change in topography to shift from informal to formal development. This transition would be highlighted by a terrace or concourse providing views east over Rock Creek Park and onward toward the Soldiers' Home. The main boulevard would lead directly to Tenley Circle while a short spur extended north to Fort Reno. The Yuma Street boulevard continued in a straight line for another 1000 feet, coming to a dramatic halt where the ground fell off sharply from the top of a narrow plateau. The outstanding scenic potential of this site would be maximized through the construction of a projecting concourse affording expansive vistas to the north and west. This more developed and formal landscape feature would provide a dignified destination and offer an appealing contrast to the informal scenery that dominated the northwestern portion of the park system. Because of its western orientation, the outlook would be an ideal location for enjoying sunsets. Combining this under-appreciated sensitivity for local topographical nuances with its more widely acknowledged reverence for European precedents, the commission illustrated the effect it hoped to achieve with photographs of the high terrace at the Villa d'Este in Tivoli and views from the terraces at St. Germain, Paris (fig. 14).[25]

A third lateral parkway would extend west from Rock Creek Park along the valley formed by Broad Branch. Like the Rock Creek and Soapstone Parkways, this elongated park would be informally developed, with a low-level carriage drive winding alongside the stream and formal border roads located higher up at the valley edges. The main drive would pass under Connecticut Avenue. A short spur would connect with this important arterial, providing access to the park system from the rapidly building suburb of Chevy Chase. Beyond Connecticut Avenue, the parkway would wind south and then west to the highlands occupied by Fort Reno. As the highest point in the District and a site with important historic associations, this summit would be protected with a substantial reservation to preserve the hallowed terrain and protect a panorama of scenic views (fig. 15). A short length of parkway would lead to Tenley Circle, serving as another strand in the web of interconnecting reservations that the Senate Park Commission was casting throughout the city's suburbs.[26]

The most ambitious proposal for park development west of Rock Creek called for a multi-tiered parkway extending along the Potomac waterfront from Georgetown to Great Falls. Based in part on New York's celebrated Riverside Drive, this "Potomac Drive" would afford a variety of means of accessing Great Falls and prevent developers from occupying the attractively wooded hillsides that loomed above the Potomac. The commission's report contained an elaborate description of the proposed parkway along with two small renderings portraying "typical sections" for the regions above and below Chain Bridge (figs. 16, 17). At the top of the bluffs, a relatively formal border road would accommodate general traffic and provide a clear demarcation for housing frontage, ensuring that development on adjacent private land would face the parkway in an attractive and dignified

Fig. 16 Typical Section of Potomac Drive, a short distance above Aqueduct Bridge. *Senate Park Commission Report*, No. 14

Fig. 17 Typical Section of Potomac Drive, below the Chain Bridge. *Senate Park Commission Report*, No. 16

manner. A trolley line would run at a slightly lower level, offering a convenient means of reaching the cataracts and cooling groves of the upper Potomac. The primary carriage drive would occupy the most advantageous location, carefully fitted into the hillside to present an appealing mixture of expansive views and intimate woodland scenery. At the base of the escarpment, the historic Chesapeake and Ohio Canal formed a picturesque complement to the natural scenery while affording opportunities for boating, both in private canoes and aboard the traditional canal boats that plied the economically moribund waterway. Recognizing that the canal's commercial prospects were bleak, the commission urged its preservation as a scenic, historic, and recreational resource. The commission's concern for maintaining the canal's "primitive character" and ensuring that future generations would be able to enjoy "the slow, old-fashioned movement of the boats and of the people on this ancient waterway" revealed the nascent historic preservation ethic that found more explicit expression in the drive to protect the ring of Civil War forts surrounding the city.[27]

The commission made a strong plea for the creation of an official national park to protect Great Falls and the surrounding woodlands, insisting that the natural beauties of this area compared favorably with anything to be found in the American West (fig.18). While Great Falls and the more spectacular portions of the Potomac escarpment lay beyond the District's borders—and were thus technically outside the commission's mandate—the commission insisted that the stakes were so high and the potential benefits so great that artificial political boundaries should no be

Fig. 18 The Great Falls of the Potomac. *Senate Park Commission Report, No. 197*

allowed to prevent their incorporation in the park system. Since Great Falls and the upper Potomac had long served as de facto public parks for visitors to Washington and residents alike, it was time to devote the government's resources to ensuring that these treasured landscapes would be protected in perpetuity and developed to their full recreational potential.[28]

Similar logic propelled the commission to comment on the desirability of connecting Washington and Mount Vernon with "an agreeable and dignified approach." In addition to accommodating the ever-increasing stream of tourists flocking to the historic site, a grand boulevard or parkway extending from Washington to Mount Vernon would offer impressive views of the lower Potomac region. The commission embraced the general outlines of the U.S. Army Corps of Engineers' 1890 report on potential routes and design treatments. Olmsted personally inspected the various alignments suggested by the engineers and endorsed a route that carried the roadway along the chain of ridges from Arlington Cemetery to Mount Vernon. With a few modifications, he declared, this arrangement could be developed into "the most refreshing and delightful drive to be had in any direction from the Washington and not to be equaled at any great capital in the world." The commission urged the acquisition of this alignment as soon as possible to secure it at a reasonable price before the Virginia suburbs developed further.[29]

Rounding out its recommendations for the region west of Rock Creek, the commission called for the creation of a series of smaller reservations to protect the sites of Civil War era fortifications such as Battery Parrot, Fort Kemble, and Battery Vermont. These historically significant sites were ideally suited for park development, since they occupied commanding heights that afforded impressive views and had generally escaped the development pressures that were rapidly transforming the city's environs. The report also recommended taking advantage of park-like features that had been preserved for unrelated purposes, such as the grounds of the receiving reservoir for Washington's water system, which straddled the Maryland line at the western edge of the District. This heavily wooded 281-acre site could easily be adapted to park purposes. While Arlington Cemetery also lay beyond the commission's geographic mandate, the report praised its value as a soothing and reflective landscape and decried the impact of recent trends in funerary art, which had compromised the burial ground's "harmonious and sober" appearance through the introduction of eclectic and pretentious monuments. The fate of the marshy island nearby, then known as Analostan Island, was also discussed. Since the island was still in private hands, the commission urged its acquisition to ensure the protection of this "important and beautiful part of all the views over the Potomac." The commission believed the swampy tract could be acquired at minimal cost, making it "a very desirable and inexpensive addition to the park system."[30]

Fig. 19 Beach Drive, Rock Creek Park. Vintage postcard, author's collection

The major existing reservations such as Rock Creek Park and the National Zoo were briefly discussed with an eye toward defining their roles within the framework of the broad park system. Minor additions were recommended to round out the borders of both properties and appropriate development strategies were suggested. The commission advised that any new structures or landscape features in the Zoo should follow the picturesque design strategy established by Frederick Law Olmsted, Sr., despite the growing preference for neoclassical public buildings. Construction in Rock Creek Park should be kept to an absolute minimum, pending the development of "a systematic plan prepared by landscape architects."[31] This stipulation reflected misgivings about the capabilities of the park's current custodians, the Army Corps of Engineers. Under the leadership of Captain Lansing Beach, the corps was in the process of building a road alongside Rock Creek (fig. 19). While the commission acknowledged that it was imperative to make the park more accessible to the general public, and allowed that portions of the new roadway were "very skillfully laid out," it complained that several sections of the drive had "appreciably injured the scenery." Future road construction should be very carefully considered, the commission warned, with serious thought given separating the main park drive from the creek itself. Locating the roadway along the

Fig. 20 Section of proposed Savannah Parkway. *Senate Park Commission Report*, No. 17

hillsides above the creek would require additional grading and tree-cutting and be significantly more expensive, but it would prevent further damage to the park's most precious scenic resources.[32]

Shifting its attention to the region east of Rock Creek Park, the commission sung the praises of the Soldiers' Home grounds as a place of popular resort. The commission declared the construction of a substantial parkway between Rock Creek Park and the Soldiers' Home to be "of the utmost importance" as a means of "bringing into organic relation two of the largest and most beautiful places of recreation" in the city. This transition would be accomplished in two stages reflecting the varied characteristics of the intervening scenery. A picturesque parkway would follow the course of Piney Branch, which the report described as "one of the most charming passages of natural valley scenery in the District." This informal parkway would terminate at the grounds of the municipal hospital, where a formal plaza would effect the transition to a more traditional boulevard following the existing alignment of Savannah Street to the Soldiers' Home. The commission provided a plan and hypothetical section for the "Savannah Parkway," which would be 200-feet wide and comprised of a central pleasure drive and flanking border roads shaded by six rows of regularly spaced trees (fig. 20).[33]

On the east side of the Soldiers' Home a series of short parkway segments would connect smaller reservations and provide a continuous link to the substantial recreational developments the commission intended to establish on the Anacostia River. Eckington Parkway would traverse the region between the Soldiers' Home and Gallaudet University, answering local residents' demands for additional recreational facilities. Leading south and east from the Soldiers' Home, it would preserve a "charmingly wooded" valley that was threatened with encroaching development. The first half-mile or so would be informally landscaped, taking advantage of terrain the commission praised for its "natural park-like effect." Where the natural topography became less characterful, the parkway would adopt a more formal mien.[34]

Just west of the grounds of Gallaudet University, the proposed parkway entered an attractive property known as the Patterson estate, which was centered on a prominent rise affording views east toward the Anacostia and south toward the Capitol dome. The estate's rolling hills, shady groves, and picturesque plantings prompted the commission to declare that there was "no better example in the whole District of the 'park-like' type of landscape." The lower part of the property consisted of more level terrain ideally suited to the development of recreational facilities, which the commission declared to be "of the utmost value to the future population of the surrounding region." The existing mansion could be converted into a facility for selling refreshments and staging various activities and amusements. A potential drawback to this plan lay in the fact that Congress had authorized the Baltimore & Ohio Railroad to relocate its lines across the property. The commission expressed confidence that this incompatible development could be accommodated with a tunnel located well below the surface of the park. The proposed extension of New York Avenue also posed problems, since this thoroughfare would run directly through the top third of the park. Again, the commission maintained the threat could be ameliorated, in this case with a sunken roadway reminiscent of the transverse roads that carried cross-town traffic unobtrusively through Central Park. Unfortunately, the construction of these transportation facilities seriously compromised the site. The lower portion was eventually put to use as athletic fields for a local school, but the picturesque hilltop was carved into an unsightly array of transportation facilities and maintenance yards. The only trace of the commission's vision for this prime location is a small amount of greensward and double row of paltry plantings flanking a fragment of curvilinear roadway generously titled Brentwood Parkway.[35]

Proceeding east through undistinguished terrain, a formal parkway would curve around the north edge of Mount Olivet Cemetery to Mount Hamilton, the next major reservation in the commission's sprawling park system. Mount Hamilton was a steep, heavily wooded promontory that stood out as one of the highest summits between Rock Creek and the Anacostia. In addition to offering sweeping views in every direction, it formed a highly visible landmark from many locations in the eastern half of the city. The commission believed it was imperative to protect the peak's wild, undeveloped character as an example of the typical mountain scenery that had largely disappeared from the region. To this end, improvements would be limited to paths and minimal conveniences, with a single driveway providing access to the summit. A white marble pavilion would be erected at the apex, to provide shelter and "accentuate the peak as seen from a distance."[36]

Another short stretch of informal parkway would provide the final link to the proposed Anacostia water park. Of all the planned improvements to the city's park system, the rehabilitation of the Anacostia River and its surroundings posed the greatest challenges. This shallow freshwater estuary was barely tolerable at high tide, when rising waters flooded acres of marsh and low-lying meadows, rendering a large amount of potentially valuable land useless for recreational or productive purposes. When the waters receded, they exposed vast expanses of reeking mud flats and rotting vegetation. The unpleasant odor and threat of malaria and similar diseases permeated the area, making life miserable for the region's poor inhabitants and for the workers and residents of the government installations located nearby. Congress had already authorized numerous studies to ameliorate the problem. The commission availed itself of the Army Corps of Engineers 1898 report, which called for a comprehensive program of draining and filling to create a deeper watercourse surrounded by dry and solid land. Under the engineers' plan, a considerable portion of the shoreline along the lower portion of the river would be devoted to commercial purposes. The commission acquiesced to this treatment but proposed that a series of quays and viaducts be built to allow recreational passage through the area in the same manner proposed for the Potomac waterfront. At the height of commercial navigation, a low dam would eliminate tidal deviations so that a consistent shoreline could be established. This would be stabilized by a retaining wall, which would be raised and clearly visible in the engineers' proposal or more subtle and naturalistic in the park commission's formulation. Dredging would create a clear channel that would widen into a diversified array of lakes and

basins that could be used for informal boating and organized regattas. Draining and stabilizing the surrounding meadows and tidal flats would create significant areas devoted to recreational facilities and landscaped park-land. Paths and drive would provide complementary circulation networks. Boat houses, bath houses, and shelters would cater to the seasonally varying needs of

Fig. 21 Henley – A suggestion of Anacostia Park. *Senate Park Commission Report*, page 109

Fig. 22 Potomac Park. *Senate Park Commission Report,* No. 194

local residents. The commission's report included photographs of well-dressed boaters and spectators at Henley and Oxford to illustrate the sort of riverine landscapes and recreational practices it hoped to foster (fig. 21).[37]

The commission devoted considerable thought to the development of East Potomac Park (fig. 22). This area had already been reclaimed from the tidal flats of the Potomac, though filling continued to raise the island's surface further above the tide level. Rows of poplars and willows had been planted along the edge of the island to shelter recreationists and stabilize the shoreline by binding the soil together. The commission approved of this arrangement but maintained that the bulk of the island should remain informally developed to resemble the open meadow landscapes of natural river bottoms. The fringe of trees would frame these broad clearings and afford welcome shade without obstructing the cooling breezes off the river—another example of the commission's efforts to harmonize aesthetic and environmental factors. A carriage drive bordered by pedestrian paths would circle the island's perimeter but additional roads would be kept to a minimum to maintain a predominantly naturalistic appearance. The inherent appeal of this simple informal landscape would be heightened, the commission observed, by the pointed contrast it presented to the "strongly formal and elaborate scheme of the central group." The commission also considered the idea of using East Potomac Park as the location for a new national arboretum, maintaining that a great variety of trees and shrubs could be planted along the east side of the park without detracting from the desired naturalistic effect.[38]

The gently rolling hillsides east of the Anacostia afforded numerous opportunities for the park commission to further its goal of spreading recreational facilities throughout the city. The most substantial of the eastern parks would be a large reservation occupying a large portion of the hillside on either side of the line of Massachusetts Avenue. The commission asserted that this area was "so admirably adapted" to park development that it should not be lost residential construction, but only a modest area north of Massachusetts Avenue was protected from development, in association with the preservation of Fort Dupont. The commission also called for the creation of several minor parkways along the steep and narrow drainages of the Anacostia highlands. Stickfoot Creek Parkway would follow the tributary of this name through the grounds of St. Elizabeth's and then proceed down to the Anacostia bridge. Giesboro Parkway would wind along the ridge from St. Elizabeth's to Bald Eagle Point, preserving a notable grove of beautiful oaks, protecting the hillside below from development, and presenting sweeping views of the confluence of the Anacostia and the Potomac, along with the parks, monuments, and public buildings beyond.[39]

This primary ring of parks and parkways was to be loosely paralleled by an outer circuit linking the Civil War fort sites that occupied prominent hill crests in the northern and eastern parts of the city. Fort Drive exemplified the dual concerns for scenery and historic preservation that played an under-appreciated role in turn-of-the-century park-making efforts. The principle forts included in this proposal, listed in clockwise progression from Rock Creek Park, were Fort Steven, Fort Totten, Fort Slemmer, Fort Bunker Hill, Fort Thayer, Fort Chaplin, Fort Sedgwick, Fort Dupont, Fort Davis, Fort Baker, Battery Ricketts, Fort Stanton, and, further down along the proposed Giesboro Parkway, forts Carrol and Greble. The commission realized it would be unrealistic to acquire and develop the broad leafy corridors allotted to the major parkways, but suggested the drive be wider and more attractively landscaped than ordinary city streets. Though not as elaborately developed as the primary parks and parkways, and occupying considerably less ground, Fort Drive would afford a delightful suburban excursion of considerable scenic and historic interest.[40]

While this impressive system of outlying parks and parkways would clearly vault Washington into the front ranks of American park system development, the commission realized its job would not be complete unless it also provided smaller neighborhood parks and playgrounds to accommodate the recreational needs of citizens who lacked the time and means to make excursions to outlying parks. L'Enfant had equipped the inner city with a well-dispersed array of minor parks and reservations, but the commission believed these could be improved to greater practical benefit. During the late-nineteenth century, the city's squares and circles had been ornamented with an eclectic variety of sculptural and horticultural decoration. The commission applauded the commemorative sentiment that informed much of the sculptural display and acknowledged that the tidy lawns and colorful plantings added to the city's "cheerful and comfortable character." Sounding more like twentieth-century functionalists than nineteenth-century aesthetes, however, the commission called for additional development aimed at "giving each area a more distinct individuality" and "providing for more special forms of recreation chosen with a view to the surroundings and capabilities of each particular area." More people would be encouraged to use the city's parks,

Fig. 23 Wading Pool, Riverside Park, Hartford, Connecticut. *Senate Park Commission Report*, No. 193

Fig. 24 The Girl's Gymnasium, Charles Bank, Boston. *Senate Park Commission Report*, No. 201

the commissioners advised, if they could enjoy them as vibrant social spaces rather than as sterile aesthetic displays or stern patriotic sermons. Bandstands, water features, illuminated fountains, fireworks displays, and more diversified horticultural treatments were proposed as means of luring residents into the city's parks, to their moral, physical, and mental benefit.[41]

In addition to building facilities for social amusements within existing parks, the commission called for a concerted effort to provide playgrounds for every area of the city. Individualized play-grounds, or at least discrete areas within the same playground should be devoted to specific ages or activities. Facilities for young children might include sand boxes, swings, seesaws, and wading pools. Older children and adults would benefit from gymnastic apparatus, running tracks, ball courts, and playing fields. The commission declined to specify design schemes or locations for these facilities. Contrary to the stereotype of City Beautiful planners as autocratic aesthetes, the commissioners advised that it would be best to leave such decisions to local officials who were better equipped to respond to the practical needs of particular neighborhoods. A number of local citizens' groups had already been agitating for playground development. Several of these organizations contributed pleas for neighborhood recreational facilities to the compendium of local park proposals assembled by Charles Moore to assist the commission in it deliberations.[42] Underscoring the manner in which the Senate Park Commission reflected broader trends and drew on a wide variety of contemporary precedents, this section of the report was illustrated with photographs of playgrounds, outdoor gymnasiums, and wading pools in Boston and Hartford (figs. 23, 24). An illustration of an open-air restaurant in Vienna's Prater reflected Harvard President Charles W. Eliot's advice that the best way to encourage sedentary American's to adopt the "outdoor habit" was to equip parks with European-style beer gardens. Eliot also suggested the construction more and better roads would further increase the popularity of parks and parkways by catering to the popularity of recreational carriage driving.[43]

While the commission believed that local playground development should be left to the discretion of neighborhood groups, it called for a centralized authority to ensure that its broader park system proposals would be fulfilled in a comprehensive, unified, and professional manner. Without a permanent park authority, the commission feared, its ambitious schemes might never be realized. Since the proposed parklands were spread throughout the metropolitan region among various official jurisdictions, important elements of the overall plan might fall by the wayside, or be poorly executed due to economic limitations, political pressures, or professional incompetence. Time was also of the essence. The longer it took to act on the Park Commission's proposals, the more difficult it would be to achieve its goals. Real estate prices would inevitably rise, development would encroach on coveted private lands, and changing circumstances would introduce additional complications and produce new priorities that would compete for limited funds, political capital, and open space.[44]

The Senate Park Commission's concerns were well-placed. It would take two decades for Congress to authorize a centralized park development authority and much longer than that for many of its proposals to be realized. Remarkably, however, the broader outlines of the commission's comprehensive park program were largely completed (fig. 25). The process was not easy and success was by no means guaranteed, but committed park supporters worked diligently with various commissions and government agencies to fulfill a large portion of the comprehensive plan. The Commission of Fine Arts played a crucial role following it establishment in 1910, with Olmsted taking a particularly active part as the first commissioner for landscape architecture. The Commission of Fine Arts's attention was divided among many concerns, however, and the focus of key members and staff was directed more toward the Mall and related public building issues.[45] It was not until 1924, with the establishment of the National Capital Park Commission, that a centralized authority undertook the oversight of Washington park development as its principal task. Strengthened and renamed the National Capital Park and Planning Commission (NCPPC) in 1926, this board was charged with overseeing the development and refinement of the city's comprehensive park plan. Importantly, it was also authorized to acquire and develop lands in related areas of Maryland and Virginia, providing a legal basis to further the Senate Park Commission's more wide-ranging agendas. The NCPPC produced a succession of general plans for the Washington region that were strongly influenced by the Senate Park Commission's proposals, though various details were altered to adapt to changing circumstances. Olmsted instilled a strong sense of continuity by serving on the initial iteration of

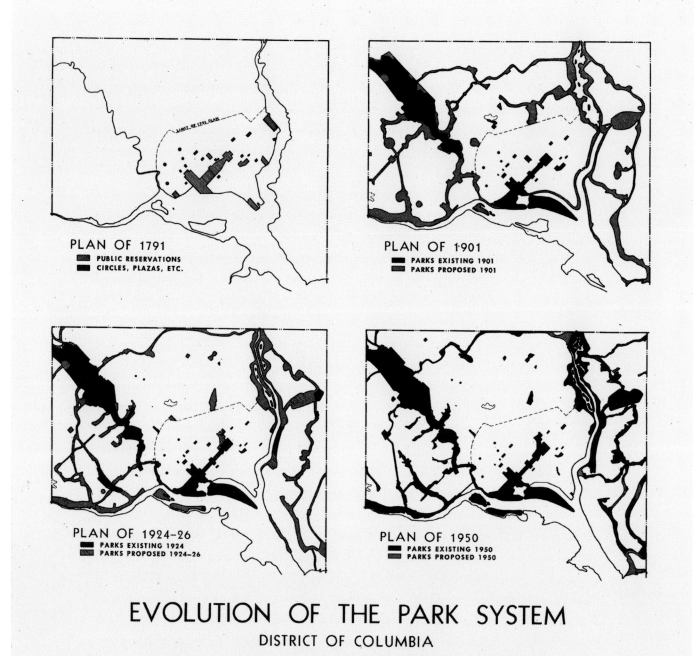

PLAN OF 1791
■ PUBLIC RESERVATIONS
■ CIRCLES, PLAZAS, ETC.

PLAN OF 1·901
■ PARKS EXISTING 1901
▨ PARKS PROPOSED 1901

PLAN OF 1924–26
■ PARKS EXISTING 1924
▨ PARKS PROPOSED 1924–26

PLAN OF 1950
■ PARKS EXISTING 1950
▨ PARKS PROPOSED 1950

EVOLUTION OF THE PARK SYSTEM
DISTRICT OF COLUMBIA
SHOWING MAJOR PARKS, PARKWAYS, AND OTHER PUBLIC AREAS USED AS PARKS
NATIONAL CAPITAL PARK AND PLANNING COMMISSION

Fig. 25 Evolution of the Park System of the District of Columbia. *Washington Present and Future*, National Capital Park and Planning Commission, 1950; Map 22

this body as well. A key achievement of the NCPPC and its supporters was the 1930 Capper-Cramton Act, which finally provided significant funds to support Washington park improvements and realize the broader metropolitan dimensions of the Senate Park Commission's plan.[46]

Even after the creation of the NCPPC, individual projects were generally attended to by the government agencies that owned the relevant land, often in conjunction with various special commissions and consultants. One such commission was appointed in 1913 to oversee the development of Rock Creek and Potomac Parkway, a lengthy process that was eventually completed through the infusion of Depression-relief funds in the 1930s.[47] Most federal lands in the District remained under jurisdiction of the Army Corps of Engineers, which did an admirable job of overseeing projects until the National Park Service took over Washington-area parks in 1933. The George Washington Bicentennial Commission engaged the U.S. Bureau of Public Roads (BPR) to construct the Mount Vernon Memorial Highway between 1928 and 1932. This project fulfilled most of the goals associated with the proposed boulevard to Mount Vernon, though the location and design evolved considerably to accommodate automobile traffic and other changing concerns.

From the 1930s to the 1960s, the BPR and its successor agencies, the Public Roads Administration and the Federal Highway Administration, worked closely with the NCPPC and the National Park Service to extend this project along both sides of the Potomac River. The resulting George Washington Memorial Parkway largely realized the Senate Park Commission's goal of preserving the banks of the Potomac between Washington and Great Falls.[48] Just as the commission had hoped, both Great Falls and the Chesapeake & Ohio Canal were granted national park status. While the proposed Georgetown Parkway was never completed, the creation of Glover-Archbold Park preserved a much larger portion of the Foundry Branch watershed than the commission had envisioned. Not all of the minor parkways west of Rock Creek park were developed as planned, but many of the smaller stream valleys identified in the original plan were protected. The NCPPC worked with its counterpart, the Maryland National Capital Park & Planning Commission to extend the Senate Park Commission's policy of informal parkway development to preserve the remainder of Rock Creek north of the District line and protect Sligo Creek and other picturesque stream valleys in suburban Montgomery County. Other regional parks and parkways were gradually developed by the National Park Service, the surrounding counties, and the states of Maryland and Virginia (fig. 26).

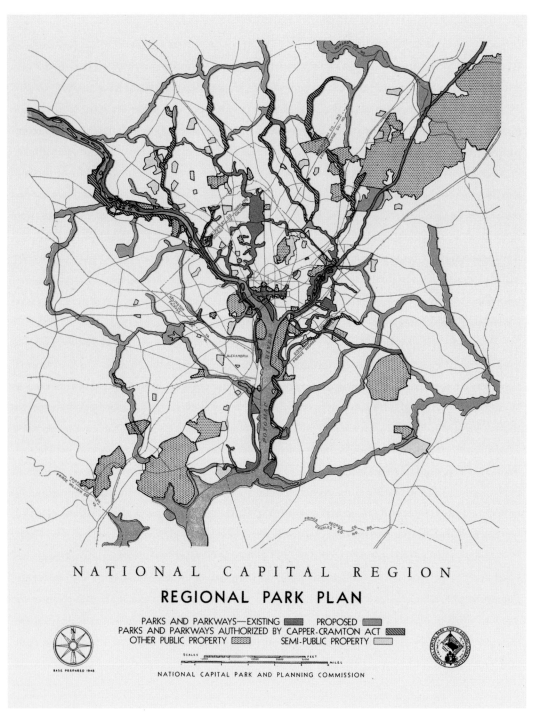

NATIONAL CAPITAL REGION

REGIONAL PARK PLAN

PARKS AND PARKWAYS—EXISTING ▨ PROPOSED ▨
PARKS AND PARKWAYS AUTHORIZED BY CAPPER-CRAMTON ACT ▨
OTHER PUBLIC PROPERTY ▨ SEMI-PUBLIC PROPERTY ▨

NATIONAL CAPITAL PARK AND PLANNING COMMISSION

Fig. 26 Regional Park Plan, 1950. *Washington Present and Future,* National Capital Park and Planning Commission, Washington, 1950; Map 17

The story east of Rock Park was less sanguine, reflecting both the less compelling nature of the existing terrain and the unfortunate history of racial and economic discrimination in the provision of public amenities, both in Washington and the nation as a whole. Piney Branch Parkway was developed more or less as planned, but the proposed parkway stretching all the way to the Anacostia foundered as a result of competing developments, the fading appeal of formal boulevards, and a reluctance to commit resources to this economically deprived, politically weak, and increasingly African-American portion of the city.[49] While crucial connecting parkways remained unbuilt and the recreational potential of the Patterson tract was squandered, Mount Hamilton escaped development through its incorporation in the expansive National Arboretum—an attractive solution that had not figured in the commission's original deliberations. Traces of the commission's plans for parkways east of the Anacostia can be found in Suitland Parkway and the Anacostia Freeway, but these cursorily landscaped roadways received a fraction of the funding and attention lavished on recreational developments west of Rock Creek Park and along the Potomac River.

The most egregious example of the disparate allocation of park resources and the most dramatic deviation from the Senate Park Commission's comprehensive plan was the failure to transform the neglected and polluted Anacostia River into the clean, safe, and appealingly diversified recreational environment extolled in the original report. Revitalizing the Anacostia waterfront remains the single greatest challenge facing Washington park planners. The National Capital Planning Commission has recognized this failing and cast the improvement of the Anacostia and its environs as one of the top priorities of its Legacy Plan, a highly self-conscious attempt to extend the Senate Park Commission's goals and methods into the 21st Century (fig. 27).[50] The National Park Service, meanwhile, has more quietly undertaken the task of breathing new life into another unfinished aspect of the Senate Park Commission's vision by resuming studies that may some day lead to the completion of the long-delayed dream of a circumferential greenway linking the remains of the city's Civil War forts.

While the Senate Park Commission's plans were not completely fulfilled, the underlying goal of providing Washington with a unified and comprehensive park system was achieved in admirable fashion (fig 28). The park system of the nation's capital is the equal of any in the country, exceeding many larger metropolises in the acreage devoted to public use and the diversity and scenic quality of its recreational resources. Few cities in the world can boast a comparable array of preserved natural landscapes, artistically ornamented parks, and broadly distributed facilities for active outdoor recreation. As an example of the practical and aesthetic possibilities of comprehensive city planning, Washington's park system epitomized the City Beautiful movement's faith in the ability of carefully coordinated civic improvements to elevate the social, economic, and aesthetic qualities of American urban life.

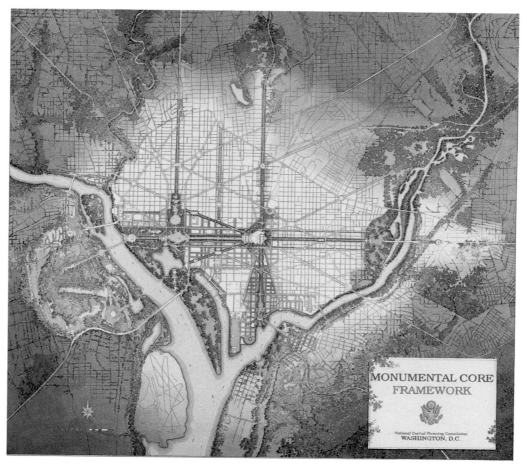

Anacostia Waterfront

Kennedy Center, River Entrance

Fig. 27 *Extending the Legacy*, National Capital Planning Commission, Washington, 1997

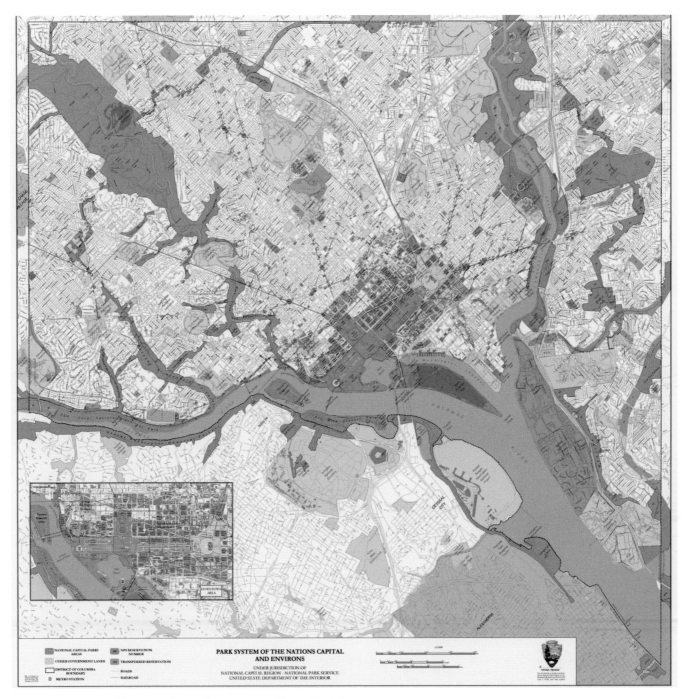

Fig. 28 Park System of the National Capital Region, 2001. National Park Service

Given its widely acknowledged success and the emulation it spurred on the part of cities throughout the country, it is surprising that the park system component of the Senate Park Commission's plan would be so thoroughly overshadowed by the development of the Mall and its environs, which offered a compelling and triumphant tale but had far less relevance to the development of ordinary American cities. A number of practical, biographical, and historiographical factors have contributed to this trend. They range from the visual imagery used to promote the proposals, to the politics of the plan's inception and realization, to the professional affiliations and intellectual predispositions of the principle chroniclers of American planning history. The location, physical characteristics, and intended audiences of the two components of the plan also contributed to the Mall's preeminence in the historical record.

The most fundamental reason for the Mall's ascendance is that the monumental core is clearly one of the world's most visually striking and symbolically powerful civic spaces, while the outlying park system is difficult to appreciate as an impressive artistic accomplishment and profound cultural statement in its own right. The disparity between these two visions was not always so distinct, however. While park systems are now taken for granted as integral components of urban life, anyone familiar with the unhealthy and unattractive appearance of most American cities and significant portions of the nation's capital would have appreciated the ambitious scope of the commission's proposals. Changing cultural concerns have also contributed to the park component's fall from prominence. The ideological implications of the American park movement may no longer be as apparent as the grandiose symbolism that characterizes the monumental core, but contemporary viewers understood that the creation of a broad-ranging park system represented an equally sincere and sophisticated attempt to shape, express, and uphold American values. Parks were prized as democratic and emphatically American institutions, where the beneficent influence of nature would uplift the spirits of over-stressed urbanites while the informal interaction in safely structured surroundings would remind everyone of their mutual interdependence as members of the same body politic. Modern audiences may no longer view parks as politically charged or uniquely American landscapes, but nineteenth-century sophisticates considered parks to be quintessential embodiments of the national culture, as emblematic of American values as Doric temples were to ancient Greece or cathedrals were to medieval France.[51]

The persistent emphasis on the monumental core can also be ascribed to the strengths and limitations of the available visual representations. The commission's proposals for the Mall, monuments, and surrounding buildings were strikingly rendered in a compelling series of lavishly colored illustrations that received considerable exposure through publication in the *National Geographic* and other prominent venues. Daniel Burnham's famous dictum about the efficacy of grandiose plans was clearly reflected in these commanding visions. The dark, diminutive parkway sections, in contrast, possessed little of the requisite "magic to stir men's blood." Basic geographical realities also contributed to the Mall's dominance. The outlying parks and parkways were literally marginalized in the few prominent images in which they figured, appearing as vague green spaces at the fringes of the boldly delineated monumental core. The same is true of the famous models, where the waterfront section of Rock Creek Parkway is the only park element depicted. Though the park drawings bore a greater resemblance to the executed designs, the images themselves have largely faded from historical consciousness. The Mall and memorial images are often reproduced, but it requires a trip back to the original report to uncover the tiny sections, dry diagrams, and prosaic photographs that illustrated the park proposals.[52] Subsequent iterations of the Washington plan perpetuated this disparity, with the monumental core appearing in charismatic renderings and the broader park system relegated to technical diagrams and lackluster land-use maps.

The disparate visual treatments and historical presentations of the park system and the monumental core reflect fundamental differences in the goals and audiences of the plan's two elements. The diffuse and heterogeneous qualities that made the broader park system difficult to convey in a single striking image may have hindered its historical reception, but they were essential to its success as a broad-based public amenity. By spreading its diverse benefits throughout the region, the park system catered to the practical needs of local citizens, unlike the monumental core, whose impressive but primarily symbolic appeal was directed toward a national, or even international, audience. This dichotomy was reflected in the primary sources of support for the plan's two components. The monumental core proposals were championed by the American Institute of Architects (AIA), a national body that sought to elevate the profession and demonstrate that American designers could rival their Old World predecessors in the production of monumental civic art. The AIA presented the restoration of L'Enfant's vision as the primary aim of the Senate Park Commission and cast its classical formality as the defining characteristic of the nation's capital. Given that the AIA leadership was heavily invested in presenting Beaux-Arts neoclassicism as the preeminent national style, the self-proclaimed "rediscovery" of L'Enfant and concomitant emphasis on ennobling the monumental core with grandiose architectural statements may have had as much to do with contemporary professional agendas as with the restoration of historical ideals.

The Washington Board of Trade and local officials charged with improving the quality of life for city residents held a different perspective on the capital's history and destiny. The "old Washington" these local leaders sought to preserve and nurture was an overgrown village steeped in Jeffersonian ideals and embellished with the aesthetic and ideological refinements of the Anglo-American park movement. From Downing's romantically configured Mall and Olmsted's picturesque Capitol grounds to the tree-lined streets whose leafy canopies provided soothing shade throughout the summer months, this Washington embodied the American ideal of pastoral simplicity, closeness to nature, and unostentatious civility. From this perspective, the architectural community's grandiose urban extravaganza could have appeared to be not just ahistorical, but un-American, autocratic, meretricious. The Board of Trade insisted Washington should continue to develop along lines that reflected its historical role as "a forest city" that had been "adorned with all the resources of the landscape gardener's art." The greatest need, the board asserted, was not to engage in ostentatious architectural displays but to provide "health-giving breathing places for the benefit of that portion of the people who must rely on fresh air and natural scenery on parks close at hand."[53] Both the Washington Board of Trade and the District Commissioners went out of their way to emphasize park development in their endorsements of the commission's efforts. "No other labor of the centennial year is more inspiring of notable results in increasing the attractiveness of the capital," the Board of Trade proclaimed, "than that of developing Washington as the city of parks."[54]

The Board of Trade had been developing park proposals for a decade or more when the AIA bustled to center stage in 1900 with its conference on the improvement of Washington. When the concomitant attempt to convince Congress to support the architects' plans for the monumental core failed, the Board of Trade's support was pivotal in securing the Senate Park Commission's authorization, with the AIA's emphasis on public buildings deleted and the commitment to a comprehensive park system confirmed. Since the AIA and its supporters played a dominant role in writing the history of the commission, the subsequent celebration of the architects' influence and emphasis on L'Enfant and the monumental core could reflect a desire, either conscious or unconscious, to downplay the Board of Trade's contributions and focus attention on aspects of the plan that elevated the AIA's stature while supporting a more formal and architectural agenda. Professional rivalries may also have influenced the construction of the historical record. The Board of Trade maintained a generally positive relationship with the Army Corps of Engineers, whose custodianship of Washington parks and public buildings the AIA and its associates tended to view as detrimental. For decades after the report's release the AIA and the Commission of Fine Arts were frequently at odds with the Army Corps of Engineers and the District Commissioners over the realization of the plan and related issues.[55]

Even the language used to chronicle the commission's history displayed a subtle bias against the park dimensions of the plan. The ascendancy of the term "McMillan Commission" followed the common practice of honoring congressional sponsors, but this linguistic turn also answered the architectural community's need for a more neutral term than "Senate Park Commission," which called attention to the proposal's broader goals and complex political heritage. Now that the original participants and their immediate successors have departed the scene and historians have taken a more measured view of the City Beautiful that places greater emphasis on the contributions of the nineteenth-century movement and other broad-based influences, the term "Senate Park Commission" has returned to favor.

Perhaps the most important reason for down-playing the park components was that they complicated efforts to present the Senate Park Commission's plan as a revolutionary document that sprang full-formed from the commission's collective brow and radically altered the landscape of American city planning. The monumental core proposals were striking, to be sure, and the combination of traditional park and parkway development with Chicago World's Fair-influenced architectonic excess was arguably a significant step forward, but the broader park dimensions of the plan were deeply rooted in local and national precedents and conspicuously demonstrated the proposal's close relationship to mainstream traditions of American civic improvement. The original commissioners made no secret of this at the time, acknowledging the value of existing local studies and invoking examples from park developments throughout the country. The Boston park system, in particular, was repeatedly hailed as an important predecessor, both as a source of design precedents and as a framework for the report's underlying goals and organization.

While architects and historians emphasize the legacy of the Chicago World's Fair, landscape architect Charles Eliot's 1893 report to the Boston Metropolitan Park Commission had equal or greater impact, both on the Senate Park Commission and on the broader course of American City planning. By transcending municipal boundaries to consider the needs of an entire metropolitan region and addressing a wide variety of scenic, recreational, and practical concerns in a detailed and methodical manner, Eliot pioneered an approach to comprehensive urban analysis that served as an explicit model for the Senate Park Commission's efforts and profoundly influenced the development of modern city planning.[56] Olmsted and others repeatedly pointed out the virtues of Eliot's approach as the commission's goals and methods were being refined. Olmsted's place on the commission was predicated in large part on his familiarity with the Boston park system, and he brought Eliot's ideas into the discussion long before Burnham appeared on the scene. Burnham was a larger than life personality, however, while the younger Olmsted was a modest technocrat who publicly deferred to his more famous colleague. Eliot had passed away before the commission undertook its endeavors, silencing his powerful personae and prolific pen. While Burnham and his admirers subsequently credited the Chicago World's Fair as a leading influence on the Senate Park Commission, the actual report made scant reference to this supposedly seminal project, repeatedly invoking the Boston park system as a model and employing maps, diagrams, and photographs from Boston.[57]

Another reason for down-playing Eliot's influence along with the broader park system plans that served as his direct legacy was that the 1893 Boston document was not just more innovative than the Senate Park Commission's report, but significantly more wide-ranging as well, belying assertions by the commission and its supporters that the Washington plan was "the most comprehensive ever provided for the development of an American city."[58] The Senate Park Commission undeniably made major strides in the realm of monumental urban design, but the Boston report was far more encyclopedic, moving well beyond traditional civic art matters to address practical transportation problems, public health concerns, water and sewage provisions, and urban development patterns. Eliot's co-author Sylvester Baxter went into considerable detail on pragmatic financial issues and legislative strategies and even provided a prescient assessment of the problems of urban sprawl, calling for the construction of model garden apartments as an alternative to poorly planned and shoddily built suburbs.[59] The Boston report lacked the monumental architectural component that attracted so much attention to the Senate Park Commission plan, but as an illustration of comprehensive urban analysis, it was far more indicative of the measured and functional approach that informed the field's rise to prominence in the Progressive Era.

While the Senate Park Commission's plan may not have been as well-rounded as its Boston predecessor, it was significantly more comprehensive than conventional caricatures of the City Beautiful Movement would suggest. This points to a final reason for the ongoing emphasis on the monumental core at the expense of the broader park system proposals. For critics and supporters of the City Beautiful Movement alike, the monumental core components of the Senate Park Commission plan became an icon of the Baroque grandeur that ostensibly infused this controversial chapter in American planning history. When the City Beautiful was in its heyday and Burnham and other ambitious architects were attempting to impose similar schemes on other major metropolises, emphasizing the monumental core and down-playing the park dimensions helped differentiate the new movement from its predecessors and elevate the reputations of its practitioners. For those who viewed the City Beautiful as an atavistic exercise in architectural excess perpetrated by priggish aesthetes bent on imposing imperialistic order on unruly urbanites, or as an intellectually bankrupt folly that retarded the development of modern architecture and city planning, the commission's grandiose designs for the monumental core served as the perfect stereotype for defining and denigrating the movement.

The park system proposals confounded both of these popular misconceptions by demonstrating the City Beautiful Movement's broader dimensions and underscoring its continuity with previous planning traditions.

The lingering stereotype of the Senate Park Commission plan as an expanded and politicized version of Chicago's White City serves a convenient heuristic purpose. According to the standard pedagogical progression, the City Beautiful Movement burst onto the scene with the Chicago World's Fair, reached its apogee of artistic and intellectual refinement in the Senate Park Commission's plan for the nation's capital, then came crashing to earth with Burnham's unrealized plans for Chicago, New York, and San Francisco. This compelling teleology has long enjoyed popularity —and the associated imagery makes for an impressive undergraduate lecture or textbook narrative—but the chimerical tale relies on the same half-truths and interpretive biases that have long distorted the historical reputation of the Senate Park Commission plan. While a few American cities constructed—or at least contemplated—grandiose civic centers inspired by the Mall and the Chicago World's Fair, most municipalities embraced the Senate Park Commission's broader legacy and focused on the development of wide-ranging park systems and other practical improvements. In fact, the park dimensions of City Beautiful plans were almost always their most successful attributes, responding to the practical needs of local residents and remaining popular long after the Baroque excess of monumental civic centers appeared mannered and out-of-date.

Recent historians have challenged the standard interpretation of the City Beautiful by calling attention to the broader motivations and practical achievements of the movement, but the Senate Park Commission is still remembered primarily for its monumental proposals for the Mall.[60] Reinvigorating the monumental core was certainly no mean feat, but the continued preoccupation with the Mall and its environs sustains outmoded stereotypes, discounts its affinity with contemporary planning efforts, and disregards its subtle adaptations to local political and environmental considerations.[61] By ushering nineteenth-century park-planning principles into the twentieth-century in a compelling and context-sensitive manner, the park system proposals profoundly benefited the citizens of Washington while serving as inspiration for comprehensive park development programs throughout the country. The analysis of such broad-based planning concerns may not elicit the same fervor as the exegesis of extravagant architectural gestures, but restoring the park system proposals to their historical prominence provides important insights into the Senate Park Commission's goals and accomplishments while underscoring its profound importance to the history of American urban planning and landscape design.

NOTES

[1] General histories of American planning reduce the park system component of the Senate Park Commission plan to a sentence or two, while even the most detailed analyses of Washington's development rarely grant it more than a few paragraphs. The Mall and its environs, meanwhile, have generated numerous studies, most notably John Reps, *Monumental Washington: The Planning and Development of the Capital Center* (Princeton: Princeton University Press, 1967) and Richard Longstreth, ed., *The Mall in Washington, 1791-1991* (Washington, D.C.: National Gallery of Art, 1991, 2002). Reps's more comprehensive survey, *The Making of Urban America; A History of City Planning in the United States*. Princeton, N.J.: Princeton University Press, 1965), devotes an entire chapter to the Senate Park Commission plan, but focuses on the politics and aesthetics of the neoclassical core and passes over the broader park system in a sentence or two. The longtime standard on American landscape history, Norman Newton's *Design on the Land: The Development of Landscape Architecture* (Cambridge: Harvard University Press, 1971) similarly dwells on the plan's Beaux Arts monumentality and covers the park system component in one terse paragraph. Thomas Hines's popular biography of Burnham scarcely mentions the broader Washington park system at all (Thomas Hines, *Burnham of Chicago: Architect and Planner* [New York: Oxford University Press, 1974]). Hines's essay "The Imperial Mall: The City Beautiful Movement and the Washington Plan of 1901-1902" in *The Mall in Washington* (79-99) epitomizes the reductive reading of the Senate Park Commission plan as an architectonic exercise in baroque urbanism. Richard Guy Wilson also short-changed the contributions of landscape architects to the City Beautiful Movement, elevating Burnham to demigod status and insisting that architecture was the "controlling art form"of the era (Richard Guy Wilson, Dianne H. Pilgrim, and Richard Murray, *The American Renaissance: 1876-1917* [New York: Brooklyn Museum/Pantheon, 1979], 75-82). Frederick Gutheim's *Worthy of the Nation: The History of Planning in the National Capital.* (Washington, D.C.: Smithsonian University Press, 1977) seems almost generous in comparison, devoting four full paragraphs of its chapter on the Senate Park Commission to a summary of the plan's sixty-plus pages of park proposals. In his classic *American City Planning Since 1890* (Berkeley, CA: University of California Press, 1969) Mel Scott acknowledged the strong influence of nineteenth-century park system development on the Senate Park Commission plan, characterized the broader park system proposals as its "most commendable feature" (55), and went on to describe it in more detail than other chroniclers (four whole paragraphs!) but he, too, focused on the commission's efforts to transform the Mall into a neoclassical showpiece, which he cast as a typical example of the City Beautiful movement's unfortunate emphasis on aesthetics over practical reforms. Even the more recent accounts by scholars such as Jon Peterson and William Wilson, which point to the diverse and complex origins of the City Beautiful movement and dissect the Senate Park Commission's activities in great detail, give short shrift to the broader park system component when it comes to the actual exegesis of design features and development processes; both acknowledge the plan's roots in local and national park and parkway planning efforts, but seem less interested in discussing the park components than in addressing the plan's monumental aspects and recounting the efforts to revise the central core, which provide a more compelling case for the commission's role as catalyst of a new era in city planning history (Jon A Peterson, "The City Beautiful Movement: Forgotten Origins and Lost Meanings," *Journal of Urban History* 2 [August 1976], 417-28; idem, "The Nation's First Comprehensive City Plan: A Political Analysis of the McMillan Plan for Washington, D.C., 1900-1902," *American Planning Association Journal* 51 [April 1985], 134-50; idem, "The Mall, the McMillan Plan, and the Origins of American City Planning" in *The Mall in Washington*, 101-115; William Wilson "The Ideology, Aesthetics, and Politics of the City Beautiful Movement," in Anthony Sutcliffe, ed., *The Rise of Modern Urban Planning* [New York: St. Martins, 1980],165-98; idem, *The City Beautiful Movement* [Baltimore: Johns Hopkins University Press, 1989]). Visual depictions of the monumental core dominate all these accounts, with the broader park system represented, if at all, by a lackluster map or two. While they were not as lavish as the color graphics prepared to promote the Mall and its environs, the original report contained dozens of drawings and photographs explicating various elements of the park, parkway, and playground system.

[2] In terms of cold statistics, the commission devoted about thirty-five pages of its1902 report to aspects of the monumental core, while its discussion of outlying parks, parkways, playgrounds, and other recreational features ran well over fifty pages and was bolstered by another twenty-odd pages of appendices and augmented by dozens of illustrations and several enormous maps. The report's introduction repeatedly emphasized that the commission was not simply concerned with improving the appearance of the monumental core. The commission's aim was to propose a "comprehensive plan" that would address "the location of public buildings, of preserving spaces for parks in the portions of the District beyond the city limits of Washington, of connecting and developing existing parks by attractive drives, and of providing for the recreation and health of a constantly growing population." This

broad scope was outlined in the senate resolution of March 8, 1901 that authorized the commission and charged it with the task of preparing "plans for the development and improvement of the entire park system of the District of Columbia." (U.S. Congress, Senate Committee on the District of Columbia, *The Improvement of the Park System of the District of Columbia*, Senate Report No. 166, 57ᵗʰ Cong. 1ˢᵗ sess. [Washington: Government Printing Office, 1902] , quotes, p.7). Hereafter, *Senate Park Commission Report*.

³ *Senate Park Commission Report*, 19.

⁴ *Senate Park Commission Report*, 7-24, quoted, 19, 23.

⁵ The best overviews of nineteenth-century American park development are David Schuyler's *The New Urban Landscape: The Redefinition of City Form in Nineteenth-Century America* (Baltimore: Johns Hopkins University Press, 1986) and Albert Fein, "The American City: The Ideal and the Real, in *The Rise of an American Architecture*, ed. Edgar Kauffman, Jr., (New York: Praeger Publishers, 1970), 51-112. More critical interpretations of the American park movement that emphasize the park's role as elitist retreat and agent of social control can be found in Paul Boyer, *Urban Masses and Moral Order in America, 1820-1920* (Cambridge: Harvard University Press, 1978), Christine Boyer, *Dreaming the Rational City: The Myth of American City Planning* (Cambridge: MIT Press, 1983), and Roy Rosenzweig and Elizabeth Blackmar, *The Park and the People: A History of Central Park* (Ithaca, N.Y.: Cornell University Press, 1992).

⁶ Mary C. Robbins, "Park Making as a National Art," *Atlantic Monthly* (January 1897), 86-98; Robbins elaborated on similar themes in "The Art of Public Improvement," *Atlantic Monthly* (December 1896), 742-51.

⁷ Underscoring the competitive nature of contemporary park development activities and the prevailing sentiment that Washington was unconscionably outpaced, the Washington Board of Trade declared, "Certainly there has never been a time when the citizens of the capital have been more deeply impressed with the necessity of keeping abreast of the times in the way of public improvements, not the least of which are its public parks," [from "Report of the Committee on Parks and Reservations, November 8, 1899," reprinted in W.V. Cox, "Park Improvement Papers No. 1. Action of the Board of Trade in Relation to the Park System of the Park System of the District of Columbia," in *Park Improvement Papers: A Series of Seventeen Papers Related to the Improvement of the Park System of the District of Columba; Printed for the use of the Senate Committee on the District of Columbia* (Washington: Government Printing Office, 1902). Cynthia Zaitzevsky chronicled the development of Boston's "Emerald Necklace" in *Frederick Law Olmsted and the Boston Park System* (Cambridge: Harvard University Press, 1982). The Buffalo park and parkway system is

discussed in Francis Kowski, ed., *The Best Planned City: The Olmsted Legacy in Buffalo* (Buffalo, N.Y.: Burchfield Art Center, 1991). The Minneapolis park system is summarized in several of the previously mentioned secondary sources and detailed in Horace W.S. Cleveland, *Suggestions for a System of Parkways for the City of Minneapolis* (Minneapolis: Johnson, Smith and Harrison, 1883); and idem, *Public Parks, Radial Avenues, and Boulevards: Outline Plan of a Park System for the City of St. Paul* (St. Paul: Globe Job Office, 1885). Wilson summarized the goals and methods of Kansas City planners in *The City Beautiful*, 99-125.

⁸ The development of Washington's park system is recounted in numerous sources including Frederick Gutheim/National Capital Planning Commission, *Worthy of the Nation: The History of Planning in the National Capitol* (Washington: Smithsonian Institution Press, 1977) and John Reps, *Washington on View: The Nation's Capitol Since 1790* (Chapel Hill: University of North Carolina Press, 1991). The creation and early development of Rock Creek Park is detailed in Cox, "Park Improvement Papers No. 7. Notes on the Establishment of A National Park in the District of Columbia and the Acquirement and Improvement of the Valley of Rock Creek for Park Purposes," in Moore, ed., *Park Improvement Papers*, 107-176.

⁹ *Report of the Advisory Committee on the Bathing Beach of the District of Columbia for the Year Ending June 30, 1901* (Washington: Government Printing Office, 1901)

¹⁰ The Senate Park Commission borrowed this graphic technique, along with a number of key maps, from Charles Eliot's 1893 report to the Boston Metropolitan Park Commissioners. ([Boston, Massachusetts] Metropolitan Park Commission, *Report of the Board of the Metropolitan Park Commissioners, January 1893*).

¹¹ The U.S. Army Corps of Engineers' plans for the Anacostia section were submitted in U.S. Congress, House, Executive Doc. No. 30, Report of Lieut. Peter C. Hains, U.S. Army Corps of Engineers, 52ⁿᵈ Cong., 1ˢᵗ sess; and U.S. Congress, House, House Doc. No. 87, Report of Col. C.J. Allen, U.S. Army Corps of Engineers, 55ᵗʰ Cong., 3ʳᵈ sess. The engineers also hired noted New York City landscape architect Samuel Parsons, Jr. to prepare plans for the improvement of the Mall and provision of a link with Rock Creek Park; these proposals were presented in U.S. Congress, House, *Plans for Treatment of That Portion of the District of Columbia South of Pennsylvania Avenue and North of B Street SW., and for a Connection Between Potomac and Zoological Parks*, Doc. No. 135, 56ᵗʰ Congress, 2d sess., December 1900. The Washington Board of Trade presented detailed proposals for a Rock Creek Parkway and Fort Drive in W[illiam] V. Cox. "Park Improvement Papers No. 1. Action of the Washington Board of Trade in Relation to the Park System of the District of Columbia," in Charles Moore, ed., *Park Improvement Papers*, 1-17,

and "Report by Henry B. Looker for the Committee on Parks and Reservations of the Washington Board of Trade, December 15, 1899," Appendix I to Cox, "Park Improvement Papers No. 7. Notes on the Establishment of A National Park in the District of Columbia and the Acquirement and Improvement of the Valley of Rock Creek for Park Purposes," in Moore, ed., *Park Improvement Papers*, 145-48. The various alternative proposals for Rock Creek and Potomac Parkway are described in Timothy Davis, "Rock Creek and Potomac Parkway: The Evolution of a Contested Urban Landscape," *Studies in the History of Gardens and Designed Landscapes*in 19 (April-June 1999), 123-237. Late-nineteenth-century efforts to create a Mount Vernon Memorial Avenue are recounted in Timothy Davis, "Mount Vernon Memorial Highway and the Evolution of the American Parkway," Ph.D. diss., University of Texas at Austin, 1997; and idem, "Mount Vernon Memorial Highway: Changing Conceptions of An American Commemorative Landscape," in *Places of Commemoration, Search for Identity and Landscape Design*, ed. Joachim Wolschke-Bulmahn, (Washington, D.C.: Dumbarton Oaks, 2000), 123-177. Among the groups agitating for the development of playgrounds and local recreational outlets were the Columbia Heights Citizens' Association, the North Capitol and Eckington Civic Association, the Takoma Park Citizens' Association, and an organization known as the Washington Civic Center ("Park Improvement Papers, No. 3. The Need of Additional Playgrounds, Parks, and Reservations" in Charles Moore, ed., *Park Improvement Papers*.

[12] *Senate Park Commission Report*, 17 ("one great composition"), 24 ("modern park system").

[13] Olmsted later characterized Langdon as the "staff landscape architect to the Park Commission" and promoted his application for the position of chief planner for the National Capital Park Commission when that body was being formed in 1925, asserting that Langdon knew more about the Senate Park Commission's intentions than any other individual; Charles W. Eliot, Jr. was eventually awarded the post, however, due in part to his own considerable connections and in part to Langdon's reputation as a rather prickly character (letter, Olmsted to Horace Peaslee, 23 April 1925; Olmsted Associates Papers, file no. 365, Library of Congress; numerous letters documenting the evolution of the park system component of the plan and underscoring Langdon's role can be found in Charles Moore's papers at the Library of Congress Manuscript Division, primarily in Box 2, Olmsted Letters, 1901-1903). Landscape historian Cynthia Zaitzevsky described Langdon's working relationship to the senior Olmsted in *Frederick Law Olmsted and the Boston Park System*, 152; Reps noted Langdon's contribution to the Senate Park Commission's plans in *Monumental Washington*, 90.

[14] This material was compiled by Moore and later reprinted as *Park Improvement Papers: A Series of Seventeen Papers Related to the Improvement of the Park System of the District of Columba; Printed for the use of the Senate Committee on the District of Columbia* (Washington: Government Printing Office, 1902).

[15] *Senate Park Commission Report*, 25-31; figures 148, 147, 175, 84, 173, 63, 86, 105, 78, 79, 101, 177, 100, 149, 196 (figure numbers reflect the placement of images in the original exhibition; this sequence reflects their placement in the commission's report between pages 25-31).

[16] *Senate Park Commission Report*, 47-53; "Appendix A, Public Bathing Places," 124-29; quote, p. 28.

[17] *Senate Park Commission Report*, 75-77, quote, p. 75.

[18] Ibid., 75-77.

[19] Ibid., 83-84.

[20] U.S. Congress, Senate, *Communication from the Engineer Commissioner, District of Columbia, submitting estimates of the Cost of Converting Rock Creek into a Closed Sewer, in Response to a Resolution of July 22, 1892*, Misc. Doc. No. 21, 52nd Cong., 2nd Sess., 1893; "Report by Henry B. Looker for the Committee on Parks and Reservations of the Washington Board of Trade, December 15, 1899," Appendix I to Cox, "Park Improvement Papers No. 7. Notes on the Establishment of A National Park in the District of Columbia and the Acquirement and Improvement of the Valley of Rock Creek for Park Purposes," in Moore, ed., *Park Improvement Papers*, 145-48. The development of Rock Creek and Potomac Parkway is detailed in Timothy Davis, "Rock Creek and Potomac Parkway: The Evolution of a Contested Urban Landscape," *Studies in the History of Gardens and Designed Landscapes* 19 (April-June 1999), 123-237.

[21] The improvement of Rock Creek was discussed in the report's introduction, in the general overview of park features, and in a special appendix (*Senate Park Commission Report*, 11, 85-86, 137-42). Related illustrations appeared on or opposite pages 10, 11, 85, 86, 87,140, and 141.

[22] Sears Gallagher and Percival Gallager were credited for these renderings and the subsequent parkway sections in *Senate Park Commission Report*, 147, fn. 1.

[23] *Ibid.*, 85.

[24] *Ibid.*, 97-98.

[25] *Ibid.*, 91-94.

[26] *Ibid.*, 91-94.

[27] *Ibid.*, 94-95.

[28] *Ibid.*, 95-97.

[29] *Ibid.*, 121-22.

[30] *Ibid.*, 57-59; 91-98.

[31] *Ibid.*, 10.

[32] *Ibid.*, 87-89; quote, p. 88.

[33] *Ibid.*, 98-101.

[34] *Ibid.*, 101-102.

[35] *Ibid.*, 102-103.

[36] *Ibid.*, 103 -104.

[37] *Ibid.*, 105-109, 115.

[38] *Ibid.*, 117-19.

[39] *Ibid.*, 113-14.

[40] *Ibid.*, 111-12, 167.

[41] *Ibid.*, 79-82.

[42] Statements from the Columbia Heights Citizens Association, the North Capitol and Eckington Citizens' Association, and several other groups were compiled in "The Need of Additional Playgrounds, Parks, and Reservations, Park Improvement Papers No. 3" in Moore, ed., *Park Improvement Papers*.

[43] *Senate Park Commission Report*, 79-82. Charles W. Eliot, "The Utilization of Public Reservations. Park Improvement Papers, Second Series, No. 1," in Charles Moore, ed. *Park Improvement Papers* (Washington: Government Printing Office, 1903), 247–57. This was essentially a second edition of the initial volume, containing a few additional entries.

[44] *Senate Park Commission Report*, 18.

[45] For an overview of the Commission of Fine Arts activities, see Sue Kohler, *The Commission of Fine Arts: A Brief History, 1910-1995* (Washington, D.C.: Government Printing Office, 1996).

[46] Frederick Gutheim provides a compelling overview of the NCP&PC's activities and Washington park and planning efforts in general in *Worthy of the Nation*.

[47] The development of Rock Creek and Potomac Parkway is detailed in Timothy Davis, "Rock Creek and Potomac Parkway: The Evolution of a Contested Urban Landscape," *Studies in the History of Gardens and Designed Landscapes* 19 (April-June 1999), 123-237.

[48] The original segment of George Washington Memorial Parkway, linking Washington and Mount Vernon, was initially called Mount Vernon Memorial Highway. Completed in 1932 under the official aegis of the U.S. George Washington Bicentennial Commission, it was transferred to the National Park Service in 1933. For more on the development of Mount Vernon Memorial Highway and George Washington Memorial Parkway, see Timothy Davis, "Mount Vernon Memorial Highway and the Evolution of the American Parkway," Ph.D. diss., University of Texas at Austin, 1997; and idem, "Mount Vernon Memorial Highway: Changing Conceptions of An American Commemorative Landscape," in *Places of Commemoration, Search for Identity and Landscape Design*, ed. Joachim Wolschke-Bulmahn, (Washington, D.C.: Dumbarton Oaks, 2000), 123-177.

[49] Howard Gillette expounds on this theme in his encyclopedic *Between Justice and Beauty: Race, Planning and the Failure of Urban Policy in Washington, D.C.* (Baltimore: Johns Hopkins University Press, 1995).

[50] National Capital Planning Commission, *Extending the Legacy: Planning America's Capital for the 21st Century* (Washington, D.C: National Capital Planning Commission, 1997).

[51] Historian Albert Fein made this comparison and embellished on the analogy in his essay, "The American City: The Real and the Ideal," 51.

[52] The entire park system was meticulously delineated in the maps folded into the back of the original report, but these diagrams were too unwieldy for easy perusal when new, and have now become too brittle for all but the most audacious investigators to assay.

[53] Cox, "Park Improvement Papers No. 1. Action of the Washington Board of Trade in Relation to the Park System of the District of Columbia," in Moore, ed., *Park Improvement Papers*, 5 ("forest city," "landscape gardener's art" and "breathing places"), 7 ("Old Washington").

[54] Cox, "Park Improvement Papers No. 1. Action of the Washington Board of Trade in Relation to the Park System of the District of Columbia," in Moore, ed., *Park Improvement Papers*, 2. In their letter of endorsement reprinted at the beginning of the Senate Park Commission's report, the District Commissioners make no reference to L'Enfant or to the provision of public buildings and monuments, but assert that they, other district officials, and the city's residents eagerly awaited "a comprehensive scheme of improvement of the park system" (*Senate Park Commission Report*, 14).

[55] Petersen chronicles the politics of the commission's authorization in his essay in this volume and in previous writings on this subject ("The City Beautiful Movement: Forgotten Origins and Lost Meanings," *Journal of Urban History* 2 [August 1976], 417-28; "The Nation's First Comprehensive City Plan: A Political Analysis of the McMillan Plan for Washington, D.C., 1900-1902," *American Planning Association Journal* 51 [April 1985], 134-50; and "The Mall, the McMillan Plan, and the Origins of American City Planning" in Longstreth, ed., *The Mall in Washington*, 101-115). A transcript of related negotiations was reprinted as "Park Improvement Papers, No. 5. Informal Hearing Before the Subcommittee of the Committee on the District of Columbia, United States Senate," April 1, 1901, in Moore, ed. *Park Improvement Papers*, 76-79. Burnham, Brown, and their AIA associates may have viewed the park commission aspect as a political subterfuge to enable them to pursue their agenda for the Mall, but Olmsted, the Washington Board of Trade, and other local interests took this component of the commission's mandate with utmost seriousness.

[56] Charles Eliot, "Report of the Landscape Architect," in [Boston, Massachusetts] Metropolitan Park Commission, *Report of the Board of the Metropolitan Park Commissioners, January 1893*, 82-110. Eliot's report was reprinted along with many of his other writings in Charles W. Eliot, *Charles Eliot Landscape Architect* (Boston: Houghton, Mifflin and Company, 1903). Eliot's career

and the details of Boston's metropolitan park system are discussed more fully in Newton, *Design on the Land*, 318-36, Schuyler, *The New Urban Landscape*, 138-46, and Scott, *American City Planning*, 17-26.

[57] The introduction to the commission's report identified Olmsted as "the consulting landscape architect not only of the vast system of parks and boulevards which make up the metropolitan system of Boston and its suburbs but also of large parks in various cities (*Senate Park Commission Report*, 9) Olmsted presented Eliot's report as a model for the commissions endeavors in "Park Improvement Papers, No. 5. Informal Hearing Before the Subcommittee of the Committee on the District of Columbia, United States Senate," April 1, 1901," in Moore, ed. *Park Improvement Papers*, 84-86; when Daniel Burnham's participation was being discussed, William Boring, chairman of the American Institute of Architect's committee on legislation, insisted that the Chicago architect had not yet been consulted in the matter and knew nothing about it (p.79).

[58] *Senate Park Commission Report*, 16.

[59] Sylvester Baxter, "Secretary's Report," in *Report of the Board of the Metropolitan Park Commissioners, January 1893*, 1-81.

[60] Despite his excellent analysis of the broader origins and diverse goals of the City Beautiful movement, Wilson ultimately characterizes the Senate Park Commission plan in typically reductive form as "a stunning neoclassical scheme for the revitalization of Washington, D.C." (*The City Beautiful Movement*, 38). Even Schuyler, who masterfully explicated the practical, aesthetic, and ideological agendas of the late-nineteenth century park movement in *The New Urban Landscape*, casts the Senate Park Commission's plan as the antithesis of naturalistic park system development. Peterson's numerous essays pay greater heed to the plan's park dimensions, but his focus is still drawn to the Mall and the battles over its development.

[61] In his important recent volume *Between Justice and Beauty* (88-108), for instance, Howard Gillette correctly notes that the focus on the Mall replicated a common Washington pattern by privileging national interests at the expense of local concerns. By taking the standard approach of equating the Senate Park Commission plan with the monumental core scheme, however, he fails to credit the commission for its broader concerns and for the more widespread benefits afforded by the locally focused park system proposals.

Dupont Circle fountain soon after its completion in 1921. Daniel Chester French, sculptor; Henry Bacon, architect for base. Commission of Fine Arts.

Opposite page: One of six pavilions in the Washington Monument gardens. Watercolor on paper, 19x13 inches. Collection: Commission of Fine Arts.

PLATES

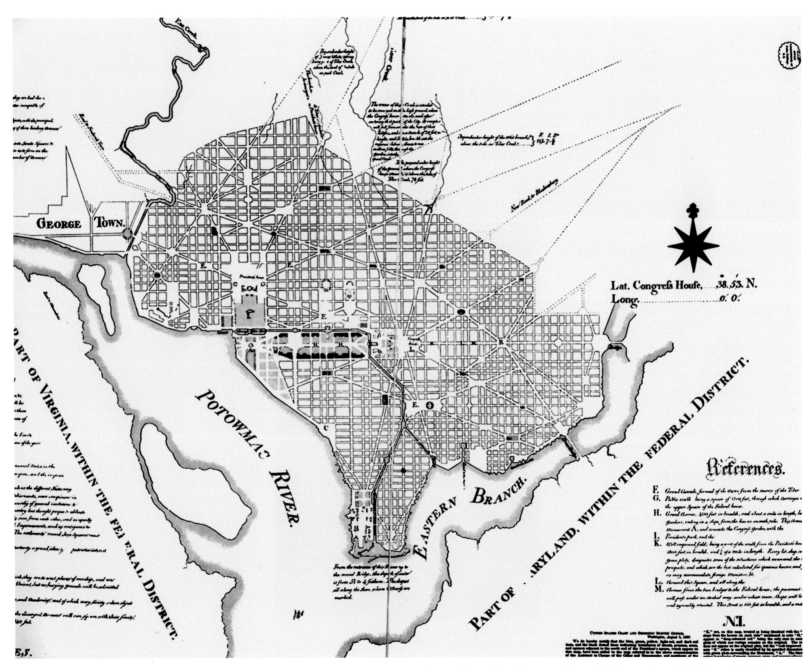

Plate I. L'Enfant plan of 1791, as reproduced by the U.S. Coast and Geodetic Survey, 1887. This would have been the version known by the members of the Senate Park Commission. Library of Congress, Geography and Maps Division

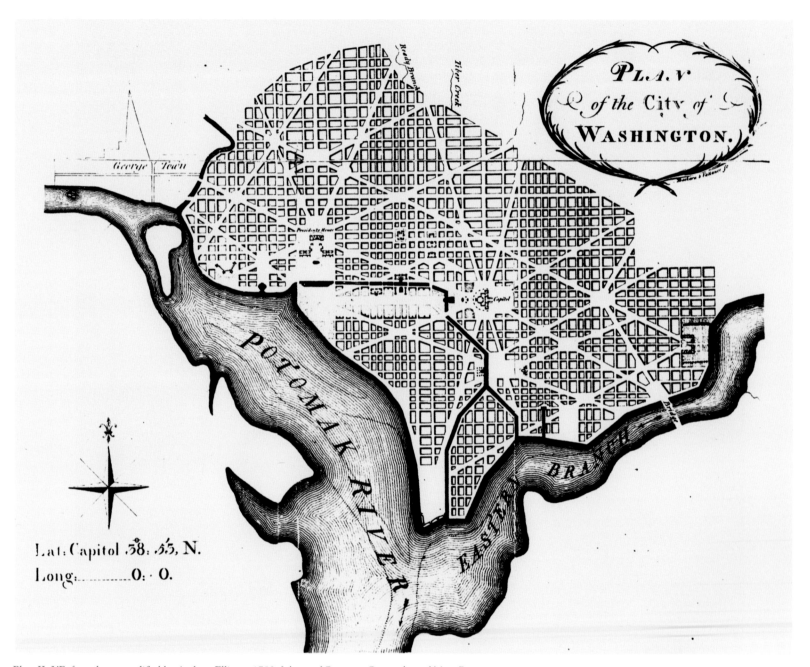

Plate II. L'Enfant plan as modified by Andrew Ellicott, 1792. Library of Congress, Geography and Maps Division.

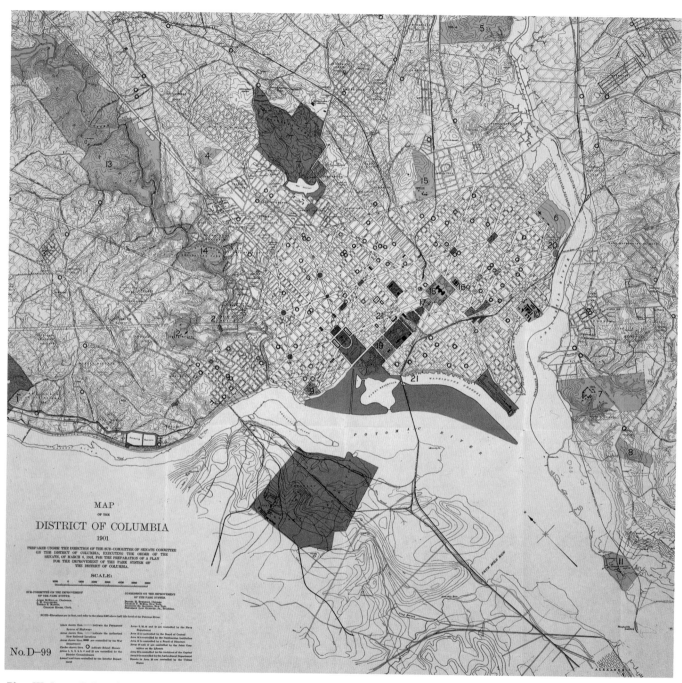

Plate III. James G. Langdon, map of the District of Columbia prepared for the Senate Park Commission, showing the existing park system in 1901 and giving other information. Library of Congress, Prints and Photographs Division

Plate IV. Map showing the existing District of Columbia park system (green) and the additions proposed by the Senate Park Commission (dark green). D.H. Burnham and E. H. Bennett, *Plan of Chicago*, 1909.

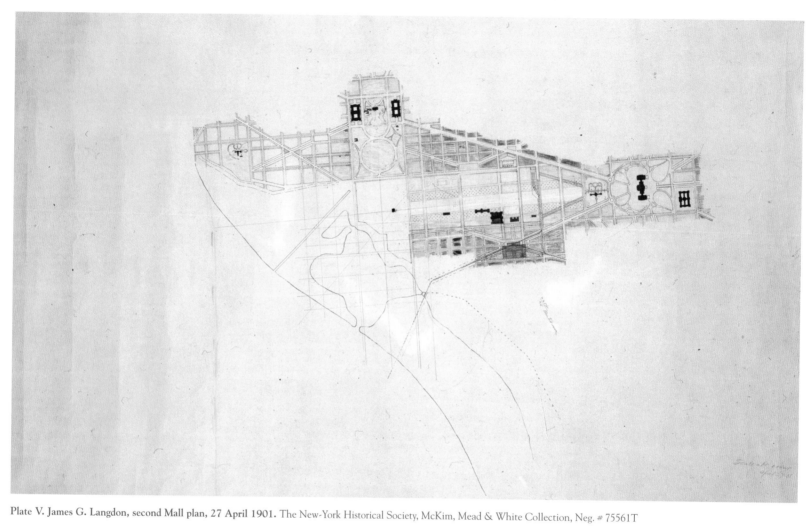

Plate V. James G. Langdon, second Mall plan, 27 April 1901. The New-York Historical Society, McKim, Mead & White Collection, Neg. # 75561T

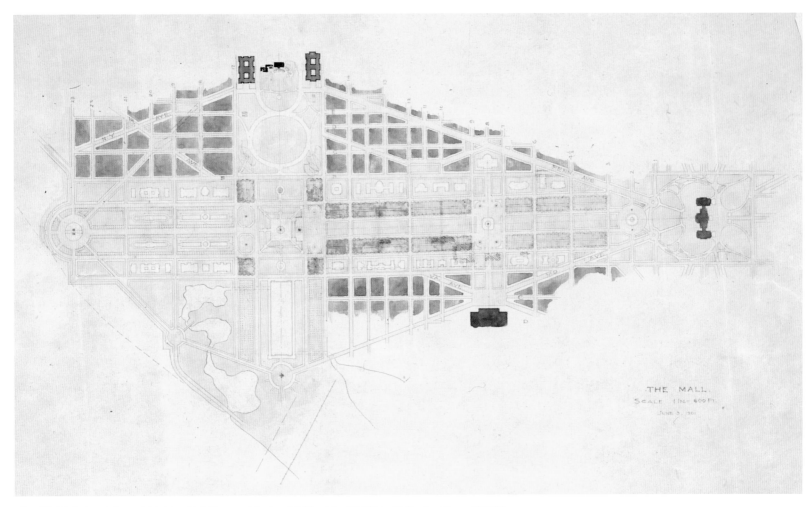

THE MALL
SCALE 1 IN = 600 FT
JUNE 3, '01

Plate VI. Mall plan, 3 June 1901. New-York Historical Society, McKim, Mead & White Collection, Neg. # 75560T

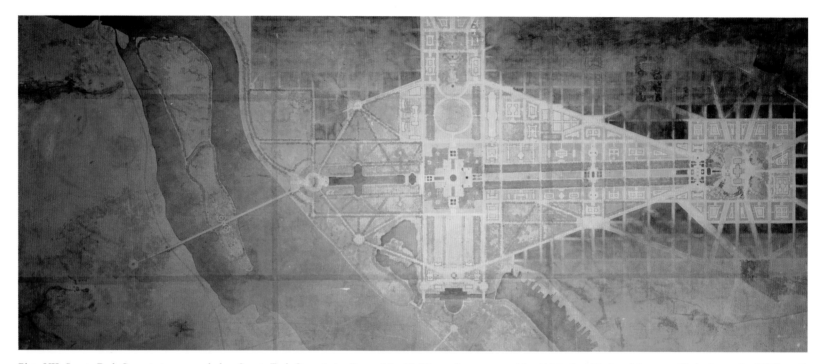

Plate VII. Senate Park Commission, general plan. Senate Park Commission Report No. 19. Watercolor on paper, 46 x 110 inches. Unsigned, but very likely the work of William T. Partridge, as alluded to in his "Personal Recollections." Partridge laid out all the exhibition drawings in pencil before turning them over to the illustrators to render them in color.
Collection: Commission of Fine Arts

Plate VIII. Senate Park Commission rendering of the plan from a point 4,000 feet above Arlington, by Francis L.V. Hoppin, signed and dated 1902. Senate Park Commission Report No. 20. Watercolor on paper, 34 x 72 inches. Collection: Commission of Fine Arts

Plate IX. Senate Park Commission rendering of the Washington Monument Gardens and Mall, looking toward the Capitol, from the original rendering by Charles Graham. Senate Park Commission Report No. 58. Watercolor on paper, 37 x 68 inches. Collection: Commission of Fine Arts. Photo: Lee Stalsworth

Plate X. Senate Park Commission rendering of Union Square, at the head of the Mall, by Charles Graham. Senate Park Commission Report No. 37. Watercolor on paper, 40 x 62 inches.
Collection: Commission of Fine Arts. Photo: National Gallery of Art

Plate XI. Senate Park Commission rendering of the proposed development of the site for the Lincoln Memorial, seen from the east; from the original rendering by Robert Blum. Senate Park Commission Report No. 49. Watercolor on paper, 24 x 59 inches. Collection: Commission of Fine Arts. Photo: Lee Stalsworth

Plate XII. Vaux-le-Vicomte, the gardens. These gardens, one of Le Nôtre's finest achievements, held a particular fascination for the commission. They spent a day at the chateau, the guests of the owners, M. and Mme. Sommier, who turned on the garden fountains for them so that they could see Le Nôtre's intended effect.
See Charles Moore, *The Life and Times of Charles Follen McKim*, p.196. Photo: Sue Kohler

Plate XIII. Birds-eye view taken from a point 4,000 feet over Saint Elizabeths Hospital. Senate Park Commission Report No. 21. Unfortunately the original has been lost as it was the companion piece to the View from Arlington. This color photograph appeared in the September 1918 issue of *The New Country Life*, p. 49.

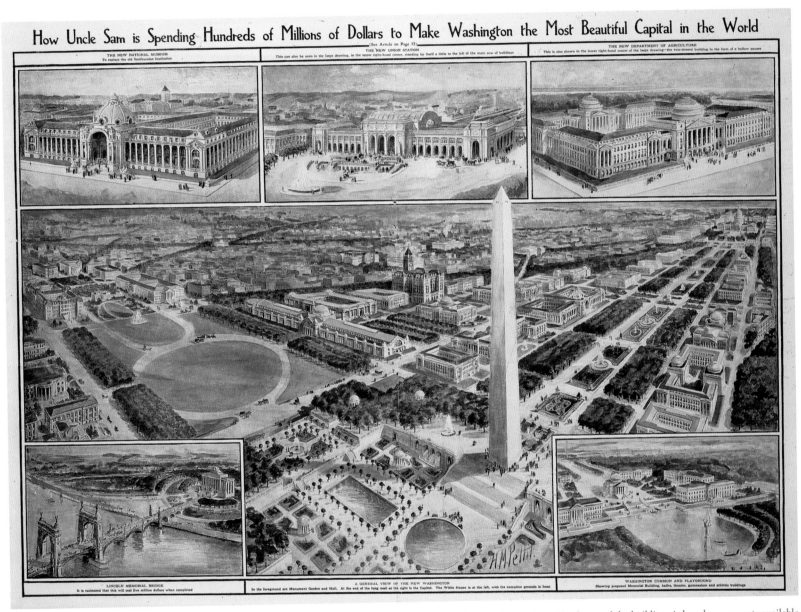

How Uncle Sam is Spending Hundreds of Millions of Dollars to Make Washington the Most Beautiful Capital in the World

(See Article on Page 32)

THE NEW NATIONAL MUSEUM
To replace the old Smithsonian Institution

THE NEW UNION STATION
This can also be seen in the large drawing, in the upper right-hand corner, standing by itself a little to the left of the main row of buildings

THE NEW DEPARTMENT OF AGRICULTURE
This is also shown in the lower right-hand corner of the large drawing—the two-domed building in the form of a hollow square

LINCOLN MEMORIAL BRIDGE
It is estimated that this will cost five million dollars when completed

A GENERAL VIEW OF THE NEW WASHINGTON
In the foreground are Monument Garden and Mall. At the end of the long mall at the right is the Capitol. The White House is at the left, with the executive grounds in front

WASHINGTON COMMON AND PLAYGROUND
Showing proposed Memorial Building, baths, theater, gymnasium and athletic buildings

Plate XIV. An artist's conception of how Washington might look if developed according to the Senate Park Commission plan. The design of the buildings is based on concepts available at the time. The text accompanying the illustration reflected the great enthusiasm the Park Commission's plans had generated. It said, in part: "Washington will be a place of public buildings, massive, magnificent, beautiful. Unter den Linden, Princes Street [Edinburgh], the Champs Elysées, will pale into insignificance; the Rome of the Caesars will rise again in a new world." *Woman's Home Companion*, February 1905. Collection: Dana Dalrymple

Plate XV. Senate Park Commission model, 1902, showing existing conditions in the central area of Washington, looking east. William T. Partridge, in his "Personal Recollections," remarks on the unusual accuracy of these models, due to the taking of hundreds of photographs by landscape architect James D. Langdon. Originally given to the Commission of Fine Arts with the other remaining Park Commission material, the models were kept in storage until 1974, when they were transferred to the Smithsonian Institution and completely restored for exhibition in the bicentennial exhibition, "The Federal City: Plans and Realities." Although the Smithsonian still owns the models, the National Building Museum is now their custodian; at this writing, further restoration is planned. Photographs from the Olmsted Associates' scrapbook. Collection, Commission of Fine Arts.

Plate XVI. Senate Park Commission model, 1902, showing existing conditions, looking west.

Plate XVII. Senate Park Commission model, showing Park Commission's proposals, looking east.

Plate XVIII. Senate Park Commission model, showing Park Commission's proposals, looking west.

Plate XIX. Daniel Hudson Burnham, as painted by Anders Zorn, 1899. Oil on canvas, 30x25 inches. Collection: Commission of Fine Arts, gift of the Burnham family, 1958. Photo: Lee Stalsworth

Plate XX. Charles Moore, as painted by Eugene Savage, 1935. Oil on canvas, 39x34 inches. Collection: Commission of Fine Arts.
Photo: Lee Stalsworth

Plate XXI. Alfred Githens' humorous "Coat of Arms" of the Senate Park Commission, and Olmsted's recollection of how it happened, as well as an account of some parts of the plan that, because of the rush to meet the exhibition deadline, were "unavoidably hurried to a finish." See also William T. Partridge's comments in his "Personal Recollections" under topic F. "Final Days of Preparation," in Kurt Helfrich's essay in this volume. Collection: Commission of Fine Arts.

NOTES ON GITHENS' CARICATURE COAT OF ARMS FOR THE SO-CALLED "SENATE PARK COMMISSION OF 1901"

My recollection of the story as McKim told it to me is as follows:

When the bunch of draughtsmen, under W.T. Partridge as head draughtsman, were working under great pressure to finish the drawings for the "Central Area" of the Plan of Washington in 1902 in the office set up for that purpose on the floor above McKim, Mead & White's office in New York, Mr. McKim on coming in one day saw Githens surreptitiously cover up a drawing he was working at, and went and uncovered it. McKim was so amused by the caricature that he had it reproduced and sent several copies to members of the Commission and other friends.

There had been endless discussion especially by me and by McKim, about "typical elms", and of course about the "Dome" and the "Monument", and about Guerin's technique in the drawings made by him. The hydra heads of the Commission are, from top to bottom, those of McKim, Saint-Gaudens, Burnham and myself; all amusingly recognizable caricatures except perhaps Burnham's. The most amusing touches in the sketch, we all thought, lay in the symbolic representation of the pressure under which all hands were then working to get the drawings completed on time—driven to death with the pressure and the mercilessness of the Commission in "socking it to 'em".

It was in that eleventh-hour rush to finish the drawings that some parts of the plans had to go through without the same deliberate study and unanimous unqualified approval by the Commission as a whole which was given to the major decisions. Among the parts thus unavoidably hurried to a finish were the designs for the eastern end of the Mall vista, from the Capitol to and including "Union Square"; those for the rearrangement of the Tidal Basin area; and those for some of the details of the Washington Monument Gardens: by way of distinction from the major and earlier decisions dealing with the width and character of the main Mall vista and its enclosing rows of elms; the framing of the Washington Monument by an orderly expansion of the frame of elms flanking the Mall, first devised in plan by McKim and me on a piece of quadrille paper in a train en route from Budapest to Paris in 1901; the development, on the site afterwards assigned to the Lincoln Memorial, of a great terminal monument of a form non-competitive with the Capitol Dome and the Washington Monument; the introduction west of the Monument Grounds of a long reflecting basin; the opening through of the White House axis to the southward, at a relatively low elevation, past the west side of the Washington Monument; and the development of a southern monumental focal point on the White House axis at its intersection with the line of Maryland Avenue in such a way as to leave the axial view from the White House down the river unobstructed by any bulky monument on the axis itself.

Frederick Law Olmsted
November 1935

Plaster mock-up of design of front of east wing of the Department of Agriculture building, April 1905. Author's collection.

Agriculture, Architects, and the Mall, 1901–1905:

THE PLAN IS TESTED

By Dana G. Dalrymple

A T the turn of the twentieth century, the U.S. Department of Agriculture was a bustling and crowded scientific enterprise. It was, rather oddly, largely located on the Mall, with jurisdiction over the block between Twelfth and Fourteenth streets and what are now Independence and Constitution avenues (then B streets, South and North). Its principal offices and laboratories were on the south side of the Mall or in rented quarters across Independence Avenue. The department had long sought expanded and improved laboratory space, but it was not until 1901 that Congress approved funds to plan a new building. Concurrently, the Senate Committee on the District of Columbia, headed by James McMillan of Michigan, established the Senate Park Commission to provide a master plan for the orderly development of Washington. The inadvertent combination of location and legislation thrust the Department of Agriculture into an unexpected role in civic planning on a grand scale. The key issue proved to be establishing a building line for the Mall (the width of the central greensward from the front of the buildings on the north side to those on the south), but there were a host of other architectural and political issues as well. Their resolution was critical in realizing the Senate Park Commission's vision for the development of the Mall.[1]

BACKGROUND: THE 1800s

The Department of Agriculture was preceded on the Mall, and located between, the Smithsonian Institution (begun in 1847) on the east and the Washington Monument (begun in 1848) on the west (fig. 1). Both had followed a fairly formal legislative path to the Mall, and their placement, particularly that of the monument, played a very substantial role in the later discussions about alignment and building line. The Department of Agriculture, however, won a prized Mall location more by happenstance than design.

Fig. 1 The Washington Monument and surrounding area, 24 September 1850, as drawn by Montgomery Meigs. The Jefferson Pier, which marks the true axis of the Mall, is located in the left center foreground at the edge of Tiber Creek. Smithsonian Institution (Neg. 38876B).

President James K. Polk and most of the Smithsonian's regents originally favored the present Department of Agriculture site for the Smithsonian because of its relatively high elevation. They were opposed by Washington mayor, William W. Seaton, a regent who favored the present Smithsonian site between Ninth and Twelfth streets because it was closer to the city's business hub. This latter location was ratified by Polk on 17 January 1847. The question of where to place the Smithsonian's building had been considered as early as 9 December 1846, when it was resolved to put it at least 250 feet south of the center of the Mall. The regents decided on 20 March 1847 to place the center of the building on the center of the lot from north to south, which would have put its center 380 feet from the Mall's central axis. When its cornerstone was laid on 1 May 1847, the Smithsonian's front facade was 300 feet south of the real axis, leaving a central greensward, or parkway, 600 feet in width.[2]

The site for the Washington Monument had been debated for about a decade before Robert Mills's design for a 600-foot-tall obelisk surrounded by a circular pantheon 200 feet in diameter was adopted on 18 November 1845. On 31 January 1848, Congress granted the Washington National

Monument Society access to "the public grounds or reservations," and on 2 February the society chose Reservation No. 3. Two months later the society decided to build only the present obelisk. The process followed in selecting the present site on this large plot is unclear. The proceedings of the Board of Managers of the Monument Society indicate only that on 21 March 1848 it was "resolved that previous to excavating the foundation the Board of Managers shall designate the precise spot on which the Monument is to be erected and that a well be dug to ascertain at what depth the surest foundation can be had...." The spot turned out to be on the top of a small hill 371.6 feet east and 123.17 feet south of the location proposed for an equestrian monument to Washington by Pierre Charles L'Enfant's 1791 plan and occupied since 1802 by the Jefferson Stone. This stone represented the intersection of an east-west line from the center of the Capitol and a north-south line from the center of the White House. While there has been considerable speculation, generally relating to foundation conditions (the site was on the edge of Tiber Creek), about why the society selected a location other than the one designated by L'Enfant, no contemporary evidence has been found that explicitly states why this decision was made. We only know from accounts of the period that the monument's excavation was begun on 17 April and was completed by 16 May 1848. It was reported a few months later that, as specified, "A well was first dug some little distance, which indicated favorably" and that the site "is most appropriate and commanding."[3]

Shortly thereafter, the Agricultural Division of the Patent Office, the precursor of the Department of Agriculture, came into the picture. The division, which was established in 1839, subsequently sought land "on or near the Mall," for "the purpose of cultivating and propagating seeds and cuttings." On 23 May 1856, it was assigned five acres of "public space immediately north of the canal between Four and One-half and Sixth streets," formerly part of the marshy bank of the Tiber Creek. Two years later, following drainage and development work, these grounds—now occupied by part of the National Gallery of Art—were formally designated the Propagating Gardens, and greenhouses were built.[4]

The next phase was triggered by the establishment of the Department of Agriculture on 15 May 1862. The enabling legislation stated that the Commissioner of Agriculture "shall receive and have charge of all the property of the agricultural division of the Patent Office...including the fixtures and property of the propagating garden." Subsequent entreaties by Commissioner Isaac Newton for more land paid off on 7 April 1863, when Benjamin B. French, the Commissioner of Public Buildings, offered the use of Reservation No. 2 between Twelfth and Fourteenth streets for use "as an experimental garden for Agricultural purposes" (fig.2). French stated that "no power but Congress can interfere with your use of it for public purposes, and I do not think that they will have

Fig. 2 The newly acquired grounds of the Department of Agriculture between 12th and 14th streets and North and South B streets on 13 August 1863, as photographed by Titian Ramsay Peale. The land was assigned to the Department on 7 April 1863, but was then part of the Washington Monument cattle yards and was not occupied by the Department until 5 April 1865. University of Rochester Library.

any desire to do so." In 1867 responsibility for the administration of Washington's public grounds was transferred to the Chief of Engineers of the War Department, but their authority did not extend to the Agriculture Department's reservation.[5]

The Department of Agriculture gained possession of Reservation No. 2 on 5 April 1865, following its use as a component of the Washington Monument cattle yard during the Civil War. Field trials, the first to be initiated by the fledgling department, were initiated on much of the land, but were largely discontinued by 1868. The first Department of Agriculture building (fig. 3), designed by Adolf Cluss, was begun on 2 August 1867, and was ready for occupancy on 1 September 1868. It was centered on Thirteenth Street, which because of the varied widths of the city's blocks (and hence the Mall's reservations), put it closer to Twelfth than Fourteenth Street, and set slightly back from the Smithsonian Institution's facade line. A conservatory was built on its west side, roughly on the same alignment. Several lesser buildings were later erected to the south of these structures. From 1867 to 1879, the grounds on the north and south of the building were landscaped into an attractive Victorian garden and arboretum, while several acres to its south continued to be cultivated. In 1873, when the Washington Canal was filled, the propagating garden was closed and exchanged for four acres formerly occupied by the canal along the north side of the department's grounds.[6]

Proposals during the next three decades for additional Department of Agriculture buildings proved futile and space problems became increasingly severe (there were five times as many employees in the Mall area in 1894 as there had been in 1871, an increase from 84 to 433), particularly in the case of chemistry laboratories. The department was given cabinet status on 9 February 1889, and the secretary's report for 1894 stated that "there is hardly a university or agricultural college in the United States which has not better constructed, better lighted, better ventilated laboratories than those used by the Department of Agriculture." In 1900, the department requested $200,000 from Congress to construct laboratory buildings but had to resubmit the request in 1901 (fig. 4).[7]

INITIAL DEVELOPMENTS, 1901

On 2 March 1901, Congress approved $5,000 "to enable the Secretary of Agriculture to have prepared, under his direction, plans for a fireproof administrative building, to be erected on the grounds of the Department of Agriculture and to be transmitted to Congress at its next regular session." While no mention was made of the laboratory buildings that had been the focus of the department's requests, they were part of the subsequent package. A few days later, Secretary of Agriculture James Wilson was quoted as saying, "We want a handsome building— nothing too

Fig. 3 A somewhat fanciful depiction of the Department of Agriculture buildings and grounds. The main building was completed in 1868, the Conservatory on the right in 1870, and this portion of the grounds in 1871. *Report of the Commissioner of Agriculture for the Year 1868*, frontispiece.

Fig. 4 The Mall and the Department of Agriculture complex, foreground, in the summer of 1901, at the time the work of the Park Commission and the architectural competition for the new Department building were underway. Martin Luther King Jr. Library, Washington, D.C., Washingtoniana Division (Neg. 154688).

elaborate, but we want it to be good in all ways." He wanted it to be constructed of stone, and he favored a quadrangle with interior courtyards for light and air. Phased construction was foreseen, first the laboratory wings followed by the administration block.[8]

Wilson chose Supervising Architect of the Treasury James Knox Taylor as his expert advisor, a function Taylor often served for government buildings other than those directly under his control. Taylor established an architectural advisory group consisting of the members of the recently appointed Senate Park Commission: Daniel H. Burnham, Charles F. McKim, Frederick Law Olmsted Jr., and Augustus Saint-Gaudens. It was probably Taylor who decided to hold an architectural competition, its design parameters laid out in a draft "Program and Conditions of a Competition for a Building for the Department." In commenting on the program on 13 June 1901, the Senate Park Commission members suggested that "the new building be built to the South and rear of the present building, in order to conform with the proposed avenue which will form part of the scheme upon which we are to report." They went on to say that "neither you nor we are in a position to determine exactly how far South" but they did think that the Thirteenth Street axis "should be recognized." The advisory group enclosed a list of ten architectural firms which should be invited to compete, preference being given to those "who have not already received a government contract." Eight of the firms had some association with either McKim or Burnham.[9]

Invitations were sent to the firms on 18 June. The "programme and conditions" for the building stated that the competition was to select an architect "for a design to be approved by Congress at the next session." The architect would then "prepare such design or designs as may in the judgment of the Supervising Architect…be necessary to meet the conditions finally adopted by him." The cost of the building was not to exceed $2 million, be of fireproof construction, and "classic in character." The laboratories "should be in wings away from the principal administrative and executive work." The architects were also forewarned that the building's actual location had not yet been determined.[10]

On 23 August, McKim, on behalf of the advisory group, sent Taylor "a block plan [not found], showing the proposed building line for the new building of the Department of Agriculture." The plot was "333 feet in mean width," which, given the building line on the north, would leave about 230 feet to the curb on B Street, SW. Allowing 15 feet for the sidewalk would leave about 215 feet for the building's width, "ample space" in McKim's view. The plot was long enough (1,050 feet) to allow for the construction of three buildings, including one large building in the center which would be the "Agriculture Building" (the disposition of the other two buildings is not clear).[11]

Competition entries were judged by the advisory group on 23 October 1901, and the contestants notified the next day. The submission by Lord & Hewlett of New York (fig. 5) was ranked first. Runners-up were Howells & Stokes and P.J. Webber. Key members of all three firms had previously been associated with McKim or Burnham; Austin Lord had worked for McKim, Mead & White from 1890 to 1894. The Lord & Hewlett design was described in the 28 October *Evening Star* account as "being of white marble, four-stories in height, of adapted Greek design and with a decorated facade. … According to Secretary Wilson's plans it will stand somewhat south of its present location, with a wide plaza in front, and the [laboratory] wing at the westward will be constructed first. The department force now in the main building will then move into the wing and its present quarters—condemned frequently during the past ten years—will be razed." By 20 December the

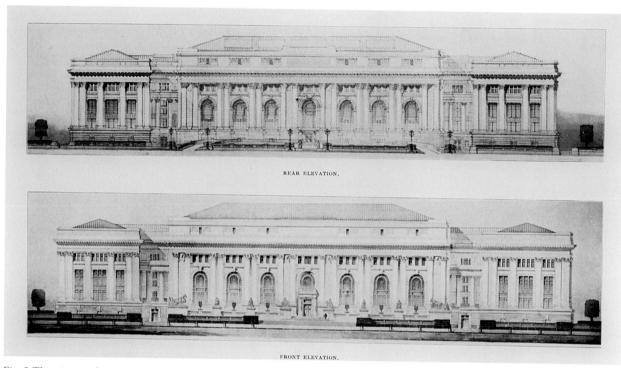

REAR ELEVATION.

FRONT ELEVATION.

Fig. 5 The winning design in the architectural competition for the Department of Agriculture building by Lord & Hewlett of New York. *The Inland Architect and News Record, December 1901.* Photo courtesy of the American Institute of Architects Library and Archives, Washington, D.C.

Evening Star carried a picture of the winning design and reported its cost at $2.5 million. The article noted the building would stand about 50 feet south of the existing structure and be about 400 feet long and 200 feet deep with laboratory wings flanking the central administration wing. Congressional reaction was "still uncertain."[12]

Nebraska Congressman David H. Mercer, chairman of the Committee on Public Buildings and Grounds, had introduced a bill in the House of Representatives on 18 December (H.7207) calling for the building "to be constructed in accordance with the approved plans," but limiting its cost to $2 million, the amount specified in the invitation for the competition. With respect to location, Mercer's bill said only "on such portion of the ground of the Department of Agriculture [as the Secretary of Agriculture] may deem expedient." Secretary Wilson later noted that "after careful consultation with Messrs. Lord & Hewlett and with Mr. Taylor…it was decided that a building suitable for the Department would cost approximately $2,500,000."[13]

THE PARK COMMISSION REPORT AND CONGRESSIONAL REACTION, 1902

Meanwhile, the Senate Park Commission was completing its report to Congress, presented on 15 January 1902. The Mall was to be shifted to the south so as to align its central axis with the Washington Monument. With respect to buildings, the report stated that "areas adjoining B St. north and south, averaging more than four hundred feet in width…afford spacious sites for buildings devoted to scientific purposes and for the great museums." It further noted that "with the approval of the Secretary of Agriculture and the Secretary of the Treasury, the Supervising Architect consulted the commission at every stage in the selection of an architect for and the location of the new building for the Department of Agriculture." Moreover, "the structure to be erected for the Department of Agriculture on the site of the present building marks at once the building line and the type of architecture which should be adopted throughout the Mall system." Further, the Department of Agriculture, "being the nucleus of a great number of laboratories requiring a maximum of light and air, may properly have its new building located as present proposed, on the grounds in the Mall, now set apart for its uses."[14]

Although the Senate Park Commission had officially completed its original assignment, its individual members continued to work officially and unofficially to insure implementation of their plan. McKim consulted with Secretary of War Elihu Root (who had general control over public grounds and buildings) and Secretary Wilson, in part for his political wisdom and his prior experience as a member of the House of Representatives from Iowa in the 1870s. Wilson reportedly responded to McKim rather grandly that "the only thing I know about your plans is that, if they are not the finest ever made, the people of the Unites States will have none of them." Olmsted subsequently sent McKim a diagrammatic plan of the Mall, dated 5 October 1902 (fig. 6), "embodying the results of my study for the grades," as well as cross sections. He also suggested a meeting with the architects to "discuss this whole matter of grades and other rules governing the mass of the buildings," but nothing seems to have come of it.[15]

Everything appeared set, except for one critical factor: the opposition of Illinois Congressman Joseph G. Cannon, chairman of the House Appropriations Committee from December 1901 to July 1902 and Speaker of the House from November 1903 to 1911. As one of Cannon's biographers later wrote: "The experience in erecting the new building would have tested the composure of a saint." Cannon's opposition was not surprising. He "felt deeply about the prerogative of the House of Representatives to initiate appropriation measures." Cannon also was culturally conservative and repeatedly expressed "criticism of government expenditures for elaborate buildings" and "had expressed hostility toward any but the most spartan building plans." Funding of the Senate Park Commission by the Senate Committee on the District of Columbia usurped Cannon's authority, and the elaborate design for the Agriculture building violated his political and aesthetic principles. According to Glenn Brown, secretary of the American Institute of Architects (AIA), "Cannon said that he would rather see the Mall sown in oats than treated as an artistic composition."[16]

While the Senate Park Commission plan was never formally submitted for Congressional approval and hence did not give Cannon a direct target, the Department of Agriculture depended on

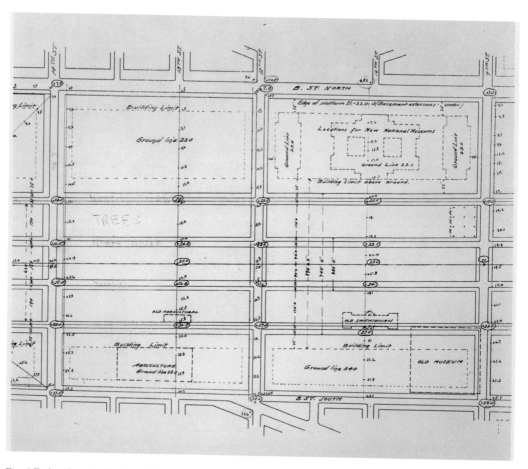

Fig. 6 Early schematic drawing of the proposed arrangement of the Mall in the area of the Department of Agriculture and the Smithsonian Institution by the Olmsted Brothers, 5 October 1902. Specifications show the proposed width of the Mall (890 feet between building lines) and existing and proposed grades. National Park Service, Frederick Law Olmsted National Historic Site, (Job #2828, Plan 6).

Congressional authorization and appropriations. The Mercer bill of 1901 (H.7207) was submitted to the House Committee on Public Buildings and Grounds where it died. On 24 March 1902, Indiana Senator Charles W. Fairbanks, chairman of the Committee on Buildings and Grounds, introduced a similar bill (S.4722) which raised the authorized funding level to $2.5 million. On 10 June, the Senate Committee on Buildings and Grounds reported favorably on it, quoting Wilson's strategy: "the idea is to fix the limit of the cost and then to secure from time to time the amounts necessary to put up the building as a whole…the administrative features could be looked after next." The Senate approved the bill on 25 June.[17]

The Senate bill was referred to the House on 26 June, then sent to the House Committee on Buildings and Grounds. Twenty years later, B. T. Galloway, chief of the Bureau of Plant Industry, whom Wilson placed in charge of the building committee, wrote that at these House hearings, "it was indicated by members of the Committee that they favored buildings of nonclassic type…[and] thought that for the utilization of terra-cotta and brick construction, $1,500,000 would be adequate." Galloway added that this attitude "was in part due to some opposition to broad plans for the Development of Washington," recommended by the Senate Park Commission. On 16 December 1902, Wilson wrote that the House "[has] reduced our appropriation for a building to $1,500,000. I expect to have it put back in the Senate. I am going to have a good building, or none at all." Two days later, the House Committee on Buildings and Grounds reported the bill out with two significant amendments, the addition of the phrase "immediately to the rear of the present building" concerning its location and the reduction of the authorization to $1.5 million.[18]

CONGRESSIONAL AND ARCHITECTURAL CHALLENGES, 1903

On 22 January 1903, Secretary Wilson wrote Speaker of the House David Henderson of Iowa stating that if the bill were to be passed, "we would ask $400,000 to begin the work" and that "it would be many years before the full amount would be necessary." The Speaker replied, "I have consulted with friends and we have agreed to get the bill up if possible, provided, however, that certain amendments which I have submitted to Chairman Mercer be adopted in order to make certain the limit shall not go over a million and a half dollars." Henderson added a handwritten postscript. "It will be impossible to increase the limit. Efforts in that direction may be fatal. Guard the Senate against that."[19]

The only time Congressman Cannon's views were publicly recorded was during the debate on the House floor on 24 January 1903:

It seems that it is contemplated to erect a building down here on the Mall to house the Department of Agriculture. It ought to be done. That is a valuable Department—subject to some abuses as all departments; but it ought to be housed properly. It is carrying on its business now largely in rented buildings. The proposition is made on the part of the House to spend a million and a half dollars to house that Department—quite enough, as we already have the site.

Cannon went on to note that he had received several letters from state agricultural experiment stations protesting the reduced authorization level of $1.5 million (Wilson had evidently mustered the troops) but none from "any man who follows the plow or works upon the farm." Cannon concluded that "of course, we shall appropriate twice that amount, if necessary, but 'enough is as good as a feast.'"[20]

When the bill came up on the floor on 2 February 1903, Mercer moved to suspend the rules and pass S.4722 as amended by the committee. However, the bill as read was different from the committee bill. The three most significant changes were: (1) the addition of the phrase "including all of its bureaus and officers now occupying rented quarters in the District of Columbia;" (2) the committee's wording on location "in the rear of the present building" was changed to "in the vicinity;" and, (3) the phrase "the approval of plans heretofore secured in pursuance of the provisions of the Act of Congress" was replaced with a more general reference to "plans to be procured." Even under individual suspension, changing the language of a committee bill before it is introduced on the floor is most unusual. In any case, this strategy worked, and on 9 February the bill to erect the new Agriculture building became law. Three months later Galloway wrote that "As a matter of fact…and as a matter that is not recorded, the Committee of the House did not want to consider this plan [the Lord & Hewlett design] at all, and this was the chief reason why an entire new bill was drafted." We shall probably never know either the full story of this rather obscure parliamentary maneuver, nor how widespread was congressional opposition to the Senate Park Commission's proposals, but both had significant implications for what was to follow, particularly with respect to relations with the architects.[21]

Passage of the authorization bill set in process several concurrent aspects of the design and construction phase. Within the Department of Agriculture two principal steps were taken: establishment of the Building Committee and placement of construction under the Army Corps of Engineers. Galloway chaired the Building Committee, its other members being D. E. Salmon, chief of the Bureau of Animal Industry, and A. C. True, director of the Office of Experiment Stations. Capt. John S. Sewell, who was placed in charge of general construction work on 2 May, had overseen the erection of the new Government Printing Office and the War College. At the express wish of Congress, Army engineers had been in charge of constructing Washington's public buildings beginning in 1867. Sewell's contributions proved to be a bone of contention when it came time for calculating the architects' fees.[22]

Lord & Hewlett sat out 1902 while the authorization and appropriation process was underway. Because the funding for the proposed building had been cut from $2.5 million to $1.5 million, some significant changes in their design would seem to be necessary. But the process did not proceed quite in the order one might expect. Fragmentary contemporary documents and Galloway's account written twenty years later leave some unanswered questions, but it is clear that the relationship between the architects and the department was not harmonious and that there were significant gaps in communication. Some of the problems dated back to the winning design. In Galloway's view:

> They submitted a really beautiful design but not at all adapted for laboratory purposes. We endeavored to bring the architects to our point of view and to the need for laboratory facilities and for the kind of light and space generally required for this kind of science. In this effect we were not successful. After several months of discussion and negotiation there developed in the minds of our building committee the germ of an idea for a series of buildings all eventually to be connected and forming one more or less harmonious whole.[23]

On 17 February 1903, Lord & Hewlett were sent a letter outlining space needs, followed by a second letter two months later that contained two scenarios proposed by the Building Committee. The first suggestion was for "three buildings to be established with the funds at hand and other buildings to be erected when additional funds are available." This plan called for placing the administrative building and two flanking laboratories immediately to the rear of Cluss's building. The space between the old and new buildings would be limited, adversely affecting light and ventilation and would also necessitate demolishing several other structures. Hence the committee viewed this solution as "not practicable."[24]

The Building Committee's second proposal led to considerable controversy. It called for placing a new building of the same configuration "directly in front of the old structure, about forty feet from it." This arrangement would allow "ample space for five additional buildings." The proposal met "the hearty approval of the Secretary." Galloway's letter of 17 March to the architects went on to say that "we offer no suggestions in regard to the so-called boulevard or parkway, believing that this is a matter which does not really need serious attention at the present time." He also stated, incorrectly, that the proposed building placement of the second proposal would be in line with the Smithsonian. No written response from Lord & Hewlett survives, but Galloway remembered their reaction. "Mr. Hewlett, was not only cold but actually hostile to our suggestions. Mr. Hewlett seemed firmly convinced that we should erect one classical building. … When I showed Mr. Hewlett the squares and blocks representing our ground plan and their connections he rather sarcastically remarked that the sketches looked more like a 'school of fish' than anything else."[25]

Moreover, when the architects visited the department on 13 April, as Galloway recalled in his testimony when the case went to court in 1908, they "were in doubt as to what could be done with the $1,500,000." They suggested that "it might be well to start the building on a $2,500,000 proposition, with the idea of securing additional funds at forthcoming sessions." While this was a variant of what Wilson had proposed to Congress in January 1902, the secretary did not react well to it and told Galloway to fire the architects and relieve James Knox Taylor of his advisory duties. The day following this meeting, Lord and Hewlett—who were evidently unaware of the Secretary's attitude—wrote Galloway: "We are sending herewith a block plan embodying as far as possible the general scheme of arrangement which we understood at our conference on Monday you propose to submit to the Secretary of Agriculture for his approval." They also suggested that they prepare detailed drawings and specifications to get cost estimates to determine "how many sections…can be undertaken within the limits of the present appropriation and which [can be] deferred until further appropriations can be obtained. … At your suggestion we have indicated in dotted lines a scheme of possible enlargement for the future, which would place the Administration Building in the center of the entire group of buildings." The architects went on to state that "we feel very strongly that the establishment of a main axis at any point but the center of the lot and the erection of buildings on the north [side of the Mall] would be a grave mistake."[26]

Meanwhile, Galloway followed Wilson's instructions and wrote the architects on 15 April (their letters must have crossed in the mail) that "I am directed by The Honorable Secretary of Agriculture to inform you that it appears from the statement made by you and Mr. Taylor…that there seems to be some doubt as to his [the secretary's] ability to carry out the spirit and letter of the law with respect to the proposed buildings for this department…[and] he wishes to terminate present relations." The architects were understandably puzzled by this turn of events, writing on 17 April that they understood "the purpose of our recent conference was merely to determine the most advisable method of procedure." They requested an interview. Evidently things then cooled down a bit and following further legal consultations in the department, a contract was forwarded to Lord & Hewlett on 11 May. However, it set the architects' fee at 3.5 percent, not the 5 percent established by the AIA as its members' fee. From the department's end, the lower figure was justified because Capt. Sewell was providing some of the services normally provided by private architects. This was not acceptable to Lord & Hewlett, and on 12 May they declined to sign the contract. Wilson wrote them that he would "look elsewhere for assistance in this matter." Lord & Hewlett wrote the Senate Park Commission members, the AIA, and others. In 1908, they took their grievance to the Court of Claims, lost, appealed to the Supreme Court in 1909, and again lost.[27]

The Building Committee's alternative sites outlined in Galloway's 7 March 1903 letter to Lord & Hewlett initiated a lengthy correspondence that "grew increasingly more vehement." On 19 June 1903, President Theodore Roosevelt wrote Wilson:

> From some comments which Mr. Galloway and other members of the Committee who are to deal with the new Agricultural Building are reported to have made, I feel that my entire trust in them from a scientific standpoint hardly extends to an equally unquestioning acceptance of their views on architecture. Please have Mr. Burnham… consulted before any plans are made and submit them to me with his remarks before anything definite is decided upon.

Wilson responded on 14 July that the "question of the improvement of the Mall has been brought into the controversy, but this has at no time had any particular bearing on the case as I prefer not to consider the location of the buildings until something definite as to their nature should be at hand."[28]

The location of the Agriculture Building coincided with a discussion about where to place the proposed Hall of Records. Senate Park Commission chairman Burnham wrote Secretary of the Treasury Leslie M. Shaw on 24 July 1903, pointing out that "if one of these buildings be now erected upon the Mall but not upon its true axis, then the state of disorder will have been made permanent." He concluded his letter: "Must the Agricultural Building go on without reference to any future plan?" Shaw evidently showed the letter to Roosevelt, who wrote Wilson on 28 July asking, "will you look over the enclosed? I wish you would get into touch with Mr. Burnham in the matter. I am very reluctant to spoil Washington's plan."[29]

Wilson, who seemingly hadn't followed the president's earlier advice to consult with Burnham, rather angrily wrote to Burnham asking, "to what axis [do] you have reference? …We have not come to the location of the building and will not for several months." On 5 August, Burnham replied with "a soft answer," enclosing a copy of the Senate Park Commission's plan. Burnham later elaborated:

> I sent a beautiful map of the Mall to Secretary Wilson and one to the President. These had movable facings of tissue paper on which strong red lines indicated the east and west axis of the buildings beside the Avenue, thus explaining to the Secretary the meaning of "its true axis." These drawings are about two feet by two feet six inches and will make things clear to the President and his Cabinet.[30]

These drawings are not known to have survived, but Wilson's query had some validity. Was the Mall's "true axis" L'Enfant's or the Senate Park Commission's?

During the summer of 1903, the Department of Agriculture negotiated with the Philadelphia firm of Rankin, Kellogg & Crane. The outcome was reported to Roosevelt on 21 September:

> A number of architects were consulted after this, but all positively refused to take action as long as there was any question as to Lord & Hewlett's connection with the matter. Rankin and Kellogg came into the work from the fact that Capt. Sewell, and others of the Committee, knew them to be good architects and that they were engaged upon important government projects and were giving perfect satisfaction.

Four days later Wilson wrote Roosevelt explaining that "Mr. Kellogg had been associated with Mr. McKim and would be fully in sympathy with his views with reference to the beautification of Washington." Thomas M. Kellogg was born and raised in Washington and worked in the McKim, Mead, & White office from 1884–1891.[31]

The siting of the buildings was an ongoing point of discussion. Enclosing a draft contract, Galloway wrote Rankin, Kellogg & Crane on 14 August:

> One other consideration with the Secretary that is highly important, is that, after a full conference with the Secretary, we believe the wisest plan will probably be to consider the space north of the boulevard [the Mall's central greensward] rather than south of it. We have nearly 500 feet in this space for the building, whereas south of the line we have only a little over 275 feet, according to the latest measurements, which I think now are certainly correct. By going on the north side of the line we are following in the steps of the Smithsonian people, who are putting their building there [the present Museum of Natural History]. I think this will be a satisfactory solution of the whole proposition, and will not put us to any extra expense in the matter of tearing down present structures.

There were no real impediments to placing the new building on the wider north side of the Mall, which was only occupied by some wetlands then laid out as ornamental gardens and ponds.[32]

In any case, the Building Committee provided "full and detailed statements with reference to the various requirements of the Department," and Rankin, Kellogg & Crane set to work developing block and building plans. On 5 September the firm provided drawings of a proposed block plan (fig. 7) consisting of a series of buildings connected by pavilions, which Acting Secretary Bingham reported to the president conformed "fully to the scheme for beautifying the Mall." An article in the *Evening Star* on 23 September commented on the concept of a series of buildings, noting that the "day of a single Agriculture Department building has passed." This was followed by an editorial expressing concern

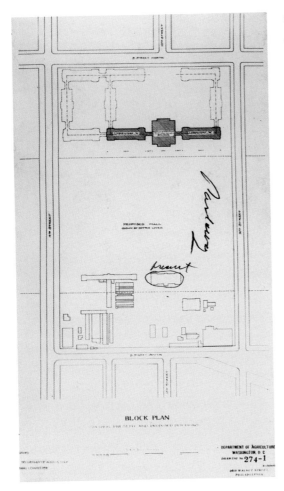

Fig. 7 Block Plan for the Department of Agriculture building complex by Rankin, Kellogg & Crane, 5 September 1903, to be located on the north side of the Mall. Provision is made for up to nine laboratory buildings and an administration building. Like the old Administration Building (circled) the three new buildings would be centered on 13th street. National Archives, RG 16, Series 167.

about the implications of the loss of park space due to the expansion of such a structure.[33]

A month later the architects were told to "proceed at once with the preparation of sketch plans for the executive building and laboratories 'A' and 'B'," followed by a request to "bring the buildings as near the north line of the parkway as the scheme will permit." Galloway asked that they "Prepare for us a sketch showing our grounds with the Parkway scheme running through them, inserting in the north lot, in accordance with our plans, the buildings which you have already laid out and a sketch of which you have submitted to us. This will enable us to present to the Secretary definitely the location of the buildings with respect to the park improvement scheme. The Secretary will undoubtedly want to lay the matter before the President."[34]

A note from the architects accompanying eight preliminary drawings delivered on 10 November confirmed that three buildings would be constructed initially, and that they would accommodate "all of those Bureaus and Divisions which are now paying rent." Two days later, Galloway wrote the firm: "I went over the plans with the Secretary, who seemed very satisfied with them. I also brought up the question as to the advisability of abandoning at present the erection of the administration building, confining our efforts to the three laboratory buildings. The Secretary expressed the opinion that probably this would be the best line of action."[35]

The Building Committee met on 24 November and formally approved the building's location on the north side of the Mall, its organization into three wings, and its design features.

However, "in view of the tentative estimates obtained, it does not seem feasible, at this time, to erect two laboratory buildings and an administration building, but that three laboratory buildings may be completed for the amount authorized by Congress." These recommendations were approved by Wilson and forwarded to the architects on 25 November. They in turn requested "a chart showing the exact location of the axis line…and the definite width to allow for the proposed mall." They also inquired whether the laboratory buildings were to be oriented toward the Mall or Twelfth Street, NW; this issue was evidently not resolved for it came up later. On 18 December Galloway indicated that the preliminary sketches for the laboratory buildings had been approved.[36]

Rankin, Kellogg & Crane's plans made the newspapers, first in the *Evening Star* on 9 December and in greater detail in the *Washington Times* on 13 December. Wilson was quoted as saying that "the Department of Agriculture is different in its requirements, so far as buildings are concerned, from other branches of government. Our work is largely of a research nature. Laboratories, therefore, are essential and form a considerable portion of the room required." The article noted that the boulevard at the center of the Mall, "800 feet wide," would sweep right past the buildings.[37]

CONTROVERSIES ABOUT THE SITE, 1904

At the beginning of 1904, after the considerable tumult of previous years, it appeared that everything had been worked out: the Agriculture Department building's location on the Mall's north side complied with the Senate Park Commission's plans, while it also met the department's needs. But it was not to be. On 14 September 1903 the late Senator McMillan's secretary, Charles Moore, wrote McKim that "I fear [Cannon] is going to make all possible trouble in mean little ways." Trouble soon arrived and it was not minor. On 13 January 1904, a subcommittee of the House Committee on Agriculture, which heretofore had not been heard from, visited the department. Galloway reported to Rankin the next day that "they were of the opinion that the buildings could be put up in front of our present structure, which, of course, would bring up the whole question again of interference with the parkway plans." They also felt that "the buildings cannot be made as attractive on the north lot as they could if placed where the present buildings stand." Galloway pointed out that buildings on the Mall's south side could not comply with the section of the authorization bill requiring that all staff in rented facilities be accommodated in the new building. The costs of removing the old structures and providing interim quarters would leave only enough money to erect two laboratory buildings.[38]

The stakes were raised when the chairman of the House Agriculture Committee, New York Representative James W. Wadsworth, met with Roosevelt on 27 January. Wadsworth, according to a newspaper account, vowed that his committee was "unalterably opposed" to the north Mall site. "This will set the building in a veritable hollow where it will make no showing in the world ." Wadsworth not only wanted the building "near" the existing building, but also wanted the Mall's greensward narrowed from 800 feet to 600 feet. Glenn Brown of the AIA alerted McKim who contacted Roosevelt, Root, and the Speaker of the House but "nothing positive was accomplished."[39]

Wadsworth and eleven (possibly all sixteen) House Agriculture Committee members—a remarkable display of interest in civic planning—met with the president on 5 February. Galloway reported that "the question hinged on whether a Parkway 800 feet in width should be reserved… or whether this should be reduced to 600 feet in order to properly accommodate the Department of Agriculture buildings and to retain the Smithsonian Institution building." When Roosevelt asked the assembled committee members if they favored the 600-foot-wide Mall they unanimously assented. The president thereupon replied that the matter should stand in that way, and the Secretary of Agriculture issued instructions at once that "we proceed with the plans on the basis that the buildings would be erected in conformity with the 600-foot proposition."[40]

Accordingly, Galloway wrote Rankin, Kellogg & Crane on 6 February, reporting that "we will build right up to the 600 foot line [on the Mall's south side], so as not to necessitate tearing down or moving the present statistical building." The architects responded with "we regret very much that it has been decided to do this, and we believe that a very great mistake is being made that will adversely affect not only the Agricultural buildings, but the plans for a monumental Washington and that this will become more and more apparent as time passed." Rankin, Kellogg & Crane wrote McKim on 9 February that they had designed the buildings for the Mall's south side "located as we think that they should be, preserving the full width of the Mall. This is now being rendered by Prof. [Paul] Cret and will be finished tomorrow." In subsequent correspondence with Galloway, the architects reaffirmed their regret at the decision, especially as "this ground [on the Mall's north side] might be so easily reclaimed and when the buildings, if located there, could readily and would unquestionably be raised to a proper height." They also stated that "it appears impossible to obtain nearly as good a result either politically or artistically, on the south location."[41]

Roosevelt's meeting with the House Agriculture Committee prompted McKim to action. He wrote the president on 10 February, requesting further review of the parkway's width but acknowledged that "perhaps you deem it best to avoid a formal hearing." Roosevelt responded the next day that the "House Committee was a unit in favor of reducing the width below 600 feet and accepted

600 feet as a compromise. The architects of the Commission should appear at once before a Senate committee." A week later McKim wrote the other Senate Park Commission members as well as Brown and Moore about Roosevelt's letter. He glumly remarked that it "confirms statements made in the newspapers that he had already given such consent." On 11 February, McKim had written Olmsted, commenting that the real purpose of the House committee's demand was to "build their group of new buildings upon their present site."[42]

On the first of March McKim met with Nevada Senator Francis G. Newlands, who had shown some sympathy to his cause. However, New Hampshire Senator Jacob H. Gallinger (who became chairman of the District Committee after McMillan's sudden death on 10 August 1902) said his committee thought that 600 feet was "wide enough for anything." Newlands insisted on a hearing and Gallinger gave in. Newlands also introduced a short bill (S.4845)—which McKim claimed he helped draw up—on 7 March that stated "no building shall be erected on the Mall of Washington, District of Columbia, within four hundred feet of a central line stretching from the center of the Dome of the Capitol to the center of the Washington Monument."[43]

The bill was discussed on the Senate floor on 8 March, with Newlands vigorously supporting the Senate Park Commission's position. Wilson wrote him a day later, pointing out that the 800-foot line would, because of the southern tilt of the Mall's west end, run "at least 100 feet south of the present Agricultural building, leaving only about 200 feet of building space…. While it was said that the Department was proposing to erect the new building in front of the existing structure, this is a mistake. Our new buildings will go back of the present structure and will be further south than the Smithsonian Institution." This statement did not provide much support for the Newlands bill, but given the House Committee's view, Wilson probably saw little choice.[44]

Newlands's bill and his correspondence with Wilson referred to an 800-foot-wide parkway in the Mall's center. Yet Olmsted's schematic drawing of the Mall, dated 5 October 1902 (see fig. 6), placed its width as 890 feet, and in a letter written on 1 March 1904 he referred to a similar distance. This discrepancy was to pose an unnecessary point of confusion in the Senate hearing. The Senate Committee on the District of Columbia, with Gallinger presiding, held its hearing on 12 March. The primary issue was the width of the building line; the location of the Agriculture buildings on the north or south side of the Mall was of secondary importance. The hearing was well attended, including eight senators, the Senate Park Commission members, and leaders of the AIA. Wilson did not participate, but was represented by Galloway.[45]

Galloway testified that on the basis of a 600-foot-wide parkway, its center aligned with the Washington Monument, 350 feet would be left on the Mall's south side for the Agriculture Department buildings. If, on the other hand, the Mall's central line ran straight west from the Capitol, "our lot would be about 450 feet which would serve every purpose." In both cases, the buildings were to be centered on Thirteenth Street. He argued that laboratory work made it "absolutely essential to cut off certain sections of the building," precluding a single monumental structure. Galloway acknowledged that the architects he had talked to preferred the north side, and that plans had been made for both locations. While he was concerned with the low-lying site on the Mall's north side, Galloway conceded that none of the architects felt it to be a problem.[46]

Concerns of a more mundane and previously unrecorded nature emerged in Galloway's testimony. Wilson, it seems, was hesitant to build on the north side because he wanted to keep it as a natural park area. The Agriculture Department was also now fearful that buildings on the north side "would be set up against a lot of lumber yards and things of that nature" and "we would be within a stones throw of not only houses of ill repute but of the old power house and lumber yard and all the rattle traps of the day." Galloway asserted: "That is the thing that brought the matter more clearly to the attention of the members of Congress than anything else, and that is all." One wonders. Burnham, ever the visionary, commented that the north Mall site "being available, is sure at no distant date to be covered with noble buildings. We say that the government is going to need that and ever more ground." The question of the actual proposed width of the central greensward surfaced, perhaps unconsciously, in Newlands's questioning of Gallinger, when he referred to a vista of 890 feet. It was not clarified until Burnham's testimony. Newlands, evidently reading from a display map, referred to 890 feet for the first time (fig. 8). West Virginia Senator Nathan Scott tried to get this sorted out: "Eight hundred and ninety feet?" Mr. Burnham: "Yes sir." Senator Newlands: "Mr. Chairman I will state that I find I have made a mistake in stating that as 800 feet in the bill. I supposed that was the width called for."[47]

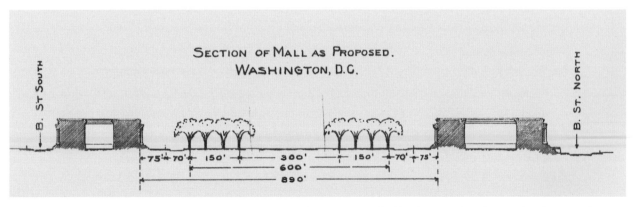

Fig. 8 Cross section of the Mall, showing proposed dimensions, including an 890-foot building line. May have been used in the Senate hearing on the Mall, 12 March 1904. Published in the *Boston Herald*, 14 March 1904. National Park Service, Frederick Law Olmsted National Historic Site (Job #2828, Plan 26).

Newlands also asked, according to Burnham, "if the building could not go somewhere else, and I said certainly we can." Rhode Island Senator George Peabody Wetmore perceptively asked Galloway: "Why should you not condemn some land back of where you plan to put the buildings on the south side?" Galloway responded that "The policy of the government is against it," although it is not certain that this was the case. Joseph C. Hornblower, architect of the Smithsonian Institution's new National Museum (now the Museum of Natural History), commented that if a building were located on the Mall's south side, he saw "no reason why it should not extend across B St., which is a street of unimportant character." Samuel P. Langley, Secretary of the Smithsonian Institution, noted that the 600-foot line passed through the rear of the original Smithsonian Institution, while the 800-foot line fell to its south. Wetmore wondered if it might be possible to move the building. Langley responded: "That is rather a question for an engineer, but my own impression is that either that can be moved to the south or that even the monument can be moved, if the gentleman will allow me that question. [Laughter.]" Burnham later commented, with respect to the Smithsonian, "It can be moved. We frankly confess that our scheme would result in moving back the Smithsonian Institution so far as it now projects into the composition…it ought not to stand in the way of a grand improvement."[48]

On the same day as the hearing, and presumably as a result of it, Roosevelt wrote Wilson (unaware of the error between 800 and 890 feet), "I am having great trouble about that Mall. The best architects and artists and most cultivated people I know feel that it is an outrage to encroach on the 800 feet. I very earnestly wish that under my administration we could refrain from such encroachment." The Senate Parkway Hearings were reported in Washington papers on 12 and 13 March and in the *Boston Herald* on 14 March, illustrated by four engravings. McKim wrote Nicholas Butler (president of Columbia University) on 14 March that "as a result (and a most unexpected one)… the Senate Committee rendered a unanimous report, signed by all the members, including Sen. Gallinger, favoring adherence to the plan as reported by the Park Commission, calling not for 800 but 890 feet in width between buildings! It now remains to go before the House Committee."[49]

In legislative terms, the Newlands bill, with the distance from the Mall's adjusted centerline to building facades amended to 445 feet, came up on the Senate floor on 30 March and was passed. A similar bill had been introduced in the House on 14 March (H. 13926) but was superseded by House consideration of the Senate bill (S. 4845). It was referred to the House Committee on Buildings and Grounds where, McKim wrote Root on 18 March, "It is very much feared that it may remain there without action." The AIA mounted a massive campaign in support of the Newlands bill, but to no avail as far as the House of Representatives was concerned.[50]

The Senate parkway hearings may have clarified the desired Mall width, but they left the Department of Agriculture with unanswered concerns. Galloway explained the department's dilemma to Kellogg on 14 March:

> I do not believe that the House will ever pass a bill committing the Government to the Parkway scheme. [On one hand] with all the members of the House Committee [on Agriculture] on record as unalterably opposed to the north location of our buildings, we are, it seems, liable to have our opportunities for growth weakened, if we decide to go in the face of this sentiment. On the other hand, if we take the other tack and locate our buildings without reference to the Parkway scheme, we will undoubtedly have an influential body of men opposing us.[51]

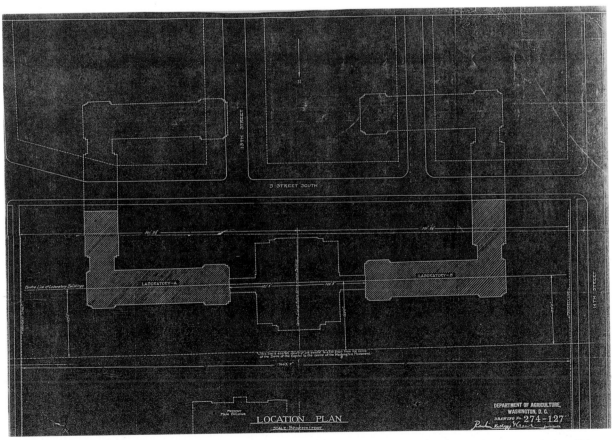

Fig. 9 Block plan for relocating the Department of Agriculture building on the south side of the Mall. Further construction would have required either bridging or blocking B St. National Archives, RG 16, Series 167.

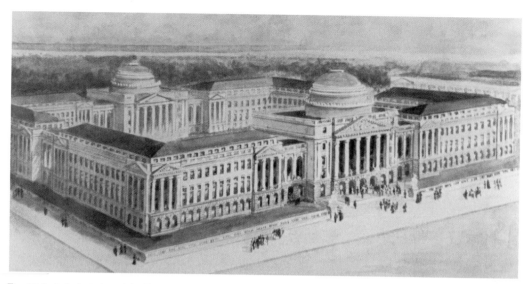

Fig. 10 Artistic depiction of the Department of Agriculture building on the south side of the Mall from a larger montage by H. M. Petit, presumably drawn in 1904, and published in *Woman's Home Companion*, February 1905 (see pl. XIV). The drawing is remarkably accurate in terms of the revised plans, but does differ in its depiction of the length of the front wings and the arrangement of the side wings. It also includes a domed structure at the center of the south side, which was not included in plans of the time, though space was left for it (see figs. 7, 9).

Even so, the Building Committee began to make plans to build on the Mall's south side. On 11 March, the day before the Senate parkway hearings, the Building Committee considered "the revised block plan [submitted by the architects] with new buildings grouped on the site south of the contemplated Parkway." On 19 March, they agreed to place the buildings on the Mall's south side facing north, with the front of the administration building on a line 445 feet south of the parkway axis, and to retain the design of its front. They further agreed to center the buildings on Thirteenth Street and extend the laboratory wings as far as B Street, SW.[52]

The Building Committee sent these revisions to Rankin, Kellogg & Crane the same day and broached the question of future expansion. "One other matter we have considered and which is, of course vital in this connection, is the securing of property at some future date across from B Street, SW. There are two squares that are easily available." On 2 April 1904 Galloway wrote the architects that "we must be prepared to either make [our current design] complete...or to prepare plans with the idea that the buildings will be extended at some day across B St." Some block plans and drawings of the period show the core group of buildings originally designed for the Mall's north side simply moved to the south side, crossing B Street, SW (figs. 9, 10). The Building Committee and architects also realized that by aligning the building with the tilted Mall axis as proposed by the Senate Park Commission, its sides would not be parallel with Twelfth and Fourteenth streets, which "would throw the west wing so far out as to project into South B St."[53]

The House Agriculture Committee remained adamant about a 600-foot-wide parkway, ostensibly to preserve the Smithsonian Institution. On 22 April, Wadsworth again met with Roosevelt, raising the committee's objection to a location on the Mall's north side even though the Agriculture Department had decided to go to the south side over a month earlier. He told the president that the Senate bill for an 890-foot-wide parkway would never get through the House, which was hardly news. His committee also wished to preserve the Mall's existing natural park appearance, and reported that Wilson agreed with the Agriculture Committee. The *Evening Star* reported that "Under such conditions the President is not pleased." Wadsworth invited Roosevelt to visit the site and see the situation for himself. The architects, however, wrote Olmsted that "We have not received the slightest intimation that any change is contemplated in location, but, on the contrary the officials…appear to consider the matter definitely settled." All of this may have left some understandable confusion about the Agriculture Department's intentions.[54]

On 7 May the *Washington Post* reported that "President Roosevelt personally inspected the site of the proposed new building of the Department of Agriculture and decided that the location of that structure should conform to the Parkway scheme for the improvement of the Mall." The

Fig. 11 Revised plan for the Department of Agriculture building as relocated on the south side of the Mall, ca. April 1904. The wings were built as shown, but the building base was lowered and the first floor became a partial basement. The central administration building, in a lighter tone, was not constructed until the late 1920s and the dome was eliminated. The design of the connecting walkways between the central building and the wings was also modified. *Yearbook of the United States Department of Agriculture, 1903*, frontispiece.

890-foot clearance was maintained. A few weeks later Roosevelt wrote Butler that "this year I have forced the erection of the new buildings of the Agricultural Department, in accordance with the ... McMillan plan, preserving the ... Mall. Congress did not do it. I did it." Though not overly modest, nor the whole story, there is considerable truth to Roosevelt's boast. Rankin, Kellogg & Crane's plans were completed in August 1904 (fig. 11) and reviewed by the Building Committee on the nineteenth, with advertisements for proposals appearing the same day; the contract was awarded on 14 December, with groundbreaking held a few days later.[55]

CONTROVERSIES ABOUT BUILDING PLACEMENT, 1905

The year started, by past standards, rather quietly; that is, no problems arose in January, and excavation got well under way. Early in the year, a full-sized plaster mock-up of a vertical slice of the front of the east laboratory wing was erected (frontispiece). But on 25 February, the contractor was ordered to stop work.[56]

On 16 February Bernard Green, a civilian employee of the Corps of Engineers in charge of constructing the Smithsonian's new National Museum and superintendent of construction at the Library of Congress, had written Sewell, who was still in charge of construction of the Agriculture Department Building. In his letter, Green reported that as part of some joint consultations about the proper grade line "for buildings on the north side of the Mall as affected by the new Museum," McKim had been "considering the grade line at the site of the Agricultural building." On the same day, Kellogg met McKim in New York about the height of the base of the Agriculture building. At the same meeting, McKim "expressed great disappointment that the new buildings have been laid out to center on 13th Street instead of being equidistant from 12th and 14th." The next day, Rankin, Kellogg & Crane wrote Galloway that McKim expressed "great concern" about the difference in level of the National Museum and Agriculture Department buildings.[57]

The key players met in Rankin, Kellogg & Crane's Philadelphia offices on 23 February. McKim requested that the elevation of the Agriculture building be reduced by seven or ten feet "in order that the base line might conform more nearly to that of future adjoining buildings" and that the Agriculture complex be centered between Twelfth and Fourteenth streets. Rankin, Kellogg & Crane agreed and specifically recommended that the buildings be lowered and moved approximately 106 feet to the west. McKim also said that he had recently met with Speaker Cannon "who had withdrawn his opposition to the plans of the Park Commission and had announced that he would favor the appointment of a permanent commission to carry out the work."[58]

A quarter century later Glenn Brown recalled that the "engineer in charge, with the approval of Secretary Wilson, [1] set the building about a hundred feet farther east and [2] fixed its ground line some eight feet higher than the Park Commission indicated." Brown joined McKim on the site and remembered that "the point that disturbed McKim most was the intention to *raise* the ground level, which would throw the base of this building above the base of the Washington Monument." This would have negated "one of the most important elements in the Mall plan [which] is the continuous upgrade from the Grant Statue to the Washington Monument."[59]

Contemporary documents raise questions about both aspects of Brown's account. In the first case, the proposed buildings had been centered on Thirteenth Street from the outset (as noted, for instance, in correspondence from McKim on 13 June 1901). This placement had also been clearly stated by Galloway in the Senate hearing on 12 March 1904. McKim was involved in both events but evidently either did not recall this detail or changed his mind (the Park Commission drawings of 1901–2 placed generic sets of buildings equidistant between Twelfth and Fourteenth streets). The second item concerning height is more perplexing. Olmsted's drawing dated 5 October 1902, entitled "Tentative Plans for Grades" recorded both actual elevations and proposed new grades. The Agriculture Department's sites for both the old and new buildings were the highest on the Mall at about 35.8 feet, but the "tentative grade" projected for the new building just behind the old Agriculture building was 30 feet (see fig. 6). Thus it appears that the existing site would have to be *lowered* nearly 6 feet to conform with the commission's wishes, and perhaps the real question was whether the department was planning to do this. Curiously, no references have been found revealing the Senate Park Commission's views on the height for Mall buildings, although the same group (except Olmsted) had established a cornice line of 60 feet for buildings erected at the 1893 Columbian Exposition in Chicago; the issue was also raised later with McKim.[60]

Members of the Building Committee learned at their 6 March 1905 meeting that implementing the changes suggested by the Senate Park Commission would cost $36,000, but they were disposed to follow the recommendations. This may not have been entirely altruistic. The committee thought that if they conformed with the commission's ideas, the latter would help them secure additional buildings and the property south of B Street, SW. On a more practical level, Capt. Sewell pointed out that lowering the buildings would "make available a much better bearing soil for the footings," thus reducing the net cost increase to only $6,000, down from $36,000. But with a look over their shoulder towards Congress, the Building Committee decided they needed clearance for the expenditure.[61]

On 7 March they wrote Wilson that "it would be wise and justifiable to make the change proposed by the architects, reserving the exact change in location for future determination, though, it seems, from an engineering point of view 10 feet would be better than 7 feet ... Should the Secretary of Agriculture feel that some official sanction of the Park Commission plans is necessary to justify the proposed changes, it is respectfully suggested that higher authority be consulted." The Building Committee then unfairly chastised the architects for not having "fully considered all conditions at the time the present location of the buildings was decided on." On 8 March the committee wrote the architects that the "Secretary has fully discussed the question with the Cabinet and the President and the general consensus…is that the Secretary would not be warranted in involving the Department in the additional expense."[62]

Rankin, Kellogg & Crane forwarded the letter to McKim, stating that "when we saw Dr. Galloway in Washington some days ago, he did not seem disposed to oppose the suggested changes." McKim wrote Burnham and contacted Secretary of War William Howard Taft who spoke with Roosevelt. At McKim's memorial service in 1909, Taft, who was then president, recalled that Roosevelt "at once agreed that we ought to change [the Agriculture building's height and location]. 'But,' said he, 'the trouble is with Uncle Jimmy [Cannon] who has a real cause of complaint. He says these architects have delayed too long and the public money cannot be wasted and expended in this way.'"[63]

Taft, McKim, Wilson, Sewell, and Green met with Roosevelt at the White House on 13 March and ritually flogged the architects. Glenn Brown (who did not attend the meeting) later reported that Roosevelt asked Wilson to give way to the architects and he agreed. After the meeting, Taft reported in 1909, "McKim and I walked up the steps of the War Department. I said, 'Mr. McKim, I congratulate you on your victory!' He turned and looked at me for a moment, and said, 'Was it a victory? Another such and I am dead.'" The following day Roosevelt issued an Executive Order "appointing a Consultative Board of Architects to secure uniformity and harmony in the public buildings hereafter to be constructed." Green was appointed its chairman with McKim, Burnham, Olmsted, and Saint-Gaudens the board's invited members. Green and McKim corresponded and agreed that the buildings should be equidistant between the street building lines and that they should be lowered 10 feet "in order to insure the best future grade for this and the future buildings along the south side of the Mall in consideration of the grade of the base of the Washington Monument."[64]

When the Building Committee met on 21 March, Green reported, "Mr. Kellogg hated very much to put his building, even temporarily, in the depression. I think I consoled him…by the statement that it could hardly be very long before the ground about the building would be properly graded down." In the meeting minutes Kellogg called it a "hole without a base." Evidently a diplomat, Green told Kellogg that "such a building in a hole would make the hole respectable."

He also stated that "while the papers might criticize the location, if the building were lowered 10 feet…thoughtful men would know that the buildings were lowered with some object in view in accordance with a general scheme." Green estimated the costs of lowering the grounds at $70,000, noting that the soil could be used for fill on the north side of the grounds.[65]

A few more issues came up in early April. One was the old question of how aligning the building with the tilted Mall would affect its alignment with Twelfth and Fourteenth streets. Sewell wrote McKim that "it is expected ultimately to extend the Agricultural Buildings until the total depth from

Fig. 12 Construction of west wing of the Department of Agriculture building, April 1906. Shows brick bearing wall construction and extensive tile flue system for ventilation of laboratories. View is to the northeast, with Conservatory and old Post Office building at top left, old Department building at top center, and Smithsonian castle at top right. Author's collection.

north to south will probably be as much as 500 or 600 feet," and that this deviation "would become increasingly unpleasantly apparent." Interestingly, McKim said that he would "unhesitatingly advise that the wings be made parallel with 12th and 14th Sts.," agreeing that the deviation would be "immediately observable and disturbing to the eye." His advice does not seem to have been followed.[66]

With final attention devoted to details such as these, the debate about the building line and placement essentially came to an end. Ironically, about the only aspect of the project that did not prove to be controversial was the architecture itself. What may have seemed a never-ending flow of petty annoyances, more substantial problems, and even perils was, in retrospect, a defining moment for the Mall as we know it. In this respect, it was a beginning as well.[67]

AFTERMATH

The two laboratory wings, after all the controversy, were quietly constructed (fig. 12) and completed on 17 March 1907, and the Building Committee dissolved. But the struggle to complete the complex continued. On 3 January 1905, Sewell wrote Galloway, submitting a "tentative draft of a bill for the erection of an Administrative building." Iowa Senator Jonathan P. Dolliver subsequently introduced a bill calling for demolition of the Cluss building (the original department building) and construction of the center wing for $1.75 million. It was referred to the Committee on Buildings and Grounds and died there. Nothing further happened for 25 years.[68]

As a result, the Department was left with a rather odd cluster of main buildings: in the words of one recent critic, the Cluss building resembled "a much despised Second Empire structure ... a decayed tooth amid limestone [sic] grandeur" (fig. 13). There was also another problem, not visible from the Mall, at the back of the new complex where the ends of the two wings facing B Street were left unfinished (fig. 14, following endnotes).[69]

The situation was even worse with respect to secondary structures, some erected by department carpenters. While some of these temporary buildings had been torn down with the new construction, they were largely rebuilt on the northern side of the grounds, one out of salvaged materials. The latter drew particular criticism in 1908:

> It is said to be not quite clear whose specific duty it is to protect the Mall from what is termed the latest desecration, apparently without the authority or consent of Congress, the President, or even the Park Commission. But it is declared to be the duty of at least someone to at once stay the building work, remove the blot and to take such action that hereafter no one may even start to erect a stable at the front door of an architectural monument of the nation.[70]

On the eve of leaving office, on 19 January 1909, Roosevelt issued an Executive Order that created a Council of Fine Arts to advise on the design and placement of future public buildings. In 1910, President Taft reaffirmed the renamed Commission of Fine Arts. At the hearings to establish this commission held on 9 February 1910, Illinois Representative James R. Mann raised the example of the "enormous crime as was perpetuated in the construction of the Agriculture Building," having noted "the first story below the level of the ground" and "two wings . . . constructed widely separated." He concluded: "A future place will never be hot enough to properly singe the man [responsible] for the present Agricultural Department constructed as it is." The hearing record continued: "Mr. [James L.] Slayden [from Texas]: Who did it? Mr. Mann: The art commission was responsible for it. Mr. [John J.] Fitzgerald [from New York]: The gentleman is mistaken. Mr. Mann: ...President Roosevelt ordered it done at the request of the Burnham art commission."[71]

Fig. 13 The Mall in the summer of 1908, showing the newly completed Department wings on the right, before some of the older buildings in front of the west wing had been removed. Also shows Museum of Natural History nearing completion on the left. *Washington, the Nation's Pride* (Philadelphia, Pa., Avil Publishing Co., no date); author's collection.

NOTES

I wish to acknowledge the encouragement and assistance of Helen Dalrymple, Sue Kohler, and Pamela Scott over many years of research on the development of the Mall and of the Department of Agriculture complex. Pamela stimulated me to move on from research to writing this chapter and made many contributions.

[1] This is a much larger and more complex story than may be evident from the existing literature. David J. Murphy, a Ph.D. candidate in history at the University of Maryland, did extensive archival research on the subject and presented a talk on "Architects, Engineers, and the New Agriculture Department Buildings: A Reinterpretation of the Fight Over Implementing the McMillan Plan" at a meeting of the Society for American City and Regional Planning, in Richmond, in November 1991. His paper was not published. Murphy, moreover, did not complete his graduate program and efforts to locate him have been unsuccessful.

[2] Kenneth Hafertape, *America's Castle, The Evolution of the Smithsonian Building and Its Institution, 1840–1878* (Washington, D.C.: Smithsonian Institution Press, 1984), 26, 46–47; George Brown Goode, "The Smithsonian Building and Grounds," in *The Smithsonian Institution, 1846–1896; The History of Its First Half Century*, ed. George Brown Goode (Washington, D.C.: Smithsonian Institution, 1897), 255; Allan Nevins, ed., *Polk, The Diary of a President, 1845–1848* (New York: Longmans, Green and Co., 1929), 124–25, 264, 272–73; *Smithsonian Institution, Report from the Board of Regents*, 29th Cong., 2d Sess., 1847, S. Rept. 21, 7–10, 15–17; Smithsonian Archives, Record Group 95, Box 68, large folios; Daniel D. Reiff, *Washington Architecture 1791–1861: Problems in Development* (Washington, D.C.: U.S. Commission of Fine Arts, 1971), 120.

[3] Louis Torres, *To the Immortal Name and Memory of George Washington* (Washington, D.C.: Historic Division, Office of Administrative Services, Office of Chief Engineers, 1984), 14–16; Nevins, ed., *Polk, Diary of a President*, 273, 323; Frederick L. Harvey, *History of the Washington National Monument and Washington National Monument Society*, 57th Cong., 2d Sess., 1903, S. Doc. 44, 41–43; "Proceedings of the Board of Managers" (Washington Monument Society), National Archives and Records Administration (NARA), Record Group (RG) 42, Series (S) 420, Box 9, 144–45, 160–66, 182; H. P. Caemmerer, *Historic Washington, Capital of the Nation* (Washington, D.C.: Columbia Historical Society, 1954), 48; Silvio A. Bendini, *The Jefferson Stone: Demarcation of the First Meridian of the United States* (Frederick, Md.: Professional Surveyers Publishing Co., 1999), 23–40, 61–127; "Washington Monument," *National Intelligencer* (Washington, D.C.), 17 April, 1848, 1; "Cornerstone of the National Washington Monument," *National Intelligencer*, 17 May 1848, 4; "Washington National Monument," *National Intelligencer*, 15 September 1848, 4.

[4] John B. Black, Commissioner of Public Buildings, to Charles Mason, Commissioner of Patents, 23 May 1856, NARA, RG 42, S 371, Drawer 10–101, Reel 7; *Report of the Commissioner of Patents for the Year 1858, Agriculture* (Washington, D.C.: 1859), hereafter *RCP*, frontispiece, 280–83; *RCP 1859* (1860), 1; *RCP 1861* (1862), 28–34.

[5] *U.S. Statutes at Large* 12, (Washington, D.C.: Government Printing Office, 1862): 387–88; *U.S. Statutes at Large* 13 (1864): 381; *Report of the Commissioner of Agriculture, 1862*, (Washington, D.C.: Government Printing Office, 1863), 540–41, hereafter *RCA*; *RCA 1864*, 11–12, 547–48; B. B. French to Isaac Newton, 7 April 1863, NARA, RG 42, Microcopy No. M371, Roll 7, Vol. 14, 206; *RCA 1863*, 12–13; George J. Olzewski, *History of the Mall* (Washington, D.C.: Department of the Interior, Office of History and Historic Architecture, Eastern Service Center, March 1970), 20, 25; Charles Greathouse, *Historical Sketch of the U.S. Department of Agriculture; Its Objectives and Present Organization* (Washington: U.S. Department of Agriculture, Division of Publications, Bulletin 3, 1907), 9, 10, 41; Glenn Brown, *Memories, 1860–1930: A Winning Crusade to Revive George Washington's Vision of a Capital City* (Washington, D.C.: W. F. Roberts, 1931), 275.

[6] *RCA 1864*, 12; *RCA 1865*, 5–6, 25–32; *RCA 1866*, 9–10; *RCA 1867*, 14, 16–29; William Saunders to Horace Capron, 15 December 1867, Library of Congress, Papers of Horace Capron, Container 2; Greathouse, *Historical Sketch*, 9–13; *RCA 1867*, xviii; *RCA 1868*, 15–16, 192–93; *RCA 1874*; Reiff, *Washington Architecture*, 110–11.

[7] *Yearbook of the Department of Agriculture, 1894* (Washington, D.C.: Government Printing Office, 1895), 62–64, hereafter *YDA*; *YDA 1899*, 65; *YDA 1900*, 76; *Cong. Rec.*, 56th Cong., 1st Sess., 21 April 1900, 4508; *Cong. Rec.*, 56th Cong., 2d Sess., 7 May 1900, 5208; *Cong. Rec.*, 56th Cong., 2d Sess., 31 January 1901, 1712; *Cong. Rec.*, 56th Cong., 2d Sess., 1 February 1901, 1768; and *Cong. Rec.*, 56th Cong., 2d Sess., 7 February 1901, 2052. Data on changes in number of employees based on unpublished, non-archival information.

[8] *U.S. Statutes at Large* 31 (1901): 938; "For a New Wing," *Evening Star* (Washington, D.C.), 8 March 1901, 11.

[9] Advisory Group to James Knox Taylor, 13 June 1901, Charles F. McKim Papers, Letterbooks, vol. 10, 118–21, Library of Congress, Manuscript Division, hereafter McKim Papers, LC.

[10] Taylor to invited competitors, 18 June 1901, NARA, RG 16, S 162, Box 1, 1903; "Notes and Clippings," *American Architect and Building News* (6 July 1901), 8; "Programme and conditions of a competition for a building for the Department of Agriculture in Washington, D.C.," (probably 18 June 1901), 284–87, in *Austin W. Lord et al. v. the United States*, No. 24809, Decided March 9, 1908, in *Cases Decided in the Court of Claims at the Term of 1907–08*, vol. 43 (Washington, D.C.: Government Printing Office, 1909).

[11] Charles McKim to Taylor, 23 August 1901, McKim Papers, LC, vol. 10, 179–81.

[12] Charles Moore, *Daniel H. Burnham: Architect, Planner of Cities* (Boston: Houghton Mifflin Co. 1921), 1:162; Augustus Saint-Gaudens, *The Reminiscences of Augustus Saint-Gaudens, Edited and Amplified by Homer Saint-Gaudens* (New York: Century Co., 1913), 1:277; *Lord & Hewlett v. United States*, Appeal from the Court of Claims, No. 162, Argued 20 April 1910, Decided 2 May 1910, in *United States Reports*, vol. 217; *Cases Adjudged in the Supreme Court at October Term, 1909* (New York: The Banks Law Publishing Co., 1910), 342; *The Inland Architect and News Record*, December 1901, 40, folio; "Building for the Department of Agriculture, NARA, RG 16, S 167, Box (folio) 15; "Plans for a New Building," *Evening Star*, 28 October 1901, 1; "A New Building," *Evening Star*, 20 December 1901, 3; "Lord, Austin W," *Macmillan Encylopedia of Architects*, ed. Adolph K. Placzek (Free Press, 1982), 3:32. Lord was the first director of the American Academy in Rome and later director of the School of Architecture at Columbia University.

[13] U.S. Congress, H.7207, 57th Cong., 1st Sess., 18 December 1901; *Cases Adjudged in the Supreme Court*, 342; Wilson statement taken from *Building for the Use of Department of Agriculture*, 57th Cong., 1st Sess., 1902, S. Rept. 1852, 2.

[14] Senate Committee on the District of Columbia, *The Improvement of the Park System of the District of Colombia*, 57th Cong., 1st Sess., 1902, S. Rept 166 (Washington, D.C.: Government Printing Office, 1902), 13, 44, 95.

[15] Charles F. McKim to Daniel Burnham, 28 August 1901, enclosure (sent to Moore, 4 September 1901), Charles Moore Papers, Park Commission Correspondence, Container 2, Library of Congress, Manuscript Division; *The Commission of Fine Arts, Twelfth Report, July 1, 1929 to December 31, 1934* (Washington, D.C.: Government Printing Office, 1936), 7, 11; Wayne D. Rasmussen and Gladys L. Baker, *The Department of Agriculture* (New York: Praeger, 1972), 10; Frederick L. Olmsted Jr. to Charles F. McKim, 31 October 1902, Olmsted Associate Papers, Library of Congress, Manuscript Division, Box B 135,

File 2828, Mall, hereafter Olmsted Papers, LC. The cross sections are on file at the Olmsted National Historic Site, Brookline, Mass., Archives, Job No. 2828, Plans 6 and 8.

[16] Early Vernon Wilcox, with Flora H. Wilson, *Tama Jim* (Boston: The Stratford Company, 1930), 26; John W. Reps, *Monumental Washington, The Planning and Development of the Capital Center* (Princeton: Princeton University Press, 1967), 144; William Rea Gwinn, *Uncle Joe Cannon: Archfoe of Insurgency* (publication place unknown: Brookman Associates, 1957), 7, 63, 67; Brown, *Memories*, 3, 99, 283.

[17] U.S. Congress, S.4722, 57th Cong., 1st Sess., March 24, 1902; *Building for the Use of Department of Agriculture.*, 57th Cong., 1st Sess., 1902, S. Rept 1852, 1–2; *Cong. Rec.*, 57th Cong., 2d Sess., 25 June 1902 (vol. 35), 7382–7383.

[18] S.4722, as marked up in the House, 18 December 1902; *Building for Department of Agriculture*, 57th Cong., 1st Sess., 1902, H. Rept. 2911, 18; James Wilson to D. E. Salmon, 16 December 1902, NARA, Microfilm Series M-440, Roll No. 36; B. T. Galloway, "Memorandum for Committee on Permanent Housing for Department of Agriculture," 19 June 1922, B. T. Galloway Files, Box 1, Folder 3, National Agricultural Library, hereafter Galloway Files, NAL.

[19] Wilson to H. B. Henderson, 22 January 1903, NARA, Microfilm Series M-440, Roll No. 36; Henderson to Wilson, 23 January 1903, NARA, RG 16, S 162.

[20] *Cong. Rec.*, 57th Cong., 2d Sess., 24 January 1903 (vol. 36), 1215.

[21] *Cong. Rec.*, 57th Cong., 2d Sess., 2 February 1903 (vol. 36), 1585; "Gets a New Building," *Evening Star*, 2 February 1903, 1; *Cong. Rec.*, 57th Cong., 2d Sess., 4 February 1903 (vol. 36), 1674; *U.S. Statutes at Large* 32 (1903): 806; Galloway to R. B. Talcott, 16 May 1903, NARA, RG 16, S 162, Box 1 or 2.

[22] *YDA 1905*, 525. Biographical material on Galloway can be found in *Science* (29 December 1933): 598 and (1 July 1938): 6; Advisory Board to Wilson, 30 April 1903, NARA, RG 16, S 162, Box 1, 1903; Wilson to Taylor, 30 April 1903, ibid. John Sewell to Wilson, 4 May 1903, NARA, RG 16, S 165, Box 23; *Lord v. United States*, Court of Claims, 288; Leland M. Roth, *McKim, Mead & White, Architects* (New York: Harper & Row, 1983), 282.

[23] Galloway, "USDA Buildings: The Why of Two Wings," circa 1930, 2–3, Galloway Files, NAL, Box 1, Folder 3.

[24] Lord & Hewlett to Galloway, 25 February 1903, NARA, RG 16, S 162, Box 1, 1903; Galloway to Lord & Hewlett, 17 March 1903, ibid.

[25] Ibid. Other accounts attribute this general idea to Cannon: Brown, *Memories*, 99, 283; "Wilson's Wings,"

USDA Newsletter, 4 June 1942; Galloway, "USDA Buildings," 4.

[26] "Statement of Beverly T. Galloway … in Reference to the Case of Lord & Hewlett vs. U. S.," NARA, RG 6, S 160, Building Book (hereafter BB) 3, 103–4, undated; Lord & Hewlett to Galloway, 14 April 1903 (author's collection).

[27] *Lord v. United States,* Court of Claims, 293–94; Galloway to Lord & Hewlett, 15 April 1903, NARA, RG 16, S 162, Box 1; Lord & Hewlett to Galloway, 17 April 1903, ibid; "Statement of B. T. Galloway," Galloway to F. L. Evans, 9 May 1903, and Evans to Galloway, 12 May 1903, ibid.; Galloway to Lord & Hewlett, 11 May 1903, ibid; Lord & Hewlett to Advisory Committee, 12 May 1903, ibid.; Wilson to Lord & Hewlett, 13 May 1903, ibid.; *Lord v. United States,* Court of Claims, 282–99; *Lord & Hewlett v. United States,* Supreme Court, 340–48.

[28] Reps, *Monumental Washington,* 144; Theodore Roosevelt to Wilson, 19 June 1903, Library of Congress, Theodore Roosevelt Letters, Reel 331, hereafter Roosevelt Letters, LC; Wilson to Roosevelt, 14 July 1903, NA, RG 16, S 161, Claims Lord & Hewlett & Co., 1903–1904.

[29] Moore, *Burnham,* 1:206–7; Reps, *Monumental Washington,* 145; Roosevelt to Wilson, 28 July 28, Roosevelt Letters, LC, Reel 331.

[30] Moore, *Burnham,* 1:213–15; Reps, *Monumental Washington,* 145–46.

[31] J. H. Brigham to Roosevelt, 21 September 1903, NARA, RG 16, S 1601, BB no. 1, 20–22; Wilson to Roosevelt, 25 September 1903, NARA, RG 16, BB no. 1, 34; Sandra L Tatman and Roger W. Moss, *Biographical Dictionary of Philadelphia Architects: 1700–1930* (Boston: G. K. Hall, 1985), 437, 643.

[32] Galloway to Rankin, Kellogg & Crane, hereafter RK&C, 4 August 1903, NARA, RG 16, S 162, Box 2.

[33] RK&C to Galloway, 25 August 1903, NARA, RG 16, S 162, Box 3; "New Department Building," *Evening Star,* 2 September 1903, 2; *YDA 1904,* 526; RK&C to Galloway, 5 September 1903, NARA, RG 16, S 162, Box 3; Brigham to Roosevelt, 21 September 1903, NARA, RG 16, S 160, BB no. 1, 20–22; "Group of Buildings," *Evening Star,* 23 September 1903, 10; "Public Building Groups," *Evening Star,* 24 September 1903, 4.

[34] Galloway to RK&C, 8 October 1903, NARA, RG 16, S 160, BB no. 1, 31; Galloway to RK&C, 24 October 1903, NARA, RG 16, S 160, BB no. 1, 38.

[35] "Plans of the U.S. Department of Agriculture Buildings," 5 November 1903, NARA, RG 16, S 162, Box (folio) 15; *YDA 1903,* 102; *YDA 1904,* 526; attachment to minutes of meeting of Building Committee, 6 April 1904; NARA, RG 16, S 164; Galloway to RK&C, 12 November 1903, NARA, RG 16, S 160, BB no. 1, 45.

[36] Building Committee to Wilson, 24 November 1903, and Galloway to RK&C, 25 November 1903,

NARA, RG 16, S 160, BB no. 1, 52, 55; RK&C to Galloway, 27 November 1903, NARA, RG 16, Box 3; Galloway to RK&C, 15 & 18 December 1903, NARA, RG 16, S 160, BB no. 1, 71–73.

[37] "Plans Approved," *Evening Star,* 9 December 1903, 12; "New Department of Agriculture Plans Accepted," *Washington Times,* 13 December 1903, 10.

[38] Charles Moore to McKim, 14 September 1900, New-York Historical Society, McKim, Mead & White Papers, hereafter MM&W Papers, NYHS (courtesy of Pamela Scott); Galloway to Rankin, 14 January 1904, NARA, RG 16, S 160, BB no. 1, 92; Rankin to Kellogg, 16 January 1904, NARA, RG 16, S 162, Box 3.

[39] "Against the Plan," *Evening Star,* 27 January 1904, 6; "The Mall and the Park Plan," *Evening Star,* 29 January, 1904; Glenn Brown to McKim, 29 January 1904, NARA, RG 801, S 1.1 (AIA Secretary Letterbook, Box 8, S 19a, vol. 26); McKim to Kellogg, 3 February 1904, McKim to Burnham and 3 February 1904, MM&W Papers, NYHS, 139.

[40] B. T. Galloway, "Minutes relative to meeting held in office of the President, 5 February 1904, in reference to location of Department of Agriculture," NARA, RG 16, S 163, Box 22; also reproduced in *The Mall Parkway Hearing before the Committee on the District of Columbia* (Washington, D.C.: Government Printing Office, 1904), 6, hereafter *Mall Parkway Hearing.*

[41] Galloway to RK&C, 6 February 1904, NARA, RG 16, S 165, Box 23; also RG 16, S 160, BB no. 1, 115; RK&C to Galloway, 8 February 1904, NARA, RG 16, S 162, Box 3; also RG 16, S 160, BB no. 1, 117 (a further letter was sent to RK&C on 11 February 1904 with more detail, NARA, RG 16, S 165, Box 23 and NARA, RG 16, S 160, BB no. 1, 120); RK&C to McKim, 9 February 1904, Olmsted Papers, LC, Box B-135, File 2823; RK&C to Galloway, 18 February 1904, NARA, RG 16, S 162, Box 3).

[42] RK&C to Galloway, 6 February 1904, NA, RG 16, S 162, Box 3; McKim to Moore, 8 February 1904, McKim Papers, LC, vol. 12, 319; McKim to Olmsted, 11 February 1904, Olmsted Papers, LC, Box B-135, File 2823; Moore Papers, LC, Box 7; McKim to Roosevelt, 10 February 1904, Olmsted Papers, LC, Box B-135, File 2823 (also in Moore, *Burnham,* 1: 218–19); Roosevelt to McKim, 11 February 1904, Roosevelt Letters, LC, Reel 333; McKim to Olmsted, 11 February 1904 , Olmsted Papers, LC, Box B-135, File 2823; McKim to Senate Park Commission members, 19 February 1904, McKim Papers, LC, vol. 12, 338–43. Brown, *Memories,* 275–76, provides a somewhat different account of this period.

[43] McKim to Francis G. Newlands, 1 March 1904 and Newlands to Olmsted, 5 March 1904, Olmsted Papers, LC, Box B-135; McKim to Brown, 8 March 1904, McKim Papers, LC, vol. 12, 337–58; U.S. Senate, S.4845, 58th

Cong., 2d Sess., 7 March 1904; Brown, *Memories*, 275; Moore, *Burnham*, 1: 219; Reps, *Monumental Washington*, 147.

[44] *Cong. Rec.* 58th Cong., 2d Sess., 8 March 1904, 2970–2972; "The Newlands Bill," *Evening Star*, 8 March 1904, 2; Wilson to Gallinger, 9 March 1904, NARA, M-440, Roll 43.

[45] Olmsted to C. M. Robinson, 1 March 1904, Olmsted Papers, LC, Box B-135, File 2828; *Mall Parkway Hearing*, 3–6. Some of the visual aids may have been reproduced a few days later in "Building Plans for Washington," *Boston Herald*, 14 March 1904, Olmsted Papers, LC, Box B-135, File 2828. They and other possible candidates are on file at the Olmsted National Historical Site under Job No. 2828 (Item 12, a painting, is a likely prospect).

[46] *Mall Parkway Hearing*, 5–11.

[47] Ibid., 16, 18, 20.

[48] Ibid., 9–10, 18, 20, 26. In 1933 it was estimated that it would cost about $1 million to dismantle and move the Washington Monument to a new foundation (*Improvement of the Washington Monument Grounds*, 72d Cong., 2d Sess., 1934, H. Doc. 528, 13).

[49] Roosevelt to Wilson, 12 March 1904, in *The Letters of Theodore Roosevelt*, ed. Elting E. Morrison, (Cambridge, Mass: Harvard University Press, 1951), 4:750–51; Reps, *Monumental Washington*, 147; "Improving the Mall," *Evening Star*, 12 March 1904, 2; "No Building Lines—No Buildings," *Evening Star*, 12 March 1904, 4; "Clear Space on the Mall," *Washington Post*, 13 March 1904, 2; "Building Plans for Washington," *Boston Herald*, 14 March 1904; "From Mall to Avenue," *Washington Post*, 17 March 1904; McKim to Nicholas Murray Butler, 14 March 1904, McKim Papers, LC, vol. 12, 371.

[50] "Mall Bill Reported," *Evening Star*, 22 March 1904, 12; *Cong. Rec.*, 58th Cong., 2d Sess., 30 March 1904, 3974–3975; U.S. Congress, H.13926, 58th Cong., 2d Sess., 14 March 1904; McKim to Elihu Root, 18 March 1904, McKim Papers, LC, vol. 12, 380–82; William B. Bushong, "Glenn Brown, the American Institute of Architects, and the Development of the Civic Core of Washington, D.C." (Ph.D. diss., George Washington University, 1988), 149–51.

[51] Galloway to Kellogg, 14 March 1904, NARA, RG 16, S 160, BB no. 3, 142–43.

[52] "Minutes of the Building Committee," 11–12 March 1904, NARA, RG 16, S 164, Box 20.

[53] Galloway to RK&C, 19 March 1904, NARA, RG 16, S 160, BB no. 1, 147; *YDA 1904*, 527; RK&C to Olmsted, 31 March 1904, Olmsted Papers, LC, Box B-135, File 2828; Galloway to RK&C, 2 April 1904, NARA, RG 16, S 160, BB no. 1, 156–57; Galloway to Building Committee, 4 April 1904, ibid., 159; "Minutes of the Building Committee Meeting," 6 April 1904, NARA,

RG 16, S 164, Box 20; RK&C to Galloway, 12 April, 1904, NARA, RG 16, S 162, Box 3; Galloway to RK&C, 16 April, 1904, NARA, RG 16, S 160, BB no. 1, 1, 172; RK&C to Galloway, 18 April 1904, NARA, RG 16, S 162, Box 3; RK&C to Galloway, 23 May 1904, ibid.

[54] "At the White House," *Evening Star*, 22 April 1904, 1; Olmsted to Rep. Samuel Powers, 26 April 1904, Powers to Olmsted, 27 April 27 1904, and RK&C to Olmsted, 27 April 1904, Olmsted Papers, LC, Box 135.

[55] "President Champion of the Mall," *Washington Post*, 7 May 1904, 6; Roosevelt to Butler, 3 June 1904, in Morrison, *Roosevelt Letters*, 4:814 and cited in Reps, *Monumental Washington*, 147, fn. 41. The contracting process is summarized in *YDA 1904*, 98, and *YDA 1905*, 525–26.

[56] "Begins in Few Weeks," *Evening Star*, 20 March 1905, 15.

[57] Bernard Green to John Sewell, 16 February 1905, NARA, RG 16, S 165, Box 26; RK&C to Galloway, 16 February 1905, NARA, RG 16, Proj. Files, Box 1, Agr. Adm., Folder 1; RK&C to Galloway, 16 February 1905, NARA, RG 16, S 162, Box 5.

[58] RK&C to Galloway, 1 March 1905, ibid.

[59] Brown, *Memories*, 277–78 (italics added); Reps, *Monumental Washington*, 147.

[60] McKim to Taylor, 13 June 1901, McKim Papers, LC, vol. 19, 118–21; *Mall Parkway Hearing*, 8; David F. Burg, *Chicago's White City of 1893* (Lexington: University Press of Kentucky, 1976), 78 [McKim, Mead &White designed the Agriculture building at the Exposition]; Olmsted to McKim, 31 October 1902, Olmsted Papers, LC, Box B135, File 2828, Mall; see Scott essay, this volume.

[61] *YDA 1905*, 526; "Minutes of the Building Committee," 6 March 1905, NARA, RG 16, S 162, Box 5.

[62] Building Committee to Wilson, 7 March 1905; Sewell to McKim, 7 March 1905, MM&W Papers, NYHS; Building Committee to RK&C, 8 March 1905, NARA, RG 16, Series 165, Box 26. RK&C responded on 11 March, stating that "the subject was brought to the attention of the Department as soon as possible after it was known to us [middle of February]," NARA, RG 16, S 162, Box 5.

[63] RK&C to McKim, 9 March 1905, MM&W Papers, NYHS; McKim to Burnham, 9 March 1905, McKim Papers, LC, vol. 14, 173; Moore, *Burnham*, 1:227 (based on an address by Taft at the McKim Memorial Meeting of the AIA, 15 December 1909); Reps, *Monumental Washington*, 147.

[64] McKim to Roosevelt, 13 March 1905, McKim Papers, LC; Reps, *Monumental Washington*, 149–50; Moore, *Burnham*, 1: 228; Brown, *Memories*, 278–79; Executive Order 306, The White House, 14 March 1905 (Congressional Information Service (CIS) Transcription of National Archives Microfilm Publication No. M1118), amended 18 March 1905;

RK&C to Galloway, 15 March 1905, NARA, RG 16, S 162, Box 5; Galloway to RK&C, 29 March 1905, ibid.

65 Green to McKim, 20 March 1905, Green to Galloway, 21 March 1905; Green to McKim, 21 March 1905, MM&W Papers, NYHS; "Meeting of the Building Committee," 21 March 1905, NARA, RG 16, S 164, Box 20. The Mall area was lowered about 3.5 feet in front of the new Agriculture Building in 1930, but this still left the first floor essentially at basement level.

66 Sewell to McKim, 3 April 1905, MM&W Papers, NYHS; McKim to Sewell, 6 April 1905, NARA, RG 16, S 165, Box 26; Sewell to Galloway, 10 June 1905, NARA, RG 16, S 165, Box 24; Galloway to Wilson, 9 October 1905, NARA, RG 16, S 162, BB no. 3, 82.

67 In September, Burnham commented to Green that "it seems to be proper architecture and there is nothing objectionable," Burnham to Green, 25 September 1905, Daniel H. Burnham Collection, Ryerson and Burnham Library, Art Institute of Chicago, roll 7, vol. 15 (courtesy of Cynthia Field). The commission members evidently were not asked to comment on the RK&C design.

68 Sewell to Galloway, 3 January 1907, NARA, RG 16, S 163, Box 22; U.S. Congress S4174, 60th Cong., 1st Sess., 29 January 1908; "The New Building," *Evening Star*, 7 March 1907. Construction of the center wing was finally started in 1927 and completed in 1930, when the old Agriculture building was torn down ("Old Makes Way for New," *Washington Daily News*, 30 August 1930, picture).

69 Richard Guy Wilson, "High Noon on the Mall: Modernism vs. Traditionalism, 1910–1970," in Richard Longstreth, ed., *The Mall in Washington, 1791–1991* (Washington, D.C.: National Gallery of Art, 1991, 2002) 153; The rather glaring shortcoming af the unfinished wings was left unresolved, evidently without creating a fuss, for some three decades. Since the building complex was originally designed for a much deeper site on the north side of the Mall (figs. 6, 7) and simply switched to a much shallower site on the south, a compromise had to be made in adapting to the new property lines. This was done by simply and abruptly cutting off the southern portion of the wings as originally designed. The ends (fig. 14), moreover, were very plain brick painted white (somewhat analogous to several portions of the Federal Triangle) and adorned by metal fire escapes. They remained in this unattractive state until 1936 when the bridges were constructed across what was by then a considerably widened Independence Ave. (renamed in 1934) to the new South Building, the remaining wall area covered in marble, and the roofs tapered. It not certain what the Building Committee had in mind when they left the wings in this condition; but future extension of the wings across B St. (as suggested on pp. 211-212 and in figs. 9, 10) was certainly a possibility.

In 1933, a representative of the department told the National Park and Planning Commission that "the idea of an arch over B St. has been in the minds of the Agriculture Department for the past 25 years" (extract from the minutes of the 75th meeting of NCPPC, March 16-17, 1933; NARA, RG 328, box 36).

70 "Red Stable Rears Its Head," *Sunday Star*, 25 October 1908, part 7, 12 (with picture); Moore, *Burnham*, 1:218.

71 Sue A. Kohler, *The Commission of Fine Arts, A Brief History, 1910–1995* (Washington, D.C.: Government Printing Office, 1996), 1–7; Moore, *Burnham*, 1:124–25; *Cong. Rec.*, 61st Cong., 2d Sess., 9 February 1910, 1659.

Fig. 14 Unfinished business: the end of the west wing facing B Street in 1913. The structure to the right is the heating plant for the new complex. B Street at the time was a two-lane road running along the north side of what is now Independence Avenue. This view remained much the same until 1936 (see n. 69). National Archives, RG 16-G, box 5.

MR CHARLES MOORE,
I WAS DELIGHTED TO HAVE
EVEN THIS SMALL PART IN
THAT MEMORABLE DINNER TO YOU!
CORDIALLY AND SINCERELY
1937

A Berryman cartoon, appearing in the *Evening Star*, on the occasion of Charles Moore's retirement as chairman of the Commission of Fine Arts, 1937. Commission of Fine Arts

The Commission of Fine Arts:
IMPLEMENTING THE SENATE PARK COMMISSION'S VISION

By Sue Kohler

URING the waning days of 1901 a small band of young architects toiled almost without respite in the New York office of noted architects McKim, Mead & White, under the personal direction of Charles F. McKim, to finish the work on the exhibition of the Senate Park Commission plan, which was to open on 15 January 1902 at the Corcoran Gallery of Art in Washington, D.C.[1] The model builders were also putting the finishing touches on their work—two large models of the central area of the capital, one showing existing conditions and the other the proposals of the Senate Park Commission. One imagines that the holiday season that year played second fiddle to the inevitable frenzied activity that precedes the opening of an exhibition.

A few months earlier McKim had convinced Michigan Senator James McMillan, chairman of the Senate District Committee and responsible for the Senate Resolution establishing the commission, that laymen would never understand architectural plans and elevations, and for the exhibition to be successful the concepts had to be conveyed through the use of perspective drawings by the country's finest illustrators. Approximately forty views were rendered in watercolor, many of them of impressive size and in full color. Additionally, there were maps, plans, and large photographs of sites that had impressed the commission members during their earlier European study tour as having applications for Washington; a number of these photographs were taken by commission member Frederick Law Olmsted Jr., most likely with a simple tourist folding Kodak.[2]

The exhibition was a great success. President Theodore Roosevelt and a large number of other dignitaries attended the opening, and the local newspapers devoted an astonishing amount of space to it, describing the plan in great detail. Newspapers from other cities reported on it also; the *New York Times* published an article in the supplement to the 19 January 1902 issue by noted architectural critic Montgomery Schuyler, which was highly favorable to the plan. Schuyler also reported on it in the May 1902 *Architectural Record*, in a long article meant to appeal to the professional architects who read the magazine. The *Century Magazine* published articles in both its February and

March 1902 issues written by Charles Moore, Senator McMillan's aide, entitled "The Improvement of Washington City." The members of the Senate Park Commission agreed to give talks, serve on professional juries, and design buildings, and there were requests for Congress to fund the plan immediately. In short, the Senate Park Commission plan for Washington got off to a rousing start, and there was a feeling of euphoria within the art and architectural circles not only of the capital but of major cities across the country.

Before discussing the happenings of the next eight years, culminating in the establishment of the Commission of Fine Arts, it may be helpful to backtrack and comment briefly on a number of movements related to this event that had been gathering strength during the last decade of the nineteenth century. The awakening of interest in the appearance of Washington and the quality of public architecture was evident in the architectural press at this time. In the 7 May 1892 issue of the *American Architect and Building News*, Washington journalist and civic activist Frank Sewall talked about the importance of proper siting and design of public buildings as well as the desirability of establishing a federal art commission. He said:

> What is really needed to enable all these movements to reach the best result is some provision which the government should now make for a bureau of public building or a commission of architecture, which shall take a comprehensive survey of the whole field, both of the design and the location of our public buildings and monuments, and see that the vast expenditures of the people's money, which sooner or later will have to be made for these purposes, are turned to the best results in enhancing the beauty and the dignity of the national capital. This can only be effected by following a well-conceived plan, like that of L'Enfant, in laying out the city. If left to haphazard selection, the opportunity that comes but once to a capital and government like ours will be lost for an indefinite time, if not forever.[3]

In this article, Sewall seemed to be asking for both a commission to devise a city plan, such as the Senate Park Commission, and for one to oversee the implementation of its plan, such as the Commission of Fine Arts.

The American Institute of Architects (AIA) was also interested in improving the quality of federal architecture—and securing more government contracts for its members—and to this end lobbied hard for the passage in 1893 of the Tarsney Act, which provided that the Treasury Department's secretary could, "in his discretion"—the directive was not mandatory—obtain plans for public buildings through competition among private architects, rather than turning the design over to the department's supervising architect, as was the usual practice. Although the act made no provision for any kind of review body, the well-publicized controversy that ensued brought attention to the mediocre quality of most government work; also, the act created an opening for the more active participation of architects and artists in federal projects.

The controversy centered around the refusal of Secretary of the Treasury John G. Carlisle to order any competitions for government buildings; it took the form of correspondence in 1894 between Carlisle and Daniel Burnham, then president of the AIA. At this time Burnham was a powerful man in his field. Firmly committed to the City Beautiful and Civic Reform movements, he was already a major Chicago architect and one of the leaders of the Western Association of Architects. He was chief of construction for the 1893 World's Columbian Exposition in Chicago, and through this position had developed strong friendships with prominent eastern architects, painters, and sculptors. His efforts on behalf of the Tarsney Act undoubtedly sharpened his skill in dealing with politicians and bureaucrats and made his name a familiar one in Washington, factors of considerable importance for his future roles as chairman of the Senate Park Commission and ultimately as chairman of the Commission of Fine Arts.

There were a number of efforts, in the form of congressional bills, beginning as early as the 1850s, to establish some kind of control over federal art and architecture. Some were concerned only with statues and paintings, others only with architecture, while a third group would oversee all the arts. Those concerned with architecture were generally limited to the supervision of competitions, selection of architects, allowable fees and other costs, and supervision of construction—in short, functions similar to those of the current General Services Administration; they were not meant to establish true architectural review agencies.

Congressional bills advocating the third, all-inclusive type of art commission, with review power as we know it, did not appear until the last decade of the century. These bills were prepared by an organization called the Public Art League, organized in 1895 by the Washington chapter of the AIA and the Cosmos Club of Washington. Its members consisted of distinguished men from all over the country, and its purpose was to secure enactment of a law establishing a commission of experts to decide upon the merits of works of art and architecture acquired or commissioned by the federal government. Its officers included artists, art critics, and heads of museums. The president was Richard Watson Gilder, editor of *Century Magazine*. Charles F. McKim, Augustus Saint-Gaudens, painter John LaFarge, and architect Glenn Brown were among the officers, and included in the list of directors were Daniel H. Burnham, Frederick Law Olmsted Jr., sculptor Daniel Chester French, and painter Francis D. Millet. Nearly all these men were later associated with the Senate Park Commission or the Commission of Fine Arts, or in some cases both entities.

The driving force behind the League was the AIA's secretary, the indefatigable Glenn Brown. He was behind the Public Art League's first attempt, in 1897, to get a bill through Congress establishing a fine arts commission. This bill provided for a commission composed of the presidents of the AIA, the National Academy of Design, and the National Sculpture Society, with two other members to be appointed by the president. It was to pass on architecture, sculpture, landscape design, painting, medals and coins, and all objects of art; compliance with its decisions was to be mandatory. According to Glenn Brown, it was not successful because Congress would not accept the mandatory compliance clause and objected to the *ex officio* members; it was thought that the commission should be composed entirely of congressional or executive appointees.[4]

By January 1900 Brown and the Public Art League again succeeded in having a bill introduced, but it, too, was unsuccessful. Brown kept pushing, but in fact, McKim was opposed to more pressure on Congress when Brown wrote him late in 1901, requesting an opinion. (Brown wrote as well to Burnham and George Post, a former AIA president.) McKim's return letter to Brown said, in part:

> After talking it over at some length, the general opinion seemed to be that while the consummation of the scheme to place the work of the Government under the direction of a Commission or Bureau, created for the purpose, was eminently to be desired, that it would be unwise to press this question upon Congress until after the work of the Park Commission has been submitted and passed upon by the Congress, and its value estimated; that it should be remembered that this Commission was created through the efforts of the Institute of Architects, and to propose the appointment of another Commission, before the work of the first has been publicly justified, would seem premature and unwise.[5]

Charles Moore agreed, adding, in a letter to McKim, that there were "one or two complications that are beyond the scope of the Institute work, which make it inadvisable at this time to press the subject of a permanent Art Commission." One obstacle was that the District's finances were not in the best shape at that time, and the other was that there had been criticism from some quarters about the cost of the Park Commission's work. He did believe, however, that it was time to think about a new draft of legislation. His feeling was that the president and one or two members of the cabinet should be *ex officio* members, or that the members should be appointed directly by the president, "putting him virtually in command." He thought results had shown that the best work would be secured by taking it away from Congress entirely and putting it in the hands of the president.[6]

That was the way things stood in 1902 at the time of the exhibition at the Corcoran and the issuance of the Senate Park Commission's report. The plan was enthusiastically received, and members of the AIA and the Public Art League felt the future development of the city was in good hands. However, the report only made recommendations; there remained the problem of congressional approval and of implementation. The commission itself had no legal standing once its report had been made. Furthermore, the method of establishing it had made a bitter enemy of Joseph Cannon, chairman of the House Appropriations Committee and Speaker of the House after 1903. Years later Elihu Root, Theodore Roosevelt's secretary of war, described the situation:

> McMillan started a commission to advise on the development of Washington. This was the McKim-Burnham Commission of 1900–01 [sic]. It was a great fight. Joe Cannon was very angry because the Senate paid the expenses of this commission out of its Contingent Fund. Cannon claimed they should have gotten an appropriation through the House, and he was right. The Senate had no idea how much it would cost. They thought it would be a few hundred dollars and it ran up to fifty or sixty thousand. The plan involved the location of the Grant and Lincoln memorials, the Department of Agriculture building and other things. The fight grew very hot.[7]

The projects mentioned by Root came to the forefront soon after the Park Commission's report to the Senate Committee on the District of Columbia was issued; the Grant Memorial controversy will serve to illustrate the complexity of the situations the commission was called upon to consider. The memorial had been authorized by Congress just before the commission came into existence. Two tentative sites were mentioned, both on the Ellipse south of the White House. When the commission's report was issued, however, it showed the memorial as a focal point at the foot of the Capitol, in the area referred to as Union Square, at that time part of the Botanic Garden (pl. X). On the committee designated to select the memorial's sculptor were commission members Burnham, McKim, and Saint-Gaudens; in their report recommending the relatively unknown Henry Merwin Schrady, they argued against the Ellipse sites and for the Union Square location. They were supported in this by President Roosevelt, who felt strongly that no monuments should be placed on the Ellipse. In 1903 contracts were signed with Shrady and architect Edward P. Casey and work began; however, the site still had not been been specified. After many meetings and much effort by McKim, Root, and Senator George Peabody Wetmore, the Grant Memorial Commission selected the Union Square site. By this time, however, the pedestal had already been designed for one of the Ellipse sites, and more work was required to modify the design to fit the new site. Both McKim and Olmsted Jr. were on the committee to select the exact location for the sculpture. When the new location was staked out, it was found that some of the finest trees in the Botanic Garden fell within its boundaries. An uproar ensued with the *Evening Star* and the superintendent of the Botanic Garden leading the fight against the Senate Park Commission. Whereas the *Star* had heaped praise

Fig. 1 The new National Museum and the old Mall. The romantic beauty of the informal placement of specimen trees makes it understandable that many Washingtonians were loath to see them removed and replaced by the Park Commission's more formal rows of elms on either side of a French *tapis vert*. Undated photograph, ca. 1910. Commission of Fine Arts

on the commission's plan after the opening of the 1902 exhibition, six years later, almost to the day (14 January 1908), it blasted the plan and particularly McKim, who was condemned for his fondness for "trees in tubs," as seen in the renderings made for the exhibition, and for his proposal "to root out all the noble old trees on the Mall and replace them with formal trees planted with painful precision on straight lines" (fig.1). Although in extremely poor health, McKim had continued to attend meetings for several years and to press for the commission's preferred site. At the height of the controversy he wrote Burnham: "Upon the adjustment of this matter depends the upholding or reversal of our plan by Congress."[7]

The battle to place the Lincoln Memorial on the site recommended by the Senate Park Commission involves a long and complicated history beyond the scope of this essay. The final site selection was not made until February 1912, nearly two years after the Commission of Fine Arts had been established. Speaker Cannon, of course, was against anything proposed by the Senate Park Commission. Union Station Plaza, Meridian Hill, and the Soldiers Home grounds were suggested as sites, with the most improbable suggestion being that the memorial take the form of a highway from Washington to Gettysburg. Again, McKim, Root, Brown, and the AIA led the fight. McKim, of all the Senate Park Commission members, was most closely involved as he had been the one in charge of developing this part of the Mall. Unfortunately, his death in 1909 occurred before the controversy was settled, and it was his close friend Henry Bacon who was chosen as architect.

The placing of the Grant and Lincoln memorials on the sites recommended by the Senate Park Commission was considered critical, because when so placed they would "compel" (to use Elihu Root's word) the development of the Mall according to the plan.[9] The siting of the Agriculture Department building was equally important, as it would establish the width of the Mall and thus a building line for all future Mall buildings. The determination of its correct placement generated one of the biggest crises the Park Commission members faced.[10] On the other side of the Mall, the new National Museum building (now the Museum of Natural History) required McKim and Olmsted to spend months on grading plans for the Mall, so the museum would be on the proper base line. It also raised questions of architectural style. It began to look too French, which conflicted with the commission's decision during its European tour that although the plan for Washington might be French in origin, the style of the architecture was to be Roman. All members of the commission wrote letters to Bernard Green, the government official in charge of construction, objecting to the design of the facade. In the end, it was Roman. It should be remembered that through all the years of controversy the Senate Park Commission members had their own busy practices; not one of them lived in Washington, and two, McKim and Saint-Gaudens, were in poor health. Also, there was no payment for any of this work.

Charles McKim's role in implementing the Senate Park Commission plan from 1902 until 1909, when there was no properly organized, legally established commission to do so, has not received sufficient emphasis. Without a doubt, he was the most active of the commission members during this period. Saint-Gaudens and Olmsted were by no means silent and were consulted frequently, but they were not as personally involved in the constant battles with members of Congress and other government officials. Saint-Gaudens, often ill, was not oriented toward the political battlefield by reason of personality, and Olmsted was still a relatively young man, in his early thirties. Burnham, while very effective politically, was extremely busy in these years working on city plans for Cleveland, San Francisco, the Philippines, and Chicago; consequently, he traveled frequently. At times, McKim chided him for not paying enough attention to the Washington work.

And so the major burden fell on McKim. He accepted it conscientiously, writing to Glenn Brown in 1904: "Don't forget to send me a copy of the *Congressional Record* when there is anything to read. I am prepared to go to Washington at any moment that I can be of use."[11] However, he was not well, and it is not an exaggeration to say that a great part of the little energy he had left was expended in defense of the Washington plan and in overseeing the work at the American Academy in Rome. The academy was another of the influential art organizations founded at the end of the nineteenth century, and it is interesting, but not surprising, that many of its directors and other officers became members of the Commission of Fine Arts in its early years.

While the Senate Park Commission members were battling to save their plan, there were frequent discussions among them about the burden of being called in constantly to solve problems and about the difficulties of trying to operate while having no legal standing. As early as 1902 McKim wrote Charles Moore: "The function of the Commission should be to defend and develop the general features of their plan, but it would be very undesirable, I feel, even if it were feasible, to set the precedent of calling them in on all occasions to determine the details...."[12]

The question of a permanent commission was also being discussed by the Senate Park Commission members, as well as by the AIA and government officials. During the Agriculture Department building crisis, McKim had stressed the necessity for such a commission in one of his letters to Roosevelt, asking for a commission "acceptable to yourself and both houses of Congress." At the same time he wrote Olmsted: "After consulting with Mr. Root, my own opinion is that the Park Commission, having made its report, and its existence acting as a red flag in the House of Representatives, that the sooner it goes out of existence the better, as it will never be recognized by the House of Representatives, for the reasons discussed with Mr. Root, and indicated in my letter to the President. Both the President and Mr. Root are strong in their view that Mr. Cannon's sympathy and interest should be enlisted immediately." The last word had been inserted and was handwritten.[13] Regarding this permanent commission, Olmsted wrote to Charles Moore: "What is to be the function of the proposed permanent Park Commission? Advisory and impotent, or executive and overburdened?"[14]

Early in 1905 McKim, after consulting with Moore, Saint-Gaudens, and Secretary of War William Howard Taft, met with Speaker Cannon in an attempt to enlist his support for some kind of advisory commission. Afterward he wrote Roosevelt saying that "Mr. Cannon and the Park Commission are now friends" and that Cannon recognized the need for a commission.[15] This was, perhaps, a bit of wishful thinking, but Cannon apparently did not object to Roosevelt's next step, taken a few days later, which was to create by executive order what was called the Consultative

Board, consisting of the Senate Park Commission members and Bernard Green, superintendent of buildings and grounds for the Library of Congress, who had been helpful to the commission in the past.[16] The order provided that the board be consulted before any public buildings could be located or the plans approved, and that the board's examination should be confined to the location and the artistic effect of the exterior of the buildings. Lacking the sanction of Congress, the Consultative Board was still only a stopgap measure, but it held out some hope of relief to McKim, who wrote Burnham: "I have had to bear the brunt for months—time, expense, and worry—and there must be an end to what has become too heavy a load."[17]

In 1906 Glenn Brown and the Public Art League made another attempt to get legislation establishing an art commission through Congress, but it was not successful. The *Architectural Record* commented that the reason for failure was apparently the feeling that the Senate Park Commission had "satisfied all the necessities."[18]

Burnham was becoming increasingly unhappy with the lack of organization and confusion in Washington, and in 1907 he suddenly sent a telegram to Roosevelt announcing his resignation from the Consultative Board. After much persuasion on the part of the other members, particularly McKim, and also Charles Moore, he agreed to stay on, but expressed his feelings in a letter to Moore:

> What we need in Washington is a system—a Secretary probably.... As things are, one
> hears casually, when he hears at all, that something is happening, or has happened, and,
> now and then, that a member or two of the Commission has skimmed over something that
> this or that Government official purposes to do. Not thus can the power possessed by the
> Commission be brought to bear....[19]

In the meantime, Glenn Brown continued to bring pressure to bear on Congress to pass legislation establishing an art commission along the lines advocated by the Public Art League and the AIA. He worked with Senator Francis G. Newlands of Nevada, who had taken Senator McMillan's place as the great friend of the Park Commission plan, to draft a bill establishing such a commission, but it did not arouse much interest.

On 19 January 1909, following an exchange of letters with the AIA and a meeting with Glenn Brown, architect Cass Gilbert, and painter Frank Millet, President Roosevelt issued Executive Order No. 1010, establishing a Council of Fine Arts with thirty members. Those chosen had been selected by the AIA's Executive Committee and approved by Roosevelt. In fact, the nature of the council itself and its responsibilities had been set forth by the Executive Committee in a letter to the president on 11 January, further evidence of the power wielded by this private professional organization at the time. The letter said, in part:

We suggest:

1. That the council should consist of architects, painters, sculptors, landscape architects and laymen, appointed by the President, from nominations made by the Directors of the American Institute of Architects.

2. That the Supervising Architect of the Treasury should be the executive.

3. That the object should be to have the Council advise upon the character and design of all public works of architecture, painting, sculpture; all monuments, parks, bridges, and other works of which the art of design forms an integral part; and to make recommendations for the conservation of all historic monuments.

4. That the details of carrying out this arrangement should be left to the direction of the American Institute of Architects, in collaboration with the Supervising Architect of the Treasury.[20]

Why Roosevelt decided to establish the council at the very end of his administration, and why it had so many members, is not certain. It is likely that the AIA had convinced him of the urgency of settling the Lincoln Memorial question, as he had written the institute saying he would "request the Council immediately to report [on]…the Lincoln Memorial, as suggested…by the Board of Directors of the American Institute of Architects."[21]

The large number of members may have been Roosevelt's idea, as a maneuver to avoid the criticism that all crucial decisions were being made by the Senate Park Commission members, who were only four in number. In the same letter Roosevelt advised the AIA "to take immediate steps to secure the enactment of a law giving permanent effect to what I am directing to be done." To this end, a bill was introduced by Senator Newlands on the same day the executive order was issued. It was a rather complicated bill, providing for a Bureau of Fine Arts as well as an advisory council, and it was never reported out of the committee to which it had been referred.[22]

Twenty-one architects were nominated to the council, as well as four painters, four sculptors, and one landscape architect—Frederick Law Olmsted Jr. The architects included Burnham, McKim, Gilbert, and Brown, and others who were well known and active in the AIA. The painters were John LaFarge, Frank Millet, E. H. Blashfield, and Kenyon Cox. Sculptors were Daniel Chester French, Herbert Adams, H. A. McNeil, and K. T. Bitter.

The council met on 9 February 1909 and approved the Senate Park Commission's site for the Lincoln Memorial. McKim, very ill, attended for a few minutes but later on resigned. Burnham was not present and was uncertain whether he would accept the appointment. Olmsted was out of the country. Apparently, Charles Moore was asked to serve after the list of names had been released. Although his name was not on the list—strictly speaking, he did not fall into any of the professional categories—he wrote Brown from Europe on 13 February 1909 accepting the appointment. But he expressed his reservations about the council, the way in which it was created, and its large number of members. "I cannot help fearing," he wrote, "that so formed it will begin life with very serious handicaps."[23]

The idea of an arts council received enthusiastic support in the press, but there was a realization in the editorials that Congress would not accept this extra-legal creation, especially since the council's advice had to be followed unless the president, not Congress, directed otherwise. Refusing to accept any commission which might limit its power over appropriations, Congress included in the Sundry Civil Bill of 4 March 1909 a clause that denied any appropriations for the Council of Fine Arts and for any projects approved by it.

William Howard Taft became president on 4 March 1909; on 21 May he issued Executive Order No. 1074, abolishing the Council of Fine Arts. In a letter to Cass Gilbert, president of the AIA, Taft explained his reasons, saying that Congress had already directed specific legislation against the council, and furthermore, he doubted if there had ever been any power to appoint such a council in the first place. He said, however, that he hoped to secure from Congress authority to appoint a fine arts commission, since he was strongly in favor of it. "I shall have to take my own way to bring this about," he said, "since it is a matter of considerable delicacy."[24]

The successful legislation creating the Commission of Fine Arts was finally introduced in the House of Representatives by Samuel McCall of Massachusetts in early February 1910.[25] The bill was steered through the Senate by Elihu Root, who had long been a staunch supporter of the Park Commission plan, first as secretary of war, then as secretary of state, and finally as a senator from New York. It was most appropriate that his name was associated with the successful legislation for a design review body to safeguard the plan. Much later, when talking to his biographer, Philip Jessup, he said: "I came to be the man in the Government to whom they could come to find sympathy and get to the President. They were a lot of artists and architects, like lost children in the woods when they came to Washington."[26]

The debate on the bill comprises some 150 typewritten pages, double-spaced. It brings out the fears of those who were against it that Congress was about to relinquish its authority to a "coterie of artists" who would be impractical and visionary—outsiders who would not understand what was best for Washington. Some members brought up the location of the Grant Memorial, still disputing its location in the Botanic Garden and blaming the Senate Park Commission for it. Although the bill under consideration covered only statues and monuments, with no mention of buildings, others assailed the siting of the Agriculture building, "below the ground." Still others were afraid the proposed commission might abandon the L'Enfant plan, thinking no doubt of the Senate Park Commission's new plans for the Mall and its extension to the river. The commission was frequently denounced as "illegal" or "unauthorized." It was sometimes referred to as a "sky-line commission." It is interesting that it was never called the McMillan Commission and seldom the Senate Park Commission, but almost always the Burnham Commission.

Several amendments were made to the bill by the Senate; the most important was Root's recommendation that the phrase that gave the commission authority to "decide" on the various projects submitted be changed to "advise." He was wise enough to see that Congress would accept it no other way, and thus the commission's function became purely advisory.[27] In the original House bill, the appointments were for "seven artists of repute," later changed to "seven well-qualified judges of the fine arts"; review of fountains was added by Senator Jacob H. Gallinger of New Hampshire, who observed that Washington had "too many statues and too few fountains." In conference with the House, the requirement that the appointments be made "with the advice and consent of the Senate" was dropped. Root's explanation to fellow senators was that because it was decided that the members of the commission would not be paid a salary, but only their expenses, they did not fall within the category of those appointments traditionally requiring Senate approval. An important amendment that confirms the deep-seated congressional distrust of any amount of control by an art commission was offered by Senator Weldon B. Heyburn of Idaho, and accepted. It said that the provisions of the act would not apply to either the Capitol or the Library of Congress. Senator Root did not oppose the amendment but thought it unnecessary because the bill merely provided for advice. It is interesting that during the Senate-House conference, the position of this sentence in the bill was moved, so that it came after the general provisions of the act but *before* the sentence reading: "The commission shall also advise generally upon questions of art when required to do so by the president, or by any committee of either House of Congress." This made it possible for the president or Congress to ask for advice regarding the Capitol or the Library of Congress if they wished to do so. The final version read:

> Be it enacted by the Senate and House of Representatives of the United States of America in Congress assembled, That a permanent Commission of Fine Arts is hereby created to be composed of seven well-qualified judges of the fine arts, who shall be appointed by the President, and shall serve for a period of four years each, and until their successors are appointed and qualified. The President shall have authority to fill all vacancies. It shall be the duty of such commission to advise upon the location of statues, fountains, and monu-

ments in the public squares, streets, and parks in the District of Columbia, and upon the selection of models for statues, fountains, and monuments erected under the authority of the United States and upon the selection of artists for the execution of the same. It shall be the duty of the officers charged by law to determine such questions in each case to call for such advice. The foregoing provisions of this Act shall not apply to the Capitol building of the United States and the building of the Library of Congress. The commission shall also advise generally upon questions of art when required to do so by the President, or by any committee of either House of Congress. Said commission shall have a secretary and such other assistance as the commission may authorize, and the members of the commission shall each be paid actual expenses in going to and returning from Washington to attend the meetings of said commission and while attending the same.

The bill became Public Law 181, 61st Congress, on 17 May 1910.

It will be noted that the legislation made no mention of public buildings. Still smarting from the Agriculture building affair, several members objected, during the debate, to giving up any control over the design or location of public buildings. It was pointed out to them that this prerogative was not mentioned in the legislation. One member, however, said this jurisdiction could be easily slipped in later under the clause that read: "The commission shall also advise generally on questions of art when required to do so by the President…." On 25 October 1910 President Taft did that very thing by issuing Executive Order No. 1259, adding "plans" for public buildings to the commission's jurisdiction. No mention was made, however, of "locating" these structures.

President Taft announced his appointments to the Commission of Fine Arts in June 1910. Among his papers in the Manuscript Division of the Library of Congress are a number of interesting letters and lists relating to the appointments. Evidently, Senator George Peabody Wetmore took it upon himself to send letters to prominent architects and artists asking them to recommend six architects, sculptors, painters, landscape architects, and laymen.[28] Those who sent names were architects Daniel Burnham, Whitney Warren, Thomas Hastings, Irving K. Pond, and William Mead; sculptors H. A. MacNeil and Lorado Taft; and painter Frank Millet. Together they submitted the names of twenty-two architects, twenty-one painters, thirteen sculptors, seventeen landscape architects, and thirty laymen. In two cases those who received the most votes were appointed to the commission—Daniel Chester French as sculptor and Frederick Law Olmsted as landscape architect. Olmsted was on everyone's list except Burnham's, whose only choice in this field was Edward H. Bennett. Warren wrote that he had a hard time coming up with the names of six landscape architects. He said, "the majority of these men are little better than amateur gardeners…and when

Fig. 2 Earliest known photograph of the full Commission of Fine Arts, between 1912 and 1915. From left to right: Charles Moore, seated at end of table; Peirce Anderson (succeeded Daniel Burnham); Edwin H. Blashfield (succeeded Frank Millet); Frederick Law Olmsted Jr.; Daniel Chester French, chairman; Colonel William W. Harts, secretary; Thomas Hastings; Cass Gilbert. Commission of Fine Arts

one thinks that their occupation is to juggle with nature it would seem that only those who have devoted much time to the study of nature's architecture should be fit to practice."[29]

The top three in each field were: architects Walter Cook, S. B. P. Trowbridge and Frank Miles Day (tied with Cass Gilbert); painters E. H. Blashfield, John W. Alexander, and Frank Millet; sculptors Daniel Chester French, Paul Bartlett, and Herbert Adams; landscape architects Frederick Law Olmsted, W. H. Manning, and Charles W. Leavitt; and laymen Henry Walters, Charles L. Freer, and Theodore N. Ely. Glenn Brown was listed only once, by sculptor H. A. MacNeil, although Frank Millet noted that he had not placed him on his list because he thought he would serve best as secretary.

Actually chosen by the president were architects Daniel Burnham (chairman), Thomas Hastings, and Cass Gilbert; sculptor Daniel Chester French; painter Frank Millet; landscape architect Frederick Law Olmsted; and as layman, Charles Moore, who had been so closely associated with the Senate

Park Commission as to seem almost a fifth member. McKim and Saint-Gaudens had both died by this time, Saint-Gaudens in 1907 and McKim in 1909.

Unfortunately, by June 1912 the commission had lost both its chairman, Daniel Burnham, and its vice-chairman, Frank Millet. Millet was one of those lost in the *Titanic* disaster in April, and Burnham died in Germany in June. Burnham's place was taken by Peirce Anderson of his own firm, and E. H. Blashfield filled Millet's vacancy. Daniel Chester French was appointed chairman, to be succeeded in 1915 by another original member, Charles Moore, who held the position until 1937 and remained a member of the commission until 1940.[30] Frederick Law Olmsted left the commission in 1918, but was a member of the National Capital Park and Planning Commission from 1926 until 1932 and active in Washington planning circles until the early 1950s. Thus the commission retained strong personal ties with the Senate Park Commission through the first half of the century.

During its first year of existence, the commission reviewed forty-one cases; ten were for statues, fountains, and monuments, as specified in the organic act, and fourteen were for public buildings and works, the latter made possible by President Taft's executive order. These included the Burnham firm's city post office, just to the west of Union Station; the current building for the Bureau of Engraving and Printing; and new buildings for the departments of State, Justice, and Commerce and Labor. The latter were never built but were the forerunners of the Federal Triangle project of the late 1920s. The commission was also asked for its advice on such subjects as height limitations for buildings to be erected on the east and west sides of Lafayette Square, a new system of lighting for Pennsylvania Avenue, and the use of the Connecticut Avenue (Taft) Bridge by streetcars. The remaining projects were congressional committee referrals, mostly involving paintings and "miscellaneous" items, which were primarily for monuments outside the District of Columbia.

In its early years, both the Commission of Fine Arts and the applicants before it were feeling their way as to what should be or could be submitted. The commission was soon confronted with a formal request, under the wording of the Panama Canal Act, to report to the president on "the artistic character of the structures of the canal." Upon being questioned as to what kind of advice he desired, Colonel Goethals, chairman of the Isthmian Canal Commission, suggested that the Commission of Fine Arts might want to visit the Canal Zone before making its report. Chairman Daniel Chester French and member Frederick Law Olmsted were appointed a committee of two to make the trip; they spent three weeks in February 1913 inspecting the structures of the canal itself, the surrounding landscape, and the towns in the area that would house permanent workers, including the plans for the new town of Balboa, which was to contain the administrative offices. This was

Fig. 3 Panama Canal Zone, looking west from top of Ancon Hill, showing early construction in the new town of Balboa, before the Commission's inspection trip, and the Pacific entrance to the canal in the distance. Photograph dated 29 September 1912. Commission of Fine Arts

a difficult assignment, and the commission realized it; it was a bit like being asked to gild the lily. The thirteen-page report said:

> The canal itself and all the structures connected with it impress one with a sense of their having been built with a view strictly to their utility. There is an entire absence of ornament and no evidence that the aesthetic has been considered except in a few cases as a secondary consideration. Because of this very fact there is little to find fault with from the artist's point of view. The canal, like the Pyramids or some imposing object in natural scenery, is impressive from its scale and simplicity and directness. One feels that anything done merely for the purpose of beautifying it would not only fail to accomplish that purpose, but would be an impertinence. In such a work the most that the artist could

hope to do would be to aid in selecting, as between alternative forms of substantially equal value from the engineering point of view, those which are likely to prove most agreeable and appropriate in appearance.[31]

And so the commission did what it could, considering that many of the structures, such as navy-yard shops and docks, were already in place, as were a number of navigational aids—concrete lighthouses, range lights, and tripods; unfortunately, nearly all of them were considered "open to criticism as to details of appearance"; it was too late, however, to modify the designs. The commission did recommend a new design for a lighthouse for a prominent location at the Atlantic end of the canal. The design was the work of Austin Lord, the official architect of the Canal Commission, but it was never built because of "excessive cost and lack of room."[32] Other locations marked for lights were found to be impractical for anything monumental because of soil conditions; on the other hand, the report said, "there are points of interest as one approaches the canal from the Pacific with which it would be unwise to attempt to compete by any structure built for artistic reasons alone. The shore itself, with its rugged range of mountains, is inspiring, and the islands guarding the entrance are interesting in the extreme."[33]

Fig. 4 Panama Canal Zone, the Tivoli Hotel, Ancon. The hotel is typical of the architectural style of buildings approved for the Canal Zone. Undated photograph. Commission of Fine Arts

The committee also turned its attention to the preliminary plan for the new town of Balboa, pointing out in particular that the orientation of the main axis as proposed was not satisfactory, as the view of the canal was cut off by navy-yard shops, and the vista ended in a foundry. A myriad of other proposals were examined, right down to the recommendation of an interior design architect for the hotel in Colon. When French and Olmsted returned, their proposals were reviewed and discussed with the other members of the commission prior to preparing the report (figs. 3, 4).[34]

At the other end of the scale, as far as submissions were concerned, was a letter the commission received in June 1921 from the city manager of Petersburg, Virginia, requesting advice regarding the laying out of a city park and asking the members to make a personal inspection of the area. A letter was sent explaining that it would not be possible for the commission to spend several days in Petersburg, but the city manager was not told that the commission's authority extended only to federal projects; instead, he was politely informed that the commission would be happy to look at any sketches or plans when available and would like to see photographs of the area as well.

The Commission of Fine Arts looked at many federal projects outside Washington in the early years, in fact, well up into the 1960s. In the days when the City Beautiful Movement still had some meaning, congressmen often thought it would add a bit of prestige to new post offices in their districts if the commission approved them; proposals for murals and sculpture for the interior of these and other federal buildings were also frequently submitted. The National Park Service, while still working closely with the commission today on the design for parks and memorials in Washington and its environs, used to submit plans regularly for various buildings and other structures in the national park system throughout the country. A Zion National Park hotel, plans for "Yosemite Village," bridges for Smoky Mountain, Yosemite, and Acadia national parks, and a bathhouse for Hot Springs, Arkansas were all on the commission's agendas in the 1920s; in 1928 landscape architect member Ferruccio Vitale was asked by the director of the National Park Service to make an examination and report on various submissions affecting Glacier and Yellowstone national parks.

The most important submissions during the commission's first twenty-five years, of course, were related to the implementation of the key elements of the Senate Park Commission plan. The Lincoln Memorial was one of the first major projects taken up by the commission. The Act of Congress providing for the memorial had specifically authorized the Lincoln Memorial Commission "to avail itself of the services or advice of the Commission of Fine Arts."[35] On 4 March 1911 the Memorial Commission asked the Commission of Fine Arts for suggestions as to the location, plans, and designs for the memorial, and for the best method of selecting the architects, sculptors, and other artists. The minutes of the 17 March meeting stated: "The subject was thoroughly discussed with a view to ascertaining the ideas of each member, and plans for future procedure were tentatively outlined." In July 1911 the commission unanimously recommended the Park Commission's preferred site in Potomac Park, and in June 1912 the final design of the commission's recommended architect, Henry Bacon, was approved. This memorial, the linchpin of the Senate Park Commission's Mall plan, occupied the Commission of Fine Arts until its dedication in 1921. At the same time, plans were being reviewed for the adjoining Reflecting Pool and the landscaping of the entire area (fig. 5). Arlington Memorial Bridge and the approach to Arlington National Cemetery, both designed to conform to the Senate Park Commission plans, were reviewed in the later 1920s and early 1930s.

As it concentrated on carrying out the Park Commission plans for the monumental core of the city, the commission became acutely aware of eyesore conditions that threatened the beauty of the

Fig. 5 Construction site, Lincoln Memorial, with site of Reflecting Pool immediately beyond. Undated photograph, ca. 1914. Commission of Fine Arts

Fig. 6 In the days when soft coal was the primary fuel for heating and power plants, both smoke and smokestacks marred the views from the Mall. This photograph shows the effect on the wings of the new Agriculture Building, before the center section was erected and the old buildings demolished. The Commission of Fine Arts, during the January 1916 meeting, objected strongly to the proposed construction of a central heating plant at 14th Street and the Washington Channel, roughly the area in the left background of this photograph. It was to have had four stacks, each 16 feet in diameter and 188 feet high. The commission noted the effect of both the smoke and the stacks from the Mall, the Lincoln Memorial and other new Mall buildings, the Washington Monument, and the White House. The heating plant was not built. Undated photograph, ca. 1920. Commission of Fine Arts

Mall and nearby areas, and it mounted campaigns in the press and within Congress against such abominations as smoke-belching chimneys, unsightly billboards, and lines of parked cars spoiling the beauty of tree-lined avenues (fig. 6).

After Burnham's death in 1912, Frederick Law Olmsted was the only Park Commission member on the Commission of Fine Arts. His knowledge of the intent of the Senate Park Commission members was invaluable, and even after he left the Commission of Fine Arts in 1918, he was frequently consulted. It is interesting to note, however, as one reads the minutes of the meetings of the commission, how often Olmsted was willing to depart from details seen on the Senate Park Commission plans—more so than the other members who were farther removed. For example, he voted to remove the cross arms of the Reflecting Pool when a temporary World War I building prevented the immediate construction of the northern arm, and he was not averse to the removal of the watergate steps at the Lincoln Memorial when that came up in the late 1920s. In the early 1930s he was asked to design Union Square, and when he brought his design to the Commission of Fine Arts in April 1934, he was criticized for abandoning the formal treatment shown on the Senate Park Commission renderings. In a long statement submitted to the Commission of Fine Arts, Olmsted stated his reasons, citing changes to the area since 1901, and added:

> This portion of the plan of 1901 received less mature and deliberate study by the Commission as a whole than the portions of the central composition further west, and was embodied in the report under pressure of time as a tentative solution in spite of expressed doubts within the Commission as to some of its features. My further study of the problem, especially since I have been called upon to prepare definitive plans for Union Square, has tended to reenforce these doubts....[36]

A major feature of the Senate Park Commission plan, and one that was dear to the hearts of early Commission of Fine Arts members, was the elaborate proposal for the Washington Monument Gardens (pl. IX). There was no question that this had been carefully thought out, that it was considered the jewel of the Mall plan, especially by its designer, Charles McKim. Legislation was introduced in Congress in 1928 to complete the development in time for the George Washington Bicentennial in 1932, but doubts about soil conditions around the foundations of the monument caused both the Commission of Fine Arts and the National Capital Park and Planning Commission to call for a full engineering report. The report recommended that the design of 1901 be abandoned because the areas requiring either excavation or heavy loading were located where they would seriously affect the stability of the monument. The Commission of Fine Arts looked at two simpler designs—one with an informal character by Olmsted and the other a strictly formal design by William Adams Delano—but found neither satisfactory when compared to the "elegance, taste

Fig. 7 Federal Triangle area, undeveloped, ca. 1915, showing the new National Museum on the Mall at the end of 10th Street, NW. The Department of Justice building is now on the left, and the Internal Revenue Service on the right. Commission of Fine Arts

and beauty" of the treatment of the grounds of the Capitol and the Lincoln Memorial. Also, the members criticized the designs for not recognizing the White House axis in any appropriate way.[37] Even these plans, according to the engineers, were not feasible unless the foundations of the monument were carried down to bed rock, and that, Director of Public Buildings and Public Parks Ulysses S. Grant III told Charles Moore, could invite "immediate and complete disaster, with no possibility of correction."[38] This possibility, plus the lack of funds during the Depression, brought an end to the discussion, and the monument still stands today on its unadorned mound.

A number of other projects proposed by the Senate Park Commission were undertaken until the Depression, followed by World War II, curtailed construction; some were built essentially as outlined in the Senate Park Commission's report to the Senate, others underwent significant changes or were never completed. The Federal Triangle was the largest of the building projects and was certainly faithful to the Senate Park Commission's vision for Pennsylvania Avenue, although as originally proposed, this complex was to be composed of District of Columbia, not federal, buildings (fig. 7). On the crucial site south of the White House, which was to terminate the north-south axis of the Mall, only a single memorial to Thomas Jefferson was placed on a site reserved for both a memorial, possibly to the Founding Fathers, and a grouping of public buildings. The Mall was landscaped early in the 1930s according to the plan, and the Freer Gallery of Art in the early 1920s and the National Gallery of Art in the mid-1930s continued the precedent established by the present-day Museum of Natural History, erected under the supervision of the Senate Park Commission members before the creation of the Commission of Fine Arts. However, the Smithsonian Castle stayed right where it was, interrupting the Mall building line established after the Department of Agriculture building imbroglio. Around the Capitol, the Senate Park Commission had recommended an enclosure of legislative buildings, and the first Senate and House office buildings were erected only a few years after the plan was presented. Additional Senate and House buildings went up in the 1920s, but gaps remained. The

Fig. 8 The Senate Park Commission proposal for Lafayette Square, ringed with government buildings, as envisioned by Cass Gilbert, ca. 1917. Commission of Fine Arts

Fig. 9 Arlington Cemetery, Civil War section. Commission of Fine Arts

Supreme Court, although not a legislative building, filled one of these spaces in 1935. On Lafayette Square, the plan to demolish the small houses surrounding the square and replace them with government buildings of uniform height and style was begun in 1917 with the Treasury Annex, followed by the U.S. Chamber of Commerce in 1922 (fig. 8), but that was as far as it went, probably because of the vexing problem of how to explain the demolition of such historic buildings as the Blair, Decatur, Dolley Madison, and Tayloe houses, together with St. John's Church. In the landscape department, work on the Anacostia Water Park, a project not usually thought of as an integral part of the Senate Park Commission plan, was begun in 1915 and worked on actively in the 1920s. The Rock Creek and Potomac Parkway, also part of the Park Commission plan, was authorized by Congress in 1913 and completed in 1936. It was the first federally authorized parkway.[39]

Lastly, mention should be made of the commission's efforts to guide the development of Arlington Cemetery according to the Senate Park Commission's strong statements in its final report regarding the need, throughout the cemetery, to use only the simplest white headstones, placed in uniform rows, such as could be seen in the old Civil War section of the cemetery (fig. 9). These words were taken verbatim from a draft written by Saint-Gaudens, and offer only one example of the many, mostly behind-the-scenes contributions of the noted sculptor to the work of the Park Commission. They offer a vivid contrast to the more circumspect language used throughout the report by authors Moore and Olmsted. For example: "There is nothing that needs proper supervision and planning more than the modern cemetery, for there is certainly nothing that suffers more from vulgarity, ignorance, and pretentiousness on the one side, and grasping unscrupulousness on the other;…the eye and the feelings are constantly shocked by the monstrosities…."[40]

Fig. 10 Arlington Cemetery, contemporary adaptation of the Charles Platt World War I gravestone. Commission of Fine Arts

The Commission of Fine Arts began thinking about the preparation of a general plan for Arlington as early as 1913. Saint-Gaudens's plea for appropriate headstones in this military cemetery came to the forefront with the nation's participation in World War I, and the sad realization that the number of graves would soon increase dramatically. The three architect members of the commission agreed to submit designs for the headstones to the Quartermaster General's department, with the result that the one designed by member Charles Platt was selected to be used for all World War I graves, not only in Arlington, but in whatever national cemetery they might be located (fig. 10).

With such a record, the Commission of Fine Arts could take some satisfaction in the work it had done to bring the Senate Park Commission plan to fruition. Down to the present day, the commission has always considered itself the successor to the Park Commission. On the other hand, there has never been a feeling that the plan was immutable. As early as the mid-1920s, the commission's *Tenth Report* noted that the agency's position was that the L'Enfant plan of 1791 was the fundamental one for the District of Columbia, and that the plan of 1901 was "a restatement of the authority of the L'Enfant plan, together with such extensions of that plan as were necessary to make it apply to increased areas and changed conditions. This Commission have [sic] never held that the plan of 1901 might not in its turn require changes and extensions."[41] Years later, in 1938, Charles Moore, although still ultra-conservative in his architectural tastes, said in a letter to chairman Gilmore Clarke: "The Plan of 1901 has been outgrown, as Burnham anticipated it would be when he prophesied that our descendants would do things that would astonish us. The trouble is that needs have outstripped the capacity of planners; and pressing necessities have prevented a broad, comprehensive, logical plan for the future."[42]

On 23 May 1935 the commission celebrated its twenty-fifth anniversary with a dinner at the Century Club in New York, attended by present and past members. Charles Moore and Frederick Law Olmsted, members of the original commission of 1910, were there. Moore, still chairman, was presented with two gifts commemorating his twenty-five years of service: a medal designed by sculptor Lee Lawrie (fig. 11) and a portrait painted by Eugene Savage; both artists were members of the commission. The portrait hangs today in the commission's offices, along with paintings of its other chairmen. Senator Elihu Root, who had played such a key role in convincing Congress of the importance of carrying out the 1901 plan and establishing the Commission of Fine Arts, could not be present but sent Charles Moore a letter expressing his regrets and recalling the circumstances under which the legislation was steered through Congress. The letter closed with the following paragraph:

And so, without creation of any power of legal compulsion, there was brought to the service of the Government the authority of competent opinion upon questions of art arising in the course of administration, and widespread and habitual deference to such an opinion has saved the Government and the community from God knows how many atrocities.[43]

No one at the dinner could have foreseen the cataclysmic political and cultural events that were to follow in the next ten years, and even the inevitable abandonment of the classical style that had dominated architecture since the Chicago Fair of 1893 was probably not uppermost in the minds of those who attended. This was a time to recall the names of Burnham, McKim, Olmsted, and Saint-Gaudens, and the conception and implementation of one of the truly significant city plans of the twentieth century. With many of the most important features of the Senate Park Commission plan either in place or well underway, in spite of a world war and years of severe economic depression, the commission could, justifiably, congratulate itself on a job well done. As it celebrates the 100th anniversary of the plan of 1901 and looks forward to its own centennial in 2010, the Commission of Fine Arts today salutes those early members, who took to heart Senator McMillan's advice:

> Remember, Washington is the Capital of the United States. Nothing is too good for the United States Capital. When a problem is to be solved, see that the most competent men in the country are called to solve it—and then see that their advice is realized.[44]

Fig. 11 Sculptor Lee Lawrie's medal honoring commission chairman Charles Moore, presented to him at a dinner in 1935, commemorating the twenty-fifth anniversary of the commission. Commission of Fine Arts

NOTES

This chapter is an outgrowth of a paper entitled "Artists and Architects in Government Planning: the Beginnings of the Commission of Fine Arts," read at the National Collection of Fine Arts (today's Smithsonian American Art Museum) symposium, *Art in Washington: Some Artists, Patrons, and Institutions in the Nineteenth and Early Twentieth Centuries*, 15 May 1980.

I would like to thank Pamela Scott for sharing her extensive research on the Senate Park Commission plan, particularly her work in the McKim, Mead & White papers at the New-York Historical Society and the Burnham papers at the Art Institute of Chicago.

To my son, Eric Kohler, I express my thanks for his encouragement and for sharing his knowledge during the production of this book.

[1] The members of the Senate Park Commission were architects Daniel H. Burnham and Charles F. McKim, sculptor Augustus Saint-Gaudens, and landscape architect Frederick Law Olmsted Jr.

[2] In regard to these exhibition items, the commission noted in its *Annual Report, 1911* (Washington, D.C.: Government Printing Office, 1911), 5: "They have been stored for several years in the cellar of the Library of Congress, where most of them still are. Careless handling and the lack of proper storage facilities have damaged many of the plans, and none of the photographs are in condition for exhibition purposes, being punctured, soiled, or with frames broken; several of the original plans can not be located. The Commission had the plans put in as good condition as possible, but, in order to insure their proper safeguarding, better storage facilities are required." The Commission of Fine Arts has, at present, one hundred large mounted photographs, five large watercolor renderings, three small watercolor renderings, and one ink-and-wash rendering. The rest are presumed lost.

[3] Frank Sewall, "Washington and Its Public Buildings," *American Architect and Building News* 36 (May 1892): 87. Another article, "Washington's Architectural Need," had appeared earlier in the same magazine, 35 (February 1892): 107–8. Both articles had also appeared in the *Evening Star* newspaper.

[4] Glenn Brown, *Memories, 1860–1930: A Winning Crusade to Revive George Washington's Vision of a Capital City* (Washington, D.C.: W. F. Roberts, 1931), 364. Glenn Brown's firsthand account of the events and people involved in the development of Washington and the formation of the Commission of Fine Arts is invaluable.

[5] McKim to Brown, 7 December 1901, McKim, Mead & White Papers, New-York Historical Society, hereafter MM&W Papers, NYHS. It should be noted that Congress never did approve the Park Commission plan

as a whole, only individual elements, such as the Lincoln Memorial.

[6] Moore to McKim, 16 December 1901, MM&W Papers, NYHS.

[7] Philip Jessup, *Elihu Root*, (New York: Dodd, Mead & Co., 1938) 1:279; hereafter Jessup, *Root*.

[8] Charles Moore, *Daniel H. Burnham: Architect, Planner of Cities*, (Boston: Houghton Mifflin Co., 1921), 2:25; hereafter Moore, *Burnham*.

[9] McKim to Burnham, ca. late January 1907, in Moore, *Burnham*, 2:16.

[10] The Agriculture Department building controversy is discussed in Dana Dalrymple's chapter in this volume.

[11] McKim to Brown, 8 March 1904, Charles F. McKim Papers, Box 5, Library of Congress, Manuscript Division, hereafter McKim Papers, LC.

[12] McKim to Moore, 25 July 1902, Box 6, McKim Papers, LC.

[13] McKim to Theodore Roosevelt, 10 February 1904; McKim to Olmsted, 11 February 1904, Box 6, McKim Papers, LC.

[14] Olmsted to Moore, 14 February 1904, Charles Moore Papers, Box 7, Library of Congress, Manuscript Division; hereafter Moore Papers, LC.

[15] McKim to Roosevelt, 13 March 1905, Box 5, McKim Papers, LC.

[16] Executive Order No. 306, 14 March 1905, Library of Congress, Law Reading Room.

[17] McKim to Burnham, 13 March 1905, in Moore, *Burnham*, 2:81.

[18] H. Rept. 17630, 59th Cong., 1st Sess., 31 March 1906; "Notes and Comments, Public Art League," *Architectural Record* 20 no. 3 (September 1906), 250.

[19] Burnham to Moore, 16 February 1907, in Moore, *Burnham*, 2:21.

[20] This letter became part of the executive order, along with other correspondence with the AIA. A copy of the order is in the Archives of the AIA, RG801, SR1.2B, Box 2, Folder 5.

[21] Theodore Roosevelt to the AIA, 11 January 1909; printed as part of the executive order.

[22] S.8606, 60th Cong., 2nd sess., 19 January 1909.

[23] Moore to Brown, 13 February 1909, Moore Papers, LC.

[24] William Howard Taft to Cass Gilbert, 25 June 1909, Archives of the AIA, RG 801, Box 41, Folder 1909G.

[25] H. Rept. 19962, 61st Cong., 2nd sess., 2 February 1910.

[26] Jessup, *Root*, 1:280.

[27] Since 1910 several pieces of legislation have required that the commission's approval be obtained, including the American Battle Monuments Act of 1923, which dealt with the design of war memorials overseas, and the Commemorative Works Act of 1986, which required the

approval of both site and design of all commemorative works on certain federal lands in the District of Columbia and its environs.

[28] George Peabody Wetmore to William Howard Taft, 21 May 1910, William Howard Taft Papers, Series 5, Reel 333, Case File 801, Library of Congress Manuscript Division.

[29] Whitney Warren to Wetmore, 11 May 1910, ibid.

[30] French resigned from the Commission of Fine Arts in May 1915, citing his upcoming work sculpting the figure of Lincoln for the Lincoln Memorial.

[31] A Report by the Commission of Fine Arts in Relation to the Artistic Structures of the Panama Canal, 63rd Cong., 1st Sess., S. Doc. 146 (Washington, D.C.: Government Printing Office, 1913), 5; hereafter Panama Canal Report.

[32] Minutes of the Commission of Fine Arts, 25 September 1913, 3; hereafter Minutes.

[33] Panama Canal Report, 11.

[34] For the work of Austin Lord and other American artists in Panama, see Richard Guy Wilson, "Imperial American Identity at the Panama Canal," Modulus (fall 1981): 23–29.

[35] Public Law No. 346, S.9449, 9 February 1911. See Edward F. Concklin, ed., The Lincoln Memorial, Washington. Prepared under the direction of the Director of Public Buildings and Public Parks of the National Capital (Washington, D.C.: Government Printing Office, 1927), 19.

[36] Minutes, 23 April 1934, Exhibit I.

[37] Minutes, 4 October 1932, Exhibit L.

[38] Minutes, 18 November 1932, Exhibit G-1

[39] See Timothy Davis's chapter in this volume.

[40] Senate Committee on the District of Columbia, The Improvement of the Park System of the District of Columbia, 57th Cong., 1st Sess., 1902, S. Rept. 166 (Washington, D.C.: Government Printing Office, 1902), 58. Saint-Gaudens's original draft can be found in The Reminiscences of Augustus Saint-Gaudens, Edited and Amplified by Homer Saint-Gaudens (New York: Century Co., 1913), 2:275.

[41] Tenth Report of the Commission of Fine Arts, 1 July 1921 to 31 December 1925 (Washington, D.C.: Government Printing Office, 1926), 9.

[42] Minutes, 28 July 1938, Exhibit I.

[43] Thirteenth Report of the Commission of Fine Arts, 1 January 1935 to 31 December 1935 (Washington, D.C.: Government Printing Office, 1940), 2.

[44] Minutes, 9 March 1939, Exhibit C.

William T. Partridge viewing model of Monument Gardens, ca.1932. Library of Congress, Prints and Photographs Division

"Beloved Ancien":
WILLIAM T. PARTRIDGE'S RECOLLECTIONS OF THE SENATE PARK COMMISSION AND THE SUBSEQUENT MALL DEVELOPMENT

By Kurt G. F. Helfrich

I N late September 1939 the American Institute of Architects held its annual convention in Washington, D.C. Its gathering in the nation's capital was important because it was deliberately timed to coincide with the meeting of the International Congress of Architects and was meant to showcase America's architectural development during the 1930s by bringing together national and international designers and planners to discuss the state of contemporary design. Unfortunately, this intended joint meeting was postponed by the outbreak of war in Europe following Germany's invasion of Poland earlier that month.[1] Despite this postponement, the American Institute of Architects convention featured a series of tours and exhibitions that examined planning and development in Washington since 1900. It was at the 1900 Washington convention that the Institute's secretary, Glenn Brown, had skillfully orchestrated a program of lectures and discussions that set the stage for appointment in 1901 of the Senate Park Commission by the Senate Committee on the District of Columbia.[2] The recommendations of the Senate Park Commission—known familiarly as the McMillan Commission, after its Senate benefactor James McMillan—formed the basis for planning and design changes to the Mall and its environs that continue to shape the monumental core of Washington today.

The 1939 American Institute of Architects convention was a less historically momentous affair, whose only note of controversy centered around an exhibition mounted by members of the Washington, D.C., chapter. The exhibition, titled *Washington: The Planned City Without a Plan*, was intended as a plea to reevaluate the Senate Park Commission's 1902 design in light of contemporary planning challenges facing the city, including the continued impact of unregulated suburban growth combined with what was already being perceived as a decaying urban center. Spearheaded by the chapter president, Alfred Kastner, and a young associate architect, Chloethiel Woodard, the show consisted of photographic panels tracing the historical, social, and economic development of Washington, whose message emphasized the need for integration of modern requirements into the historical plan.[3] Consigned to a small room in the Willard Hotel, Kastner and Woodard's show was overshadowed by the larger exhibition, *The Plan of Washington,* organized by the Commission of Fine Arts and the National Capital Park and Planning Commission in the top floor Art Gallery of the Interior Department. While their plea for a more unified plan for Washington linking the monumental core with the surrounding city was lost in the larger debate between modernists and traditionalists, it helped spur the National Capital Park and Planning Commission's work on a regional comprehensive plan for Washington developed after World War II.

As a part of its proceedings, the 1939 American Institute of Architects convention also saw the elevation to fellowship status of the Washington architect William Thomas Partridge (1866–1955; frontispiece). Partridge had been associated with the work of the Senate Park Commission and its report, having served as chief draftsman for the project in the autumn of 1901. He worked under the direction of the noted Beaux-Arts architect Charles Follen McKim (1847–1909) overseeing the preparation of drawings and models.[4] Partridge's 1939 American Institute of Architects Fellowship nomination package testifies to the high quality of his architectural training and his subsequent career and included glowing letters of endorsement by highly placed colleagues, friends, and former students including Frederic A. Delano, William Adams Delano, Colonel Ulysses S. Grant III, Louis Justement, and Frederick Law Olmsted Jr. Partridge's friend, the Washington architect Horace W. Peaslee, summed up Partridge's accomplishments in his fellowship nomination by poetically noting, "In private practice and in public office, William Partridge, Architect and Adviser … has taught as he worked, helping young men to understand, and understanding, to produce, advancing his profession while serving the public…'Beloved Ancien—A Worthy Fellow.' "[5]

Born in the District of Columbia in 1866, Partridge's ancestors included Scottish shipwrights and English builders. He first apprenticed with the Washington architect James Rush Marshall (1851–1927), before attending the newly established architectural program at the Columbia School of Mines in New York City from 1883 to 1886.[6] At Columbia, he was exposed to the architectural principles of the École des Beaux-Arts under the tutelage of William Rotch Ware (1832–1915). Moving to Boston, Partridge worked as a paid delineator for Ware's magazine, *American Architect,* which, as he later recalled, provided "the profession with a valuable service by enabling architects to obtain perspectives and renderings of their designs at minimum cost."[7] Partridge's work for the *American Architect* involved laying out plans and perspective elevations in pencil and ink, which would then be rendered or colored in by professional artists, among them D. A. Gregg and J. Eldon Deane. Partridge's drafting skills soon caught the attention of Charles McKim who hired him as an unpaid apprentice, along with his friend Paul Gmelin, to help with work on drawings for his Boston Public Library competition entry from 1887 to 1888.[8] Partridge cherished the time he spent working on the library for McKim, who affectionately nicknamed him "Bird" during this period.

Winning the Rotch Traveling Scholarship in 1889, Partridge traveled to France and Italy, where he attended the Atelier Duray in Paris and spent much time at the Chateau of Blois, making measured drawings of the wing constructed by the French king François I (1494–1547).[9] In Italy the following year, Partridge, in a typical example of his dry wit, remembered checking up on "Vignola's digressions." By 1896 he was back at Columbia University as an assistant professor at the School of Architecture, teaching "the free use of orders" as an outgrowth of his travel studies.[10] During this period he helped complete competition drawings with John Galen Howard and others for the 1901 Pan American Exposition at Buffalo, the Carnegie Residence in New York City, and the campus plans for Carnegie-Mellon and Stanford universities. McKim kept a watchful eye over his young protégé's career, recommending the thirty-year-old junior instructor in 1896 for the position of director of the newly founded American Academy in Rome.[11]

In the autumn of 1901, McKim asked Partridge to help oversee completion of the visual materials needed for the Senate Park Commission's exhibition and report. Partridge took a leave of absence from Columbia and worked with McKim in New York during this period, producing the final plan and laying out over forty drawings that were rendered by noted artists, including Jules Guerin and Charles Graham. He also supervised the construction of two models of the Mall area, by the Boston-based geographic sculptor George Carroll Curtis, showing existing conditions and planned improvements.[12] While Partridge's time with McKim on the Senate Park Commission work was a brief four months, it set the course for his future career as an architect and planner in government service helping to implement the commission's goals for improving Washington, D.C.

Following his work on the Senate Park Commission models and drawings, Partridge returned to private architectural practice in New York and continued to teach at Columbia until 1902. In 1907 he married Alma B. Austin. Born in Red Bank, New Jersey, in 1880 and trained as a teacher, Alma Austin taught at the Ethical Culture School in New York and was one of the first women to receive a law degree from George Washington University.[13] Partridge returned to Washington in 1918, where he worked for the Navy Department's Bureau of Yards and Docks until 1927. During this period he served as a consulting architect on a number of projects, including the development of a comprehensive plan for the Naval Academy at Annapolis, studies for the Naval Hospital in Washington, D.C., and a design for the dirigible airship hangar erected at Lakehurst Field in New Jersey. Partridge was also instrumental in establishing an advisory committee on design for the Bureau's new structures, composed of two architects and two engineers. The committee encouraged the development of an "aesthetic" doctrine for engineering structures. Partridge specifically remembered working on a project to refine the design of radio mast lines.[14]

In 1928 Partridge was asked by Colonel Ulysses S. Grant III to join the staff of the National Capital Park and Planning Commission. Established in 1924 as the National Capital Park Commission, by 1926 the commission's mandate had broadened to cover all elements of city and regional planning for Washington and its environs, and its name was changed to the National Capital Park and Planning Commission. Partridge's first assignment for the National Capital Park and Planning Commission concerned, fittingly enough, supporting a design element within the Senate Park Commission plan that had been set aside: construction of a memorial bridge across the Potomac River linking Washington with Arlington National Cemetery. In 1928 the members of the Commission of Fine Arts had approved the final design by the firm of McKim, Mead & White, which left out the shore drive underpass on the Washington side. The idea of an arched opening within the stone abutment was suggested by the Senate Park Commission's 1902 report in two drawings of recommended improvements, but according to Partridge had not been included on the 1902 model due to lack of time. Partridge helped organize a meeting with the Commission of Fine Arts members in New York in the summer of 1928, during which they voted to reverse an earlier decision and retain the underpass shown in the 1902 report.[15] With this victory, Partridge established himself as a powerful advocate in Washington for adherence to the goals of the Senate Park Commission plan. To aid himself in this task, Partridge strengthened his knowledge of its goals through an intensive study of the surviving archival documents relating to Pierre Charles L'Enfant's plan for Washington from the 1790s. His findings were published as a part of the National Capital Park and Planning Commission *Annual Report* in 1930.[16]

During the early 1930s Partridge was involved in plans for the creation of the Federal Triangle development and assisted in the creation of a documentary film on the campaign to improve public architecture in Washington, started under President Herbert Hoover.[17] In the mid-1930s Partridge oversaw the creation of a new National Capital Park and Planning Commission model of the central core area of the city, one that updated the changes to the area made since the Senate Park Commission model of 1902 (fig. 1). Partridge's model traveled to a number of national expositions during the decade, helping to inform Americans about planning changes being made to their nation's capital.[18]

Partridge was hired by the National Capital Park and Planning Commission in the late 1920s because of his direct knowledge of the Senate Park Commission's plans for improving Washington. Employed as an architectural consultant, rather than a full-time staff employee, Partridge's pre-

Fig.1 View of National Capital Park and Planning Commission model designed by Partridge on exhibit at the Interior Department Gallery, 1939. Commission of Fine Arts

ferred method of work was as a behind-the-scenes advisor. Despite his low-key nature, he was instrumental in helping to extend the Park Commission's planning goals outside the confines of what he termed the "Shield-Kite" Mall area. Beginning in the late 1930s, Partridge helped to formulate designs for the Northwest and Southwest Rectangles, the Municipal Center, and the extension of the Mall east of the Capitol Building through the creation of a monumental Avenue of the States that would have replaced East Capitol Street (fig. 2).[19] These efforts, if completed as proposed, would have transformed Washington's central area. America's entry into World War II put the various proposals on hold, and they were abandoned with the National Capital Park and Planning Commission's postwar emphasis on urban renewal and regional planning to create a more dispersed and anti-monumental suburban city.

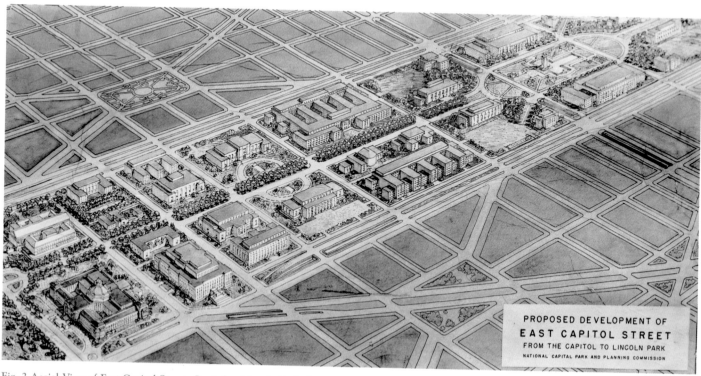

PROPOSED DEVELOPMENT OF
EAST CAPITOL STREET
FROM THE CAPITOL TO LINCOLN PARK
NATIONAL CAPITAL PARK AND PLANNING COMMISSION

Fig. 2 Aerial View of East Capitol Street, Capitol to Lincoln Park. Drawing by William T. Partridge, 1945. Commission of Fine Arts

Partridge began recording recollections of his time working with Charles McKim and the Senate Park Commission in a series of short drafts beginning in 1930. These early drafts may have been spurred by a desire to document his own role in the project, which had been neglected by Charles Moore in his 1929 biography of McKim.[20] Partridge began a more serious attempt at recording his recollections beginning in 1940, during an enforced period of rest after a serious illness.[21] By 1941, assisted by a National Capital Park and Planning Commission stenographer and typist, Partridge had expanded the scope of his writing to include subsequent developments in Washington planning, much of which he gathered from firsthand knowledge working for the National Capital Park and Planning Commission. This longer manuscript, focusing on the history and development of the Mall, was periodically amended by Partridge, even after his retirement from the National Capital Park and Planning Commission in 1951 and his subsequent move to Red Bank, New Jersey.[22] It remained in the holdings of the National Capital Park and Planning Commission, following Partridge's death in New Jersey in 1955, along with a series of rich historical data files he compiled relating to aspects of Washington's architectural and urban development from the 1790s to the late 1940s. The collection was transferred to the National Archives in the late 1960s.

Partridge's manuscript, "Mall: History and Development," is over 150 typed pages and includes a number of appendices on particular topics. Its fifteen chapters deal with a wide variety of issues including a chronological account of the development of Washington from L'Enfant's 1791 plan to the Senate Park Commission's plan of 1902, as well as an in-depth account of the role which the American Institute of Architects, particularly its secretary, Glenn Brown, played in paving the way for the Park Commission's work. Other chapters deal with the Lincoln Memorial, the Capitol Grounds, the Executive Group, and East Capitol Street.[23] For obvious reasons only a portion of the manuscript has been reproduced here. I have chosen to include his chapters on L'Enfant's plan for Washington, his time working for the Senate Park Commission, and sections on the Lincoln Memorial and the development of the Shield-Kite, including the partially completed Northwest and Southwest Rectangles and the Federal Triangle. These sections contain information that is not readily available in the published literature on Washington's architectural and urban development.

It is fitting that portions of William T. Partridge's unpublished reminiscences are now made available to scholars and the general public in this volume that celebrates the centennial anniversary of the completion of the Park Commission's report, *The Improvement of the Park System of the District of Columbia*, or *Senate Park Commission Report* (see note 4). Partridge would no doubt be pleased. Writing his friend and former Columbia University pupil, William Adams Delano, in 1940, he was candid about the role of his cherished mentor, Charles McKim, in developing the Mall in 1901:

> Now McKim was not an originator, but a wonderful adaptor and modifier, if you can use such a term architecturally. He could take a suggestion from Letarouilly or from some existing Colonial house, and by careful study, working his draftsmen to death, he would have something in the end which was not a copy, which was McKim expressing his power and strength and beauty, weaving his delicate appreciation of details into a warp of exquisite proportion....Everyone gives McKim credit for the Mall. Adopting a modification of the L'Enfant idea, he changed the central road, replacing it with a *tapis vert*, lined with elms and bordered with buildings. Was this McKim's idea? No. It was Olmsted's (Frederick Law Olmsted Jr.'s) design, with modifications which made it a McKim product. You have only to read the speech of Olmsted before the A.I.A. in 1900 to learn where McKim obtained the idea for the Mall for which he has been given the credit.[24]

Partridge had strong beliefs about the continued potential of the Senate Park Commission plan

as a guide for the development of Washington, an observation he communicated in his recollections and his work for the National Capital Park and Planning Commission. At once a visionary
and a pragmatist, he was interested in ensuring that the Senate Park Commission recommendations—particularly their overall clarity of design—continued to govern the development of Washington, D.C.'s monumental core. This comes through in his insistence on the need to restudy the
grounds surrounding the Washington Monument in the early 1930s, as well as the completion of the
post-1901 proposed Northwest and Southwest rectangles, and the creation of a more effective connection between the Mall and the Jefferson Memorial. These are planning challenges that still face
Washington. Termed the "Grand Old Man of Architecture, who has *never* grown old" by his friend
Horace W. Peaslee, on the occasion of his retirement from public service in 1951, Partridge's hith-
erto forgotten recollections can serve as inspiration for a renewed examination of the Senate Park
Commission's goals and their meaning for Washington, D.C., as it enters the twenty-first century.[25]

William Thomas Partridge
"MALL: HISTORY AND DEVELOPMENT" (1941)

I. INTRODUCTION

In 1901 the Committee on the District of Columbia of the Senate, acting under the instructions of that body, was directed to have prepared a report upon the development and improvement of the entire park system of the District of Columbia, and to secure the services of such experts as might be necessary to that end. With the advice and cooperation of the American Institute of Architects two such experts were selected, and these in turn chose two others.

This body of four men, each pre-eminent in his profession, devoted their services for a year without compensation. The group was known as the "Park Commission of 1901" but more generally called, after their Senate sponsor, "The McMillan Commission."[26]

The scope of a plan covering so broad a field, the short time allotted for its solution, the many phases of the design proceeding simultaneously make it now exceedingly difficult for any one person, no matter how closely associated with the project, to gather together the information necessary to present a complete and well balanced picture.[27] Despite these difficulties, there are certain major facts which may be recorded and which cannot be read from the finished drawings and do not appear in the official reports. It is important that the reasons be known for the acceptance of certain solutions, for the selection of certain forms to the exclusion of others in the evolution of the design. These were learned only through working at first hand with the designer during the creative period, while, through endless discussions and arguments, the final form was taking shape.

As the appointment of this Commission was the result of an historic event in the progress of the city's development—the centennial celebration of its occupancy as the national capital—it is thought necessary to go back these one hundred years to the very beginning, to the work of L'Enfant, its original designer, in order to gain a proper perspective and to better understand the problems confronted in this study of the city's future development. The Washington, D.C. of 1900 was a far cry from that city envisioned by its founders [fig. 3].

Not only did the members of the new Commission study all available material bearing upon the history of the first plan but they felt it necessary to sacrifice no small part of the very limited time allotted them for study, to visit those cities in Europe wherein could be found examples of that seventeenth-century planning which reached its perfection at Versailles and which may have had an influence upon the design.

Fig. 3 The Mall in 1901. Note Pennsylvania Railroad Station (far left, middle ground), shed, and tracks crossing the Mall at Sixth Street.
Commission of Fine Arts

The Commission spent five weeks abroad following an itinerary laid out by Mr. Olmsted, which had been based upon the work of Le Nôtre and his contemporaries. Additional visits were made to other cities which afforded examples of good or bad solutions of those problems with which the Commission had been called upon to deal.[28]

Plans of the original city and of the District of Columbia were carried with them and furnished food for discussion throughout their journey. Mr. Olmsted relates how the design of an important feature of the Mall was discussed and settled upon during a train ride to Budapest, the sketches for it having been made upon a pad of cross section paper.[29]

Whether the Commission reached any conclusion on this trip as to the influence of precedent on L'Enfant's plan for the National Capital is not recorded. It is still today a matter of discussion.

II. HISTORIC BACKGROUND

It is generally conceded that the plan for the national capital was conceived in the formal manner of LeNôtre, but the chief concern of its designer was for the conformation of his layout to the natural topography of the site [fig. 4]. While in some details the plan of Versailles may have influenced the design, it is generally considered today that the conception was an original one, evolved from topographical conditions.

It is true that L'Enfant wrote Mr. Jefferson for some plans of continental cities which he had collected in his travels abroad, but L'Enfant takes particular care to state that he would "reprobate the idea of Imitating," that he wished to prepare a plan "on a new and original way" and desired these maps only in order to refine and strengthen his judgement. In his reports and later memorials he stressed the uniqueness and originality of his scheme.[30]

Fig. 4 William T. Partridge's drawing, "Existing Topographical Conditions." National Capital Park and Planning Commission, *Reports and Plans, Washington Region: Supplementary and Technical Data to Accompany Annual Report*, 1930.

These reports or descriptions relate his endeavor to make the plan fit the ground and only secondarily offer aesthetic reasons for his avenue and street layout. His work reflects his dual ability as engineer and artist. His descriptions show a consideration of the problems of city and regional planning that would be a credit to an expert city planner of today. His carrying of water traffic into the very heart of the city to centrally located market basins is an illustration of the working of a practical engineering mind, while his vision of this canal being filled from "under Congress House" whence Tiber Creek deflected would pour in a cascade forty feet high and a hundred feet wide, is the blessing or curse, perhaps, of the artist strain of his paternity—L'Enfant's father was an artist of some note, several of whose pictures were hung in the Palace of Versailles—and was suggested doubtless by his recollection of the cascade at Saint Cloud.[31]

In formulating his plan, first consideration was given to the selection of the sites for the two principal buildings—the Capitol or "Congress House," located on the west side of a high plateau known as Jenkins Hill and described as "a pedestal awaiting a monument."[32] The site chosen for the President's Palace was not so easily settled upon. The President had, upon a personal view of the situation, selected for its location the high ground of the present Naval Hospital Hill. This choice, however, was set aside by L'Enfant in making his plan and its location was moved farther east, where though the elevation was lower, a better view was obtained down the straight stretch of the river. There were probably two other considerations which won the final agreement of the President to this change, for it is on record that he wanted his original choice of site restored. One was the possibility of here extending the grounds of the "Palace" south across the mouth of Tiber Creek over a tongue of land to the Potomac River. Had the high hill site been retained there would have been room only for a very shallow park south of the "Palace" and above all no possibility of a Public Walk directly connecting the "President's Palace" with the "Congress House," the one outstanding feature of L'Enfant's plan.

Thomas Jefferson prepared the first sketch plan for the proposed city in which the President's House was located on this high hill favored by the President, with the Capitol placed where the present White House stands [fig. 5]. He indicated "public walks" connecting the two buildings bordering the Potomac River. While this feature may have suggested the public walk of L'Enfant, it had here no latent possibilities of monumental development.[33]

The second advantage of this position of L'Enfant for the "Palace" over any other was that a line extended south through the center of the proposed building would cross the mouth of Tiber Creek and traverse the tongue of land lying between the creek and the river. A line extended westward through the center of the "Congress House" would intersect this north-south axis of the "Palace"

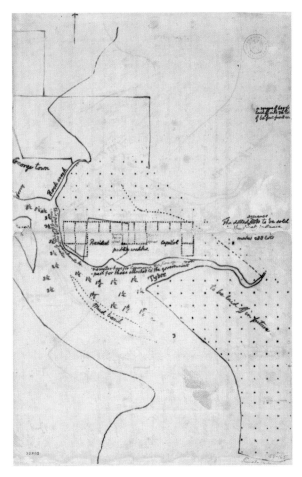

Fig. 5 Jefferson's plan for Washington, 1791. Library of Congress, Manuscript Division

and the proposed President's garden, creating a most important central point.

Here was the ideal site for that equestrian statue of General Washington which had been authorized for some time. No other location for the President's House would have produced so fortuitous a result. Thus, even the layman can understand that the city plan was based upon a double axis, an "L" shaped central area dictated by the locations of the two main buildings.

But we here ask, why two buildings and not three? The Government was a trilogy of legislative, executive, and judicial branches.

Where was the Supreme Court in the choice of locations for the principal public buildings? This third arm was allotted a site where the City Hall was afterwards erected. Although there is a major building here shown on L'Enfant's plan there is no direct reference to it in the "Legend" and only one mention of it in any of his reports. This site was one about midway between the Capitol and the "Palace" and played but a secondary part in the structure of the plan.

Across the city L'Enfant spread a plaid of streets running parallel to the cardinal points of the compass and coordinating these two main building sites [fig. 6]. Across this gridiron, from the sites of the two principal buildings as major, and from a few minor foci, were spread fans of radial avenues symmetrically arranged in pairs forming more or less complete Maltese or masonic crosses. The aim of these radials was "principally to connect each part of the city with more efficacy making the real distance less from place to place."[34] The intersections of these radial avenues determined the location of the principal streets of the plaid.

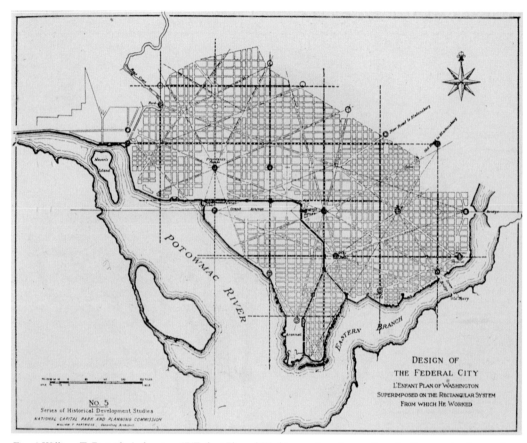

Fig. 6 William T. Partridge's drawing, "L'Enfant Plan of Washington Superimposed on the Rectangular System from which He Worked." National Capital Park and Planning Commission, *Reports and Plans, Washington Region: Supplementary and Technical Data to Accompany Annual Report*, 1930.

The secondary foci marked the sites of the City Hall, where lies today Garfield Park; the Itinerary Column site, now Lincoln Park; and the plaza at the eastern end of East Capitol Street—the bridgehead.[35] It can be readily seen that this interlacing plaid of streets and radial avenues, once laid out, could not very well be changed without disrupting the entire system.

A drawing, which was described by L'Enfant as "altered" according to the direction of the President, was submitted to Congress on December 13, 1791, and in later years (1797) was returned to the three Commissioners with an accompanying letter from the President calling their attention to the marks in pencil made by Mr. Jefferson showing the engraver what avenues to omit. This original drawing, though probably not the first, is today in the custody of the Map Division of the Library of Congress.[36] It is much damaged from well meaning but ignorant attempts to preserve it. It is best known through lithographic reproductions of a tracing made in 1887 by the Coast and Geodetic Survey [pl. I].

It may be recalled that L'Enfant refused to allow his drawing to be shown at the first auction sale of lots and was thought to have deliberately so delayed the preparation of an engraving of the plan that the task was assigned to Andrew Ellicott.[37] Changes were made during this process which brought forth violent protests from L'Enfant when discovered.

Now we find from a recently recovered "progress chart" that the laying out on the ground of that section west of the Capitol was considerably advanced by August 1791 and it is probably due to that fact that there occur no radical differences in that section between L'Enfant's plan of August and the later engraved plan of Ellicott [pl. II]—save for the omission of an undesignated feature, together with several radials on upper Sixteenth Street.[38] The most radical alterations were made by Ellicott in the southeast section of the City.

L'Enfant's antagonism to any authority save that of the President caused his dismissal and he is said to have taken the large working plan with him on his departure. The engraved plan of Ellicott was thereafter used as the official plan until 1797 when a third plan was prepared by Dermott and signed by both President Adams and George Washington.[39]

Although the McMillan Commission had pledged themselves to a strict adherence to the plan of L'Enfant, its details had been so changed and mutilated by many hands in a hundred years that only its spirit could be followed.

President Washington himself was responsible for the loss of the carefully planned vista of the White House from the Capitol. The size of the President's Palace had been considerably reduced (sic) by his orders and in directing that the original northern building line be retained, the southern semi-circular portico was forced north so it no longer could be seen from the Capitol.[40]

The change, however, producing the most far-reaching results upon the plan of the city was the shift in departmental locations. L'Enfant placed his three departments of State, War and Treasury in a single building located in the Mall itself, half way between the Capitol and the President's House. When President Adams decided to erect buildings for each of the now four departments, there had been no attempt to canalize the Tiber and this site fell practically on the very shore of the creek. He therefore suggested a location in the vicinity of the Capitol. Ex-President Washington then over-ruled that proposal and insisted the buildings should be in the immediate vicinity of the President. His reasons were not alone the convenience of the President. He stated that while in Philadelphia the departmental officials were so over-run with visits of the members of Congress that they had often to seek their homes in order to do their current work.[41]

Therefore, in accordance with the ex-President's direction four buildings were located within the grounds of the President's Palace. This established a tradition that the Executive Departments should be located in the immediate vicinity of the President which has held until today.

Nor could either of them have dreamed of the final form the memorial to General Washington, the "Hero of the Revolution," was to take. The equestrian statue, authorized by Congress, was located in the very center of the city, very near the center of the District itself. The only concern of the President was over the classic costume in which he was to be immortalized. Over forty years elapsed before any action upon a memorial was taken and that a private one—the gift of the site by Congress of this section of the Mall was its only contribution, and this was a reservation from which they had long been trying to disentangle themselves.[42]

A competition was held by the Washington National Monument Society, in which Mr. Robert Mills, Architect of the Treasury building, won the award.[43] His design resembles little the shaft of today.

The failure to canalize the Tiber as proposed by L'Enfant caused the site for the proposed equestrian statue to fall upon the very edge of the mouth of the creek. Therefore the location of this huge shaft was moved some four hundred feet southeast where there was a slight mound in the middle of the tongue of land formed at the mouth of Tiber Creek which apparently afforded better foundation conditions. This location was fatal to the axial relationship of L'Enfant's design. The new monument was 177 feet south of the original site and some 377 feet east—off axis in both directions. The scale of the gigantic shaft, some 555 feet high, was to strike an entirely different note in the future development of the central area.

Congress at an early date had donated part of the Mall to the Smithsonian Institution, which erected a brown stone structure scarcely in harmony with anything L'Enfant conceived.[44] Fortunately it was placed considerably south of the center of the Mall. That section of the Mall nearest the Capitol was turned over to the Columbian Society which instituted the Botanic Gardens.[45] A building for the Department of Agriculture as well as a huge National Museum and an Armory were also erected south of the Capitol-Monument axis line. The Tiber Canal which instead of L'Enfant's wide channel had been made so narrow and shallow that it had become a noisome ditch was filled in 1871 and the creek diverted into a large sewer. Four new squares had been carved out of the Mall by the insertion of two new avenues—Maine and Missouri Avenues—parallel to Pennsylvania and Maryland Avenues between Second and Fourth Streets, NW.[46]

In 1872 the Baltimore and Potomac Railroad was granted a right of way across the Mall and land for a station and train shed at Sixth and B Streets, N.W., and in 1901 at the time of the appointment of the McMillan Commission, Congress had granted a larger area for the use of the railroad in consideration of the surrender of street trackage and the proposed elevation of the tracks within the city.[47]

IV. APPOINTMENT OF A COMMISSION

Several speakers at this Convention [American Institute of Architects convention, 12 to 15 December 1900] had mentioned in their addresses the desirability of a board or a commission of experts to make an intensive study of the problem [the railroad]. This aroused the interest of Mr. Charles Moore, Senator James McMillan's secretary, and he in turn called the attention of the Senator to the effect on the public of a campaign for the artistic development of the national capital. As we noted earlier, the District of Columbia had long been indebted to the Senator for many practical benefits and now he was to give his untiring efforts to its beautification and later advanced from his private banking account a large sum in order to finance the expenses of the Commission he created.[48] Through his efforts the suggestions advanced by the assembled architects were successfully converted into action.

A conference was held with the officers of the Institute [of Architects], and to use a modernism, he [Senator McMillan] was sold the idea of a commission of experts. A resolution was introduced in the Senate on December 17, 1900—four days after the memorable meeting of the Institute of December 13.[49] The joint resolution called for a commission consisting of two architects and one landscape architect to consider the subject of the location and grouping of public buildings and monuments to be erected in the District of Columbia and the development and improvement of the entire park system. This committee of three was to report to Congress in December 1901. Ten thousand dollars was appropriated. This was never acted upon for fear of the opposition of Speaker Joseph Cannon who consistently opposed any expenditure of public money for "Art."[50]

It was thought best to handle the matter in another way, and on March 8, 1901, three months after the 1900 meeting, Senator McMillan reported from the District Committee a resolution directing that the committee report to the Senate a plan for the improvement of the entire park system of the District of Columbia. The committee was thereby authorized to employ experts, the necessary expenses to be paid from the contingent fund of the Senate.[51] These costs, some $60,000 were advanced by Senator McMillan and were eventually repaid him.

The resolution having been adopted, a subcommittee was appointed which met Mr. Robert Peabody, the President of the Institute. Mr. Boring for the architects recommended Mr. Daniel H. Burnham of Chicago and Mr. Frederick Law Olmsted, Jr. of Brookline, Massachusetts, to prepare the desired plan and authorized them to select a third member to act with them. These recommendations being adopted, Mr. Charles F. McKim was requested to serve as the third member and consented.[52]

The personnel of the commission is so well known to all that any account of the men or their work seems superfluous. Nevertheless, for the benefit of the younger generation, let us relate that Daniel H. Burnham, an architect of Chicago, was probably the first and by far the most successful of the "promoter architects."[53] As was necessary in the business side of the profession of architecture, he possessed rare executive ability. This practical ability was apparent in the organization and construction of the World's Columbian Exposition at Chicago in 1893, and placed that exposition in the front rank of international expositions. Aesthetically, it influenced public taste for a decade after. It was a revelation to the American citizen, unfamiliar with continental group planning and its resulting grandeur and impressiveness.

Mr. Charles McKim was recognized in his profession as without a peer in his particular field in design. His work was noted for its simplicity, directness, with a feeling for scale and proportion; in his detail he was exquisite. He was not an original designer and had no scruples in seizing any architectural precedent which suited his purpose, and in passing through his hands it became imbued with his own personal qualities. In his defense it may be said that in the past all architectural style variations have been produced by exactly this same process. The Greek architecture owes much to the Egyptians; the Romans tried to copy the Greek; the Gothic trained workmen, and in trying to copy the classic, produced the Renaissance.[54]

As stated before, two members of the Commission were appointed by Senator McMillan and these selected the third associate, Mr. McKim. How Saint-Gaudens legally became a member is not clear to the writer. McKim appears to have written to Burnham that he would prove a valuable addition and that Senator McMillan be so informed. Saint-Gaudens was then invited to become a full member of the Commission and accepted.[55]

Mr. Saint-Gaudens by common consent was recognized as preeminent among the world's sculptors, but it was his instinctive feeling for sites, for statues and buildings which had impressed McKim profoundly. Mr. Olmsted, Jr. added to an inherited taste, an unusual training in landscape architecture, both practical and theoretical—despite his youth he had enjoyed a wide experience in planning of large park projects.

V. PREPARATION-PRESENTATION-REALIZATION

A. PREPARATORY WORK OF THE COMMISSION

From the very beginning the Commission sought for no originality in design. They stated in their final report that "the more they studied the first plan of the Federal City, the more they became convinced that the greatest service they could perform would be done by carrying to a legitimate conclusion the comprehensive, intelligent, yet simple and straightforward scheme devised by L'Enfant under the direction of Washington and Jefferson." [56]

Their method of procedure too, followed closely that of the original designer. L'Enfant states in his first letter to Thomas Jefferson that he "arrived late in the evening after having traveled part of the way on foot and part on horseback, leaving the broken stage behind." He first viewed the ground, "riding over it on horseback as I have already done yesterday through the rain to obtain a knowledge of the whole."[57] He described enthusiastically the topography and possibilities of defense and notes the abundant water supply.

Similarly, the Park Commission began its work by making a personal survey of the District, but "behind spanking bays," as a caustic critic stated, going first through every part of the city in order to familiarize themselves with the character of the buildings and grounds within the city limits. Tours were then made around the outskirts. They examined the shores of the Potomac as far as Great Falls in order to learn at first hand the nature of the scenery and character of the water supply.

L'Enfant stresses in his report the possibilities of defense. The Commission visited the defending forts of the Civil War and sought the best vistas from the encircling hills.

L'Enfant worked less than a year upon his plan. The Commission spent but a similar length of time. L'Enfant wrote Jefferson asking for certain plans he had collected of continental cities, not for the purpose of "imitating" but "to strengthen his judgement."[58]

The Commission preferred to see these continental cities in person. From the very first, Mr. Burnham insisted on a trip to Europe in order to refresh the minds of the Commission and, with the problems of the Washington plan in view, to see at first hand what others had done before them. With the details of their visit the writer is not a first hand familiar, but they were often referred to by Mr. McKim in discussion of precedents, and interesting accounts of it may be read in the life of McKim and Burnham, both written by Mr. Charles Moore.[59]

An additional parallel lies in the fact that the plan of L'Enfant was never formally approved by Congress or the President, nor has the plan of the McMillan Commission ever been officially authorized, but both plans carried such force and conviction through merit alone that despite later changes, they have never been radically departed from.

B. ORGANIZATION OF WORK

Upon the return of the Commissioners to New York, the organization of the staff was now the first consideration. Offices were leased above those of McKim, Mead and White for the convenience of Mr. McKim in the transaction of his private practice, which, however, was completely ignored

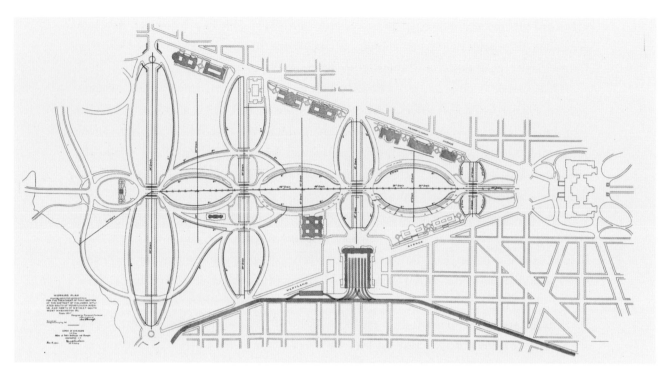

Fig. 7 Parsons and Pentecost plan for the Mall, prepared for Colonel Bingham, 1900. Collection: Pamela Scott

during the later phases of the work.[60] These offices might better have been in Washington save for the convenience it afforded Mr. McKim's partners to plead, often in person, for his attention to some of the firm's problems. I often recall how Mr. Stanford White would storm the new offices and literally carry off McKim to a conference in the rooms below.

Mr. McKim wished Henry Bacon to take charge of the preparation of the drawings but he was involved in the competition for the Department of Agriculture Building and was thereby debarred from government employment. Bacon suggested the name of the writer who had but a short time before been associated with him in preparing the plan of that project for a new Mall designed by Parsons and Pentecost for Colonel Bingham [fig. 7].[61]

The main considerations for my selection in Bacon's stead was the fact that I had been born and brought up in Washington, D.C., and was therefore thoroughly acquainted with the city, and I was also familiar with the tastes and methods of McKim through contacts in the preparation of the design for the Boston Public Library.[62]

After working nearly a year upon this Boston Public Library design, I had spent two years abroad as a Rotch Traveling Scholar. Indeed, Mr. McKim believed that this experience so qualified me for the directorship of the American Academy in Rome that he asked me to take Mr. Austin W. Lord's place as director.

At that time, I was assisting Professor William Ware in the School of Architecture at Columbia, who asked me to decline the invitation as he thought I could be of more service to more students here in New York than in Rome.[63] However, when the opportunity to help on the Washington plan came along he considered the new work of national importance and consented to my undertaking it. Mr. William Parsons proved a more than satisfactory substitute at the school during my year's absence.

Arrangements were quickly made for starting the preliminary studies on the Washington plan and directing the work of the gradually increasing drafting force.

C. BACKGROUND OF METHODS AND PROCEDURE

As previously stated, I had worked with Mr. McKim upon the design for the Boston Public Library. The Washington work started with the same enthusiastic spirit and on much the same basis as in the days, and nights, of work in Boston. The environment, however, was totally different and the atmosphere of the New York office did not inspire the personal confidences which arose from contacts when work was being carried on in his residence on Beacon Street.[64]

Mr. McKim's work upon the Boston Public Library design particularly in its preliminary stages and later in bending those in control to his will, was so characteristic of the man and his methods that an account of it is not here out of place.

In these Library studies not only were ideas and suggestions seized, tried and ruthlessly discarded, but designers as well. Letang of Technology fame, the first Beaux Arts professor of architecture to teach in this country, C. Howard Walker, and others—all skilled men—contributed their ideas of what a library should be and their efforts were simply filed away among many other discarded drawings.[65] Like Henry Bacon, I early discovered a method of working with Mr. McKim which enabled me to outlast his other assistants, that consisted chiefly in first working longer than he did and in addition possessing a facility of rapidly putting his ideas on paper. With the offices in his residence, the draftsman working late was often asked to share his dinner and seldom after a long evening session were beer and sandwiches omitted. In studies of the elevation, which particularly worried him and for which he had received no inspiration from earlier draftsmen, I made a systematic series of some thirteen elevations employing every possible columnar or pilaster treatment.

At the foot of the staircase on the first floor of the office-residence hung a large transparency of the Colosseum in Rome. After a discouraging day and a restaurant dinner to change the scene, we entered the house. Mr. McKim turned on the transparency light, sat on the bottom step studying the arcade treatment with its three-quarter columns which we had several times tried unsuccessfully to mold to the Library elevations. Suddenly he exclaimed, "Bird, look at the difference between the two sides. How much finer it looks where the columns have been stripped off and only the pier treatment is left. Pier treatment! Come upstairs quickly. Let's take off all the columns!" I made a quick tracing of the last study but without columns, the arches with imposts similar to the stripped section of this famous ruin. The greatest amount of study that night was devoted to the basement fenestration, to the relation of the basement windows to the arcade above and whether their heads should be round or square.

Staggering into the office the next morning, I found Kellogg, the head draftsman, studying the previous night's work. At that moment Mr. McKim also came in. Kellogg exclaimed, "Why, Mr. McKim, this is the Library of Sainte-Genevieve."[66]

"Get the photos," he replied.

Sure enough, there was such a similarity between the two compositions that today McKim's reputation as a copyist is more firmly fastened upon him. He would have had, however, no compunction in taking any suggestion bodily from the Paris Library, but in this instance the precedent for the Boston design was a classical one and not the Paris example. So in the Washington plan studies, no matter the source, McKim had no scruples in appropriating any suggestion.

There is every evidence that the original idea for the Mall treatment was proposed by Mr. Olmsted, yet Mr. McKim, perhaps unconsciously, made every one feel his was the authorship. It may be that McKim's charm worked upon Mr. Olmsted as it did on others of us who were closely associated with him, namely we were so proud that McKim thought enough of our efforts to claim them his own that it never occurred to us to dispute the parentage of our ideas.[67]

The value of an exhibit in advancing the public interest in a project was illustrated in the Boston Library example, later duplicated, but on a larger scale, in the Washington scene. In the Boston example the reason for publicity was the asking of an additional appropriation for the Library. Like many of Mr. McKim's projects, during the studies, cost never entered his mind, but later he usually succeeded in somehow inducing his clients to spend the additional money. In the case of this Library he had the Board of Aldermen to contend with in addition to the Library trustees. For weeks we worked upon an exhibition, plans, perspectives in line and color; a curvilinear perspective of the courtyard was made by the writer and mounted on a curved background and viewed only from a peephole.

When the exhibit was ready, the first attack for more funds was made upon the trustees at a dinner given ostensibly to the staff, but the trustees were all invited and were seated indiscriminately among the office boys and draftsmen, an arrangement not at first a complete success, owing not to the stuffiness of any of the trustees, but to the awe and embarrassment of the draftsmen. The central decorative feature of the table was a huge cake, a caterer's queer interpretation of what was originally intended as an accurate model of the final design for the Library. Its crazy features so fascinated Mr. McKim that he hesitated having it cut. Everyone contributed something to the entertainment the final event being what today would be called a tap dance by an office boy at close range on top of the cleared dining table. The trustees then viewed the exhibit.

For the inspection by the Board of Aldermen, a different procedure was followed. The exhibit was hung in a large dining room of an exclusive Boston Club. After an examination of the drawings and a careful explanation of the design and the necessity for additional funds, the Board was asked to go into the adjoining room for their discussion, which they might wish private. Upon tables in that room were grouped all the resources of the club's kitchen and wine cellar. After an unusually long closed session, the trustees were finally informed there would be no difficulty about the additional money needed.

In this Boston incident may be seen the precedent for the manner in which the Washington plan was later handled. The success in the Boston instance justified Mr. McKim in the lavish expenditure of money and labor on the Washington plan. While politics alone prevented the official authorization of the scheme, the illustrative drawings and models carried such force that there have been but few radical departures made since, and those were due to changed conditions.

The organization of the drafting office once under way, study of the various individual problems was begun. While the official report of 1901 unfolds the proposed development in a most orderly manner; while the work of the Commission with its excellent illustrations seems to reflect long and carefully coordinated study, the reverse was the case.

In the preparation of the material each section was developed independently, and while the Mall itself had been so studied abroad by Mr. McKim and Mr. Olmsted that little was left to complete it, the same cannot be said of the other details.

The Monument Gardens [pl. IX] were in a constant state of flux and the lack of coordination left many ragged ends. The most casual inspection will show the want of any organic tie between the Monument Grounds and the Lincoln Memorial beyond. The same is true to the south in the Washington Common section. Mr. Olmsted states:

It was in that eleventh-hour rush to finish the drawings that some parts of the plans had to go through without the same deliberate study and unanimous unqualified approval by the Commission as a whole which was given to the major decisions. Among the parts thus unavoidably hurried to a finish were the designs for the eastern end of the Mall vista, from the Capitol to and including 'Union Square;' those for the rearrangement of the Tidal Basin area; and those for some of the details of the Washington Monument Gardens: by way of distinction from the major and earlier decisions dealing with the width and character of the main Mall vista and its enclosing rows of elms; the framing of the Washington Monument by an orderly expansion of the frame of elms flanking the Mall first devised in the plan by McKim and me on a piece of quadrille paper in a train en route from Budapest, to Paris in 1901; the development on the site afterwards assigned to the Lincoln Memorial, of a great terminal monument of a form non-competitive with the Capitol dome and the Washington Monument; the introduction west of the Monument Grounds of a long reflecting basin; the opening through of the White House axis to the southward, at a relatively low elevation, past the west side of the Washington Monument; and the development of a southern monumental focal point on the White House axis at its intersection with the line of Maryland Avenue in such a way as to leave the axial view from the White House down the river unobstructed by any bulky monument on the axis itself.[68]

Much study was given the problem of a proper base for the huge shaft of the Washington Monument. The location of the wide steps in reference to the monument was a perplexing question. In order to properly study this relationship, a rough model was made and one day while experimenting with the relative position of the shaft to these proposed steps, Stanford White rushed in on some business question. As he started to go Mr. McKim asked, "Stan, look at this. What do you think of the Monument placed here?" "No," said White without hesitation, seizing the Monument model, "put it there!" and rushed impetuously away. No amount of study on our part could improve that snap decision. Nothing could better reveal the difference in the characters of the two men or their approach to a problem.

Mr. Burnham once remarked to me that Mr. McKim's method of study reminded him of a canary bird taking its bath—many tentative trials before making the final plunge.

D. ORIGINS AND GROWTH OF PLAN

While in the simultaneous study of many features there may have appeared a confusion of ideas, there was a basic plan. The general scheme for the central area had been pretty well settled upon by Mr. McKim and Mr. Olmsted in their discussions abroad. The crucial problem was the inclusion in the Mall treatment of some four hundred acres of reclaimed land lying south and west of the original river shoreline. How should this be brought into the composition?

During the visit of the Commission in Paris, Mr. McKim saw instantly the possibilities of adapting the grouping of the Tuileries-Place de la Concorde-Arc de Triomphe composition. Picturing the Louvre as the Capitol, the Tuileries gardens as the Mall, the Concorde obelisk as the Washington Monument, the Arc de Triomphe furnished the answer to the question. The axis of the Capitol-Monument should be extended westward and at some point near the river a major feature with a strong horizontal line would complete a composition far superior to that of Paris.

Mr. McKim was enthusiastic over this possibility. When arrangements were made for Mr. Burnham to meet Mr. Cassatt in London in order to make a final plea for the removal of the railroad tracks from the Mall, which question had hung over their heads during the entire trip, a veritable sword of Damocles, it was resolved that the Commission ask Mr. Cassatt to return with them to Paris in order to show him the glory of an executed composition with elements remarkably similar to those in Washington and only to be achieved by the removal of the existing railroad tracks and station.

It was not necessary, however, to convert Mr. Cassatt by showing him the possibilities to be realized only by the vacating of the Mall by his railroad. He at once informed Mr. Burnham, that while the Commission was abroad arrangements had been made with the Baltimore and Ohio Railroad whereby they were willing to build a Union Station north of the Capitol provided Senator McMillan would secure an appropriation for tunneling Capitol Hill in order to make connections with the south which would then free the Mall from the intruding tracks and railroad station.[69]

While the Paris monument suggested the form and circular setting of this terminal feature, the scale, the size of the circle, the height of the mound as well as its location on the Capitol Monument axis extended, were pretty well determined on the site.

The new central area spreading over the reclaimed land was almost double the size of the Mall of L'Enfant. The new composition became a symmetrical kite shaped figure based on a Latin cross, replacing L'Enfant's "L" shaped Public Walk and President's Garden [pl.VII].

Mr. McKim often stated the reason for the selection of a strong horizontal composition for the Lincoln Memorial was that while the dome of the Capitol was a derivative of the arch, the simple lines of the Monument suggested the pier. The third architectural element was the lintel and a low colonnade would be the proper expression of that elementary form. This while originally suggested by the Arc de Triomphe in Paris, it was later felt would be better carried out by a low colonnade rather than by the Paris arch [pl. XI]. Whether this was the reason or an excuse for the adaptation of the Brandenburg Gate as an inspiration for the Lincoln Memorial is a matter for speculation.

Fig. 8 The proposed development of the site for the Lincoln Memorial, seen from the Washington Monument. *Senate Park Commission Report*, No. 52

Here now was a composition filling every aesthetic and spiritual requirement for this memorial. There was no hesitance on the part of Mr. McKim in adapting it to his purposes. He often explained that the form of the memorial was a most delicate situation. Despite the thirty-five intervening years and the unity in spirit brought about by the Spanish-American War there was still a strong sectional feeling. A memorial to Lincoln across the river from Arlington, the home of Robert E. Lee, would give offense to many irreconcilables. Not so a memorial to the memorable address of Lincoln at Gettysburg. This was a message of peace and good will to which no one could take offense. The Brandenburg Gate design solved the problem perfectly; for surmounting an imposing colonnade could be placed an attic on which this immortal speech would be engraved. The structure would be open both sides so there would be no question as to which way the monument faced. There was no back to be turned towards the south across the river. A statue to Lincoln could be placed near by.

While the Mall proper to the east followed L'Enfant's conception in being bordered with buildings here was to be a special treatment—a canal some two thousand feet long, bordered by green lawns, outlined by formal tree planting, backed by dense plantations with no competing buildings, creating an isolation of the Memorial which would greatly add to the dignity of the composition [fig. 8]. Similar examples of canals had been seen at Versailles and Hampton Court.

At the head of the canal was to rise the circular mound on which this Lincoln-Gettysburg Memorial would stand—the *rond point* suggested by the Arc de Triomphe setting at Paris. From this center were to lead the Memorial Bridge to Arlington and a formal entrance to the Rock Creek and Potomac Parkway—the basis of a system of radial avenues and paths [fig. 9].

A large part of my time in the early stages of the work was spent upon the studies for the Monument Gardens. As the main presentation plan had been left to me to prepare and I had to begin laying out the many perspectives for rendering, there was little time left for me to devote to the various studies under way. I regretted seeing their completion pass into other hands while I drew the plan, superintended the start of the models and kept the ever-increasing drafting force going in the most approved head draftsman fashion of the day.

Fig. 9 View of the Lincoln Memorial site from the old Naval Observatory. *Senate Park Commission Report*, No. 51

In later years when no longer spellbound by McKim's genius and the charm of his personality, an opportunity was presented of restudying the surroundings of the Monument and the termination of the Mall motive as proposed in 1901.

While the skill shown in the solution of the architectural problems of the Mall is beyond criticism, the estimate of the Commission of the Federal building requirements have by today's experience, proven sadly lacking. The tradition that the executive departments be located in the immediate vicinity of the White House was strictly followed and Lafayette Park was made the center of a group of six relatively small buildings. The buildings pertaining to the legislative branch were located around the Capitol—sixteen of them, fifteen new ones, and the Congressional Library which was already in place. The use of the triangular shaped tract of land south of Pennsylvania Avenue for Federal building sites had long been recommended but the Commission here placed structures for the District Government.[70]

It is no less unjust to condemn their estimates of Federal departmental growth than to criticize their failure to foretell the future effect of the automobile. The Monument Garden design was based on the premise that the visitor would drive his horse and buggy down the Mall to the high terrace on which the Monument was to stand, hitch it there and spend the afternoon among the charms of the Gardens and seek shade on the surrounding high wooded terraces. There was no way to reach the gardens from the Mall save afoot, down the steps. The only continuous drive from the Capitol to the Lincoln Memorial was outside the Mall, on B Street, NW.

One of the features of the plan of L'Enfant was the use of water effects in which can be read some influence of the work of LeNôtre at Versailles. Not only was the Tiber Canal planned for transportation purposes, but the enlarged basin at its mouth afforded aquatic recreational facilities and added to the enhancement of the President's Gardens. The Tiber Canal was to have been filled from a cascade pouring from under the Congress House, while five grand fountains were distributed throughout the city. One was to be located in Pennsylvania Avenue at Eighth Street. Examples of the use of water effects in architectural compositions had been carefully studied, in the Commission's trip abroad—there are sixteen illustrations of fountains and large basins in the published report.[71] The cascade from under the Capitol was reinstated in the new plan, in a different form because Tiber Creek, once a canal, now flowed in a sewer below.

In Union Square at the foot of the Capitol Grounds there were planned two large and six small fountains while a long basin ended or began the *tapis vert* [pl. X]. Two large fountains flanked the shaft on the upper terrace of the Monument setting, while in the Garden below a huge circular reflecting pool formed the center of a group of longitudinal basins. From the niches in the buttress wall of the main terrace poured huge spouts of water in contrast to the placid surfaces of the garden pools. As before mentioned, the most striking water effect is found in the two thousand feet long reflecting basin of the Lincoln Memorial.

While those familiar with the work of the Commission know of Mr. Olmsted's important part in the conception of the Mall at least, there is no doubt that the major credit for the design as a whole is due Mr. McKim. No matter from what source he may have gleaned precedent or inspiration or fairly copied, after it had once passed through his hands it was unmistakably his own. Time and time again his assistants would hit upon some, to them, original motive in design. Upon showing it to Mr. McKim he would praise it extravagantly and ended always in saying, "Let me have some tracing paper." What resulted was McKim, although the designer still felt the solution was his own.

Here may be related an incident which although occurring a number of years later had a direct bearing upon the credit due Mr. McKim as author of the Plan of 1901. Mr. Charles Moore, Chairman of the Commission of Fine Arts, was at the time absorbed in writing his life of Daniel Burnham and some of his enthusiasm for the ability of that individual carried over into his statements in print and into his addresses.[72] He stressed the part Mr. Burnham had played in the creative work of the Commission, to which, as its chairman, he might be accredited academically. It will be recalled that he was selected architect for the proposed Baltimore and Potomac Station, planned for Sixth and B Streets, on the Mall. He played some part in the removal of the tracks from the Mall and the establishment of the Union Station which he was commissioned to design. Whatever had been his earlier activities when the designing was under way in the New York office, his visits there were hurried, merely stopovers on his trips to or from Chicago. He would examine the sketches, praise them, and then carry Mr. McKim off to lunch. One could not fail to compare the few hours he devoted to the Commission's work with the time Mr. McKim and Mr. Olmsted devoted to the task to the neglect of their personal interests, of office hours, even at times of meals.

The day before the dedication of the Lincoln Memorial I was determined to place this matter before Chief Justice Taft who was to make the principal address. With astonishing ease I obtained an appointment for what I supposed would be but a brief interview. It lasted an hour. I told him frankly the facts as I knew them at first hand. Mr. Taft smiled and said, "it was remarkable how the character of men seems to live after them. I knew both men particularly Burnham and his work at Manila. Mr. McKim was modest, retiring, and unassuming, really shy, while Mr. Burnham was exactly the opposite and most acquisitive. Mr. Partridge, I am really indebted to you for calling this matter to my attention. I shall acknowledge tonight our debt to Mr. McKim." And he did.[73]

E. ILLUSTRATIVE DRAWINGS

After a certain stage in the studies, special features of the plan were selected for illustration and were laid out by me in perspective in pencil and rendered in color by a number of the best artists of the day. The services of most of these proved difficult to secure, for a few illustrated magazines held contracts for their exclusive services. I remember calling on Mr. Alexander Drake of the *Century* in reference to getting his permission for one of his artists to render an extra drawing or so, and his showing me at his house one of the first private collections of ship models.[74]

At that period Hughson Hawley was the architectural artist par excellence, in New York. Indeed an exhibit of the Architectural League one year consisted almost entirely of his perspectives drawn for different architects. His facility and speed were exceptional. His skill in drawing trees appeared remarkable even to a trained draftsman, until I discovered that both he and Guerin had been professional scene painters, so it was an easy task to depict at small scale what they had been doing full size.[75]

A meeting of the selected illustrators was called by Mr. McKim in order to explain to them the work and to obtain if possible some uniformity in the character of the renderings. At this conference Hughson Hawley demanded that he be given the principal drawing, a large view of the Monument and its proposed base. Mr. McKim, knowing Guerin's broad simple treatment of rendering en masse, had always had him in his mind for this chief picture, so he told Hawley that they had already selected the artist for it. Thereupon Hawley stated that unless he was given that particular drawing to do he would not render any of them. Mr. McKim said politely, "Thank you, then, for coming, Mr. Hawley. Good-day." Nothing was left for Hawley to do but take his high hat, wrap himself in his long Prince Albert coat and his dignity, and depart.

The most remarkable speed in execution was shown in the rendering of the Monument Gardens drawing [see pl. IX], for which I recommended Charles Graham whose technique I admired.[76] I took particular care in laying out this perspective, as I wanted Graham to justify my selection. After delivering the pencil drawing in person and explaining several things Mr. McKim wanted stressed, I left. On going back to his studio the next evening to give him some additional instructions, I found the drawing was just being finished. It was the most remarkable illustration of speed in execution of a large drawing rendered in detail that I have ever seen.

Graham afterwards rendered the perspective of Union Square wherein was shown the interesting suggestion of McKim to restore in a modified form the cascade L'Enfant had envisioned as coming from "under the Congress House." Here too may be noted the unique position reassigned the Bulfinch Gate Houses which had been removed from the east front of the Capitol at some period during the many changes and additions made to that conglomeration of mediocre and able architectural talent.

F. FINAL DAYS OF PREPARATION

The expiration of my leave of absence from the School of Architecture terminated further direct connection with the work by which I missed the final stages, until 1918 upon my return to Washington during the First World War.

At the end of this period of intense strain a reaction set in and some of the draftsmen left surreptitiously to set about their personal tasks. One day Mr. McKim came in quite unexpectedly and saw Alfred Githens quickly cover up a drawing. More in order to embarrass him than from curiosity, Mr. McKim insisted on seeing what he was concealing. Much to his surprise he saw a nearly completed humorous coat of arms, a cartoon which so charmed him that when it was finished he had it reproduced [pl. XXI]. It depicted in heraldic fashion, a shield emblazoned with a monument surrounded by elms. The Capitol dome became a helmet. The crest was a hydra-headed monster, the Commission, the caricatures of Burnham, McKim, Saint-Gaudens, and Olmsted were easily recognizable. This monster held in its extended hand a heraldic bird which it was belaying with its rolled up Commission. This bird represented myself, a *perdix mort*, dead partridge, driven to death by the enormous amount of work we accomplished. The motto, a Latinized favorite expression of Mr. McKim's: "Let's sock it to 'em" was "Soc Et Tuum."[77]

Much time and labor was involved in the construction of two large models under the direction of a professional model maker, George Carroll Curtis, of Boston, who styled himself a "geographical sculptor."[78]

One model shows the "disturbed conditions" as the 1901 report calls them, existing in that section extending from the Library of Congress to the Potomac River, the other, the proposed features of this rehabilitation of L'Enfant's plan [pls. XV–XVIII].

The model depicting the existing conditions was most accurately done and owes its value to the painstaking assembling of information, the taking of hundreds of photographs by Mr. Olmsted's assistant, Mr. James G. Langdon.[79]

It must not be forgotten that this description of the New York office work refers only to the development of the central area, the architectural problems. At the same time Mr. Olmsted was working in Washington equally hard upon an equally important phase, the Park System. In addition, he wrote the entire report of the Commission, ably edited by Mr. Charles Moore.[80]

Fig. 10 Designers working on Senate Park Commission model already installed in the Corcoran Gallery of Art. Photograph by Frances Benjamin Johnston, Library of Congress, Prints and Photographs Division

G. PRESENTATION

The drafting work was finally completed, the models finished and the whole forwarded to Washington for the presentation of the project to the President and Congress on January 15, 1902. Mr. Brown has related many times Mr. McKim's handling of this exhibit as something quite beyond the ordinary, but to Mr. McKim's co-workers it was but characteristic performance.

The drawings were to be shown at the Corcoran Gallery of Art in Washington and carefully prepared diagrams had been made.

Upon seeing the hemicycle, Mr. McKim was dissatisfied with both the color of the walls and height of the ceiling. These were changed by the use of unbleached cotton, hurriedly procured.

After most of the drawings were hung in accordance with the plan, he was dissatisfied and the pictures were rearranged and rehung several times. Mr. McKim sparing neither his assistants nor himself. Not until in the early hours was the arrangement finished to his satisfaction. The next day the height of the two models was changed and the entire lighting system rearranged. The opening hour approached and the room was still littered with debris. Several prominent architects invited for a preview were commandeered as janitors, led by McKim, and finished their cleaning task just as the President and Cabinet entered [fig.10].[81]

At the end of this exhibit in the Corcoran Gallery the material was moved to the Library of Congress where it remained for many years.[82]

H. DIFFICULTIES IN REALIZATION

The appointment of the McMillan Commission by the Senate District Committee identified the proposed development as a Senate project. Senator McMillan at an early date had prepared a joint resolution on the subject but in fear of antagonism in the House of Representatives changed the plan of procedure. Indeed the matter was so delicate that there was no appropriation made for the expenses of the committee of experts. The cost was some $60,000 met by Senator McMillan personally. Some time after the submission of the report and the imposing collection of drawings and models accompanying it, this sum was returned to him from the contingent fund of the Senate.[83]

. . . .

The recommendations of the Commission called for no specific appropriation, their object being to provide a logical and harmonious plan for the placing of future public buildings and to provide for additional parkways and parks in accordance with a well considered general plan, portions of which had been proposed from time to time by various interests. The new Mall plans were not original; they were but the enlargement and extension of the plan of L'Enfant—an effort to adapt the principles of his design to new and enlarged conditions.

The entire plan was looked upon as visionary and its cost as prohibitive. Some time after the submission of the report, Mr. McKim asked if I would go to Boston and substitute for him in a talk before the St. Botolph Club. After a climax of eloquence in describing the beauties shown on the slides of this future development of the National Capital, I asked if there were any questions on the subject. A voice asked the one question which I was entirely incompetent to answer, "What will all this cost, and who is to pay for it?"

The first building to be constructed in accordance with the plan of 1901 was Union Station. This was begun in 1902 and completed in 1908. The first plans called for its placement across Massachusetts Avenue, the traffic of that street to pass in a long tunnel beneath the station. This was abandoned and the proposed building moved northward to its present location. No sooner was this new station in operation than President Roosevelt ordered the old Sixth Street station razed. An amusing aftermath occurred in the introduction of a bill in Congress to enclose the train shed and use the old structure for Government offices. This Act is said to have reached the floor of the House before it was discovered the station no longer existed.[84]

The first structure proposed for the Mall after the report of the Commission had been submitted, was an administration building for the Department of Agriculture. It was first proposed to put this structure in the very center of the Mall. This was objected to by the President and in the effort to gain more ground for this administration building it was proposed to set the building line three hundred feet from the Mall axis, making the distance between the buildings of the Mall six hundred feet, instead of the nine hundred feet planned in the McMillan Commission's Plan.

Without the knowledge of any of the members of the Commission this distance was staked out. It was Mr. Brown who discovered this and immediately called Mr. McKim's attention to what was being done. [Partridge begins quoting here from Glenn Brown's *Memories*, 275-277] An interview was then arranged with Roosevelt, who said at this meeting, "They told me it was according to the Park Commission plan, just a little narrower, but wide enough for anything."

"This narrowing between building lines on the Mall," McKim replied, "would destroy the whole effect. Don't you see, Mr. President," showing him the plan, "when we plant the quadruple row of trees in front of the buildings north and south of the Mall, the principal feature of the composition, the open vista shown on L'Enfant's plan, between the Washington Monument and the Capitol will be destroyed?" "I wish," Roosevelt said, "I had known this before, but I have given my assent to the six hundred feet scheme, as the engineers told me it would be wide enough for anything and only a slight modification of the park plan. Now if you will take this up with the Senate and get them to approve the nine hundred feet between buildings, I will have an opportunity to reconsider."[85]

McKim called on Senator Newlands, who arranged for a hearing before the District Committee of the Senate. Before the meeting of the Committee McKim and I [Partridge means Glenn Brown] called upon Senator Gallinger and he informed them that the matter had been submitted to the committee, they had been down to the Mall to see it as marked by the red flags, and it was in conformity with the Park Commission plans, while it was a little narrower it was "wide enough for anything." Although the committee had made up their minds, Senator Newlands insisted on giving McKim and others a hearing and Mr. Gallinger yielded.

The drawings of the Park Commission, showing this section of the Mall, were taken over to the committee room and hung upon the wall. Sketches were made showing the disastrous effect of decreasing this open space from nine hundred to six hundred feet, and hung with the other drawings. McKim called upon Burnham, Post, Olmsted, Saint-Gaudens, Frank Millet and others to defend this insidious attack upon the integrity of the Park Commission plan. Several members of the committee informed us that they had inspected the open space as shown by the line of flags and considered it "wide enough for anything" and they really did not see the use of a hearing as they had made up their minds.

McKim, Burnham, Saint-Gaudens, Post and others explained from the drawings the disastrous effect upon the composition—the destruction of the scheme as originally laid out by George Washington, and L'Enfant.

After a short discussion by members of the committee, they voted to disapprove the six hundred feet scheme and determined to introduce a resolution in the Senate that no building in the future should be erected on the Mall inside of a line four hundred and fifty feet from a line drawn from the center of the Capitol to the center of the Washington Monument. This was according to the plan of the Park Commission.

This resolution was presented by the Committee to the Senate and passed without opposition. After this action of the Senate, Roosevelt ordered the building line of the Agricultural Building placed four hundred and fifty feet from the axial line between the Monument and Capitol. This was a great victory and morally fixed the future building line in accordance with the plans.[86] [End of quote from Glenn Brown.]

There was further trouble in the attempt to place the Agriculture Building farther east and to raise the grade higher than those called for on the Mall plans. Again, the President was called upon and directed that the building should conform to the lines laid down by Mr. McKim.

The Secretary of Agriculture was very resourceful. The appropriation allotted him not being sufficient for a building the size desired, the two wings were first constructed with the thought that an additional sum would be quickly obtained for its completion. It was—after a lapse of nearly thirty years.[87]

The second building constructed on the Mall was the Natural History Museum which was placed in conformity with the building lines now ineradicably fixed. Then there was no Commission of Fine Arts and the design for this structure having met with the approval of the officials immediately interested, the contracts were let, the foundations laid and a large amount of granite cut. Mr. McKim happening to see the design, expressed great distress. He called upon the architects,

Messrs. Hornblower and Marshall of this city, and at his request they restudied the central motive until it met with his approval. Thereupon the foundations of this section were dug up, relaid, and a very large amount of stonework discarded. Who met the extra cost is not recorded.[88]

In 1902, President Theodore Roosevelt put the restoration and modernization of the White House in the hands of McKim, Mead and White. This of course fell directly in the hands of Mr. McKim who as usual devoted so much time to its study that the work was not an asset to the firm. The small executive office to the west was looked upon by Mr. McKim as a temporary structure for he had conceived a plan for the erection of an executive office in the middle of Lafayette Park surrounded by those departmental buildings there located in the plan of 1901.[89]

The battle for the integrity of the 1901 plan knew no truce. When the office of Architect of the Capitol was left vacant by the death of Edward Clark, President Theodore Roosevelt was convinced that Brown was best fitted for that office and decided to appoint him. Upon protest from Cannon the President yielded and Mr. Elliot Woods was appointed "Superintendent." Not being an architect, the President refused to so appoint him. No sooner had Mr. Wood[s] taken office than he had sketches prepared in 1904 for the proposed Senate and House Office Buildings and a scheme for the extension eastward of the central wing of the Capitol as once proposed by Thomas Walter, the architect of the wings and of the dome.[90]

The American Institute of Architects protested against any work of that character being done save by professional architects. Therefore the designing was placed in the hands of Messrs. Carrère and Hastings of New York. Through some legal complications it was found expedient that the firm dissolve, so one structure was given to Mr. Carrère and the other to Mr. Hastings, the firm being commissioned to prepare studies of the changes in the Capitol. The two office buildings were located in exact accordance with the McMillan Plan and were completed in 1908.[91]

I. GUARDIANSHIP

In May of 1910 Congress established a Commission of Fine Arts. It was the duty of that body to advise upon the location of statues, fountains and monuments to be erected in the District of Columbia, upon the selection of artists for their designing and execution. The Capitol and Library of Congress were not to be included within the provisions of the Act. President Taft by executive order extended the power of this Commission over all public buildings erected in the District.[92]

There had been previous efforts for the establishment of such a body as early as 1895 when the Public Art League of the United States was organized. This body urged the appointment of a commission to examine and pass upon designs for buildings, monuments, paintings, sculptures, with which the government was concerned. The impossibility of securing favorable Congressional action led to the awaiting of the result of the work of the McMillan Commission. The defeat of the attempt to enlarge the White House without competent professional advice may be laid to this nation-wide organization.[93]

In 1909 the American Institute of Architects took up the subject and an effort was made to obtain Congressional action. Upon finding Congress, particularly the House of Representatives, opposed to any legislation on the subject, the matter was called to the attention of President Theodore Roosevelt. He was not only in entire accord with the proposal for such an advisory body but in view of the pending battle over the site for the Lincoln Memorial suggested the creation of such a body by Executive Order. This was accordingly done and a group of thirty architects, painters and sculptors, including one landscape architect, Mr. Olmsted, Jr., were designated as a Council of Fine Arts with the Supervising Architect as Executive Officer. They were to pass upon all plans, or grounds, or the erection of any statue.[94]

Shortly after his election to office, Taft revoked the order. Within a year, however, he had an act introduced in Congress by Elihu Root creating a permanent Commission of Fine Arts to consist of only seven members. From time to time their powers were enlarged until in 1913 they covered "all questions involving matters of art in which the Federal Government is concerned."[95] Although only advisory, the moral effect of their opinions has had great weight in the guidance of the development of Washington in accordance with the plans of the McMillan Commission. Its two most noticeable services have been the defeat of the New York Avenue bridge to Arlington and the preservation of the 1901 site for the Lincoln Memorial.

VI. LINCOLN MEMORIAL

A. THE SITE

The location chosen by the McMillan Commission for the Memorial to Abraham Lincoln was at that time a most unfavorable one so far as appearances were concerned. The land on which it was to stand had been reclaimed from the river bed and its appearance was such that Speaker Cannon is said to have remarked that a monument erected in that swamp would soon shake itself down with lonesomeness and ague.

The magnificent drawings prepared by the Commission now proved their worth, and caustic critics had only to view them to become converted to approval of the site.

Along the northern line of the new made land once ran the extension of the Chesapeake & Ohio Canal where is now Constitution Avenue. This waterway emptied into a large boat basin at the mouth of Tiber Creek, formed by the construction of a long dock or pier. On this pier, in the center of Seventeenth Street extended stood the canal tender's house. This, in recent years, was moved westward and is in use today as a comfort station and park tool house.

In the filling of this area several lakes or fishponds were formed, well remembered from boyhood days.

Two years before the preparation of the McMillan Plan of 1901, it was proposed to construct a high level bridge to Arlington on the line of New York Avenue extended. Under the direction of the Corps of Engineers of the Army, a competition was held and four prominent bridge engineers were invited to submit designs. That of William H. Burr, associated with Mr. E. P. Casey as architect was considered the best and was premiated.[96]

In 1913 the project was revived and despite the recommendations of the McMillan plan and its proposed Lincoln Memorial-Arlington low level bridge, an appropriation was made for the construction of this New York Avenue high level project.[97]

In 1922 President Harding submitted the revived project to the Commission of Fine Arts for advice. Needless to say they brought arguments to bear which were so forceful that the Congressional Committee appointed decided to follow the plans of the McMillan Commission, thus fixing definitely for all time the composition of the 1901 plans west of the Monument.

Preservation of the site of the Lincoln Memorial upon the location fixed by Mr. McKim would have been impossible had not the later high bridge project been defeated. Mr. Bacon at that time made sketches showing the disastrous effect such a structure would have upon the appearance of the memorial.

B. THE DESIGN

By the year 1909 this question of a memorial to Abraham Lincoln had become a burning issue. From many suggestions, three proposals emerged: one to carry out the plan of the McMillan Commission; one to construct a memorial peristyle or hemicycle of columns in front of Union Station; and one to abandon any architectural form and build a Memorial Drive to Gettysburg.[98]

A design for a memorial in the form of a peristyle of columns enclosing the Union Station plaza was prepared by Mr. Burnham's office and presented to Congress with his recommendation [fig. 11]. When his attention was called to the fact that he was disregarding the previous

Fig. 11 Daniel Burnham's design for a Lincoln Memorial at Union Station Plaza. Commission of Fine Arts

recommendations of the McMillan Commission of which he had been the chair, he declared there had been a mistake and his support of the bill introduced by Representative McCall was through a misunderstanding.

Mr. Brown states that Mr. Burnham explained to him personally that the plans were made by his office in order to show the unsuitability of this site. From that time on Mr. Burnham devoted his efforts to the retaining of the site shown in the plan of 1901 upon the extended Capitol-Monument axis, despite its deflection.[99]

In 1910 the National Commission of Fine Arts was created and Mr. Burnham was made chairman. This new body was asked by the Lincoln Memorial Commission to advise as to the best methods of selecting the architects, sculptors and painters to make and execute the design and to make suggestions as to its location.

The Commission of Fine Arts recommended a direct selection of a designer in preference to a competition and later named Mr. Henry Bacon as the one architect best fitted by experience, taste, and training for the solution of the problem.

To return to the early controversy—while the proposal for a memorial in front of the Union Station faded from interest after the withdrawal of Mr. Burnham's support, the same cannot be said of the Gettysburg Drive.

A powerful lobby composed of automobile manufacturers and real estate speculators became a serious menace to the realization of the 1901 plan. The American Institute of Architects and the American Federation of Arts gave the matter nationwide publicity. While the architects thought

Fig. 12 John Russell Pope's design for a Lincoln Memorial on Meridian Hill. Commission of Fine Arts

the arguments before the Memorial Committee should be confined to the aesthetic side of the question, Mr. Glenn Brown had estimates prepared and verified by Colonel W. V. Judson, the Engineer Commissioner of the District.

Two million dollars had been appropriated. Colonel Judson, appearing at the hearing, stated the estimated cost of the highway was thirty million dollars, with an annual maintenance of five million dollars. This, it was afterwards learned was the most important factor in the defeat of the Memorial Highway proposal.[100]

The most determined opponent to the McMillan Commission site was Speaker Cannon. Through his influence Mr. John Russell Pope was commissioned to make additional designs for the memorial—one to be located within the Soldier's Home Grounds and one at Sixteenth Street on Meridian Hill [fig. 12].[101]

A last proposal was to construct the Memorial in Arlington and it is related that Frank Millet was a factor in its defeat. He is said to have stated to the Democratic leader of the House that the placing of the Lincoln Memorial in Arlington reminded him of the Roman custom of erecting a triumphal arch in the countries of their defeated enemies.[102]

The Lincoln Memorial Act was passed in January 1913 and was not only the final battle for an individual site but carried with it a definite authority for the entire plan of 1901.

Mr. McKim had died in 1909, and so had no voice in the execution of that feature of the plan in which he had most interest.

In 1915 the cornerstone of the present structure was laid and the Memorial was dedicated in 1922. Mr. Bacon in a technical description of his design stated, "From the beginning of my studies I believed that this Memorial to Abraham Lincoln should be composed of four features, a statue of the man, a memorial of his Gettysburg speech, a memorial of his second inaugural address, and a symbol of the union of the United States. Each feature should be related to the other by means of its design and position, and each so arranged that it becomes an integral part of the whole."[103]

We cannot find here either the force or symbolism of Mr. McKim's conceptions. The design of Bacon violated every principle Mr. McKim laid down as influencing the design. In the 1901 concept, there was to be no memorial to Lincoln the man—save a statue at the head of the reflecting basin. There was to be no difference between the front and back of the structure. In the Bacon design the enclosed room is open to the east and the structure thereby turns its back upon Virginia and the South across the river. The thirty-six columns mean nothing. It is difficult for the casual spectator to determine the number. Few know that this was the number of states in the Union at this period. The columns are pure decoration and play no structural part in the design. The general profile, however, was made to follow the structure designed by Mr. McKim. It does not seem appropriate that a naturalistic, a life-like portrait statue should be enclosed in so formal an architectural setting. There is scant harmony between the delicate refined Greek style selected and the gaunt, ill-clad figure of the Lincoln of history.

The arrangement of the final plan is such that the Gettysburg address must have a balance of necessity of the same size and character. The preeminence and meaning of this mighty document is thereby destroyed. I feel as did Mr. Brown who when he passed the present memorial, could not refrain from picturing "McKim's open portico with a brilliant sun disappearing behind the hills of Virginia as seen through the colonnades, in contrast to the bleak cella walls of Bacon's design."[104]

C. THE REFLECTING BASIN

When the construction of the reflecting basin was under consideration, Mr. Moore desired to place its designing in my hands. For some unexplained reason, instead of writing me he requested Mr. Langdon, then visiting New York, to see me personally. Fortunately I was out of town and he was unable to get in touch with me. I say fortunately, for Mr. Moore then entrusted the problem to Mr. C. E. Howard of Mr. Olmsted's office, a trained landscape architect, experienced in this type of construction, which pertained more to the landscape than the architectural field.[105]

Fig. 13 The Washington Common and public playgrounds rendered by Jules Guerin, showing proposed memorial building, baths, theater, gymnasium and athletic buildings. *Senate Park Commission Report*, No. 54

The characteristic feature of the 1901 design of this basin was a cross arm similar in character to the canal at Versailles but local details influenced the plan [pl. VII]. The position of this cross arm was a recall of the emphasis shown in L'Enfant's plan of the north-south axis line of the intersection of New York and Virginia Avenues. In both L'Enfant's plan and on Ellicott's adaptation thereof this intersection is marked by a very large reservation and a prominent water feature—for what purpose is not known.

In the execution of the reflecting pool, the cross arms were suppressed upon the recommendation of the Commission of Fine Arts who agreed with Mr. Bacon that a rigid simplicity would be in better harmony with the severe Doric style of the Memorial. Also in the interest of simplicity, the elaborate water effects and the Renaissance arcade terminating the pool of 1901 were replaced by the present severe steps and terraces. The erection of the temporary Munitions building would have blocked all development of a cross arm, had one been decided upon. The original cross-arm treatment is still recalled however in the curved segment of the outer row of trees on the south side, which persists in the plan like a rudimentary organ.[106]

The intrusion of the temporary war buildings of 1918 sadly marred the uniform development of this feature of the McMillan Plan and even when removed their location will always be distinguishable by the differences between the growth of newly planted trees and the existing planting.

D. MONUMENT GARDENS

The inclusion of the huge shaft of the Washington Monument in the Mall composition was a difficult task. The obelisk was located off both the main axes of the original plan and was so tremendous in scale as to dwarf anything in its immediate neighborhood. The suggestion for a base consisting of a long simple flight of steps with strong buttresses was a stroke of genius on the part of Mr. McKim.

The Commission however approached the problem from the opposite side, and describes in its report the bordering elms of the Mall climbing the slope and spreading themselves to the right and left on extended terraces, strengthening the broad platform from which the obelisk rises. The description then speaks of the wide view obtained of the busy city from the groves on the terraces.[107]

Much as one may admire the excellent architectural treatment of the base of the Monument, the question arises in the minds of the auto riding laymen of today, as to how one got down to the garden level from the Mall. You walked!

There was no action taken in the construction of these gardens until in 1931 an appropriation of $30,000 was granted for preparation of plans, nearly all of which was expended in investigation of subsoil conditions, and upon expert advice from experienced engineers as to what effect such ill-balanced cuts and fills as required in the 1901 plan would have upon the stability of the shaft.[108]

South of the Monument Gardens across the Tidal Basin stretched the proposed Washington Common on the axis of the White House [fig. 13]. The end of this southern short arm of the cross was to be marked by a site for a major memorial, a Pantheon or a monument to some individual, the selection of whom was to be left to the future. This structure was to be surmounted by a low dome. Indeed, this was so favored an architectural motive with Mr. McKim that in the designs for the buildings bordering the Mall nearly every structure has one or more of them.[109]

The surroundings of this site for a Memorial were in violent contrast to the isolation sought in the location of the Memorial to Lincoln. Here was to be supplied the dearth of recreation facilities in the National Capital, "the one city in this country where the people have the most leisure." Boat houses, gymnasia equipped with all conveniences were to be grouped here; playgrounds for small children, with swings and sand piles were to be provided—all to be concentrated in a most inaccessible area. No consideration seems to have been given to how the users would get there. The future stadium is foretold in the huge playground or drill field with its enclosing terrace for spectators. All this was to be upon land reclaimed from the Tidal Basin. There was little enough left of that indispensable adjunct to the Washington Channel and that remainder was to be still further reduced by a large artificial island.

VII. THE SHIELD-KITE, NORTHWEST SECTOR, TRIANGLE, SOUTHWEST SECTOR PARK

A. THE SHIELD

One of the features of the Arc de Triomphe composition was the spreading radial avenues. In following this precedent in the emplacement of the Lincoln Memorial, there was only one enforced radial line in the desired pattern—that of the Arlington Memorial Bridge. Another was supplied by the introduction of a new avenue leading from the site to the intersection of New York and Virginia Avenues.

This diagonal line happened to suggest to the imaginative mind of McKim a shield in which might be enclosed the entire development of the Central Area. This was considered of such importance that he insisted that I emphasize it in my rendering of the plan [pl. VII]. So a brilliant treatment of buildings and parks was brought out into a shield-shape pattern by means of dark washes on the surrounding areas.

A caustic critic described this effect as a "brilliant mosaic, bounded with a neat line around all this glory, beyond which was darkness and chaos."[110]

The more prosaic in the office spoke of the figure as "Mr. McKim's kite." The poetic carried the imagery further and saw in it a crusader's shield, emblazoned with a cross with the Monument gardens at the intersection of its arms. The cross-shaped plan of the central feature may then be considered as subdivided into quadrants and in their descriptions we have fallen into the habit of designating each Federal building development within the kite, according to their relative cardinal grouping.

The northwest section was first spoken of as the Northwest Triangle until the expanding building area destroyed its outline. It is now referred to as the northwest rectangle.

B. NORTHWEST RECTANGLE

In the northwest section or quadrant of the shield of the McMillan Plan, all rectangular streets south of the bounding avenues were eliminated save Eighteenth Street. A group of buildings was proposed along Seventeenth Street facing the Ellipse, based upon the existing Corcoran Gallery of Art. This arrangement was very unstudied.[111] So small wonder when it was proposed to erect the Pan American Building in 1908, the suggested location for a building on this corner was disregarded and the structure placed in the center of the plot providing a proper approach and a setting worthy of the design. In 1924, the National Academy of Sciences was erected directly on the line of the proposed avenue from the Lincoln Memorial to the intersection of New York and Virginia

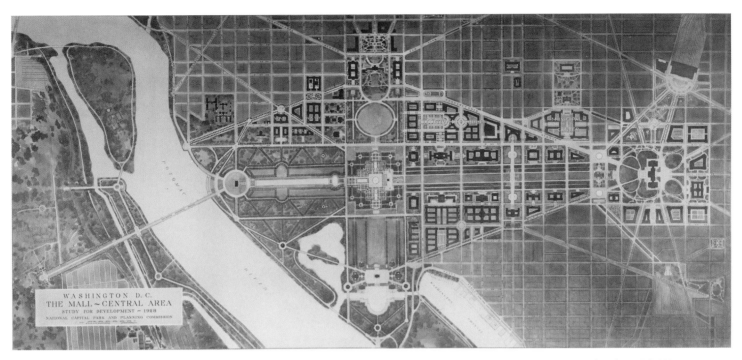

Fig. 14 The National Capital Park and Planning Commission's "The Mall—Central Area. Study for Development—1928" National Archives, RG 328

Avenues. This destroyed any chance of conserving this academic kite shaped figure within the borders of which the Federal buildings were to be grouped. It is reported the Commission of Fine Arts had considerable difficulty in compelling the architect Bertram Goodhue to abandon his latest mission style and to design something in harmony with the classic formality of the Lincoln Memorial.[112] Indeed the architect was in favor of another site where his talents would be untrammeled.

The erection of the National Academy of Sciences blocking a major radial avenue of the Lincoln Memorial surroundings, with the full approval of the Fine Arts Commission, seemed at first a grave departure from the McKim plan, but a most casual examination of that plan reveals a weakness which was remedied in placing here the proposed structure.

In the desire to conserve the Kite or Shield figure, there was left an awkward shaped area of privately owned land thrust between the Naval Hospital grounds and the proposed Northwest park area, whose tract extended south to B Street [fig.14].

Any private building or apartment house erected here would have been carried out to the building line of B Street, and not only would have ruined the appearance of that thoroughfare but would have sadly marred the background of the Lincoln Memorial.

The establishment of the present long, line of buildings of the character of the Pan American and of the Academy of Sciences was far preferable to an academic plan-form which would have been apparent only on a rendered drawing.

C. THE TRIANGLE

That section of the Central Area lying between Pennsylvania Avenue, B Street, Constitution Avenue, and Fifth Street is usually designated as "The Triangle" and not the "Northeast Triangle." Our system of nomenclature has at once failed, as did the attempt to conserve the academic shield form. In the plan of 1901 this triangular area was assigned to sites for the civic buildings of the District of Columbia. A municipal building, Courts, Armory, and a market filled nearly the entire plot.[113]

The use of this land south of Pennsylvania Avenue for public buildings had long been recognized as desirable. Several of the plans presented at that memorable convention of the American Institute of Architects in 1900 devoted this area to government use. The plan prepared for Colonel Bingham antedating the McMillan Plan, not only showed the south side of the Avenue lined with Federal structures, but the buildings are shown placed parallel to that street [fig. 7].

In 1910 despite the recommendations of 1901 it was proposed to use the area between Twelfth and Fifteenth Streets, the Avenue and B Street for three Federal buildings for Justice, Commerce and Labor. [Partridge was remembering incorrectly here. Commerce and Labor were combined in one department at that time and so required only one building; the third building was to be for the State Department.] A competition was held among the leading architects of the country and designs for these three buildings selected.[114]

In 1916 a Public Buildings Commission was appointed with a view of ultimately providing permanent quarters for all the Governmental activities within the District. They were to determine what buildings were needed and their proper locations, with due provision for future expansion. They approached the question scientifically and estimated from all the data then available, the future governmental requirements to the year 1941. An examination of these estimates of 1916 is illuminating in the light of today's requirements and disarms any criticism of the inadequacy of the provisions made for future Federal buildings by the McMillan Commission in 1901.[115]

The office building on Rawlins Square for the Interior Department had just been completed and the Commission noted in its report that "it is of great size…and it has had an important effect in shifting the center of departmental activity to the west."[116] It may be here noted that, this location was foreign to any suggestion for Federal building sites in the plan of 1901.

The Public Buildings Commission felt that in the construction of the departments of Commerce and Labor on grounds already purchased along Fifteenth Street facing the Ellipse a corrective of the westward movement would be applied.

In accordance with the 1901 plan a municipal building had been considered, and was completed in 1908, but not upon the site indicated in the plan of 1901.[117]

Federal interests had already invaded the District area as previously noted. The old, massive, Romanesque Post Office had been erected in this area in 1899 and sheltered the City Post Office as well as the Post Office Department. The report of the Public Buildings Commission states that this massive building was designed "before the necessity for an adequate amount of light and air was sufficiently recognized even by government builders. The government is fortunate in having but one example among its public buildings."[118]

Recognizing the necessities of the municipality, the Public Buildings Commission's plan provided for a market upon the same site as allotted in 1901. A smaller armory was to be placed on the site of today's Post Office Building.[119]

The matter seems to have rested here until 1919 when a continuing Public Buildings Commission was created and in 1922 submitted its first report. It pointed out the immediate needs of buildings for the storage of archives, for the Department of Agriculture, a General Accounting Office, and a building for the Bureau of Internal Revenue.

They advocated buildings of a "modern office-type structure with due regard for the safety, health, and comfort of the people who are to use it. To embark upon a program of building Greek Temples for housing the Government departments is both foolish and unnecessary. These buildings are exceedingly expensive and wasteful of space."[120] A very illuminating example of a building of this type is the Treasury Annex, located at Pennsylvania Avenue and Madison Place [fig. 15].[121]

From time to time both this Public Buildings Commission and the Commission of Fine Arts stressed the need for the construction of new government buildings, the more practical minded Public Buildings Commission calling attention to the ever mounting sum for rental in privately owned buildings, and the Fine Arts Commission urging in addition that such buildings be erected in conformity to the plan of 1901.

To add to the confusion at this period over the question of public building locations there was introduced a rider to a Public Buildings appropriation bill limiting the location of Federal buildings to the south of Pennsylvania Avenue. This was apparently aimed at the defeat of the 1901 plan for grouping such structures around Lafayette Square.[122]

Fig. 15 Rendering of Treasury Annex Building, designed by Cass Gilbert, Jr. *Public Buildings of the District of Columbia; Report of the U.S. Public Buildings Commission,* 1918, Plate B

This legislation removed the nebulous protection of the unauthorized McMillan Plan and immediately a costly hotel on the north and two office buildings on the west side were erected.[123] Although protests were made by the American Institute of Architects and bills were introduced to remedy the situation, they were without results.

D. THE SOUTHWEST SECTOR PARK

That half of the kite to the south, lying between Maryland Avenue and South B Street (Independence Avenue), balancing the Triangle, was designated in the 1901 plan as Park Area. There was but a single building here shown, the then proposed Bureau of Engraving and Printing on its former site [pl. VII]

B Street South in the existing plan of that day extended westward to Fifteenth Street and then stopped. The Lincoln Memorial, Monument, Capitol axis, as we have already noted, ran some 177 feet south of the true east-west Mall axis at the Monument thus making the space left for buildings much less on the south side than on the north side of the Mall. Had Mr. McKim carried B Street straight through to the river, the Monument gardens would have been unbalanced. Therefore he preferred sacrificing the continuity of B Street South, in favor of a symmetrical plan for the Monument grounds treatment.

This left a disrupted B Street, the offset of which, in view of today's traffic requirements presents a serious problem.

The south outline of the shield was quickly lost in the rapid developments since 1925. The refusal of the Army Engineers to allow any change in the area of the Tidal Basin destroyed all chance of executing the south arm of the 1901 composition.[124] All that could be done, when in later years a memorial to Thomas Jefferson was proposed, was to place the structure on the end of where the south arm would have been had not the practical needs of the Washington Channel taken precedence.

VIII. DEVELOPMENT SINCE 1928 FROM PERSONAL CONTACT:

D. MONUMENT GARDENS: FORTY YEARS AFTER

After many years the writer has been gradually convinced that the conception of the entire garden scheme of 1901 was wrong save for the base of the Monument, and had Mr. McKim lived and the problem been given him for execution, there would have been, without doubt, a radical revision.

A most casual study of the plan shows that in the endeavor to create a proper environment in scale with the Monument, the designer was forced to develop a central feature far too large for the whole composition, overpowering both the Lincoln Memorial and the group terminating the south arm.

This central feature took the form of a hollow Greek cross framed by high terraces surmounted by elms. The hollow of the cross-enclosed the "sunken garden," an entirely artificial conception [pl. IX]. The enclosing form concealed rather than emphasized that point of the intersection of the main axes of the plan which was considered of such importance by L'Enfant that he here suggested placing the equestrian statue of General Washington.[125]

This huge Greek cross feature formed the termination of the Mall treatment from the Capitol to the Monument, and bore no relationship to the developments west and south. It interrupted rather than carried through any continuity of treatment save on the Mall side to the east.

The structural lines of the 1901 plan for the Mall replaced L'Enfant's "Grand Avenue," bordered with gardens, by a central *tapis vert*, a carpet of grass, flanked on either side with a roadway and bordered with four rows of elms. This procession of elms gradually rose to the level of the mount on which the Monument stands. As described feelingly in the 1901 report, these rows of trees would "climb the slope up to the Monument, and, spreading right and left on extended terraces, form a great body of green, strengthening the broad platform from which the obelisk rises in majestic serenity."[126] This provided to the east of the composition a magnificent double sweep of trees, exactly the right distance apart to properly flank the Monument and form a marvelous silhouette against the western sky. From the west looking eastward these trees spread out on either side to frame a larger composition, the Monument plus two flanking fountains crowning the broad platform on which the shaft was to stand.

This need of a base to the huge obelisk has always been apparent but the scale of the Monument has made it a baffling architectural problem. With inimitable skill, Mr. McKim has here tied the steps, piers and flanking buttresses in one long horizontal base line in scale with the tremendous shaft but broken in detail in order to bring the various elements into human relationship. Had the treatment ended here, the result would have been superb. This solution, as an architectural problem, was perfect but, alas, from a practical standpoint it left much to be desired. True, the design was made in horse and buggy days. The automobile was then but an experiment. Even so, the casual visitor wanted some continuity in his buggy ride, but here the Mall drives ended; from the Monument terrace level there was no means of reaching the gardens below or the Lincoln Memorial beyond save by descending some eighty steps afoot, or by retracing one's route several blocks to B Street and making a detour around the entire Monument Gardens. The high terraces, crowned with those rows of elms, so eloquently described in the Commission's report purposed supplying views over the surrounding park, but as they were only some twenty feet high one would have been able to see only the branches of the trees on the ground below. Now there were factors disrupting this procession of "encircling elms."

The view down the river from the White House was one of the reasons for its location here, and so could not be blocked. Therefore on both the north and south enclosing terraces not only must the trees be omitted but the terraces themselves must be lowered so as to avoid blocking this all important vista. Then again, toward the west must be left an opening both for access to the gardens from the street level and to permit a view of the Lincoln Memorial from the Monument terrace, and in the design this opening is shown less than the width of the one to the east. We have as a final result a "sunken garden" enclosing terraces of varying heights. The gardens would be accessible only to pedestrians who would have to descend forty feet from the upper terrace or mount and descend again at the lower gaps on the north and south sides. The details of the enclosed gardens surpass in elaborateness anything at Versailles. There are fountains, cascades, pavilions, kiosks, clipped hedges, orange trees in boxes. The annual cost of their maintenance would have been enormous—in fact, prohibitive.

In studying the Monument Gardens model [see frontispiece] it is apparent that within the sunken garden one is forced too near the huge shaft for a comprehensive view and from the immediate vicinity, outside of the enclosure, the high terraces crowned with trees would have obscured any view at all of the shaft save from a considerable distance away. The roads and paths of the adjoining Lincoln Memorial and Washington Common nearly all of them at this central feature butt against the high terrace walls. As Mr. Moore stated, "time is not the essence of this problem," so here is an opportunity for further study.[127]

Unidentified and undated sketch by William T. Partridge, possibly a suggestion for the proposed memorial garden on East Capitol Street to the late Justice Oliver Wendell Holmes, Jr. National Archives, RG 328, W.T. Partridge Data Files, Box 106.

NOTES

Notes to Introduction

This project is dedicated to Sherry C. Birk, Honorary member of the American Institute of Architects, who in 1988 first made me aware of William T. Partridge and his memoirs when she commissioned me to compile a history of the National Capital Park and Planning Commission model of the monumental core of Washington, D.C., which Partridge helped to construct in the 1930s (now owned by the American Architectural Foundation, Washington, D.C.). I would like to express my appreciation for the guidance given me by the late Charles Atherton, Secretary of the Commission of Fine Arts, and to thank Sarah Turner, archivist at the American Institute of Architects, and architectural historians Pamela Scott, Sue Kohler, Jeffrey R. Carson, and Janet Parks for their research assistance and encouragement throughout this project. In addition, I owe a great debt to Professor Richard Guy Wilson at the University of Virginia, whose scholarship on McKim, Mead & White and American architecture and urbanism in general continues to guide me in my own work.

[1] For a review of the convention and a discussion of contemporary Washington, D.C., architectural and planning developments see "Seventy-first AIA Convention," *Pencil Points* 20 (September 1939): 540–54. See the "Program of the American Institute of Architects, Seventy-first Convention, September 25–28, 1939, Washington, D.C.," and The Fifteenth International Congress of Architects, *Report*, vol. 1, 24–25 September, 1939 (Washington, D.C.: American Institute of Architects, 1940), American Institute of Architects Library and Archives, Washington, D.C., hereafter referred to as AIALA. The postponed meeting was finally convened in London in 1946. See "Reunion in Europe: First Postwar International Meetings of Architects and Planners," *Architectural Forum* 85 (December 1946): 11.

[2] The American Institute of Architects' 1900 convention met in Washington, D.C., 12–15 December 1900 and included a series of lectures by noted designers aimed at, in the words of American Institute of Architects president Robert S. Peabody (1845–1917), making Federal architecture and planning in the city "more worthy of the greatness and intelligence of the Republic." Speakers at the convention included Cass Gilbert, Paul J. Pelz, George Oakley Totten, and Frederick Law Olmsted, Jr. Their lectures were later published as a government document compiled by the AIA's secretary, Glenn Brown. See his *Papers Relating to the Improvement of the City of Washington, District of Columbia* (Washington, D.C.: Government Printing Office, 1901). For further information on the 1900 convention see Tony P. Wrenn's essay in this publication.

[3] On the American Institute of Architects Washington, D.C., chapter's exhibition see "Program of the American Institute of Architects, Seventy–first Convention, September 25–28, 1939, Washington, D.C.," 11, AIALA; Alfred Kastner and Chloethiel Woodard, "Social Function of the Architect," in The Fifteenth International Congress of Architects, *Report*, vol. 1, 303–11; "Proposed Role for Architects in City Planning," *Architectural Record* 86 (December 1939): 56–62; Gerald G. Gross, "Young D.C. Architects Make Fiery Issue of Capital's Historic Plans," *Washington Post*, 8 October 1939, sec. B, 5; Gerald G. Gross, "Has Washington a Plan?" *Architectural Forum* 72 (December 1940): 52–53.

[4] Partridge's efforts were singled out by the four Senate Park Commission members in their final report, along with the seventeen-member team he oversaw: "To Mr. William T. Partridge, under whose able direction the drawings were prepared, and to Messrs. Baer, Butler, Chapman, Crow, de Gersdorff, Elliott, Githens, Harmon, Johnson, Kaiser, Merz, Morris, Mundy, Shephard, Trueblood, Walker and Weekes, who were associated with him in this work, the Commission desires to express its sense of obligation, not only for the skillful manner in which the work was executed, but for the interest and untiring devotion which brought it to successful completion within a very limited period." See Senate Committee on the District of Columbia, *The Improvement of the Park System of the District of Columbia*. 57th Cong., 1st Sess., 1902, S. Rept.166 (Washington, D.C.: Government Printing Office, 1902), 123, hereafter *Senate Park Commission Report*.

[5] See Partridge's "Nomination for Fellowship by Individual Members," 10 February 1939, submitted by Louis A. Simon, Fellow of the American Institute of Architects (FAIA), Walter G. Peter, FAIA, Edward W. Dunn, FAIA, Nathan C. Wyeth, FAIA, and Horace W. Peaslee, FAIA, AIALA, 6–7.

[6] Ibid., 2–3.

[7] William T. Partridge, "Memoirs of an Architect (First Revision)" undated manuscript, 2b, Avery Architectural Archives, Columbia University. I thank Pamela Scott for bringing this document to my attention.

[8] Ibid., 5b.

[9] See W. T. Partridge's three part article, "The Chateau of Blois: The Wing of Francois I," in *American Architect and Building News* 53 (18 July 1896): 19–21 and (29 August 1896): 67–68; and 54 (December 12, 1896): 87 – 88. Partridge later wrote an essay on the plan of the seventeenth-century French town of Richelieu; see his "Richelieu," *American Architect and Building News* 77 (16 August 1902): 53–54.

[10] See Partridge, "Nomination for Fellowship," AIALA, 5.

11 Charles F. McKim to C. Howard Walker 31 August 1896 in Charles Moore, *The Life and Times of Charles Follen McKim* (Boston: Houghton Mifflin Co., 1929), 155.

12 A letter to Partridge from Daniel Burnham in September 1901 confirms his work for McKim on the McMillan Commission materials at the offices of McKim, Mead & White in New York. In the letter, Burnham requested to see the materials noting, "I am informed by Mr. McKim that you will make it possible for me to look over the Washington plans upon which he is now engaged. I will, therefore, ask you to arrange so that I may see them, that is to say the work of the draftsmen of Mr. McKim and Mr. Curtis, next Sunday evening, Sept. 15, between 7 and 12 o'clock." Daniel Burnham to William T. Partridge, 9 September 1901, Daniel H. Burnham Collection, Ryerson & Burnham Archives, Art Institute of Chicago. I would like to thank Pamela Scott for making me aware of this letter.

13 See *Who's Who in the East: A Business, Professional and Social Record of Men and Women of Achievement in the Eastern States* (1930), s.v. "Partridge, Alma B."

14 See Partridge, "Nomination for Fellowship," AIALA, 6–7.

15 Partridge's account of this episode is included in the manuscript. For a more recent in-depth account of the Memorial Bridge underpass controversy, see Sue A. Kohler, *The Commission of Fine Arts: A Brief History, 1910–1995* (Washington, D.C.: Government Printing Office, 1996): 16–26.

16 Partridge's 1930 published essay, "L'Enfant's Methods and Features of His Plan for the Federal City," in National Capital Park and Planning Commission (NCPPC), *Reports and Plans, Washington Region: Supplementary and Technical Data to Accompany Annual Report* (Washington, D.C.: Government Printing Office, 1930): 21–38, drew on the work of Elbert Peets whose writings on L'Enfant and the Plan of Washington, D.C., were included in his *American Vitruvius: An Architects' Handbook of Civic Art* (New York: Architectural Book Publishing Co., 1922), coauthored with Werner Hegemann, and a series of three articles, "The Geneaology of L'Enfant's Washington," in the *Journal of the American Institute of Architects* 15 (April 1927): 115–19; (May 1927): 151–54; (June 1927): 187–91. Partridge's draft "Memoirs of an Architect (First Revision)" from the early 1930s also informed his article, "L'Enfant's Vision: A Discussion of Development from a City on Paper to a City in Actuality," in *The Federal Architect* (April 1937): 34–36; 104; 106–7.

17 See Partridge, "Nomination for Fellowship," AIALA, 9.

18 On Partridge's work on this model, originally two separate models combined as one, see my unpublished

history "NCPPC Models" (1989), in the holdings of the Prints and Drawings Collection, American Architectural Foundation, Washington, D.C.

19 See Partridge, "Nomination for Fellowship," AIALA, 8.

20 See Partridge's unpublished draft essays, "McKim," "Memoirs of an Architect (First Revision)," and "Henry Bacon," in the holdings of the Avery Architectural Archives, Columbia University.

21 See William T. Partridge to William A. Delano, 22 May 1940, and the letter from Frederic A. Delano, chairman of the NCPPC to Partridge, 13 July 1940, authorizing him to prepare a "historical statement of your old–time relations with the McMillan Commission" as well as a "record of your work with that Commission and since and of the various studies and plans you made in that connection…," National Archives and Records Administration (NARA), Historical Data Files of William T. Partridge, "Personal Recollections of the McMillan Commission," Box 105, Record Group (RG) 328.

22 Partridge continued to rewrite portions of the manuscript up until his death in 1955. As late as April 1953, John Nolen Jr., director of the National Capital Park and Planning Commission, wrote him, "We were all delighted to have the recent letter from you, particularly with its interesting account of your further writing on the background of the McMillan Commission report. We will be glad to have the opportunity of securing copies for our files of anything you write about the McMillan report and the members of the Commission…," NARA, John Nolen Jr. to William T. Partridge, 6 April 1953, Planning Files, 1924–1967, Reports, "McMillan Commission," Box 190, RG 328.

23 The full listing of the sections of Partridge's manuscript includes: I. Introduction; II. Historical Background; III. Existing Conditions; IV. Appointment of a Commission; V. Preparation-Presentation-Realization; VI. Lincoln Memorial; VII. Shield Kite; VIII. Development Since 1928 from Personal Contact; IX. The Capitol Grounds; X. Union Square: Extension of the Capitol Grounds; XI. Executive Group; XII. Municipal Center; XIII. The South Arm of the Cross; XIV. Public Buildings; XV. East Capitol Street; and appendices on Fountains; Henry Bacon and the Lincoln Memorial; Changes in Historic Buildings: Patent Office Steps; The Great Falls Power Project; Exhibitions; and Federal Architectural Styles. The full manuscript is available in Partridge, "Personal Recollections."

24 William T. Partridge to William A. Delano, 22 May 1940, in ibid.

25 Horace W. Peaslee, "Washington Says *Au Revoir* to William Thomas Partridge," *Journal of the AIA* 16 (December 1951): 258.

Notes to Partridge Manuscript

The official date of the Senate Park Commission Report is 1902, since it was presented in January of that year; however, much of its research and creation was carried out in 1901, which is why the Partridge manuscript refers to it as the plan of 1901.

[26] The special Senate Park Commission to oversee plans for what became the Senate Park Commission Report, was created in early March 1901 by the Senate's Committee on the District of Columbia. It consisted of four members: the architects Daniel Hudson Burnham (1844–1912) and Charles Follen McKim (1847–1909), the landscape architect and planner Frederick Law Olmsted Jr. (1870–1957), and the sculptor Augustus Saint-Gaudens (1848–1907), who, due to poor health, was unable to participate in an active capacity. Originally called the "Park Commission," this group later became known as the McMillan Commission, named for its principal political sponsor, Senator James McMillan (1838–1902) of Michigan. For an account of the commission's study, see Senate Committee on the District of Columbia, *The Improvement of the Park System of the District of Columbia*, 57th Cong., 1st Sess., S. Rept. 166 (Washington, D.C.: Government Printing Office, 1902), 8–10, hereafter *Senate Park Commission Report*; and John W. Reps, *Monumental Washington: The Planning and Development of the Capital Center* (Princeton: Princeton University Press, 1967), 92–93.

[27] At the time that William Partridge was writing his manuscript, 1940 to 1941, three of the four members of the Senate Park Commission were dead and the senator's former aide Charles Moore (1855–1942), was not well. McMillan himself had died in 1902. Frederick Law Olmsted Jr. survived until 1957.

[28] The commission members, except for Saint-Gaudens, along with Charles Moore, traveled to Europe on their fact-gathering trip between 13 June and 1 August 1901. They visited Paris, Rome, Venice, Vienna, Budapest, Frankfurt, Berlin, and London. For an itinerary of their visit, see Daniel Burnham's diary entries reprinted in volume one of Charles Moore, *Daniel H. Burnham: Architect, Planner of Cities* (Boston: Houghton Mifflin Co., 1921), 1:149–56.

[29] In November 1935 Olmsted recalled working out these details with Charles McKim "on a piece of quadrille paper in a train en route from Budapest to Paris in 1901." See letter from Frederick Law Olmsted Jr., "Notes on Githen's Caricature Coat-of-Arms for the So-Called Senate Park Commission of 1901," in Partridge, "Personal Recollections," and in the "Plates" section of this volume, opposite Plate XXI.

[30] Partridge's views on the plan for Washington of Pierre Charles L'Enfant (1754–1825) and the role

that George Washington played are a distillation from his longer article, "L'Enfant's Methods and Features of His Plan for the Federal City," in *National Capital Park and Planning Commission Supplementary Technical Data to Accompany Annual Report*, part 2, Studies in Continuity of Planning (Washington, D.C.: Government Printing Office, 1930), 21–38. Partridge's quotes from the 4 April 1791 letter from L'Enfant to Thomas Jefferson, then Secretary of State, are most likely taken from Elizabeth S. Kite, *L'Enfant and Washington, 1791–1792, Published and Unpublished Documents Now Brought Together for the First Time* (Baltimore: Johns Hopkins University Press, 1929), 41–42. This work included a foreword by Charles Moore, in which Moore argued that "L'Enfant claimed complete originality for his plan, and he is justified. No other person gave him substantial aid in the design, and he did not get ideas from the city plans supplied from Jefferson." Moore felt, however, that Versailles must have played a role in L'Enfant's creative imagination. "The cardinal features of L'Enfant's plan—the long vista from one focal point to another, the radiating avenues, and especially the conception of the city as a well-articulated unity—these ideas were already realized in Versailles, planned as the capital of France, the city in which L'Enfant's early years were spent," Moore quoted in Kite, *L'Enfant and Washington*, vi.

[31] L'Enfant's father, Pierre L'Enfant (1704–1787), was a painter in service to Louis XV and a professor at the Academie Royale de Peinture et de Sculpture, specializing in landscape and battle scenes. Six of his battle scenes were hung at Versailles, representing French victories during the 1740s. See Allan Greenberg, *George Washington, Architect* (London: Andreas Papadakis, 1999), 117.

[32] In an undated letter to President Washington, L'Enfant described the ideal situation for the Federal House or Congress as "the western end of Jenkin's Heights (which) stands really as a pedestal awaiting a superstructure…," Kite, *L'Enfant and Washington*, 55.

[33] Jefferson's sketch dates from March 1791. John Reps has argued, "Although the distance between the Capitol and President's house was much less than L'Enfant was eventually to provide in his plan, the spatial relationship is similar, and his 'public walks' may be regarded as the genesis of L'Enfant's great mall." Reps, *Monumental Washington*, 10.

[34] L'Enfant to President Washington, undated, in Kite, *L'Enfant and Washington*, 53.

[35] L'Enfant's original plan does not locate the City Hall or "Town House" that President Washington had promised in 1791. Reps has suggested that L'Enfant intended to locate it on the large square south and slightly east of the Capitol, facing one of the five great fountains (see Reps, *Monumental Washington*, 20). L'Enfant's Itinerary Column (to be located on the site of today's Lincoln Park) was

situated one mile from the Capitol and was to serve as the point from which all distances throughout the new Republic were to be calculated (Kite, *L'Enfant and Washington*, 64). For a detailed discussion of the features of the L'Enfant plan, see Partridge, "L'Enfant's Methods," 35–38.

[36] L'Enfant's untitled, undated plan for Washington, D.C., with later additions is in the holdings of the Geography and Map Division of the Library of Congress.

[37] Major Andrew Ellicott (1754–1820) was an astronomer and surveyor commissioned by George Washington in February 1791 to create an accurate survey of the intended site of the new Federal capital. Ellicott was not a city planner, and L'Enfant was engaged in March 1791 to draw up a plan for the new city. For a discussion of Ellicott's 1792 engraved version of L'Enfant's plan, see Reps, *Monumental Washington*, 22–25.

[38] This August 1791 "Progress Chart" showing development of land west of the Capitol is attributed to L'Enfant and is in the holdings of the Geography and Map Division of the Library of Congress.

[39] James R. Dermott's "Plan of Washington" was prepared in 1797 or 1798. Dermott was a surveyor and contractor living in the District of Columbia. See Reps, *Monumental Washington*, 20, n. 28.

[40] Partridge is incorrect here. George Washington suggested that James Hoban's design for the President's House be increased in size by one–fifth. See Pamela Scott and Antoinette J. Lee, *Buildings of the District of Columbia* (New York: Oxford University Press, 1993), 152.

[41] George Washington's aversion to locating the buildings near the new Capitol was expressed in a March 1798 letter to Alexander White. See George Washington to Alexander White, 25 March 1798, in W. W. Abbot and Dorothy Twohig, eds., *The Papers of George Washington: Retirement Series* (Charlottesville and London: University of Virginia Press, 1983), 2:159.

[42] The equestrian statue of George Washington was authorized by the Continental Congress on 17 August 1783, when, "On a motion of Mr. Lee, seconded by Mr. Bland, it was resolved 'that an equestrian statue of Washington be erected at the place where the residence of Congress shall be established.' " A further resolution was passed stipulating that the statue should be of bronze, and that Washington was to be represented in Roman garb, holding a truncheon in his right hand, with a laurel wreath encircling his head. The statue was to rest on a marble pedestal, "on which were to be represented, in bas-relief, the following principal events in the war in which General Washington commanded in person: viz: the evacuation of Boston, the capture of the Hessians at Trenton, the battle at Princeton, the action of Monmouth, and the surrender of York." The statue was to have been executed by the best artist in Europe under the supervision of the minister of

the United States at the court of Versailles. Nothing came of this elaborate and costly scheme. See S. H. Kauffmann, "Men on Horseback," in *Papers Relating to the Improvement of Washington*, ed. Charles Moore, 147–48.

[43] The plan for the Washington National Monument by Robert Mills (1781–1855) was chosen in 1845, after an initial competition held in 1836. Construction of the monument was begun in 1848, halted in 1854, and not completed until 1884. Mills's design called for a 600-foot obelisk set upon a 250-foot colonnaded base; this was later modified to the present obelisk, which rises to a height of 555 feet. For detailed accounts of Mills's work on the Washington Monument, see Pamela Scott, *Robert Mills, Architect* (Washington: American Institute of Architects, 1989) and Scott and Lee, *Buildings*, 100–2.

[44] The Smithsonian Institution was constructed by James Renwick Jr. (1818–1895) between 1846 and 1851 in the then-fashionable, crenellated Gothic-revival manner.

[45] The Botanic Garden was established in 1820, when Congress granted a triangular site of five acres at the east end of the Mall to the Columbian Institute. Its first greenhouse was erected in 1850, with larger ones constructed later, including an octagonal Gothic-revival structure from 1859, attributed to the architect Thomas Ustick Walter (1804–1887). In 1856 the garden was renamed the United States Botanic Garden and the present, newly renovated conservatory was constructed by Bennett, Parsons and Frost between 1931 and 1933. See Scott and Lee, *Buildings*, 65–66.

[46] The two streets which became Maine and Missouri Avenues were first proposed by Charles Bulfinch (1763–1844) in his 1822 plan to regularize the Tiber Creek and canal at the eastern end of the Mall. See Pamela Scott, "This Vast Empire: The Iconography of the Mall, 1791–1848," in Richard Longstreth, ed., *The Mall in Washington, 1791–1991* (Washington, D.C.: National Gallery of Art, 1991, 2002), 46.

[47] The Baltimore and Potomac Railroad Station was designed by the Philadelphia architect Joseph M. Wilson (1838–1902) and was constructed between 1873 and 1878.

[48] Educated at Harvard, Charles Moore (1855–1942) served as Senator James McMillan's aide from 1890 until the latter's death in 1902. He later served as chairman of the Commission of Fine Arts from 1915 to 1937. See "Charles Moore" in Sue A. Kohler, *The Commission of Fine Arts*, 51–52.

[49] Charles Moore, "Introduction," *Papers Relating to the Improvement of the City of Washington*, ed. Charles Moore, 9. The American Institute of Architects' annual convention was held in Washington on 13 December 1900. Glenn Brown, the AIA's able secretary, had organized a day-long symposium, at which papers were

read upon the desirability of rehabilitating Washington and the methods of accomplishing this goal.

⁵⁰ Representative Joseph Gurney Cannon (1836–1926), known familiarly as "Uncle Joe," opposed the project because he regarded the spending of public funds on "anything of an artistic character as a raid on the Treasury." Glenn Brown, *Memories, 1860–1930: A Winning Crusade to Revive George Washington's Vision of a Capital City* (Washington, D.C.: W. F. Roberts Company, 1931), 264.

⁵¹ *Senate Park Commission Report*, 7.

⁵² Ibid., 8–9.

⁵³ Partridge's somewhat negative characterization of Daniel H. Burnham as a "promoter architect" was no doubt influenced by Partridge's personal devotion to Charles McKim. Charles Moore described the Chicago–based architect's powerful drive: "His force commanded respect sometimes where it did not necessarily inspire affection in his contemporaries—outside or in his profession. One of the latter observed to me that he resembled 'a railway locomotive under full steam, holding the right of way.'" Moore, *Burnham*, 1:173. For recent scholarship on Burnham see Thomas S. Hines, *Burnham of Chicago: Architect and Planner* (Chicago: University of Chicago Press, 1979) and his "The Imperial Mall: The City Beautiful Movement and the Washington Plan of 1901–1902," in *The Mall in Washington*, ed. Longstreth, 78–99.

⁵⁴ Partridge's view of architectural history as a succession of architectural styles each copying from and building upon previous generations owed a debt to Joseph Gwilt's *Encyclopedia of Architecture: Historical, Theoretical and Practical* (London: Longmans, Green and Co., 1867), which he recalled purchasing in installments as a young draftsman in New York City. See Partridge, "Memoirs."

⁵⁵ Charles McKim wrote to Daniel Burnham on 1 June 1901, telling him of a visit with Augustus Saint-Gaudens and asking Burnham to include him (Saint-Gaudens) as a member of the Senate Park Commission "in order that he may assist us, not only for the value of his counsel in many directions, but because questions of 'SITES,' demanded in our report, is one which refers as much to sculpture as to architecture, and should be determined by the highest authority in the land." Burnham agreed to McKim's proposal and Saint–Gaudens was made a fourth member of the Senate Park Commission. Moore, *McKim*, 186.

⁵⁶ *Senate Park Commission Report*, 25

⁵⁷ L'Enfant to Thomas Jefferson, 11 March 1791, in Kite, *L'Enfant and Washington*, 35–36.

⁵⁸ Ibid., 42.

⁵⁹ On the Senate Park Commission members' tour of Europe during the summer of 1901, see Moore, *Burnham*, 1:149–58; and *McKim*, 187–199.

⁶⁰ The firm of McKim, Mead & White was established in 1879, when Stanford White joined the partnership of McKim and William R. Mead upon the retirement of William B. Bigelow. In 1901 the firm's main office was located in New York City in the Mohawk Building at 160 Broadway. On the firm's work, see Leland Roth, *McKim, Mead & White, Architects* (New York: Harper & Row, 1983) and Richard Guy Wilson, *McKim, Mead & White, Architects* (New York: Rizzoli, 1983).

⁶¹ Partridge's contemporary, the architect Henry Bacon (1866–1924), was McKim's first choice for overseeing the development of the Mall drawings for the *Senate Park Commission Report*. According to Charles Moore, "Bacon had formed a partnership with James Brite (died 1942), and they were competitors for designing the Agricultural Department building. So the Supervising Architect of the Treasury, James Knox Taylor, decided that Bacon could not take pay from the government and still be in a competition. Therefore, William T. Partridge was placed in charge of the Washington work in McKim's office and executed it in a satisfactory manner." Moore, *McKim*, 199–200. The plan for central Washington produced by the landscape architect Samuel Parsons Jr. (1845–1923), in association with Pentecost, was completed in mid–November 1900 and endorsed by Col. Theodore Bingham and Secretary of War Elihu Root, who, on 12 December 1900, sent the plan to the House of Representatives for favorable consideration prior to the centennial celebration of the District of Columbia as the nation's capital. The plan met with opposition from the AIA, particularly its secretary Glenn Brown, who urged Senator McMillan to advocate the creation of an independent professional commission to produce a comprehensive report on needed plans for improvements for Washington. See Reps, *Monumental Washington*, 78–82.

⁶² From 1887 to 1888 Partridge worked as an unpaid apprentice to Charles McKim, with the German trained architect Paul Gmelin (1859–1937), on preliminary studies and perspective elevations for the Boston Public Library, while simultaneously employed by William Rotch Ware in Boston to create illustrations for the Service Bureau for architects for the *American Architect*. Partridge had moved to Boston from New York City, where he had attended Columbia University's Architecture School to qualify for the Rotch Traveling Scholarship, which he won in 1889. See his unpublished "Memoirs" and his 1939 AIA Nomination for Fellowship application for details concerning his early career.

⁶³ In 1896 Austin W. Lord (1860–1922), who trained at the Massachusetts Institute of Technology (M.I.T.), resigned as founding director of the American School of Architecture (today's American Academy in Rome), after one year. In May 1896 the Academy instituted a three-year term for its directors. Robert Ware

proposed replacing Lord with first Robert Swain Peabody (1845–1917) and second C. Howard Walker (1857–1936), neither of whom wished to give up their architectural practices. McKim had also approached Partridge about the directorship, explaining in a letter to C. Howard Walker, "Accordingly, late in May, while negotiating with Mr. Partridge for a three year's term, and in view of certain complications which arose in his case, I received from Mr. Ware, under date of May 30, a letter suggesting your name for the first year and Partridge's for the two subsequent years of the course, to which I replied in accordance with the view that the Academy is pledged as above...." William S. Aldrich was ultimately appointed as the new director. McKim to C. Howard Walker, 31 August 1896, in Moore, *McKim*, 155.

[64] McKim's Boston office was located on two floors in one portion of the twin residences at 53 and 54 Beacon Street, which had been the home of his first wife Julia Amory Appleton's family. McKim married Julia Appelton in June 1885; she died in New York City on 3 January 1887.

[65] Eugène J. Létang (1842–1892), a graduate of the École des Beaux-Arts in Paris, came to M.I.T. in 1872 to assist William Robert Ware in teaching architecture. Létang was an advocate of precise draftsmanship and the rational classicism of his French instructor at the École, Émile Vaudremer.

[66] Thomas M. Kellogg (1862–1935) was McKim's chief draftsman in the Boston office for the Boston Public Library project. An M.I.T. graduate, he had been employed by the firm from 1885 until 1891, when he moved to Philadelphia and joined in partnership with John Hall Rankin, later practicing from 1903 to 1925 as part of the firm, Rankin, Kellogg & Crane. For Charles Moore's account of this episode, gleaned from Partridge, see his biography of McKim, 66. My thanks to Professor Richard Guy Wilson for information on Kellogg.

[67] Charles Moore notes that of the three Park Commission members, "Mr. Olmsted was the only one who had made any study whatever of the Washington problem. In a paper read before the American Institute of Architects in December 1900, he outlined a general treatment of the Mall calculated to restore the park connection between the Capitol and White House originally planned by L'Enfant— a treatment fundamentally the same as the one adopted [in the 1902 McMillan Commission Report]." Moore, *McKim*, 182–83. Moore described McKim's role in the development of the Senate Park Commission plan in the following terms: "Once embarked, however, he immediately began a detailed, systematic study of that portion of the problem with which he was particularly competent to deal—the relation of public buildings and monuments to landscape. Within nine months, under his direct personal supervision...the plans agreed upon by the Commission

after discussion were worked out.... From Burnham and Olmsted he got vitally important cooperation in criticisms and suggestions. He visualized the problem both as a whole and in its several parts, and then worked it out as he worked out all his creative problems...he strove not for originality, but for perfection." Moore, *McKim*, 184–85.

[68] Frederick Law Olmsted, "Note on Githens's Caricature Coat-of-Arms," in Partridge, "Personal Recollections." See Pl. XXI.

[69] See memorandum from Daniel H. Burnham to James McMillan, September 1901, in Moore, *Burnham*, 1:160-61.

[70] The *Senate Park Commission Report* states, "There is a present and pressing need for new buildings for existing Departments. The Department of Justice is without a home.... The State, War, and Navy Departments, now housed in a single building, are in so crowded a condition that they are occupying additional rented quarters. For the sake of convenience these Departments should be accessible to the White House, which is their common center. The proper solution of the problem of the grouping of Executive Departments undoubtedly is to be found in the construction of a series of edifices facing Lafayette Square, thus repeating for those Departments the groups of buildings for the Legislative and Judicial departments planned to the Capitol Grounds." The report also recommended that the space between Pennsylvania Avenue and the Mall be occupied by "the District Building, the Hall of Records, a modern market, an Armory for the District militia, and structures of like character," *Senate Park Commission Report*, 64 and 29.

[71] In actuality, there are more than twice that number of photographs in the report showing fountains and bodies of water seen by the commission members on their 1901 trip. Some of these photographs were taken by Frederick Law Olmsted Jr. See Appendix F, "Photographic Enlargements," in the *Senate Park Commission Report*, 151–54.

[72] Charles Moore's two-volume biography, *Daniel H. Burnham: Architect, Planner of Cities* was published in 1921.

[73] In his dedication delivered on 30 May 1930, Chief Justice William Howard Taft quoted from the 1902 *Senate Park Commission Report* concerning the siting of the proposed Lincoln Memorial, noting, "Here then was the conception of the Memorial we dedicate today. Not until 1911 was the idea carried forward.... The [Lincoln Memorial] Commission.... consulted the Fine Arts Commission, made up of Burnham, Millet, Olmsted, French, Hastings, Gilbert, and Moore, who urged the present site and recommended as the man to design and build it Henry Bacon, the student and disciple of McKim. McKim was the dean of architects of this country, and did most among us to bring the art of Greece to appreciation

and noble use. Bacon has been his worthy successor." William Howard Taft, "Address of William Howard Taft, Chief Justice of the United States, Chairman of the Lincoln Memorial Commission, in Presenting the Memorial to the President of the United States," in Office of the Public Buildings and Public Parks of the National Capital, The *Lincoln Memorial, Washington* (Washington, D.C.: Government Printing Office, 1927), 85.

[74] Alexander Wilson Drake (1843–1916) was an artist and engraver on wood who studied at the Cooper Institute in New York City and from 1870 until his death was head of the art department at *Scribners Monthly*, which became the *Century and St. Nicholas* magazine.

[75] Hughson Hawley (1850–1936) was a British-born watercolorist and architectural artist who practiced in New York City. He specialized in painting cathedrals and was noted for his rendering of skies.

[76] Charles Graham (1852–1911) was an American painter and watercolorist who specialized in rendering architectural and urban landscapes. He was best known for his series of paintings that depicted the 1893 World's Columbian Exposition in Chicago.

[77] Alfred Morton Githens (1876–1973) was a New York architect trained at the École des Beaux-Arts (1903–5), who worked for both Cass Gilbert and Charles McKim. Githens taught architecture at Columbia University (1918–21; 1925–26) and at Princeton (1927–28). His cartoon is reproduced, without any explanation as to its meaning, in Moore, *Burnham* 1:165–66. Glenn Brown also describes it in his *Memories*, 281. For Frederick Law Olmsted Jr.'s account of the creation and meaning of the piece, see his "Note on Githens's Caricature Coat-of-Arms," in Partridge, "Personal Recollections." During the busiest period in the autumn of 1901, while preparing the renderings for the *Senate Park Commission Report*, Partridge supervised a staff of over fifteen draftsman, who were listed by Charles Moore as: Baer, Butler, Chapman, Crow, de Gersdorff, Elliott, Harmon, Johnson, Kaiser, Merz, Morris, Mundy, Shephard, Trueblood, Walker, and Weekes. The *Senate Park Commission Report*, 123.

[78] The Harvard-educated explorer George Carroll Curtis (1873–1926) received gold medals for his work on "geographic" models at the Paris (1900) and St. Louis (1904) international expositions. In addition to the two large-scale models made of the Mall area before and after the proposed changes, a smaller one showing the proposed treatment of the area around the Washington Monument was also created in McKim's office. See Reps, *Monumental Washington*, 101. On Curtis, see "George Carroll Curtis, Geographic Sculptor Dies in Boston at the Age of 53," *New York Times*, 3 February 1926, 25.

[79] Olmsted's assistant was James G. Langdon. See note 105 for more information on him. See also note 13 in Timothy Davis's essay in this volume.

[80] Charles Moore notes in his biography on Burnham, "Meantime, the report to be made by the Park Commission to the Senate Committee on the District of Columbia was being prepared by Mr. Olmsted and Mr. Moore, who gathered a wealth of photographs of significant European works to supplement the reproduction and drawings. The report of the Senate Committee transmitting the Commission report to the Senate and giving a history of the undertaking, together with unqualified approval of the new plans, was written by Mr. Moore, and was unanimously approved by the [Senate] Committee [on the District of Columbia]," Moore, *Burnham*, 1:166.

[81] The models and drawings created by Partridge and his team for the Senate Park Commission were exhibited at the Corcoran Gallery of Art from 15 January to 25 February 1902.

[82] Unfortunately, the Senate Park Commission renderings (many of which were oversized, large-scale presentation drawings) presented to the Division of Prints at the Library of Congress in 1902 were subsequently dispersed or destroyed. The surviving drawings were transferred to the Commission of Fine Arts in Washington, D.C. The two models were restored in the 1980s, portions of which are now on display at the National Building Museum in Washington, D.C.

[83] John Reps has gone into great detail concerning the financing of the Park Commission's work. An original estimate of $15,000 was to be appropriated from the Senate's contingency fund. This was increased at certain points once the project was underway, not from Senator McMillan's personal funds, but from Charles Moore, himself. See the letter from McKim to Moore, 24 December 1901, in Reps, *Monumental Washington*, 103.

[84] Daniel Burnham's Union Station was constructed between 1903 and 1907. The Baltimore and Potomac Railroad Station was razed in 1907. See Scott and Lee, *Buildings*.

[85] Partridge begins a quote here fom Glenn Brown, 275–77. For an in-depth discussion of this very complicated story see, Dana Dalrymple's essay on the Department of Agriculture building in this volume.

[86] The Senate Committee on the District of Columbia Hearing was held on 12 March 1904.

[87] The Agriculture Department building's two wings, designed by Rankin, Kellogg & Crane in 1904 to 1908, were joined by a central administrative unit completed in 1930. At that time, the old Agriculture Department building to the north, located on line with James Renwick's Smithsonian Institution, was torn down.

[88] The National Museum, today's Museum of Natural History, was designed by Partridge's first employer James Rush Marshall (1851–1927) and his partner Joseph Coerten Hornblower (1848–1908) between 1904 and 1911.

89 The west wing offices of the White House, designed in 1902 by McKim, were meant to be temporary, in keeping with the idea that Daniel Burnham had proposed of constructing a permanent suite of offices in the center of Lafayette Square, surrounded by the various departments of the executive branch. For Burnham's suggestion, see his letter to Charles Moore of 14 April 1902, quoted in Moore, *McKim*, 206, n.1.

90 Elliot Woods (1865–1923) was born in Manchester, England and was appointed Superintendent of the Capitol by President Theodore Roosevelt in February 1902. He served in that position until his death in 1923.

91 In April 1904 Carrère and Hastings were retained to design the House and Senate Office buildings. Thomas Hastings (1860–1929) designed the House Office Building, which was completed in 1907. John Mervin Carrère (1858–1911) designed the Senate Office Building, which was completed the following year.

92 The legislation creating the Commission of Fine Arts was approved on 17 May 1910. President Taft's Executive Order No. 1259 was dated 25 October 1910. See Kohler, *The Commission of Fine Arts*, 3–4, 241–42.

93 Glenn Brown was an active force behind the organization of the Public Art League and was a key participant in the effort to thwart Col. Theodore Bingham's 1900 plan to enlarge the White House. See Reps, *Monumental Washington*, 83 and Brown, *Memories*, 357–65.

94 In early January 1909 an AIA committee appealed to President Theodore Roosevelt to establish a Bureau of Fine Arts to advise on plans for all future public buildings, bridges, parks, sculpture, and painting. Roosevelt approved the suggestion that month and established a Council of Fine Arts composed of thirty experts from all parts of the country. The council had one meeting, at which the location of the Lincoln Memorial as suggested by the *Senate Park Commission Report* was approved. See Kohler, *The Commission of Fine Arts*, 2–3.

95 Executive Order No. 1862, issued by President Woodrow Wilson, 28 November 1913; ibid., 242.

96 The Chief of Engineers of the Army invited four bridge engineers, L. L. Buck, William H. Burr, William R. Hutton, and George S. Morrison, to prepare plans for the bridge. The submissions were submitted to a jury composed of four experts, including Charles F. McKim's partner, Stanford White (1853–1906), and architect James G. Hill. Professor Burr's heavily decorated entry was selected, but with an estimated cost of $4,860,000, it was never constructed. See the *Senate Park Commission Report*, 56, and Reps, *Monumental Washington*, 128.

97 In 1913 the Arlington Memorial Bridge Commission was established by Congress with President Wilson as chairman.

98 The Lincoln Memorial Commission was officially created in June 1902 but did not hold its first meeting until 1904. Its official report authorized that year was not submitted to Congress until 1909. Its author, Representative James McCleary of Minnesota, set forth the idea of a monumental highway, or "Lincoln Road," from Washington to Gettysburg, as the most appropriate memorial to President Lincoln. See Reps, *Monumental Washington*, 155–56.

99 Brown, *Memories*, 284, 347.

100 Another opponent of the proposed Lincoln Memorial Highway was Secretary of War Elihu Root (1845–1937). John Reps quotes Root recalling how he dealt with the highway proposal: "I learned there was real estate speculation going on the route of the proposed highway. I got up a public meeting and went over and charged that this speculation existed, and they scuttled under their beds." Reps, *Monumental Washington*, 156; see also Moore, *Burnham*, 2:133, n.1.

101 In late August 1911 the New York architect John Russell Pope (1874–1937) was asked by the Lincoln Memorial Commission, at Speaker Joseph Cannon's insistence, to prepare additional studies for the memorial to be erected on the grounds of both the Soldiers Home and Meridian Hill. In December 1911 these plans were reviewed along with Henry Bacon's studies for the memorial in its present site in Potomac Park. The Lincoln Memorial Commission approved the Potomac Park site in February 1912. U.S. Lincoln Memorial Commission, *Lincoln Memorial Commission Report*, 62d Cong., 3d Sess., 1913, S. Doc. 965, 9–10, hereafter *Lincoln Memorial Commission Report*.

102 Francis Davis Millet (1846–1912) was an American painter who had first worked with Burnham on the 1893 Chicago World's Columbian Exposition. He was a member of the Commission of Fine Arts from 1910 to 1912 and perished on the RMS Titanic in April 1912. He is quoted by Partridge in Moore, *Burnham*, 2:135.

103 Henry Bacon quoted in *Lincoln Memorial Commission Report*, 13.

104 Brown, *Memories*, 295.

105 James G. Langdon (died 1950), a city planner and landscape architect, was Frederick Law Olmsted Jr.'s associate. Clarence E. Howard (dates unknown) was a landscape architect and longtime employee in the Olmsted Brothers firm. He designed the landscaping of the grounds between the Lincoln Memorial and the Washington Monument. See Kohler, *The Commission of Fine Arts*, 12.

106 In March 1919 the Commission of Fine Arts began studying the issue of retaining the crossarms as part of the final Reflecting Pool design. By early 1920 the members were split, with Thomas Hastings and Cass Gilbert favoring a retention of the crossarms as originally envisioned by

Charles McKim, and Peirce Anderson, Frederick Law Olmsted Jr., and James Greenleaf in accord with Henry Bacon's view that elimination of the crossarm would enhance the scale and design of the Lincoln Memorial. The members decided to build the pool without the crossarm. See Kohler, *The Commission of Fine Arts*, 13–15.

[107] *Senate Park Commission Report*, 47.

[108] The engineer's report, issued in 1931, stated that the design proposed by the *Senate Park Commission Report* for the Monument Gardens "showed heavy loading over an area where loading should be kept to a minimum; and excavation where, if anything, fill seemed to be required to increase stability." The report recommended abandoning the original plan. See Reps, *Monumental Washington*, 176–77 and Kohler, *The Commission of Fine Arts*, 34.

[109] McKim's domed pantheon would eventually become the Jefferson Memorial. Its present site was authorized in 1937, while designs for the structure were revised after the death of its designer, John Russell Pope that same year. William T. Partridge had helped to advise on the siting of the Jefferson Memorial by serving on a special commission set up by the National Capital Park and Planning Commission in 1935 to study the proposed locations for the memorial. See Reps, *Monumental Washington*, 173.

[110] Partridge's caustic critic remains unidentified but was most likely the Harvard–trained landscape architect and town planner, Elbert Peets (1886–1968). His most famous work, *The American Vitruvius: An Architect's Handbook of Civic Art* was published in 1922 in collaboration with the German urban planner Werner Hegemann (1881–1936) and included a critique of L'Enfant's plan for Washington, D.C., and its later interpretation by the Senate Park Commission. Peets was most disturbed by the 1902 plan's separation of the new monumental central core from the rest of the city. In 1927 Peets published three articles in the *Journal of the American Institute of Architects* tracing the roots and development of L'Enfant's plan for Washington, D.C. This was followed by scathing reviews of the new Federal Triangle designs and completion of the Mall as a regularized landscaped area during the 1930s. Peets served as a member of the Commission of Fine Arts from 1950 to 1954 and was also a planning consultant for the National Capital Park and Planning Commission. For a selection of his essays on Washington, D.C., see Paul D. Spreiregen, ed. *On the Art of Designing Cities: Selected Essays of Elbert Peets* (Cambridge, Mass.: The Massachusetts Institute of Technology Press, 1968).

[111] *The Senate Park Commission Report* states, "Buildings of a semi-public character may be located south of the present Corcoran Art Gallery fronting on the White Lot [the Ellipse] and extending to the park limits." Plans called for four buildings, two smaller structures fronting Eighteenth Street ranged around a larger central structure, with a fourth building fronting B Street (Constitution Avenue). See *Senate Park Commission Report*, 29.

[112] The National Academy of Sciences building designed by Bertram Grosvenor Goodhue (1869–1924) was completed in 1924. On the Northwest Rectangle, see Frederick Gutheim, *Worthy of the Nation: The History of Planning for the National Capital* (Washington, D.C.: Smithsonian Institution Press, 1977), 203–5. (Reprint 1989)

[113] *Senate Park Commission Report*, 69-71.

[114] The winners of the 1910 competition for the Justice, Commerce and Labor, and State Department buildings facing the east side of the White House grounds were Donn Barber (1871–1925), Arnold W. Brunner (1857–1925), and the firm of York & Sawyer. Plans for the three structures were approved by the Commission of Fine Arts, but appropriations to construct them were never made and the plans were deferred. See Reps, *Monumental Washington*, 167, 169, and Kohler, *The Commission of Fine Arts*, 53.

[115] See U.S. Public Buildings Commission, *Public Buildings in the District of Columbia* (Washington, D.C.: Government Printing Office, 1918), 15–43. Thomas Staples Martin (1847–1919), chairman of the Senate Committee on Appropriations, headed the special committee established in July 1916 to investigate and ascertain what public buildings would be needed in the District of Columbia for future federal expansion. Included in the document is a December 1917 letter from Charles Moore and the Commission of Fine Arts, outlining appropriate locations for new government buildings, based on the Senate Park Commission recommendations. See Charles Moore, "Letter from the National Commission of Fine Arts," in *Public Buildings in the District of Columbia*, 45–65.

[116] The Interior Department building (occupied today by the General Services Administration) was designed in 1915–1917 by Charles Butler from the Office of the Supervising Architect.

[117] The Municipal Building, today's District Building, was constructed by the Philadelphia firm of Cope and Stewardson between 1904 and 1908.

[118] See Moore, "Letter from the National Commission of Fine Arts" in *Public Buildings in the District of Columbia*, 53. Moore noted of the eclectic Romanesque-revival, towered Post Office Building, "The present Post Office Building Department was designed at the time when American architecture was in a transition state, before the necessity for an adequate amount of light and air was sufficiently recognized even by Government builders. The style of architecture adopted had its brief day of novelty and popularity; then it retired because of its failure to fulfill modern building requirements. The Government

is fortunate in having but one such example among its public buildings."

119 See *Public Buildings in the District of Columbia*, 63.

120 U.S. Public Buildings Commission, *Annual Report* (Washington, D.C.: Government Printing Office, 1922).

121 The Treasury Department Annex was designed by Cass Gilbert (1859–1934) in 1917–1918.

122 In 1925 Congress approved a public buildings bill authorizing $50 million for the construction of government offices.

123 The old Arlington Hotel was replaced by an office building in 1917, which was then occupied by the federal government. The Hay-Adams Hotel was constructed in 1927.

124 The *Senate Park Commission Report* advocated a partial in-fill of the Tidal Basin to create the proposed Washington Common, the southern component of the cross axis with the Mall centered on the Washington Monument. Partridge's lamentation that the Jefferson Memorial was not a strong enough planning element, in and of itself, was echoed by John Reps, who noted in 1960: "The unification of this southern part of the cross–axis with the rest of the great central composition was to be accomplished by the Washington Monument terrace gardens. Here is the one element of the Park Commission plans which has defied solution to the present day and which, until completed in some satisfactory manner, interferes with the appreciation and understanding of the entire design of the Mall system." See Reps, *Monumental Washington*, 176.

125 See note 42.

126 *Senate Park Commission Report*, 47. Partridge's quote is not quite correct. It should read: "climb the slope, and, spreading themselves to right and left…."

127 U.S. Commission of Fine Arts, *Twelfth Report* (Washington, D.C.: Government Printing Office, 1936), 15.

APPENDICES

Daniel Burnham's "First Draft" for the Senate Park Commission's Report to the Senate Committee on the District of Columbia[1]

DISTRICT OF COLUMBIA[2]

First draft "Improvement of the Park System of the District of Columbia"
Much more in detail than the printed bo[o]k—in places.

The Committee on the District of Columbia, acting under instructions of the Senate embodied in the resolution adopted March 8 1901:

RESOLVED, That the Committee on the District of Columbia be, and it is hereby directed to consider the subject and report to the Senate plans for the development and improvement of the entire park system of the District of Columbia. For the purpose of preparing such plans the committee may sit during the recess of Congress and may secure the services of such experts as may be necessary for a proper consideration of the subject. The expenses of such investigation shall be paid from the contingent fund of the Senate.

[R]espectfully report—

In 1889 Congress provided for the purchase of the 170 acres of land in the valley of Rock Creek which have been developed into the Zoological Park; and the next year a special act was passed, authorizing the purchase of 2000 additional acres of land extending from the northern boundaries of the Zoological Park to the District line. The amount of land actually acquired under the provisions of this act was 1,605.9 acres. This territory, beautified by nature, is undeveloped save for a few roads the location of which was obvious; and before the public can realize the advantages of the purchase, a systematic plan must be made by landscape architects.

Extending along the Potomac from the Anacostia, or Eastern Branch, nearly to the mouth of Rock Creek are the flats reclaimed by the Engineers and set apart by Congress under the name of the Potomac Park. This territory, comprising 739.42 acres (including the tidal basin) is entirely undeveloped; and its possibilities as a river park are greater than can well be stated in words.

The Anacostia flats, comprising about 2000 acres, imperatively demand reclamation in order to free the eastern portion of the city from the malarial conditions that for years have seriously retarded the development of that section, and have constantly impaired the health of those persons who

[1] This manuscript is reproduced with the permission of the Daniel H. Burnham Collection, Ryerson & Burnham Archives, The Art Institute of Chicago
[2] Editorial note: Brackets [] indicate correction of typographical errors or omitted letters or works.

have been compelled to live within its miasmal influences. Congress, recognizing the deplorable conditions to which thousands of people either in its employ or under its care are thus of necessity subjected has entered upon the preliminary work looking to the eventual reclamation of these flats; and it is believed that the time has now come to enter upon this work, with the view to create within this area a water park. In this manner can the park needs of the District be best served, and at the smallest expense.

The valley of Rock Creek from the mouth of that stream to the Zoological Park is unsightly to the verge of ugliness. Congress has had the situation studied with a view to finding a solution of the difficulty either by covering the creek entirely, or by creating a parkway through the valley. The need of a definite plan of treatment is shown in a striking manner by the fact that on the line of Connecticut Avenue a bridge is in course of construction; while the Massachusetts avenue crossing is being made by throwing an arch over the stream and filling in approaches. A decision should be reached as to whether the creek is to be covered, o[r] is to remain open; and also as to the treatment of the space in either case.

The development of the Potomac and of Rock Creek parks, the creation of a park along the Anacostia, and the increasing use of the Soldiers' Home grounds for park purposes, calls for a study of the means of connection among the parks, so as to bring into one system the diversified attractions that the parks when developed will offer. The positive squalor which to-day mars the entrance to almost every one of the parks is too apparent to need discussion.

Aside from the pleasure and the positive benefits to health that the people derive from public parks, in a capital city like Washington there is a distinct use of public spaces as the indispens[a]ble means of giving dignity to governmental buildings; and of making suitable connections between the great departments. When the city of Washington was planned under the direct and minute supervision of Washington and Jefferson, the relations that should subsist between the Capitol and the Presidents House, were carefully studied. Indeed the whole city was planned with a view to the reciprocity of sight between public buildings. Vistas and axes; sites for monuments and museums; parks and pleasure-gardens, fountains and canals; in a word all that goes to make a city a magnificent and consistent work of art were regarded as essentials in the plans prepared by L'Enfant and approved by the first President and his Secretary of State. Nor were these original plans prepared without due study of great models. The stately art of landscape architecture had been brought from overseas by royal governors and wealthy planters; and both Washington and Jefferson were familiar with the practice of that art. L'Enfant, a man of position and education, and an e[n]g[i]neer of ability, must have been familiar with those great works of the master Le Notre which are still the admiration of the traveler and the constant pleasure of the French people. Moreover, from his well-stocked library Jefferson sent to L'Enfant plans "on a large and accurate scale" of Paris, Amsterdam, Frankfort, Carlsr[uh]e, Strasburg, Orleans, Turin, Milan and other European cities, at the same time felicitating himself that the President had "left the planning of the town in such good hands".

It has so happened that the slow and unequal development of the city during the century of its existence has worked changes in the original design; and to a certain extent has prevented the realization of the comprehensive plan of the founders. As a result there has been a lack of continuity in the parks, and spaces like the Mall, that were designed for development as a unit have been cut into pieces, some of which have been improved, some have been sold to private persons, and some have been diverted to uses so absolutely at variance with the original idea as seriously to detract from the dignity of the buildings these spaces were intended to enhance.

Happily, however, nothing has been lost that cannot be regained at reasonable cost. Fortunately, also, during the years that have passed the Capitol has been enlarged and ennobled; and the Washington Monument, wonderful alike as an engineering feat and a work of art, has been constructed on a site that may be brought into relations with the Capitol and the Executive Mansion. Doubly fortunate, moreover, is the fact that the vast and successful work of the engineers in redeeming the Potomac shores from unhealthful conditions gives opportunity for enlarging the scope of the earlier plans in a manner corresponding to the growth of the country. At the same time the development of Potomac Park both provides for a connection between the parks on the west and those on the east, and also it may readily furnish sites for those memorials which history has shown to be worthy a place in vital relation to the great buildings and monuments erected by the founders of the Republic.

The question of the development of these park areas forces itself upon the attention of Congress. Either this development may be made in a haphazard manner, as the official happening to be in charge of the work for the time may elect; or it my be made according to a well-studied and well-considered plan, devised by persons whose competence has been proved beyond question. Such a plan, adopted at this time and carried out as Congress may make appropriations for the work, will make Washington the most beautiful capital city in the world. The reasons on which the foregoing assertion is based will appear in the course of this report.

The action of the Senate in ordering a comprehensive plan for the development of the entire park system of the District of Columbia is the resultant of two movements, one popular in character, the other technical. In October, 1898, the citizens of the District of Columbia began to plan for the celebration, two years later, of the one hundredth anniversary of the permanent seat of government in Washington. The project being national rather than local, was brought to the attention of the President, and by him was laid before Congress, with the result that a joint committee of the two Houses was appointed to act with the citizens committee in planning for the celebration. In December, 1900, commemorative exercises, held at the Executive Mansion and at the Capitol, were participated [in] by the Governors of the States as well as by the officials of the General Government and the representatives of foreign powers; and the celebration was brought to an appropriate end by a reception and banquet given by the Washington Board of Trade in honor of the committees and the distinguished guests.

The key-note of the celebration was the improvement of the District of Columbia in a manner and to an extent commensurate with the dignity and the resources of the American Nation. Senators, and Congressmen vied with Governor after Governor in commendation of the ideas breached by the joint committee, that the opportunities for making Washington the beautiful city its founders intended it to be should be realized without delay.

While the centennial exercises were in progress the Institute of American Architects, in session in this city, was discussing the subject of beautifying Washington; and in a series of papers making suggestions for the development of the parks and placing of public buildings, the tentative ideas of a number of the leading architects, sculptors and landscape architects of the country were put forward for discussion. As a result the Institute appointed a committee on legislation; and from consultations with the Senate Committee on the District of Columbia resulted the order of the Senate for the preparation and submission of a general plan for the development of the entire park system of the District.

On March 19, 1901, the subcommittee of the District Committee having the matter in charge met the representatives of the Institute of American Architects, and agreed to the proposition of the latter that Mr. Daniel H. Burnham, of Chicago, Illinois, and Mr. Frederick Law Olmsted, Jr., of Brookline, Massachusetts, be invited to act as experts in the preparation of park plans, with power to add to their number. These gentlemen accepted the task, and subsequently invited Mr. Charles F. McKim and Mr. Augustus St. Gaudens, of New York, to act with them.

The Committee considered itself most fortunate in securing the services of men who had won the very highest places in their several professions. As the director of works of the World's Columbian Exposition at Chicago, Mr. Burnham had achieved a reputation for artistic taste, executive ability, and that comprehensive grasp of the details necessary to carry a great undertaking to its successful issue. The monumental works with which Mr. McKim's name is connected as architect made it certain that in the preparation of plans for the District of Columbia only those elements of beauty which the world has agreed upon would find place; that a reverent and intelligent appreciation of what was good in the work of the founders would have due weight; and that the development proposed would be at once harmonious with the past and equally pleasing to a refined taste. Mr. St. Gaudens' work as a sculptor is by universal consent second to that of no other American; and among architects and artists his critical abilities are held in the highest esteem. Mr. Olmste[a]d bears a name identified with what is best in modern landscape architecture in the District of Columbia; he is the consulting landscape architect not only of the vast system of parks and boulevards which make up the metropolitan park system of Boston and its suburbs, but also of large parks in various cities. To inherited taste, he adds the highest training both practical and theoretical; and he enjoys the distinction of being the sole instructor in landscape architecture in any American university.

The nature and scope of the work having been outlined to the Commission, they entered upon their task not without hesitation and misgivings. The problem was both difficult and complex. Much must be done; much, also, must be undone. Moreover, no sooner was the membership of the Commission announced than their aid and advice was sought in relation to buildings and memorials under consideration; so that immediately the range of the work broadened. Thus the importance and usefulness of the Commission was enhanced. Such a result was anticipated by your Committee; and the most encouraging part of the work has been the cordiality and even enthusiasm with which the various officials who came into relations with the Commission have taken up the work.

The Supervising Architect of the Treasury Department from the first has been in the heartiest accord with the general ideas and aims of the Commission as to the character of the buildings and their approaches; and at his request the Commission have aided him in his efforts to obtain suitable plans for the new building for the Agricultural Department. The Secretary of War and the Secretary of the Treasury have also done the general work a service by calling upon the Commission for assistance.

After a detailed examination of the topographical features of the District of Columbia, the Commission drew up preliminary plans. They were then forced to the conclusion that an adequate treatment of the park system depended upon the exclusion of the Baltimore and Potomac Railroad from the Mall, so as to give an unrestricted passage from the Capitol to the Monument and the Executive Mansion. For years the removal of railroad tracks from the Mall has been the dream alike of citizen and legislator.

The occupation of the Mall by the railroad dates back about thirty years, at which time in their eagerness to secure competition in freight and passenger traffic the then local government of the District granted the lands, and subsequently Congress confirmed the grant. In extenuation of the original grant it may be urged that the space was then no better than a common pasture and that the railroad would but take the place of the canal which it paralleled, so that conditions would be bettered by the change, as undoubtedly proved to be the case. Be that as it may, the railroad held the property by a title good in law and in equity; and by virtue of a recent act of Congress the space to be occupied had been increased, in consideration for the surrender of street trackage and the proposed ele[v]ation of the tracks within the City of Washington.

It so happened that the chairman of the Commission, Mr. Burnham, was the architect of the Pennsylvania railroad's new station at Pittsburg[h], and after his selection as a member of the Commission the construction of the Washington station was offered to him. After consultation with the subcommittee, Mr. Burnham proposed to the President of the Pennsylvania railroad that the station be built on the south side of the Mall and lands adjoining. The architectural and other advantages of such a site were set forth with such vigor as to command serious consideration. There the matter rested for a time.

The Commission, in order to make a closer study of the practice of landscape architecture as applied to parks and public buildings, made a brief trip to Europe, visiting Rome, Venice, Vienna, Budapest, Paris, London, and their suburbs. Attention was directed principally to ascertaining what arrangement of park areas best adapts them to the uses of the people; and what are the elements that give pleasure from generation to generation and even from century to century. The many and striking results of this study will appear in the discussions that follow.

It was during the stay of the Commission in London, that President Cassat[t] announced to Mr. Burnham his willingness to consider the question, not of moving the Baltimore and Potomac station to the south side of the Mall, but of withdrawing altogether from that region and uniting with the Baltimore and Ohio Company in the erection of a union station on the site established by legislation for the new depot of that road; provided suitable legislation could be secured to make proper compensation for the increased expense such a change would involve; and, provided, also that the approaches to the new site be made worthy of the building proposed to be erected.

It should be said here that in considering the views of the Commission and in reaching his decision, the President of the Pennsylvania Railroad looked at the matter from the standpoint of an American citizen, saying in substance that he appreciated the fact that if Congress intended to make of the Mall what the founders of the city intended it to be, no railroad should be allowed to cross it; and that he would do all he could do consistent with the interests of the stockholders of his road to vacate that space.

This conditional consent on the part of the railroad removed the one great obstacle to the preparation of adequate plans for the improvement of the city. Lesser obstacles, such as the lack of surveys of the oldest parks in the District, and the difficulties of getting together the widely scattered data, have been surmounted. On the other hand, the work has been much lightened by the excellent topographical maps of the District outside of the city, prepared by the Coast and Geodetic Survey; and by the uniform courtesy of the Engineer Commissioner of the District and other officials who have willingly given all the assistance of their various offices.

On beginning work the Commission was confronted by the fact that while from the first of October till about the middle of May the climatic conditions of Washington are most salubrious, during the remaining four and a half months the city is subject to extended periods of intense heat, during which all public business is conducted at an undue expenditure of physical force. Every second year Congress is in session usually until about the middle of July; and not infrequently it happens that by reason of prolonged or special sessions during the hottest portion of the summer the city is filled with the already great and increasing numbers of persons whose business makes necessary a more or less prolonged stay in Washington. Of course nothing can be done to change weather conditions; but very much can be accomplished to mitigate the physical strain caused by summer heats. Singularly enough up to the present time the abundant facilities which nature affords for healthful and pleasant recreation during heated terms have been neglected; and in this respect Washington is far behind other cities whose climatic conditions demand much less, and whose opportunities also are less favorable.

In Rome throughout the centuries it has been the pride of emperor and pope to build fountains to promote health and to give pleasure. Mile after mile of aqueduct has been constructed to gather the water even from remote hills, and bring great living streams into every quarter of the city; so that from the moment of entering the Eternal City until the time of departure, the visitor is scarcely out of sight of beautiful jets of water now flung upward in great columns to add life and dignity even to St. Peter's; or again gushing in the form of cascades from some great work of architect or sculptor; or still again dripping refreshingly over the brim of a beautiful basin that was old when the Christian era began. The forum is ruins, basilicas and baths have been transformed into churches, palaces have been turned into museums; but the fountains of Rome are bo[th] omnipotent and eternal.

If all the fountains of Washington, instead of being left lifeless and inert as they are during most of the time, should be set playing at their full capacity, they would not use the amount of water that bursts from the world-famous fountain of Trev[i] or splashes on the stones of the pi[a]zza of St. Peter's. At the Chateau Vaux le Vico[m]te near Paris, the great landscape architect Le Notre built cascades, canals and fountains consuming five million gallons of water per day; and the fountains of Versailles are the wonder and delight of the French people.

The original plans of Washington show the high appreciation L' Enfant had for all forms of water decoration; and argument is scarcely needed to prove that the first and greatest step to be taken in the matter of beautifying the District of Columbia [is] such an increase in the water supply as will make possible the copious and even lavish use of water in fountains.

Scarcely secondary in importance to fountains are public baths. An instructive lesson in this respect is to be found in the experience of the Metropolitan Park Commission in taking over and equipping Revere Beach, immediately north of Boston. There the squalid conditions prevailing in former years have been changed radically; and a well-kept and well-ordered beach sufficient in extent to accommodate over 100,000 persons is publicly maintained; no fewer than 1700 separate rooms are provided for bathers and bathing suits are furnished at a small expense. The receipts are sufficient to pay for maintenance and yield a surplus of several thousand dollars for repairs and extensions.

In Washington the extensive use of the present bathing beach shows how welcome would be the construction of a modern building with ample facilities. Moreover the opportunities offered by an extended river front should be utilized in furnishing opportunities for free public baths, especially for the people of that section of the city between the Mall and the Potomac.

The creation of a water park on the upper stretches of the Anacostia is anticipated as calculated to furnish a much needed variety in the District park system. Those persons who have visited the Thames on the occasion of a London holiday will readily appreciate the enormous use which the people make of that narrow stream, the surface of which at times seems to be literally covered with the different kinds of light craft. In Belle Isle park in the city of Detroit, the creation of shallow lakes and connecting canals developed boating in summer and skating in winter to such an extent that often tens of thousands of people daily enjoy an island that for years was little else than a series of marshes. Given the opportunities for enjoyment the people are quick to seize upon them; and, once realized, it seems astonishing that chances for pleasure ha[ve]so long been neglected.

The creation of a water park, with driveways surrounding it, being the suggested treatment of the Anacostia above the head of navigation, the lower portion of the stream to its junction with the Potomac may well be treated as proposed by the Engineers, namely, by the construction of walls along the borders of the channel and filling in the flats. The present limited wharf frontage of Washington makes it certain that as the city increases in size, that portion of the Anacostia frontage from its mouth to the Navy Yard wil be needed for business purposes. It is important, however, that a broad parkway connection be maintained along the river in order to connect the Anacostia park with the Potomac park; and for this work a line of stone quays, [o]verlooked by terraces, as on the Seine in Paris, may be used to excellent advantage.

The long island lying between the Washington channel and the main channel of the Potomac should be treated in such a manner as to afford shaded drives and walks along the water, with frequent boat landings so as to make the park accessible to the section of the city which it adjoins. The work of the Engineers has been of such a character that the island can be developed at comparatively small expense; and at the same time a portion of the city in great need of park space will be well accommodated.

The necessity of rebuilding the frontage on Washington channel which recently has come into the undisputed possession of the District of Columbia, makes it necessary to decide as to the character of the new wharves. The War Department has recently established the Engineers' College, [on] what is known as the Arsenal Grounds, and this property will be greatly improved within the near future. The rebuilding of the wharves should be in keeping with these prospective improvements; and fortunately the rental value of the frontage will be sufficient to provide for the ultimate payment of the cost of permanent work as well as the maintenance of the same.

The ebb and flow of the tide in the channel should not be impeded by slips that collect refuse; but should be accelerated by a continuous line of masonry quays, to correspond with the miles of masonry work already constructed by the engineers to form the river walls of the Potomac Park. Then as business demands larger space, the piling should be arranged so as to provide for clear tidal flow. Then the wide thoroughfare known as Water street may be treated as a driveway between the Potomac Park and the Anacostia Park.

The valley of Rock Creek forms the natural connection between the Potomac Park and the Zoological and Rock Creek Parks. The Commission give[s] alternative plans for traversing the short space necessary to get from the Potomac park into the valley of Rock Creek, and either of these plans may be taken, as shall seem most expedient at the time. There is no question in the minds of the Commission, or of this Committee, that the most convenient, the least expensive and the most satisfactory way of treating Rock Creek is to improve the banks, build roadways along them, and secure such control of the spaces along the top of the banks as will allow adequate policing.

A stream, even a small stream, running between picturesque banks, in the midst of a city like Washington, offers opportunities for park improvement that should not be ignored. The alternative of arching over the creek and filling in between the banks for the purpose of constructing a boulevard on a level with the streets is highly expensive, [and] is dangerous in case of the sudden melting of snows or of a cloud-burst in the upper valley. In 189_ Captain (now Colonel) Lusk U. S. Engineer Corps, reported strongly in favor of the open treatment, from an engineering point of view; and the aesthetic argument reinforces the engineering position.

A plan for the systematic development of the outlying parks is absolutely and immediately necessary. Such a plan is what all progressive American cities have already adopted; and in the matter of park development the District of Columbia [i]s behind the majority of the cities of the country. The improvement of the present park areas should begin at once, and be carried out with energy and thoroughness.

Such a task the District of Columbia shares with the cities of the United States. There is, however, a peculiar duty to be done in Washington, the capital city of the Nation.

When L 'Enfant drew the plans of the city of Washington he anticipated a development of this country only less than has actually taken place; and he made provision accordingly. The ground that he laid off for a suitable setting for the Capitol and the Presidents House. In spite of many encroachments of many divisions of the territory, of mutually discordant developments of parts of the area in question, the treatment of the space known as the Mall, can now be undertaken in a manner such as even L'Enfant could never have conceived.

The plans of the Commission are both simple and rational. Starting with L'Enfant's original plan of treating the entire space as a unit, the Commission recommended certain minor departures from general plans, and also certain extensions of it.

The general outline of the Commissioners' plan is as follows: To establish a relation between the Capitol and the Washington Monument, by such a re-arrangement of the trees in the Mall as shall create a vista 300 feet in width; and to extend this axial treatment to the banks of the Potomac, there to have a suitable termination in a great arch. This arch shall be in itself a point of divergence for the drive to the Rock Creek valley on the west; to the Potomac Park on the east; and by the Memorial Bridge to Arlington on the south. The principle is the same as that in the Arc de Triumph in Paris, from which the Champs Elysees drive to the Bois de Boulogne, the [blank; streets?] radiate. This arch should form the Grant Memorial. In honor of the great General who led the armies of the Union to victory that meant the preservation of the Republic, and in memory of the brave soldiers who fought under him, what more appropriate site than one which holds vital relations on the one hand with the commander of the Revolutionary armies, and on the other hand with the last resting place of so many thousands of the brave men who gave their lives in battle for their country.

Plans for a Grant Memorial have been authorized by Congress and a competition for the selection of the artist to whom the commission shall be [e]ntrusted; so that if the site suggested shall be approved work on this portion of the plan might begin within a short time. Moreover the sentiment in favor of a memorial bridge to connect the Potomac Park with Arlington is so strong that the project must soon be carried out. The memorial bridge plans sent to Congress, with the approval of the War Department, call for a more elaborate and costly structure than will be necessary or advisable in case a Grant Memorial Arch is located as suggested. Indeed the dignified treatment of this problem is to be found in the construction of a masonry bridge, which shall derive its beauty from the harmony and proportion of its arches and the simplicity and solidity of its structure rather than from superimposed ornament.

The construction of a great bridge demands a suitable treatment of its approaches. The Grant Memorial at the Washington end, provides amply for the Washington approach. From this arch the bridge should point straight for the Mansion house at Arlington, a dignified and pleasing piece of architecture—and the high slopes on which the house stands should be treated with terraces by which the visitor would ascend easy grades from the Virginia end of the bridge to his destination at Arlington. In this way that great reservation would be brought into close relationship with the Potomac Park, so as to be but an extension of it. Moreover, the terraces are not only capable of a treatment intrinsically beautiful, but they will afford the most beautiful views imaginable of Washington and the Potomac. In this way a harmonious, thoughtful, systematic and continuous treatment can be given to a vast area.

The Capitol, the Washington Monument and the Grant Memorial thus form the main axis. The cross axis is now to be considered.

Approaching the White House from the north, the great thoroughfare of Sixteenth street extends in a straight line from the boundary of the District to Lafayette Square, the White House closing the vista. The south front of the White House looks out on the President's Gardens, then across the White Lots and the Monument Grounds to the Potomac and the Virginia hills. The Washington Monument is not on the axis of the White House, nor can it be brought into such relation by any possible treatment; but if the western slope of the hill on which the Monument stands shall be terraced and the space below shall be treated as a plaza, then this plaza will be on the White House axis. Then this axis, where it strikes the Potomac may be terminated by some large treatment that will engage, without obstructing, the view from the Executive Mansion. This latter situation may well be reserved for the memorial that will surely be built to Lincoln; and such treatment would give the great places to Washington, Lincoln and Grant as the three most illustrious men in the history of the Republic. Any treatment less comprehensive must seem inadequate and meager. A more comprehensive treatment has yet to be proposed.

THE MUNICIPAL BUILDING.

The necessity for the erection of a municipal building for the District of Columbia is so well recognized, both in and out of Congress, that no argument on the subject is needed.

The District Government occupies a rented building, constructed for offices, and provided with accommodations for a comparatively few people during a given time. No citizen enters this building without feeling that it is inconvenient, unsafe, overcrowded and shabby. The new building should be large enough to give comfortable and sanitary work-rooms to the employe[e]s, and to provide the public with reasonable facilities for the transaction of business. In its architecture it should harmonize with the best of the Government buildings, having dignity and expressing the feeling of permanence.

The location deserves very careful consideration. That is [it] should be constructed on the south side of Pennsylvania avenue has been settled probably by universal consent, but the exact location has not been discussed widely. There are considerations which would seem to point to the space now occupied by the market as the most desirable site for the building which is to represent the Government of the District of Columbia as a distinct function of the National Government. Facing the junction of Pennsylvania and Louisiana Avenues, the municipal building would hold vital relations with the District Courts on Judiciary Square, and would occupy a position about midway between the Capitol and the White House. This point seems to be the center of the business life of the community and, therefore, perhaps, the most convenient portion of the city. Moreover, the ample public spaces on every side provide opportunity for an ample and attractive setting for the building. Furthermore, for many years the District has owned the land in front of the market with the view of placing a municipal building there. Nothing but the smallness of the site has stood in the way of agreement on this location.

The removal of the market to the squares west of its present location might be made with advantage to all the interests concerned. These squares are now occupied with a class of buildings that must be removed if the south side of the Avenue is to be reclaimed; and a readjustment of the space might provide for a larger and more modern market, so constructed that it would be an ornament to the Avenue, while at the same time the increasing public who frequent it, would be much better accommodated. Then too, a place should be provided for market wagons and the streets should be cleared of the present and unsightly conditions. All this could be accomplished with increased convenience to the market men themselves; and the public would be benefited in every way.

PLAY GROUNDS

On visiting the Boston parks the sub-committee was impressed by the open air gymnasium provided for boys, and the play-garden for children on the Charles River embankment. The need of play grounds, especially prepared for the youth, is now recognized in almost all cities. In the beautiful Borghese Gardens in Rome, boys play ball on the grass, and on occasions the American game of baseball is played by the students from this country.

In Paris children build their houses, whip their tops and play games on the gravel or on the piles in the gardens of the Tuileries and Luxembourg. Everywhere in the crowded cities of Europe the parks and gardens are the play-grounds of all ages and classes of the people; and ornament, if not subordinated to utility, at least goes with it hand in hand.

In purchasing lands for new schoolhouses the appropriations should be sufficient to obtain considerable areas for playgrounds. The advantages of such action will be two-fold. First, areas for parks will thus be acquired at comparatively small expense, and as the District increases in population these breathing spaces will become invaluable. Again, in this way certain choice sites, already marked out for public occupation on the street extension plans, will be secured and put into immediate use. If the children were provided with play space, other than the streets, the present objection from property owners to the location of schoolhouses in their immediate neighborhood would be obviated.

Minute on the Life of Charles Moore

ADOPTED BY THE COMMISSION OF FINE ARTS ON JANUARY 29, 1943

In the passing of Charles Moore at Gig Harbor in the State of Washington on September 25, 1942, the Commission of Fine Arts lost a devoted friend and inspired leader, and the Nation a scholar and leader in civic affairs. His years of public service covered a period of almost half a century. During practically all of these years Dr. Moore was concerned with the development of the Plan of Washington. Since his work had a nation-wide interest, he was known in all parts of the United States and his advice on artistic matters was sought by both state and city authorities. His influence as a patron of the arts was recognized at home and abroad.

Charles Moore was born in Ypsilanti, Michigan, on October 20, 1855, and at his death he was within a month of reaching the age of 87 years. He was the son of sturdy, patriotic Americans, who instilled into the boy a love of home and country and a devout faith in God.

At a very early age he experienced an incident which seemed to predestine his work in the interest of the National Capital, to which Dr. Moore devoted so many years. Once, when he was a child, a visitor from Virginia appeared at his home, took the boy on his knee, asked him how old he was and said, "When I was your age, I sat on George Washington's knee." Dr. Moore never forgot that episode and, as he grew older the experience filled him with the desire to see the City of Washington and subsequently to act in the interests of its orderly development.

Dr. Moore received his preparatory education at the Phillips Andover Academy at Andover, Massachusetts. He matriculated at Harvard University in 1874 and graduated in the class of 1878, winning honors in several fields of activity. He gained an appreciation of the arts from his teacher Charles Eliot Norton, who about that time introduced at Harvard the first course in the History of Art in the United States. That was during President Grant's administration, when the Centennial of the Establishment of the United States was celebrated in Philadelphia in 1876. It was a period when several museums were founded, including the Metropolitan Museum of Art in New York, the Boston Museum of Fine Arts, and the Corcoran Gallery of Art in Washington. During these years the National Capital witnessed its first great period of improvement after a lapse of 50 years, which led President Grant to state that there were more paved streets in Washington than in any other city of the United States. At this time Dr. Moore was a young man of about 22 years and on one of his visits to the east he saw the City of Washington for the first time.

Upon graduation from Harvard, Dr. Moore chose journalism as a vocation and entered the employ of the *Detroit Evening Journal* as a reporter. He became a skilful writer and a master in the use of English; his writings were enriched from the Bible, which was his constant companion.

About the year 1889 Dr. Moore was sent to Washington as correspondent of Detroit newspapers, where his experience in journalism was further enlarged. His success as a newspaper correspondent soon brought him into association with Senator James McMillan of Michigan, and he became his political secretary about 1890. Subsequently, by virtue of the fact that Senator McMillan was Chairman, Dr. Moore became Clerk of the Senate Committee on the District of Columbia.

Senator McMillan was concerned with several needed improvements for the National Capital demanded by the increase in the population of the city, which had grown from 61,000 in 1860 to nearly 200,000 in 1890. Among these improvements were: the establishment of the Filtration Plant, which became a part of McMillan Park; the consolidation of the nearly a dozen street car companies (horse-drawn until about 1890) to two; the reorganization of the charitable institutions of the District of Columbia; the elimination of the railroad grade crossings; and the extension of the highway system. As Clerk of the Senate District Committee, Dr. Moore prepared the reports on all these projects.

The World's Columbian Exposition in Chicago in 1893 gave Dr. Moore a view of a monumental group of buildings built in accordance with a comprehensive plan in which architects, sculptors, painters, and landscape architects collaborated. The so-called "White City" on the shores of Lake Michigan was the impetus which resulted in bringing about a revival in the Fine Arts in the United States. The Exposition stirred the whole world as the result of the development of a beautiful and impressive group of buildings so arranged as to create a sense of unity in the composition. The landscape effects, the architecture, sculpture, and mural paintings made a vital impression upon the public mind and caused the people to recognize new standards and new ideals of artistic achievements. Thus the Exposition began a new era in civic development.

The first city to benefit as a result of the aesthetic achievements of the 1893 World's Fair was the National Capital. The construction of the Library of Congress, completed in 1897, brought many artists to Washington. In 1900 a celebration commemorating the one hundredth anniversary of the establishment of the seat of government in the District of Columbia was held in the Capital. The celebration developed an impetus to improve the District of Columbia in a manner and to an extent commensurate with the dignity and resources of the United States, which at the close of the Spanish-American War had become a world power. The population of Washington at this time was 218,196. While the centennial exercises were in progress, the American Institute of Architects was in session in the City and the subject of the development of parks and the placing of public buildings was the important subject of discussion. The tentative ideas of a number of the leading architects, sculptors, and landscape architects were heard. The Institute appointed a committee on legislation which met with the Senate Committee on the District of Columbia and subsequently, in March 8, 1901, the United States Senate authorized the establishment of the Senate Park Commission; Messrs. Daniel H. Burnham and Charles Follen McKim, architects, Frederick Law Olmsted, landscape architect, and Augustus Saint-Gaudens, sculptor, were appointed members of the Commission. Charles Moore served as secretary.

The plans and written report prepared by the Senate Park Commission, edited by Dr. Moore, which were submitted to the United States Senate, constituted the first and most notable proposal pertaining to city development in the United States advanced up to this time. It marked an important epoch in the development of the National Capital and brought about the revival of the L'Enfant Plan of 1791 for the Federal City, a Plan adopted by President Washington and Secretary of State Jefferson that had been neglected for three-quarters of a century. Champions of this new Plan of Washington were opposed by certain vested interests, but it nevertheless had many friends, among them President Theodore Roosevelt and the Honorable Elihu Root. As a result of the Commission's recommendations the railroad tracks were removed from the Mall, thereby making it possible to restore the central axis of the L'Enfant Plan. The Union Station was built from the designs of Daniel H. Burnham, and the White House was restored by Charles F. McKim to be in keeping with the dignity of the Chief Executive of the Nation. In all this work Dr. Moore took an active part.

Thereafter a series of difficulties arose; the McMillan Commission, having submitted its report, went out of existence, and the Plan was left with no one to guide in executing it. Senator McMillan died in 1902 and Dr. Moore returned to Detroit to become Secretary of the Security Trust Company.

In 1909 President Theodore Roosevelt, by Executive Order, appointed a Council of the Fine Arts consisting of 30 artists, but Congress denied the Council their traveling expenses. Thereupon, on March 21, 1909, President Taft abolished the Council and Congress on May 17, 1910, established the Commission of Fine Arts "to consist of seven qualified judges of the Fine Arts." Dr. Moore became one of the original members of this new Commission. It was a fitting recognition not only of his past services, but also of his pre-eminent qualifications to pass upon matters relating to the beautification of the National Capital. The Commission of Fine Arts held its first meeting on July 8, 1910, and elected Daniel H. Burnham, architect, Chairman. Other members of the original Commission of Fine Arts, in addition to Dr. Moore, were Frederick Law Olmsted, Jr., landscape architect, Cass Gilbert and Thomas Hastings, architects, Daniel Chester French, sculptor, and Francis D. Millet, painter.

The first project to come before the Commission was the design and location of the Lincoln Memorial, and in this the Commission reaffirmed the site in Potomac Park on the banks of the Potomac, in connection with a Memorial Bridge and a Water Gate, suggested by the Senate Park Commission.

After Mr. Burnham's death in 1912, Mr. French was elected Chairman and served until 1915. Dr. Moore was thereupon elected Chairman and served as such during the succeeding 22 years. During those years Dr. Moore was the guiding spirit of the Commission, and although he relied on the artist members for decisions on aesthetic or technical matters, they depended upon him to carry out their ideas and placed the utmost respect in his judgment. Dr. Moore was influential with the members of Congress, Cabinet Officers, and other leading officials of the Government. He was conciliatory, firm when occasions required, but nevertheless willing to compromise "in everything but the essence". The projects that came before the Commission of Fine Arts during Dr. Moore's 27 years' service as member and Chairman numbered into the thousands, and the story of the beautification of Washington has the name of Charles Moore linked with each one of its important projects. In fact from 1901 to 1937 Dr. Moore witnessed the transformation of Washington from a small, run-down community to the most beautiful capital city in the world.

A most important part in the work of transforming Washington culminated in the Public Buildings Program of 1926 adopted during the administration of President Coolidge. The President took up the problem with Dr. Moore in its earliest stages, and he in turn with the members of the Commission of Fine Arts. The outstanding result of the Public Buildings Program was the purchase by Congress of the entire 70 acres south of Pennsylvania Avenue between the Treasury Department and the United States Capitol and the resultant development of the area known as the "Triangle". Other important projects were the completion of Union Station Plaza, the enlargement of the Capitol Grounds with provision for an additional House of Representatives Office Building, the United States Supreme Court Building, the Arlington Memorial Bridge and Water Gate, the completion of the Tomb of the Unknown Soldier, and the restoration of the Arlington Mansion.

The World War of 1917-1918 brought Dr. Moore from Detroit to Washington as a permanent resident. In addition to his duties as Chairman of the Commission of Fine Arts, he became Consultant to the Librarian of Congress and Acting Chief of the Division of Manuscripts. He occupied the last named position for nine years, 1918-1927, during which period he succeeded in securing many valuable documents for the Library of Congress, in particular the letters and other papers of presidents Theodore Roosevelt and William Howard Taft.

Amidst his daily duties, Dr. Moore found time to write a number of books. In 1900 he published *The Northwest Under Three Flags*; in 1915 a *History of Michigan*; in 1921 *A Life of Daniel H.*

Burnham, Architect and Planner of Cities (two volumes); in 1926 *The Family Life of George Washington*; in 1929 *Life and Letters of Charles Follen McKim*, and *Washington Past and Present*; in 1932 *Wakefield, Birthplace of George Washington*. Dr. Moore was editor of *The Plan of Chicago* prepared by Daniel H. Burnham and E. H. Bennett, 1909. He prepared editions of *George Washington's Rules of Civility* and *Lincoln's Gettysburg Address and Second Inaugural* as well as the *Report of the Senate Park Commission* of 1901, heretofore mentioned, and a *Report on the Restoration of the White House* in 1902. Dr. Moore fully realized the value of recording subjects of importance, and his numerous reports and articles pertaining to Washington, written during a period of more than 30 years, remain as valuable records.

At the approach of the Bicentennial of the Birthday of George Washington, Dr. Moore became actively interested in the restoration of the birthplace of the first President. He was elected an officer of the Wakefield National Memorial Association, which completed the restoration of the birthplace in time for the celebration in 1932. As a part of the celebration, Congress authorized the construction of the Mount Vernon Memorial Highway, extending from the City of Washington via the Arlington Memorial Bridge, to the home of the first President at Mount Vernon. Both parkway and bridge were completed in 1932. Dr. Moore participated in the Bicentennial by serving as an Advisor in the publication of the *Writings of George Washington*, authorized by Congress, a work comprising 37 volumes.

Because of his advancing years, Dr. Moore began to feel that his service in behalf of the City of Washington was complete and he therefore retired as member of the Commission of Fine Arts on September 29, 1937. He was succeeded in the chairmanship by Mr. Gilmore D. Clarke, who had been appointed a member of the Commission soon after completing his service as Consulting Landscape Architect for the Mount Vernon Memorial Highway and later, after having been reappointed by President Roosevelt, had been elected Vice-Chairman of the Commission.

Dr. Moore was the recipient of numerous honors in this country and abroad. He accompanied the members of the Senate Park Commission of 1901 on their trip to Europe to visit the leading capital cities. In 1918 he was appointed a delegate to visit British universities on a World War mission arranged by London University. In 1923 the Secretary of War appointed him a member of the Commission to plan for the American War Cemeteries in Europe. He served as Overseer of Harvard University from 1924 to 1930. He was a life member of the American Historical Association and its Treasurer from 1917-1930; he was Vice-President of the Wakefield National Memorial Association; member of the American Institute of Arts and Letters, the Academy of Arts and Letters of Cuba, the National Sculpture Society, the American Planning and Civic Association, and Phi Beta Kappa; he was an honorary member of the American Institute of Architects, the American Society of Landscape Architects, the New York Architectural League, and the Institut Français de Washington. Dr. Moore was an Incorporator and a Life Member of the American Academy in Rome. He was President of the Detroit City Planning Commission, 1912-1919. In 1924 he was awarded the Gold Medal of Honor of the American branch, Société des Architectes Diplômes par le Gouvernement Français. France honored him with the Chevalier of the Legion of Honor in 1924; in 1928 he received the Friedsam Fellowship gold medal award; in 1927 he received the New York Architectural League Medal of Honor, and in 1937 the Carnegie Corporation award for services to the Arts in America. In 1890 George Washington University conferred upon him the degree of Doctor of Philosophy and in 1923 the degree of Doctor of Laws. Miami University bestowed upon him the degree of Doctor of Laws in 1930, and Harvard University, his Alma Mater, honored him with the degree of Doctor of Arts in 1937.

Dr. Moore had a most genial disposition; he was fond of good stories and enjoyed telling them. Thus his *Washington Past and Present* is less a chronological history of the city than it is, to quote Dr. Moore, "an endeavor to interpret those new plans in the light of the past....", and he did this entertainingly by telling stories of his experiences during the years that he was occupied with the development of the National Capital, during which time the plans were carried out only after many struggles and discouragements but, through his constant perseverance, with success. In recent years his fellow members on the Commission of Fine Arts have given testimony to the fact that Washington would not be as beautiful as it is today had it not been for Dr. Moore's untiring zeal and steadfast devotion to the Plan of Washington, accompanied by much self-sacrifice, for his work on the Commission was without compensation.

The members and former members of the Commission of Fine Arts honored Dr. Moore in 1935 on the twenty-fifth anniversary of the establishment of the Commission by presenting him with a special Gold Medal designed by Mr. Lee Lawrie, then the sculptor member of the Commission. Mr. Eugene Savage, painter member of the Commission, executed a portrait of Dr. Moore for this occasion.

After Senator McMillan's death in 1902, Dr. Moore established his home in Detroit, where his wife died in 1914. During that period he became intimately acquainted with Mr. Charles L. Freer, managing director of the Michigan Car Company, the parent organization of the American Car and Foundry Company, of which Senator McMillan was Chairman of the Board of Directors. Mr. Freer acquired a notable collection of Oriental Art numbering 8,000 objects, and Dr. Moore was helpful in persuading him to donate this collection to the Smithsonian Institution and to house it in Washington, an ideal accomplished in the Freer Gallery of Art, which was opened to the public in 1923. Mr. Freer stipulated in his will that objects of art acquired in the future for the Freer Gallery of Art must have the approval of the Commission of Fine Arts, and the Commission has continuously served in the manner outlined.

On February 18, 1937, the Washington Society of Fine Arts gave a dinner in honor of Dr. Moore, at which he summarized his experiences in the National Capital in one brief paragraph, saying:

"A cloud of witnesses encompass me tonight as the past rises before me. Dimly through the mists of time I see their faces–nine Presidents, Cabinet Officers, Senators, Representatives, officials, specialists, high-minded citizens, and a long procession of artists. Various were their contributions. Combined they are a part of the great tradition, coming from the past, flowing into the future–destined to prepare a Capital worthy of the American Nation, the city of George Washington and Abraham Lincoln."

During the last five years of his life Dr. Moore lived with his son MacAllaster Moore at Moorlands, Gig Harbor, in the State of Washington. He spent these years writing his reminiscences; he had begun a history of the District of Columbia. On Friday morning, September 25th, Dr. Moore was taken ill and, ere his son had time to call a physician, he had departed. Another son, Colonel James M. Moore, U.S. Army, also survives. A brief funeral service was held at Bremerton, Washington, and among the many friends who sent floral tributes were the President and Mrs. Roosevelt, and the members and former members of the Commission of Fine Arts.

Dr. Moore will always be remembered and revered for his illustrious service rendered on behalf of the Capital of this Nation.